# The Institutions of the Market

# The Institutions of the Market

*Organizations, Social Systems, and Governance*

*Edited by*

Alexander Ebner and Nikolaus Beck

OXFORD
UNIVERSITY PRESS

# OXFORD
UNIVERSITY PRESS

Great Clarendon Street, Oxford OX2 6DP

Oxford University Press is a department of the University of Oxford.
It furthers the University's objective of excellence in research, scholarship,
and education by publishing worldwide in

Oxford New York

Auckland Cape Town Dar es Salaam Hong Kong Karachi
Kuala Lumpur Madrid Melbourne Mexico City Nairobi
New Delhi Shanghai Taipei Toronto

With offices in

Argentina Austria Brazil Chile Czech Republic France Greece
Guatemala Hungary Italy Japan Poland Portugal Singapore
South Korea Switzerland Thailand Turkey Ukraine Vietnam

Oxford is a registered trade mark of Oxford University Press
in the UK and in certain other countries

Published in the United States
by Oxford University Press Inc., New York

© Oxford University Press 2008

British Library Cataloguing in Publication Data

Data available

Library of Congress Cataloging in Publication Data

The institutions of the market: organizations, social systems, and
governance/edited by Alexander Ebner and Nikolaus Beck.
    p. cm.
    Includes index
    ISBN–13: 978–0–19–923143–0
    ISBN–13: 978–0–19–923142–3
1. Institutional economics. 2. Evolutionary economics.
3. Economics–Sociological aspects. I. Ebner, Alexander. II. Beck, Nikolaus.
    HB99.5.I589 2008
    381–dc22                      2008008563

Typeset by SPI Publisher Services, Pondicherry, India
Printed in Great Britain
on acid-free paper by
CPI Antony Rowe, Chippenham, Wiltshire

ISBN 978–0–19–923142–3 (Hbk.)
ISBN 978–0–19–923143–0 (Pbk.)

1 3 5 7 9 10 8 6 4 2

# Contents

# Contents

# List of Figures

# List of Tables

# List of Contributors

**Nikolaus Beck**, Associate Professor, Faculty of Economics, University of Lugano, Switzerland.

**Christophe Boone**, Professor of Organization Theory and Behaviour, Faculty of Applied Economics, University of Antwerp, Belgium.

**Robert Boyer**, Professor of Economics, CEPREMAP-ENS, Paris, France.

**Alexander Ebner**, Professor of Political Economy, School of Humanities and Social Sciences, Jacobs University Bremen, Germany and Affiliate Professor, Grenoble École de Management France.

**Neil Fligstein**, Professor of Sociology, Department of Sociology, University of California at Berkeley, Berkeley, California, USA.

**Henrich R. Greve**, Professor of Strategy, Norwegian School of Management, Sandvika, Norway.

**John Harriss**, Professor of International Studies, Simon Fraser University, Vancouver, Canada.

**C. R. Hinings**, Professor Emeritus, Department of Strategic Management and Organization, School of Business, University of Alberta, Edmonton, Canada.

**Geoffrey M. Hodgson**, Research Professor in Business Studies, Business School, University of Hertfordshire, Hatfield, UK.

**Bob Jessop**, Professor of Sociology, Sociology Department, Lancaster University, UK.

**Alfred Kieser**, Professor of Business Administration, Chair of Business Administration and Organization, University of Mannheim, Germany.

**Namrata Malhotra**, Lecturer, Tanaka School of Management, Imperial College, London, UK.

**Renate E. Meyer,** Associate Professor, Institute of Public Management, Vienna University of Economics and Business Administration, Austria.

**Richard R. Nelson,** Professor of International Political Economy, School of International and Public Affairs, Columbia University, New York, USA.

**Rudolf Richter,** Professor Emeritus of Economics, Chair of Economic Theory, University of Saarland, Saarbrücken, Germany.

**Peter Walgenbach,** Professor of Business Administration, Chair of Organization Theory and Management, University of Erfurt, Germany.

**Filippo Carlo Wezel,** Associate Professor, Faculty of Communication, University of Lugano, Switzerland.

**Sidney G. Winter,** Deloitte and Touche Professor of Management, The Wharton School, University of Pennsylvania, Department of Management, Philadelphia, Pennsylvania, USA.

**Arjen van Witteloostuijn,** Professor of Economics and Business, Department of International Economics and Business, University of Groningen, The Netherlands.

# Introduction: The Institutions of the Market

*Alexander Ebner*

## 0.1. Overview

What defines the institutional specificity of markets? Which factors drive the interaction among market actors? How are markets governed? Questions like these belong to the standard repertoire of the social sciences. Certainly, this is because markets are defining institutional characteristics of economies and societies in modern capitalism. Addressing the institutional substance of markets, however, is a particularly relevant motivation for the theoretical perspective of the new institutionalism in the social sciences. Indeed, recent advances of institutionalist theorizing in economics, sociology, and political science have been concerned with the exploration of markets as specific institutional ensembles. As such, markets are part of a diversity of governance mechanisms alongside hierarchies, networks, and related hybrid forms of social coordination. The institutional dynamism of markets is accordingly derived from a variety of interrelated determinants. These include the organizational capabilities of firms as market actors, their competitive interactions in the market process as well as the governance of their market relations.

The following chapters address these aspects as a representation of the institutions of the market, viewed in the context of theoretical advances in the current debates of the new institutionalism. In focusing on the organizational, competitive, and regulative dimensions of markets, the presentation in the chapters is primarily concerned with contributions from organization studies, institutional economics, economic sociology, and institutional political economy. The underlying thesis suggests that the basic conceptual parameters of the new institutionalism are currently shifting towards an integrative framework that adheres to evolutionary concepts in accounting for the matter of knowledge, learning, and institutional change. Organizational dimensions of market operations are taken to the fore regarding their endogenous capabilities, systemic interactions, and governance relations. An evolutionary perspective thus may contribute to a profoundly dynamic understanding of the institutions of the market.

## 0.2. The Institutions of the Market and the Varieties of Institutionalism

A consensual characterization of the new institutionalism in the social sciences invokes a common understanding of institutions as sets of rules and norms that contribute to the evolution of social systems of governance, involving markets as institutional ensembles. The underlying research perspective addresses institutional diversity as a result of complex interactions in the formation and transformation of institutions (Morgan 2005; Nee 2005). Accounting for this quality of institutional change, then, a complementary definition of institutions in game theoretic terms would highlight their attributes as systems of shared beliefs about a salient way a particular game is played. This allows for reconsidering the contested character of institutions as social constructions (Aoki 2001: 10–12). Applied to the matter of markets, this means that the market process of coordinating supply and demand may be viewed as a set of games that proceed in the framework of specific rules and norms. More specifically, markets provide the terrain for transactions among autonomous actors who engage in decentralized bargaining based on contractual arrangements and price signals. This horizontal mode of coordination is well contrasted with vertical coordination in organizational hierarchies as well as with hybrid coordination in networks. However, considering the actually existing variety of markets for diverse commodities, the coordination of market processes is subject to a diversity of competitive patterns and regulation modes beyond the price mechanism (Boyer 1997; Hollingsworth and Boyer 1997: 7–9). Accordingly, the new institutionalism dispenses with the institutional sterility of the neoclassical definition of markets as decentralized allocation mechanisms. By adding institutional substance to this definition, analytical attention is directed to the organizational capabilities of the involved actors as well as to the attributes of their interactions. For that reason, aspects like rationality and efficiency play a prominent role in delineating the various strands of institutionalist reasoning.

Indeed, critical assessments of rational choice theory serve as a point of reference for demarcating the major lines of reasoning in the new institutionalism. Viewed in terms of distinct levels of analysis, rational choice institutionalism may be assessed according to its micro-focus on the incentive effects of rules and norms in governing exchange relations. This is differentiated from organizational institutionalism with its meso-focus on role-following behaviour in organizational fields and populations as well as from historical institutionalism with its macro-concern for the path-dependent change of political–economic governance structures (Campbell 2004: 2–3). Alternatively, in reconsidering their theoretical foundations, these major strands of institutionalist reasoning may be positioned in a continuum of ideas that ranges from 'calculus' to 'cultural' views on the behavioural impact of institutions. The calculus perspective claims that institutions reduce uncertainty in strategic interactions, whereas the cultural perspective addresses the institutional framing of individual rationality (Hall and Taylor 1996).

Rational choice institutionalism stands for the calculus position, which is rooted in the new institutional economics. It models institutions as instrumental outcomes of individual maximization strategies that apply to market processes as well as to politics, bureaucracy, and other domains of social coordination. In this framework, problems of monitoring and enforcement that arise from the transfer of property rights are to be solved through institutional incentives (Furubotn and Richter 1997). A major contribution to this line of reasoning is Oliver Williamson's transaction cost theory of economic organization. It highlights contractual arrangements, which economize on transaction costs that arise from the costliness of information in exchange (Williamson 1985, 2000). The latter aspect is taken up in Douglass North's theory of institutional change. It applies the transaction cost perspective to the evolution of property rights in economic development. Institutions are defined as legal rules and social norms that govern both economic and political exchange. Their path-dependent change shapes the institutional profile of cultural evolution (North 1990, 2005). In its characterization of markets, thus, rational choice institutionalism perceives market operations as strategic interactions in a competitive setting. Their dynamism underlines the comparative inertia of political institutions (Shepsle 2001). However, despite the increasing openness of rational choice institutionalism for aspects of context-specificity, bounded rationality, and institutional inefficiency, it still struggles with the recombination of its basic components; suffice to mention the problem of functionalism in the interpretation of institutional change.

Organizational institutionalism represents the cultural counterpart to the calculus framework of the rational choice approach. It highlights institutions as culturally embedded social constructions, an interpretation that applies also to markets as distinct institutional ensembles. Because of a contextual 'logic of appropriateness', institutions are related to cultural scripts and aspects of legitimation that promote role-following behaviour in an organizational context. In this manner, an integrated cultural–cognitive perspective on organizational interactions is taken to the fore (DiMaggio and Powell 1991; March and Olsen 1989). In particular, organizational institutionalism addresses the matter of identity, legitimation, and symbolism in explaining the isomorphic change of organizational patterns. This resounds arguments of classical sociology that cope with the cultural determinants of social interaction. Thus, the organizational behaviour of market actors is not subject to an instrumental calculus but rather to the perception of cultural appropriateness (Scott 2001: 51–2). The latter proposition hints at a major criticism of rational choice institutionalism. Above all, its implicit assumption of institutional efficiency is said to neglect the attributes of organizations as 'power systems' (Zafirowski 2004: 372–3). However, organizational institutionalism suffers from analytical deficits as well. Above all, its implicit tendency of cultural determinism in theorizing organizational behaviour also neglects factors such as interest, power, and conflict.

An intermediate position between both the calculus and the cultural perspectives that delineate the theoretical discourse of the new institutionalism is provided by historical institutionalism. Emerging from institutional political economy, it relates institutions to the diversity of political–economic governance structures. The corresponding focus of attention is directed at legal rules and formalized norms, which are subject to strategic compromises in institutionalized bargaining procedures (Streeck and Thelen 2005: 10–11). In this vein, the perspective of historical institutionalism approaches markets as creations of government, which are embedded in distinct sets of social and political institutions. Market regulation thus belongs to its centre of attention (Immergut 1998; Reich 2000). Because of this concern with the relationship between market and state, the national diversity of political–economic governance regimes stands out as a research issue. 'Varieties of capitalism' are derived from the organization of the private sector, which implies a reconsideration of the relational set-up of firms in a specific institutional environment (Amable 2003; Hall and Soskice 2001; Streeck and Thelen 2005). This allows for countering mechanistic perceptions of the market. Instead, historically rooted institutional modes of economic and social coordination are addressed as factors in shaping distinct trajectories of economic development (Boyer and Saillard 2002; Zysman 1994). Still, related to this implicit focus on developmental continuity, historical institutionalism is not fit to adequately grasp the matter of institutional innovation and rapid change. Therefore, it seems that an integrated framework is required to transcend the self-imposed analytical limitations of the new institutionalism.

## 0.3. Understanding Institutional Change: Towards an Integrated Framework

Recent trends in the differentiation of institutionalist theorizing are related to the analytical challenge of understanding institutional change. This differentiation reaches across the boundaries of rational choice, organizational and historical institutionalism. It also transcends disciplinary subdivisions. One example is the discursive strand of reasoning, which highlights the communication of ideas about legitimate political–economic action (Campbell and Pedersen 2001: 6; Schmidt 2006). This particular variant of institutionalist reasoning may be associated with another development in the new institutionalism, namely, an increasing acceptance of the context-specificity of individual and collective choices as a point of departure for cross-disciplinary convergence (Katznelson and Weingast 2005: 15–16). However, further suggestions address the theoretical portfolio of the new institutionalism. In particular, they highlight the need to include more explicitly the major strands of heterodox economic thought, primarily the Veblenian blend of institutionalism and Schumpeterian evolutionary economics (Nielsen 2001: 507–10).

In the light of these concerns, understanding institutional change poses the main problem of recent institutionalist theorizing. This involves questions of structure and agency in the creation and diffusion of institutions across diverse governance structures. Particularly relevant are non-equilibrium conceptions of institutions that allow for both spontaneity and design in institutional evolution (Scott 2001: 193–5;

Streeck and Thelen 2005: 19; Peters 2005: 161–2). Accordingly, theoretical developments in the new institutionalism proceed towards positions that reject the pitfalls of mechanistic functionalism in favour of a non-deterministic perspective on institutional change. Above all, the matter of learning and innovation, which is a prominent feature of evolutionary strands of institutionalist theorizing, has been gaining further influence.

These conceptual reconfigurations are most obvious in the discourse of rational choice institutionalism, and here especially in the new institutional economics. Claims of institutional efficiency have been largely abandoned. Instead, the path-dependence of institutional evolution is taken to the fore, highlighting increasing returns, lock-in effects, and multiple equilibria. Bounded rationality and diverging social interests are held responsible for the prevalence of inefficient institutional constellations, which are particularly relevant in the case of rules and norms that promote market exchange (Greif 1998; North 1990, 2005). This view on bounded rationality and path-dependence allows for the reconsideration of role-following behaviour in the market operations of organizations, thus offering references to sociological positions (Nee 1998: 10–11). Moreover, related to these concerns, the complex relationship between markets and states is reinterpreted in a manner that accounts for the institutional variety of governance mechanisms (Chang 2002).

In a similar manner, organizational institutionalism has been shifting its theoretical outlook towards an evolutionary perspective. Above all, this hints at organizational ecology with its specific interest in the disposition of evolving populations in institutional fields. Yet also the broader spectrum of evolutionary economics has been gaining ground (Hirsch 1997: 1716–17; Scott 2001). This tendency is accompanied by persistent references to the integration of structure and agency as a key concern for institutionalist theorizing. Indeed, in analysing the dynamism of markets, both context and choices need to be taken into account. Crucially, context is shaped not only by market forces but also by regulatory and normative pressures emanating from the public sphere (Greenwood and Hinings 1996: 1023–5). This reconsideration of the mutually constitutive interaction between organizations and their environment also allows for the matter of interest, power, and conflict. For instance, institutional innovations may be assessed as contested projects of entrepreneurial actors (Colomy 1998).

Historical institutionalism stands out in combining the recognition of evolutionary patterns of institutional change with the exploration of conflicting interests and their political–economic articulation. Agency and conflicts of interest remain decisive, for they inform the distinction between equilibrium order and historical processes (Clemens and Cook 1999; Thelen 1999). Accordingly, the concept of path-dependence has been transferred from the evolutionary segments of institutional economics. It refers to self-reinforcing social processes in historical time, which implies a reconsideration of contingent events and their lock-in effects in the evolution of the market system. Yet in the setting of historical institutionalism, the analytical emphasis is more explicitly on the aggregate impact of power relations and legitimization strategies (Mahoney 2000; Pierson 2000a; Streeck and Thelen 2005: 8–9). Adding to this amalgamation of theoretical positions, historical institutionalist reasoning on the social embeddedness of market operations goes well together with the matter of organizational learning in evolutionary economics (Coriat and Dosi 1998).

A striking example for this hybridization of theoretical perspectives in the new institutionalism is provided by recent debates in economic sociology. Indeed, it has been claimed that economic sociology covers the middle ground between the new institutional economics with its choice-theoretic framework and organizational sociology with its emphasis on cultural scripts (Nee 2005: 63–5). The theoretical matrix of economic sociology thus contains components of all the major variants of the new institutionalism. It addresses the social embeddedness of economic action by highlighting norms and routines as coordination devices while accounting for the impact of power relations in the formation of social structures (Beckert 2002: 291–2; Dobbin 2004). Yet owing to this eclecticism, there exists no consensus on the institutional substance of these structures. Following Granovetter, they may be perceived in terms of social networks, which reflect the embeddedness of market operations in a non-market setting of cultural and political influences (Granovetter 1985, 2002: 36, 2005: 34–5). Arguing against such a focus on personal relationships, Swedberg underlines the quality of institutions as manifestations of social interests. This corresponds to a Weberian interpretation of market competition as a struggle of conflicting interests (Swedberg 2005a: 6, 2005b: 243–4). However, despite these controversies, the reconsideration of evolutionary positions has been persistently moulding the research programme of all the major strands of economic sociology (Smelser and Swedberg 1994).

7

Basically, the sensitivity for concerns with organizational behaviour and culturally embedded social practices underlines the advantages of an evolutionary approach to institutional change. Especially, a reconsideration of the institutional dynamism of markets highlights the analytical limitations of a static perspective with its deterministic implications. An integrative approach to institutionalist reasoning needs to be set apart from the type of equilibrium considerations that have been particularly influential in rational choice institutionalism. More precisely, in approaching institutional change, an adequate perspective needs to address a multifaceted set of phenomena involving uncertainty, complexity, path dependence, and unintended consequences (Immergut 2006; Streeck 2005: 582–3). The problem of institutional change thus may be specified by invoking the notion of institutional innovation as a paradigmatic motive. It blends insights on evolutionary patterns, behavioural mechanisms, and cultural conditions of change from all institutionalist lines of reasoning (Campbell 2004: 4–6, 185–9; Hay and Wincott 1998; Hira and Hira 2000). Elaborating on these concerns in an integrative manner poses the decisive challenge for an evolutionary perspective on institutional change.

## 0.4. Organizations, Social Systems, and Governance: The Challenge of an Evolutionary Perspective

In a programmatic statement on the research perspectives of the new institutionalism, Paul DiMaggio suggests that evolutionary reasoning on institutional change provides the most promising options for transdisciplinary cooperation. Above all, he maintains that this would apply most adequately to the question of efficiency in the selective function of market competition and its regulation (DiMaggio 1998: 699–700). This suggestion hints at the problem of characterizing institutional evolution in terms of the involved mechanisms and patterns of change. On the one hand, the concept of path-dependence tends to overemphasize institutional continuity. On the other hand, the reconsideration of radical change by invoking notions like critical junctures neglects the aspect of gradual adaptation. Required is thus a differentiated set of conceptual tools that accounts for the reproduction, transformation as well as innovation of institutions (Thelen 2003: 232–3). Such a framework would have to address ideational paradigms, interest conflicts, and power relations as variables that shape the entrepreneurial provision of meaning systems and schemes of legitimation (Garud, Hardy, and Maguire 2007: 957–8). Accordingly, an evolutionary perspective that represents the matter of innovation in an adequate manner reaches beyond the concepts of path-dependence and embeddedness. Institutional innovation then resembles the entrepreneurial recombination of a local institutional repertoire that exhibits both an enabling and constraining influence on the process of change (Campbell 2004: 68–70; Crouch 2005: 17, 72).

Furthermore, the developmental character of the institutional evolution of markets needs to be specified. At this point, the widespread argument of efficiency in market competition becomes decisive. An institutionalist perspective takes the trade-off between efficiency and effectiveness to the fore, confronting the static concerns of Pareto optimality in resource allocation with the evolutionary survival and control of market organizations (Fligstein 2002: 66–9). The question is, however, how far is market competition to be understood as an efficiency-enhancing evolutionary mechanism. The latter view is still widely shared in institutionalist reasoning. It is usually accompanied by the claim that evolutionary explanations of institutional change would emphasize the efficiency of competitive selection (Ingram and Clay 2000: 527; Scharpf 1997: 20). Concurrently, despite the well-established interpretation of path-dependence as a phenomenon of market failure, all of this amounts to claiming an efficiency principle in economic evolution, which is specified through the coordinative function of the price system in market competition. The competitive pressure of the market process is accordingly said to exercise an efficiency-enhancing impact on the learning efforts of market actors (Pierson 2000b: 487–90). However, these arguments promote only a partial view of the market process, as the selective efficiency of competition has been questioned repeatedly in the debates of evolutionary economics (Nelson 2002).

Because of the widespread misrepresentation of evolutionary reasoning in modern institutional economics, it may be useful to bring up some of its basic propositions. Above all, economic evolution is defined as the self-transformation of an economic system in historical time, caused by the internal generation of innovation and its local diffusion (Nelson 1995: 57–8; Witt 1993). Evolutionary models thus cope with the role of individual and collective learning as decisive factors in the knowledge-based interactions of market actors. The market process resembles an experimental discovery procedure that involves error and imperfection in the face of radical uncertainty (Dosi and Nelson 1994: 154–5). Crucially, the evolutionary perspective on economic change addresses organizational capabilities as conditioning factors in the competitive performance of firms. Evolutionary selection patterns shape the growth trajectories of industries. Yet selective pressures are also exercised by the regulations of public policy. Accordingly, the institutional evolution of markets is driven by systemic interactions between private and public sector (Nelson and Winter 1982).

A programmatic outline of evolutionary theorizing in the new institutionalism may be summarized as follows. First, it commands a non-reductionist methodology that addresses selection on both individual and higher-order entities. Second, it accounts for historical time, involving chance events and multiple equilibria. Third, it highlights increasing returns in technology and social interactions that are based on local learning. Fourth, it allows for the embeddedness of the economy in larger social systems with co-evolving components (Bowles 2004: 478–80). All of this adds up to the insight that institutional innovations are not only constrained by their environment but also contribute to its ongoing reconstruction. In this manner, the structuration of institutional change may be described by the notion of 'embedded entrepreneurship' (Ebner 2008). Again, this points to the fundamental role of organizations, social systems, and governance mechanisms in delineating the institutions of the market. An evolutionary perspective contributes to each of these areas of analysis with a distinct set of arguments.

Institutionalist reasoning on the organizational dimension of market operations has recently drawn attention to the matter of dynamic capabilities, that is, the competitive recombination of capabilities that are specific to an organization. This topic hints at the endogenous potential for institutional innovation as a driving force in the evolution of markets. Corresponding arguments challenge those views in the literature, which emphasize market structure and pressures of competition as determinants of market behaviour (Teece, Pisano, and Shuen 2000). Furthermore, evolutionary reasoning on organizational capabilities may allow for grasping their co-evolution with governance structures. This is acknowledged as a major contribution to understanding the micro-foundations of economic growth (Dosi, Nelson, and Winter 2000). More specifically, evolutionary reasoning addresses the dynamizing impact of institutional variation through the introduction of new organizations. Adaptation to changing environments is facilitated by entrepreneurial interventions while competitive selection operates through organizational survival, which relates to retention through imitation (Aldrich and Martinez 2001).

Coping with similar issues, the approach of organizational ecology perceives markets as evolving social systems. The diversity of organizational forms is derived from an understanding of market selection that involves cultural fitness and institutional legitimation (Hannan 2005). Thus, the interactive relation between organizational actors and institutional context becomes decisive for understanding the evolution of markets. Accordingly, evolutionary concepts of institutional change may go well together with a reconsideration of the social embeddedness of competitive interactions and governance structures (Gibbons 2005: 5; Guillén et al. 2002). Clarified in a system theoretic jargon, then, markets may be characterized as diversified pluralities with a dominant structure that is accompanied by a variety of inter-penetrating components (Hodgson 1988: 167–8).

These considerations hint at the matter of governance, defined as an institutional mechanism that contributes to the maintenance of behavioural regularities and thus delineates the institutional terrain of markets (Crouch 2005: 20–1). This goes well together with Bourdieu's view of markets as socially constructed fields of power relations that are generated by distinct social forces and mediated by the state (Bourdieu 2005: 12–13). Indeed, market transactions may be viewed as contested social processes that involve common rules and understandings. State, politics, and culture are inherent components in the institutional embeddedness of markets (Krippner et al. 2004). Accordingly, market actors support specific governance structures that stabilize the market process and regulate competition. Corresponding discourses on the legitimation of these control strategies contribute decisively to the evolution of markets (Fligstein 2001: 12–16; White 1981). It follows that governance mechanisms exercise a major impact on the legitimation of organizational forms—and vice versa. Market regulation thus becomes an endogenous component of the market process (Dacin, Goodstein, and Scott 2002: 51–2). In consequence, the related operations of the state co-evolve with the market in a complex setting of institutional reproduction, adaptation, and innovation (Nelson 2002). Again, understanding the institutions of the market requires a move beyond its inherent boundaries.

## 0.5. A Guide to the Chapters of this Book

This book brings together the major lines of institutionalist reasoning on the institutional foundations of the market. It is meant to encourage cross-disciplinary dialogue, while allowing for a pluralism of conceptual frameworks and methodological positions. Because of its concern with the institutions of the market, this book focuses on theoretical positions that are rooted in organization studies, institutional economics, economic sociology, and institutional political economy. The resulting exposition is divided into three parts, which are concerned with the organizational actors, competitive interactions, and governance mechanisms of markets. Part I presents explorations into the organizational behaviour of firms as market actors. It highlights issues of knowledge and learning in the formation of dynamic capabilities and organizational interactions. Part II addresses the institutional dynamism of market competition. In approaching markets as social systems, the social construction and structuration of competition is taken to the fore. Part III examines the subject of market governance. It accounts for the social embeddedness of market operations and thus approaches governance as an institutional process in the coordination of private and public sectors. Set out in more detail, then, the chapters of this book proceed as follows.

The chapters of Part I address the organizational behaviour of firms in the institutional setting of markets. Geoffrey M. Hodgson explores the intellectual history of the idea of organizational learning. In particular, George Henry Lewes's concept of the 'general mind' and Thorstein Veblen's notion of collective knowledge are taken to the fore. Both point out that the social store of custom and tradition is made up of accumulated knowledge. Learning is thus a process of positive feedback between individuals and society. Similar conceptions have become popular once again with the rise of modern behavioural and evolutionary economics, which account for organizational learning as a determinant of the market performance of firms. The latter line of reasoning is taken up in Sidney G. Winter's chapter on dynamic capabilities. These capabilities extend, modify, or create those learned patterns of behaviour by which organizations accomplish their productive tasks and maintain their profitability. However, in differentiating adaptive and proactive patterns of change, a decisive problem is posed by the question how apparent opposites, namely, novelty and familiarity, creativity and learned routine, come into a pragmatic synthesis. This question motivates the reconsideration of a 'hierarchy of change', which implies that higher-order dynamic capabilities such as capabilities for learning to change might exist. The specific interplay of rules and routines in organizational learning is discussed in Alfred Kieser's chapter. Rules and routines not only serve as organizational memories and repositories of knowledge but also determine the relation between stability and flexibility in the evolution of an organization. Distinct steps of rule-based organizational learning involve the experimental variation, selection, and retention of rules. Yet this process comes about only when actors successfully overcome learning barriers and thus complete the learning cycle. This is a precondition for an organization to succeed in correctly interpreting feedback information from its environment. Henrich R. Greve's chapter proceeds with the question how the institutional environment relates to organizational learning. Two areas of research on organizational change are distinguished: the concept of problemistic search and the concept of inter-organizational diffusion. Research on problemistic search examines conditions that give rise to organizational problems, whereas the theory of diffusion emphasizes the availability of effective solutions. Yet both perspectives rely on a similar model of managerial cognition and its operational effects. A theoretical synthesis thus may advance the understanding of how new behaviours are adopted by organizations. The chapter by Bob Hinings and Namrata Malhotra deals with the matter of change in institutional fields. It highlights the concept of institutional archetypes as a way of understanding radical organizational change within a field. The dynamics of change involve inter-organizational relations as well as the activities of individual organizations and groups within organizations. Organizational responses to institutional change need to involve aspects like values, interest, and power. The proposed process model of institutional change then addresses the de-institutionalization as well as the re-institutionalization of organizational components as an evolutionary process.

The chapters in Part II focus on the social construction and structuration of markets as social systems. The chapter by Neil Fligstein argues that market evolution is supported by a complex array of public and private institutions. This is illustrated by two cases: the emergence of the shareholder value conception of the firm and the rise of Silicon Valley as an innovative location for the computer industry. Countering the free market narrative, Fligstein suggests that both phenomena were embedded in pre-existing social relations framed by an interventionist government. Accordingly, in order to make sense of the direction of economic change, market structures need to be viewed in their larger institutional contexts. These concerns are shared by Rudolf Richter's survey of the literature on the social structure of markets. Arguing from the position of the new institutional economics, Richter deals with the claim that the social structure of markets matters for the performance of firms and industries. Social structure is understood as a set of social relationships, which may be approached in terms of networks. Thus, markets can be understood as systems of network connections. What is in further need of clarification, however, is the role that actors and interests play in the formation of such a social system. The chapter by Peter Walgenbach and Renate Meyer maintains that organizational actors and interests need to be regarded as cultural constructions. In relating strategic action with the process of institutional innovation, a synthesis of organizational institutionalism and Giddens's structuration theory is at hand. This allows for a reconsideration of social practices through which organizational actors reproduce certain structures. Accordingly, institutional innovation is perceived as a representation of the structuring of organizations and markets through entrepreneurial efforts. A further elaboration on these concerns is given in Nikolaus Beck's chapter on organizational ecology as a theory of competition. Organizational ecology views market evolution as the development of populations of organizations that share formal rules and patterns of conduct in a similar market segment. Sociological aspects of that perspective are related to the classic works of Emile Durkheim and Amos Hawley. They actually inform those components of organizational ecology which address competition most explicitly, namely, density dependence and resource partitioning, accompanied by the spatial dimension of competition. An application of these concepts of organizational ecology to the comparative analysis of industry evolution is provided in the chapter by Filippo Carlo Wezel, Christophe Boone, and Arjen van Witteloostuijn. They derive variations of industry evolution from the timing of entry and development of national populations within the same industry. Cross-country density effects are interpreted as a result of international legitimation and competition spill-overs. Thus, pioneer countries, defined as early entrants in the history of an international industry, function not only as broadcasters of legitimation but also as disseminators of competition.

In resuming the comparative perspective on economic evolution, the chapters of Part III examine the matter of market governance. Richard R. Nelson's chapter reviews the role of institutions in economic development. Nelson underscores that the process of institutional evolution is tightly intertwined with technological change. Accounting for that fact, the way productive activities are coordinated is denoted as 'social technology'. Institutions like legal rules and social norms support certain social technologies and make others infeasible. Yet the evolution of social technologies and their supporting institutions proceeds erratically. Ideological influences and a lack of reliable performance feedback imply that societies have very limited ability to design effective institutions. In accordance with these considerations, the chapter by Alexander Ebner addresses the co-evolutionary relationship between markets and states. This relationship is perceived as a key factor in the variety of governance structures that characterize complex market systems. In exploring that topic, the chapter surveys major contributions to the governance approach that have been emerging from the new institutional economics, including the work of Oliver Williamson, Douglass North, and Mancur Olson. Their critical assessment informs the conclusion that institutionalist theorizing requires an evolutionary conceptualization of institutional innovation as a driving force in the transformation of governance structures. The chapter by John Harriss then highlights the role of politics, power, and culture in the explanation of institutional change. The rational choice framework of the new institutional economics is criticized for its apparent limitations in theorizing on these issues. Therefore, Harriss underlines the analytical advantages of historical institutionalism. The conflict among social classes and the institutional substance of power structures are of particular analytical significance. They are interrelated factors in the evolution of cultural values, as exemplified by the case of Indian economic development and its sociopolitical underpinnings. Bob Jessop reconsiders these issues from a Polanyian perspective. Jessop's chapter interprets Karl Polanyi's institutionalist analysis of the market system in the light of two institutionalist schools, namely, the regulation approach to contemporary capitalism and systems theory with its account of the market as an autopoietic system. Both maintain that the market economy is an operationally autonomous system which is socially embedded and thus requires complex forms of governance. This is particularly relevant when it comes to governance in the knowledge-based economy. Robert Boyer's chapter examines the relationship between regulation theory and Bourdieu's sociology. Regulationist research has turned to Bourdieu's concepts of habitus and fields as a micro-perspective on macroeconomic phenomena. Habitus accounts for the evolution of preferences under contextual influences. The latter are shaped by institutional fields such as markets and industries, which are subject to complex forces of change, involving the reconfiguration of power relations. A significant proportion of theories in the new institutionalism has adopted these arguments. However, they are particularly well represented in economic sociology.

## References

Aldrich, H. E. and Martinez, M. A. (2001). 'Many Are Called, but Few Are Chosen: An Evolutionary Perspective for the Study of Entrepreneurship', *Entrepreneurship Theory and Practice*, 25: 41–56.

Amable, B. (2003). *The Diversity of Modern Capitalism*. Oxford: Oxford University Press.

Aoki, M. (2001). *Toward A Comparative Institutional Analysis*. Cambridge, MA: MIT Press.

Beckert, J. (2002). *Beyond the Market: The Social Foundations of Economic Efficiency*. Princeton, NJ: Princeton University Press.

Bourdieu, P. (2005). *The Social Structures of the Economy*, trans. by C. Turner. Cambridge: Polity Press.

Bowles, S. (2004). *Microeconomics: Behavior, Institutions, and Evolution*. Princeton, NJ: Princeton University Press.

Boyer, R. (1997). 'The Variety and Unequal Performance of Really Existing Markets: Farewell to Doctor Pangloss', in J. R. Hollingsworth and R. Boyer (eds.), *Contemporary Capitalism: The Embeddedness of Institutions*. Cambridge: Cambridge University Press.

—— and Saillard, Y. (2002). 'A Summary of Régulation Theory', in R. Boyer and Y. Saillard (eds.), *Régulation Theory: The State of the Art*. London and New York: Routledge.

Campbell, J. L. (2004). *Institutional Change and Globalization*. Princeton, NJ: Princeton University Press.

—— and Pedersen, O. K. (2001). 'Introduction: The Rise of Neoliberalism and Institutional Analysis', in J. L. Campbell and O. K. Perdersen (eds.), *The Rise of Neoliberalism and Institutional Analysis*. Princeton, NJ: Princeton University Press.

Chang, H. J. (2002). 'Breaking the Mould: An Institutionalist Political Economy Alternative to the Neo-Liberal Theory of the Market and the State', *Cambridge Journal of Economics*, 26: 539–59.

Clemens, E. S. and Cook, J. M. (1999). 'Politics and Institutionalism: Explaining Durability and Change', *Annual Review of Sociology*, 25: 441–66.

Colomy, P. (1998). 'Neofunctionalism and Neoinstitutionalism: Human Agency and Interest in Institutional Change', *Sociological Forum*, 13: 265–300.

Coriat, B. and Dosi, G. (1998). 'The Institutional Embeddedness of Economic Change: An Appraisal of the "Evolutionary" and "Regulationist" Research Programmes', in K. Nielsen and B. Johnson (eds.), *Institutions and Economic Change: New Perspectives on Markets, Firms and Technology*. Cheltenham, UK: Elgar.

Crouch, C. (2005). *Capitalist Diversity and Change: Recombinant Governance and Institutional Entrepreneurs*. Oxford: Oxford University Press.

Dacin, M. T., Goodstein, J., and Scott, W. R. (2002). 'Institutional Theory and Institutional Change', *Academy of Management Journal*, 45: 45–57.

DiMaggio, P. J. (1998). 'The New Institutionalism: Avenues of Collaboration', *Journal of Institutional and Theoretical Economics*, 154: 696–705.

——and Powell, W. W. (1991). 'Introduction', in W. W. Powell and P. J. DiMaggio (eds.), *The New Institutionalism in Organizational Analysis*. Chicago, IL: Chicago University Press.

Dobbin, F. (2004). 'The Sociological View of the Economy', in F. Dobbin (ed.), *The New Economic Sociology*. Princeton, NJ: Princeton University Press.

Dosi, G. and Nelson, R. R. (1994). 'An Introduction to Evolutionary Theories in Economics', *Journal of Evolutionary Economics*, 4: 153–72.

——— and Winter, S. (2000). 'Introduction: The Nature and Dynamics of Organizational Capabilities', in G. Dosi, R. R. Nelson, and S. Winter (eds.), *The Nature and Dynamics of Organizational Capabilities*. Oxford: Oxford University Press.

Ebner, A. (2008). *Embedded Entrepreneurship: The Institutional Dynamics of Innovation*. London and New York: Routledge.

Fligstein, N. (2001). *The Architecture of Markets: An Economic Sociology of Twenty-First Century Capitalist Societies*. Princeton, NJ: Princeton University Press.

——(2002). 'Agreements, Disagreements, and Opportunities in the "New Sociology of Markets" ', in M. F. Guillén, R. Collins, P. England, and M. Meyer (eds.), *The New Economic Sociology*. New York: Russell Sage.

Furubotn, E. and Richter, R. (1997). *Institutions and Economic Theory: The Contribution of the New Institutional Economics*. Ann Arbor: University of Michigan Press.

Garud, R., Hardy, C., and Maguire, S. (2007). 'Institutional Entrepreneurship as Embedded Agency: An Introduction to the Special Issue', *Organization Studies*, 28: 957–69.

Gibbons, R. (2005). 'What Is Economic Sociology and Should any Economists Care?', *Journal of Economic Perspectives*, 19: 3–7.

Granovetter, M. (1985). 'Economic Action and Social Structure: The Problem of Embeddedness', *American Journal of Sociology*, 91: 481–510.

——(2002). 'A Theoretical Agenda for Economic Sociology', in M. F. Guillén, R. Collins, P. England, and M. Meyer (eds.), *The New Economic Sociology*. New York: Sage.

——(2005). 'The Impact of Social Structure on Economic Outcomes', *Journal of Economic Perspectives*, 19: 33–50.

Greenwood, R. and Hinings, C. R. (1996). 'Understanding Radical Organizational Change: Bringing Together the Old and the New Institutionalism', *Academy of Management Review*, 21: 1022–54.

Greif, A. (1998). 'Historical and Comparative Institutional Analysis', *American Economic Review*, 88: 80–4.

Guillén, M. F., Collins, R., England, P., and Meyer, M. (2002). 'The Revival of Economic Sociology', in M. F. Guillén, R. Collins, P. England, and M. Meyer (eds.), *The New Economic Sociology*. New York: Sage.

Hall, P. A. and Soskice, D. (2001). 'An Introduction to Varieties of Capitalism', in P. A. Hall and D. Soskice (eds.), *Varieties of Capitalism: The Institutional Foundations of Comparative Advantage*. Oxford: Oxford University Press.

—— and Taylor, R. C. R. (1996). 'Political Science and the Three New Institutionalisms', *Political Studies*, 44: 936–57.

Hannan, M. T. (2005). 'Ecologies of Organizations: Diversity and Identity', *Journal of Economic Perspectives*, 19: 51–70.

Hay, C. and Wincott, D. (1998). 'Structure, Agency and Historical Institutionalism', *Political Studies*, XLVI: 951–7.

Hira, A. and Hira, R. (2000). 'The New Institutionalism: Contradictory Notions of Change', *American Journal of Economics and Sociology*, 59: 267–82.

Hirsch, P. M. (1997). 'Sociology without Social Structure: Neoinstitutional Theory Meets Brave New World', *American Journal of Sociology*, 102: 1702–23.

Hodgson, G. M. (1988). *Economics and Institutions: A Manifesto for a Modern Institutional Economics*. Cambridge: Polity Press.

Hollingsworth, J. R. and Boyer, R. (1997). 'Coordination of Economic Actors and Social Systems of Production', in J. R. Hollingsworth and R. Boyer (eds.), *Contemporary Capitalism: The Embeddedness of Institutions*. Cambridge: Cambridge University Press.

Immergut, E. (1998). 'The Theoretical Core of the New Institutionalism', *Politics and Society*, 26: 5–34.

—— (2006). 'Historical Institutionalism in Political Science and the Problem of Change', in A. Wimmer and R. Kössler (eds.), *Understanding Change: Models, Methodologies, and Metaphors*. Houndmills, Basingstoke: Palgrave Macmillan.

Ingram, P. and Clay, K. (2000). 'The Choice-Within-Constraints New Institutionalism and Implications for Sociology', *Annual Review of Sociology*, 26: 525–46.

Katznelson, I. and Weingast, B. R. (2005). 'Intersections Between Historical and Rational Choice Institutionalism', in I. Katznelson and B. R. Weingast (eds.), *Preferences and Situations: Points of Intersection Between Historical and Rational Choice Institutionalism*. New York: Russell Sage.

Krippner, G., Granovetter, M., Block, F., Biggart, N., Beamish, T., Hsing, Y., Hart, G., Arrighi, G., Mendell, M., Hall, J., Burawoy, M., Vogel, S. and O'Riain, S. (2004). 'Polanyi Symposium: A Conversation on Embeddedness', *Socio-Economic Review*, 2: 109–35.

Mahoney, J. (2000). 'Path Dependence in Historical Sociology', *Theory and Society*, 29: 507–48.

March, J. G. and Olsen, J. P. (1989). *Rediscovering Institutions: The Organizational Basis of Politics*. New York: Free Press.

Morgan, G. (2005). 'Institutional Complementarities, Path Dependency, and the Dynamics of Firms', in G. Morgan, R. Whitley, and E. Moen (eds.), *Changing Capitalisms? Internationalization, Institutional Change, and Systems of Economic Organization*. Oxford: Oxford University Press.

Nee, V. (1998). 'Sources of the New Institutionalism', in M. C. Brinton and V. Nee (eds.), *The New Institutionalism in Sociology*. New York: Sage.

—— (2005). 'The New Institutionalisms in Economics and Sociology', in N. Smelser and R. Swedberg (eds.), *Handbook of Economic Sociology*, 2nd edn. Princeton, NJ: Princeton University Press.

Nelson, R. R. (1995). 'Recent Evolutionary Theorizing about Economic Change', *Journal of Economic Literature*, 33: 48–90.

—— (2002). 'The Problem of Market Bias in Modern Capitalist Economies', *Industrial and Corporate Change*, 11: 207–44.

—— and Winter, S. (1982). *An Evolutionary Theory of Economic Change*. Cambridge, MA: Harvard University Press.

Nielsen, K. (2001). 'Institutionalist Approaches in the Social Sciences: Typologies, Dialogues, and Future Challenges', *Journal of Economic Issues*, 35: 505–16.

North, D. C. (1990). *Institutions, Institutional Change and Economic Performance*. Cambridge: Cambridge University Press.

—— (2005). *Understanding the Process of Economic Change*. Princeton, NJ: Princeton University Press.

Peters, B. G. (2005). *Institutional Theory in Political Science: The 'New Institutionalism'*, 2nd edn. London: Continuum.

Pierson, P. (2000a). 'Increasing Returns, Path Dependence, and the Study of Politics', *American Political Science Review*, 94: 251–67.

—— (2000b). 'The Limits of Design: Explaining Institutional Origins and Change', *Governance*, 13: 475–99.

Reich, S. (2000). 'The Four Faces of Institutionalism: Public Policy and a Pluralistic Perspective', *Governance*, 13: 501–22.

Scharpf, F. (1997). *Games Real Actors Play: Actor-Centered Institutionalism in Policy-Research*. Boulder, CO: Westview.

Schmidt, V. (2006). 'Give Peace a Chance: Reconciling Four (Not Three) "New Institutionalisms'", paper presented at the Annual Meetings of the American Political Science Association, Philadelphia, PA, 31 August–3 September, 2006.

Scott, W. R. (2001). *Institutions and Organizations*, 2nd edn. Thousand Oaks: Sage.

Shepsle, K. (2001). 'A Comment on Institutional Change', *Journal of Theoretical Politics*, 13: 321–5.

Smelser, N. J. and Swedberg, R. (1994). 'The Sociological Perspective on the Economy', in N. J. Smelser and R. Swedberg (eds.), *The Handbook of Economic Sociology*. Princeton, NJ: Princeton University Press.

Streeck, W. (2005). 'Rejoinder: On Terminology, Functionalism, (Historical) Institutionalism and Liberalization', *Socio-Economic Review*, 3: 577–87.

—— and Thelen, K. (2005). 'Introduction: Institutional Change in Advanced Political Economies', in W. Streeck and K. Thelen (eds.), *Beyond Continuity: Institutional Change in Advanced Political Economies*. Oxford: Oxford University Press.

Swedberg, R. (2005a). 'The Economic Sociology of Capitalism: An Introduction and Agenda', in V. Nee and R. Swedberg (eds.), *The Economic Sociology of Capitalism*. Princeton, NJ: Princeton University Press.

—— (2005b). 'Markets in Society', in N. Smelser and R. Swedberg (eds.), *The Handbook of Economic Sociology*, 2nd edn. Princeton, NJ: Princeton University Press.

Teece, D. J., Pisano, G., and Shuen, A. (2000). 'Dynamic Capabilities and Strategic Management', in G. Dosi, R. R. Nelson, and S. Winter (eds.), *The Nature and Dynamics of Organizational Capabilities*. Oxford: Oxford University Press.

Thelen, K. (1999). 'Historical Institutionalism in Comparative Politics', *Annual Review of Political Science*, 2: 369–404.

—— (2003). 'How Institutions Evolve: Insights from Comparative Historical Analysis', in J. Mahoney and D. Rueschemeyer (eds.), *Comparative Historical Analysis in the Social Sciences*. Cambridge: Cambridge University Press.

White, H. (1981). 'Where Do Markets Come From?', *American Journal of Sociology*, 87: 517–47.

Williamson, O. E. (1985). *The Economic Institutions of Capitalism: Firms, Markets, Relational Contracting*. New York: Free Press.

—— (2000). 'The New Institutional Economics: Taking Stock, Looking Ahead', *Journal of Economic Literature*, 38: 595–613.

Witt, U. (1993). 'Evolutionary Economics: Some Principles', in U. Witt (ed.), *Evolution in Markets and Institutions*. Heidelberg: Physica.

Zafirowski, M. (2004). 'Paradigms for Analysis of Social Institutions: A Case for Sociological Institutionalism', *International Review of Sociology*, 14: 363–97.

Zysman, J. (1994). 'How Institutions Create Historically Rooted Trajectories of Growth', *Industrial and Corporate Change*, 3: 243–81.

Part I

# Market Agents: Knowledge and Learning in Organizations

# 1

# The Emergence of the Idea of Institutions as Repositories of Knowledge

*Geoffrey M. Hodgson*

## 1.1. Introduction

The term 'organizational learning' is now commonplace.[1] In a related vein, the idea of knowledge as something that is not simply in our heads, but is cued and enabled by social relations and structures, is gaining currency among economists and other social scientists (Clark 1997; Kogut 2000; Lane et al. 1996; Langlois 2001).

However, these ideas remain controversial, and others insist that knowledge and learning are nothing beyond the mental capacities of individuals. It is said that only individuals learn, and talk of institutional knowledge or organizational learning is to commit the fallacy of attributing to social structures properties that are essentially cerebral and individual.

An aim of this chapter is to show that these issues and controversies are far from new, and they can be traced back at least to the last quarter of the nineteenth century. In addition, this excursion into the history of ideas shows that answers to the individualist objection above were evident at the beginning. Consequently, methodological insights are derived from this historical excursion, which can help sustain contemporary concepts such as organizational learning.

The two principal historical figures discussed here are George Henry Lewes (1817–78) and Thorstein Veblen (1857–1929). They were both

---

[1] This chapter makes use of material from Hodgson (2003*b*, 2004).

inspired by the rise of Darwinism, and they were linked by other important thinkers, particularly Conwy Lloyd Morgan (1852–1936). However, by the 1920s there was a strong reaction against the philosophical assumptions adopted by Lewes and Veblen, and the development of analysis in this tradition was truncated. It has been revived by recent work, but largely without reference to its precursors in the history of ideas.


## 1.2. George Henry Lewes and the 'General Mind'

George Henry Lewes lived in London and was acquainted with leading figures such as Charles Darwin, Thomas Henry Huxley, and Herbert Spencer. His philosophical *magnum opus* was *Problems of Life and Mind* (Lewes 1874, 1875, 1877, 1879). Therein Lewes (1875: 412) was the originator of the concept of an 'emergent'. He inspired pioneers of the philosophy of emergent properties, such as Conwy Lloyd Morgan (1923), who was a student of Huxley. Lewes used the concept of emergent to address the relationship between the evolution of human nature and the evolution of civilization. Lewes believed neither that the mind could be explained entirely in physical or neurophysiological terms (although the mind depends for its existence on neural matter) nor that human society could be explained entirely in terms of the biotic characteristics of its individual members (although society depends for its existence on the biotic vitality of those individuals). He thus pointed to an *emergent level* of social evolution.

Indeed, Lewes connected the two problems and their responses, by taking the concept of mind at the individual level and proposing the concept of the 'General Mind' at the social level. For Lewes, the 'General Mind' was not a mystical entity, but his choice of term betrayed the Hegelian influence on his thought. It had an equivalent ontological status to ideas such as 'organizational learning' and 'collective action' that are commonly used today. But we must allow Lewes (1879, vol. 1: 161–2) to speak for himself:

The experiences of each individual come and go; they correct, enlarge, destroy one another, leaving behind them a certain residual store, which, condensed in intuitions and formulated in principles, direct and modify all future experiences. The sum of these is designated as the individual mind. A similar process evolves the General Mind—the residual store of experiences common to all. By means of language the individual shares in the general fund, which thus becomes for him an impersonal objective influence. To it each appeals. We all assimilate some of its material, and help to increase its store. Not only do we find ourselves confronting Nature, to whose order we must conform, but confronting Society, whose laws we must obey. We have to learn what Nature is and does, what our fellow-men think and will, and unless we learn aright and act in conformity, we are inexorably punished.

Accordingly, customs and laws serve as emergent stores of intuitions and experiences. They are formed by individuals, but they also form a social environment to which each individual adapts. Not only do these customs and laws emerge out of individuals and their interactions, but these also coerce and impose sanctions upon individuals. Lewes's exposition involves a notion of social structure that is not reduced to individuals. Neither is the individual explained entirely by structure. Enlarging on these points, Lewes (1879, vol. 1: 164–5) continued:

Customs arise, and are formulated in laws, the restraint of all. The customs, born of the circumstances, immanent in the social conditions, are consciously extricated and prescribed as the rules of life; each new generation is born in this social medium, and has to adapt itself to the established forms. . . . It makes a man accept what he cannot understand, and obey what he does not believe. His thoughts are only partly his own; they are also the thoughts of others. His actions are guided by the will of others; even in rebellion he has them in his mind. His standard is outside. . . . If he does not feel what all feel, he is thrown out of account, except in the reckoning of abnormalities. Individual experiences being limited and individual spontaneity feeble, we are strengthened and enriched by assimilating the experiences of others.

Lewes proposed here an articulation of actor and structure, where each was conditioned by, and dependent on, the other. His position was antithetical to the bipolar extremes of methodological individualism and methodological collectivism, at least in their reductionist versions (Hodgson 2004, 2007a, 2007b). However, while seeing this two-way interdependence of actor and structure, Lewes did not regard the relationship between actor and structure as symmetrical. For Lewes, the past dominated the present; we all adapt to a world that existed before our birth. Those now dead largely created this world, but the living can in some respects change it. Lewes (1879: 166) wrote:

Civilisation is the accumulation of experiences; and since it is this accumulated wealth which is the tradition of the race, we may say with Comte that the Past more and more dominates the Present, precisely as in the individual case it is the registered experiences which more and more determine the feelings and opinions.

Human knowledge is pre-eminently distinguished from Animal knowledge by this collective experience.

Building on Auguste Comte's ironic insight that the dead dominate social life, Lewes realized that collective experience likewise bound the individual to the past. Through social structures and customs, we are pressured (albeit often incompletely) not only to acquiesce and to conform but also to 'feel what all feel' and adopt the beliefs and preferences of others. The accumulated experiences of all 'more and more determine the feelings and opinions'. I have used the term *reconstitutive downward causation* to describe the possibility that social structures can change individual preferences to some degree (Hodgson 2003*a*, 2004).

Lewes pointed to the fact that the social store of custom and tradition is made up essentially of 'collective experience' and accumulated knowledge, built up with the growth of human civilization and accessible in part by means of language and learning. Hence Lewes pointed to the insight that social institutions are not simply rules and constraints but also *repositories of social knowledge*. He indicated that institutions could accumulate experience and knowledge in some way.[2]

Several theorists, including Karl Marx, saw social structures as reconstituting individual preferences or beliefs. For example, in the third volume of *Capital*, Marx (1981: 1020) wrote of 'specific social characters that the social production process stamps on individuals'. But this notion is less well developed in Marx's writings. Also, compared with Lewes, the more dramatic omission is that Marx did not articulate a conception of social institutions as repositories of social knowledge. Indeed, the concept of knowledge in Marx's work is one largely of natural-scientific or technical knowledge. Marx did not fully recognize that social interactions require and sustain other forms of knowledge that are an essential part of individual adaptation within society. These other forms of knowledge are partly expressed in customs, rules, and other protocols of behaviour. Part of this rich heritage of knowledge is built up in the centuries of accumulated common law. Marx lacked a developed concept of custom, and he saw common law as something conservative, to be swept aside in social revolution, rather than carefully sifted and partially retained. Following Lewes, custom eventually became a central concept in American institutional

---

[2] Other social theorists recognized social evolution as in part an accumulation of experiences and ideas. Such hints are found, for example, in Buckle (1858) and in an essay of Huxley (1894, vol. 7: 155–6) from the 1860s. But neither author placed social evolution in the context of emergent properties, as Lewes had done.

economics, thus expressing an important difference between Marxism and institutionalism.[3]

Lewes's notion that social institutions acted as emergent repositories of social knowledge resolved a particular problem that had perplexed Alfred Russel Wallace and others concerning the evolution of the human species. Wallace (1870)—Darwin's collaborator—had concluded that different races, whether in primitive or civilized circumstances, were at similar levels of intellectual potential. But he then could not explain the relatively rapid evolution of human civilization in some regions, while other humans remained in a savage state. Lewes proposed that once writing and records emerged, civilization itself could evolve at a rate much faster than the physiological and mental capacities of humans themselves, as knowledge and experience were accumulated. Human capacities could not be understood in terms of the human brain alone. Human abilities also depended on the structured environment of social interactions between individuals. The growing knowledge that was embedded in social structures provided an environment in which individuals could realize more and more of their intellectual potential, possibly without such a rapid growth in individual human capabilities.

However, Lewes did not give enough emphasis to this argument because he retained, like Charles Darwin (1859) himself, strong Lamarckian inclinations. If the Lamarckian inheritance of acquired individual human characters were possible, then the mechanism outlined in the last paragraph was not necessary to explain the growth of human civilization. It could be explained by acquired character inheritance alone. An additional mechanism, where the evolving social environment itself stimulated individuals to fulfil their potential, would not be essential. For this reason, the full impact of Lewes's additional argument was not realized, even by Lewes himself.

However, Lewes's argument had a greater impact a few years after his death, when August Weismann (1893) provided experimental evidence and theoretical arguments to undermine the idea that the Lamarckian inheritance of acquired characters was prevalent in the biological sphere. Without Lamarckian transmission at the biological level, the importance of cultural transmission of knowledge at the institutional level was more

---

[3] Note the valid criticism of Marx by Commons (1925: 686–7): 'Here is the culminating oversight of Karl Marx in his theory of socialism . . . namely, the failure to see the importance of custom, and what in Anglo-American jurisprudence is named the common law . . . between the individual and the state is a supreme principle of stabilization by custom, which both regulates the individual proprietor, on the one hand, and overrides the arbitrary will of the state, on the other hand.'

important. Morgan (1896) was persuaded by Weismann's arguments, and developed Lewes's ideas precisely in the required direction.

Several other issues were insufficiently clarified in Lewes's work. He articulated only partially an ontology of different levels. The nature of social institutions and structures was not examined in any depth. Furthermore, Lewes did not elaborate any psychological mechanism through which individual feelings, beliefs, or aspirations could be remoulded by their institutional or social circumstances. Yet he made a significant start. Partly under the stimulation of further debates within biology, Lewes's ideas would receive further development. In regarding institutions as repositories of social knowledge, and in pointing to emergent properties as a possible mean of establishing a social ontology, Lewes paved the way for a multilevel theory of selection and evolution, in which social evolution was a part.

## 1.3. Thorstein Veblen and the Community of Knowledge

Thorstein Veblen was the fourth son and the sixth child of Norwegian immigrants who had arrived in the United States in 1847. The family moved to Minnesota when Thorstein was a young boy. Like Lewes, Veblen was influenced by Darwinism and grappled with the application of the Darwinian worldview to social phenomena. He read widely in anthropology, biology, and the social sciences.

There are at least two likely routes through which the ideas of Lewes reached Veblen. The first is through the British philosopher Morgan, who visited Veblen's then university in Chicago in 1896 (Dorfman 1934: 139; Hodgson 2004). The influence of Lewes on Morgan (1896: 340) is clear in the following passage:

In the written record, in social traditions, in the manifold inventions which make scientific and industrial progress possible, in the products of art, and the recorded examples of noble lives, we have an environment which is at the same time the product of mental evolution, and affords the condition of the development of each individual mind to-day.

In addition, Lewes influenced leading American intellectuals such as the sociologist Franklin Giddings. Significantly, Giddings (1896: 132–3) recognized George Henry Lewes's concept of a 'social mind'(1879: 161–5).

Other sociologists, such as Charles Horton Cooley (1902, 1907), developed similar ideas.[4]

Possibly partly through ideas inherited from Lewes and hints provided by Morgan, Veblen took up and developed the notion that social groups and institutions carry accumulated knowledge and experiences from the past. Accordingly, Veblen argued that the social complex of interacting individual habits constituted a social stock of largely intangible knowledge that could not be associated with individuals severally. As Veblen (1898: 353–4) put it:

Production takes place only in society—only through the co-operation of an industrial community. This industrial community... always comprises a group, large enough to contain and transmit the traditions, tools, technical knowledge, and usages without which there can be no industrial organization and no economic relation of individuals to one another or to their environment. The isolated individual is not a productive agent. What he can do at best is to live from season to season, as the non-gregarious animals do. There can be no production without technical knowledge; hence no accumulation and no wealth to be owned, in severalty or otherwise. And there is no technical knowledge apart from an industrial community.

Most economists uphold that production is entirely a result of owned factors of production—such as land, capital, and labour—whose owners can be remunerated accordingly. In contrast, Veblen (1921: 28) argued consistently that production depended on a 'joint stock of knowledge derived from past experience' that itself could not become an individually owned commodity, because it involved the practices of the whole industrial community. Veblen (1898: 354) continued:

Since there is no individual production and no individual productivity, the natural-rights preconception that ownership rests on the individually productive labor of the owner reduces itself to absurdity, even under the logic of its own assumptions.

However, it is not Veblen's critique of mainstream economics that primarily concerns us here, but his contribution to the foundations of economic and social theory. Veblen's devastating critique of the concept of capital in economic theory is best encountered by reading the original essays (1908a, 1908b, 1908c). We focus here on Veblen's argument that learning and experience are accumulated within a community (1908b: 539–40):

---

[4] In turn, Cooley was an influence on G. H. Mead (1934).

These immaterial industrial expedients are necessarily a product of the community, the immaterial residue of the community's experience, past and present; which has no existence apart from the community's life, and can be transmitted only in the keeping of the community at large.

Veblen (1914: 103) repeated this point, again and again, here referring to technological knowledge and its storage in the social group:

Technological knowledge is of the nature of a common stock, held and carried forward by the community, which is in this relation to be conceived as a going concern. The state of the industrial arts is a fact of group life, not of individual or private initiative or innovation. It is an affair of the collectivity, not a creative achievement of individuals working self-sufficiently in severalty or in isolation.

However, he made it clear that the collective domain of knowledge does not devalue the role of the individual, or the fact that knowledge is always held by individuals and is a matter of individual experience. As Veblen (1908b: 521) put it:

The complement of technological knowledge so held, used, and transmitted in the life of the community is, of course, made up out of the experience of individuals. Experience, experimentation, habit, knowledge, initiative, are phenomena of individual life, and it is necessarily from this source that the community's common stock is all derived. The possibility of growth lies in the feasibility of accumulating knowledge gained by individual experience and initiative, and therefore it lies in the feasibility of one individual's learning from the experience of another.

The individual and the social aspects of knowledge are connected, because the social environment and its 'common stock' of experience provide the means and stimulus to individual learning. The social environment is the result of individual interactions, but without this social environment the individual would be stultified. Learning is thus potentially a process of positive feedback between individual and society. The above quotations make it clear that Veblen saw the social domain as the site of a potential storehouse of knowledge. But Veblen took the argument one significant step further. In the *Theory of the Leisure Class*, Veblen (1899: 193–4) wrote:

Any community may be viewed as an industrial or economic mechanism, the structure of which is made up of what is called its economic institutions. These institutions are habitual methods of carrying on the life process of the community in material contact with the material environment in which it lives. When given methods of unfolding human activity in this given environment have been elaborated in this way, the life of the community will express itself with some facility in these habitual directions. The community will make use of the forces of the environment for the purposes of its life according to methods learned in the past and embodied in those institutions.

This brought his concept of a social institution into the picture. Veblen stated here that institutions are social structures, involving individual habits and engaged with a material environment. He wrote of members of a community making use of their social and material environment for their purposes, according to methods learned in the past and embodied in their social institutions. The latter quotation is one of Veblen's clearest statements that institutions function as repositories of social knowledge.

He also discussed some of the mechanisms and means by which this knowledge is stored. Veblen (1906: 592) wrote of 'habits of thought that rule in the working-out of a system of knowledge' being 'fostered by . . . the institutional structure under which the community lives'. Veblen not only identified an environment of stored knowledge that is conducive to learning—as was the case with Lewes and Morgan—but also saw it as structured and made up of institutions. These institutions are the expression and outcome of the interaction of habituated individual behaviours, but cannot be reduced to the behaviours of individuals alone.

Veblen (1914: 38–9) explained that 'the habitual acquirements of the race are handed on from one generation to the next, by tradition, training, education, or whatever general term may best designate that discipline of habituation by which the young acquire what the old have learned'. Veblen (1914: 39) wrote: 'handed on by the same discipline of habituation, goes a cumulative body of knowledge'. In terms redolent of Lewes and Morgan, Veblen saw conventions, customs, and institutions as repositories of social knowledge. Institutional adaptations and behavioural norms were stored in individual habits and could be passed on by education or imitation to succeeding generations.

Consequently, Veblen emphasized the *double weight of the past* on human deliberation and decision-making. First, the natural selection of instincts over hundreds of thousands of years has provided humans with a set of basic dispositions, albeit with substantial 'variations of individuality' (Veblen 1914: 13) from person to person. The newborn infant comes into the world with these fixed and inherited propensities. But, second, the world of the child is one of specific customs and institutions into which he or she must be socialized. The individual learns to adapt to these circumstances, and through repeated action acquires culturally specific habits of thought and behaviour. These customs and institutions

31

have also evolved through time; they are the weight of the past at the social level. The weight of instinct results from the phylogenetic evolution of the human population. Habituation is the mechanism through which the weight of social institutions can make its mark on the ontogenetic development of each individual.

However, Veblen did not develop his analysis of the institutional aspect of social knowledge much further. The philosophical underpinnings of his approach remained underdeveloped, and he seems to have taken little notice of the key developments in emergentist philosophy that occurred in the last fifteen years of his life (Blitz 1992; Hodgson 2004).

In the absence of a stratified ontology and a developed concept of emergent properties, social theorists would always be wary of terms like 'social memory' and the notion that knowledge could be associated with routines, organizations, and institutions, as well as with individuals. Veblen's idea was the germ of a research programme that took many decades to be revived and further developed. In the meantime, there was a reaction in the social sciences against any notion that knowledge was anything more than merely an individual phenomenon.

By the 1920s, influential sociologists such as Floyd Allport (1924, 1927) argued for a version of reductionism where groups and institutions were to be explained solely in terms of individual behaviour, understood in terms of the canons of behaviourist psychology. Allport (1924: 689) saw error in attempts 'to explain social phenomena in terms of the group as a whole, whereas the true explanation is to be found only in its component parts, the individuals'.

Emergentist philosophy itself came under attack in the late 1920s, and was rendered unfashionable by the rise of logical positivism in the 1930s (Blitz 1992). Logical positivism regarded such ontological considerations as largely valueless. Consequently, deprived of theoretical and philosophical support, the idea of institutions as repositories of knowledge was marginalized.

## 1.4. The Recent Revival of the Concept of Institutional Knowledge

While structuralist and collectivist approaches became prominent in postwar sociology, the earlier conception of institutions as repositories of knowledge was largely forgotten. Although there were occasional prior appearances, similar conceptions did not begin to become popular again until the 1980s, when in economics Richard Nelson and Sidney Winter (1982) described routines as 'organizational memory' and sociologists such as Barbara Levitt and James G. March (1988) rehabilitated the concept of 'organizational learning'. But none of these key works from the 1980s refers to Lewes or Veblen.

A key point is that institutions provide an environment, consisting of routines, images, artefacts, and information, which can enhance the capabilities of individuals. Accordingly, even if knowledge is regarded as an individual phenomenon, existing solely in the memory traces of individuals, then institutions provide a structured environment consisting partly of routinized practices that can augment individual capabilities. The institutional whole is more than the sum of its individual parts.

As an example, Chris Argyris and Donald Schön (1996: 8) develop concepts of 'organizational knowledge' and 'organizational learning' that are nevertheless consistent with a view that knowledge is traceable to the memories or capacities of individuals. Argyris and Schön (1996: 12–13) write:

First, organizations function in several ways as *holding environments for knowledge* ... in an organization's files, which record its actions, decisions, regulations, and policies ... in physical objects that members use as references and guideposts as they go about their business. ... Second, *organizations directly represent knowledge* in the sense that they embody strategies for performing complex tasks ... Organizational knowledge is embedded in routines and practices which may be inspected and decoded even when the individuals who carry them out are unable to put them into words.

Learning becomes organizational when it is not only embedded in the minds of its members but also incorporated in the structures, files, or routines of the organization itself. The mark of organizational learning is a change in the environment in which the individuals operate, leading to enhanced individual or organizational capabilities.

Scott Cook and Dvora Yanow (1993) develop a similar argument, focusing also on the capacity of corporate culture to preserve and enhance capabilities. For them, organizational learning is more than the cognitions of individuals. It involves the development of cultural features, constituted in intersubjective meanings and expressed in common practices. Through such meaning-bearing activities, languages, and objects, knowledge is reproduced and transmitted in the firm. Much of this knowledge is tacit and beyond codifiable description.

Luigi Marengo (1992) and others explicitly incorporate the concept of organizational learning into the theory of the firm. David Lane et al. (1996) develop the concept of 'generative relationships'. These social relationships are part of the make-up of a firm: they are part of the corporate environment in which individuals work. Just as individuals adapt to their environment, interactions among the participants in a 'generative relationship' can change the way the participants conceive the world and act in it. They give rise to new capabilities and are partly emergent, in the sense that what develops is not predictable from knowledge of interacting individuals alone. The attributions, competences, and entities that are constructed from interactions cannot be predicted from knowledge of the participating agents alone, without knowledge of the structure and history of the interactions that constitute the generative relationships. What is common to all these explanations is the proposition that individual capabilities can be enhanced in specific institutional environments.

The concept of routines is relevant here (Becker 2004, 2005; Lazaric 2000). Michael D. Cohen and Paul Bacdayan (1994) show in specific detail how organizational routines can aid the memories of the individuals involved. They use the distinction in psychology between procedural and other, more cognitive forms of memory, such as semantic, episodic, or declarative memory. Procedural memory is triggered by social or other cues. 'Procedural knowledge is less subject to decay, less explicitly accessible, and less easy to transfer to novel circumstances' (Cohen and Bacdayan 1994: 557).

Routines depend on a group of individuals, each with habits of a particular kind, where many of these habits depend on procedural memory. The behavioural cues by some members of a structured assembly of habituated individuals trigger specific habits in others. Hence various individual habits sustain each other in an interlocking structure of reciprocating individual behaviours. The organization or group provides a social and physical environment for each individual. This environment is made up of the other individuals, the relations between them and the technological and physical artefacts that they may use in their interactions. This social and physical environment produces cues that can trigger behaviours, which, in turn, can trigger the behaviour of others, perhaps produce or modify some artefacts, and help change or replicate parts of this social and physical environment.

Partly because of procedural memory, organizations can have important additional properties and capacities that are not possessed by individuals, taken severally. The organization provides the social and physical environment that is necessary to cue individual habits and deploy individual memories. If one person leaves the organization and is replaced by another, then the new recruit may have to learn the habits that are required to maintain specific routines. Just as the human body has a life in addition to its constituent cells, the organization has a life in addition to its members. A routine derives from the capacity of an organization to energize a series of conditional, interlocking, sequential behaviours among several individuals within the organization.

The concept of a routine is a key building block in the literature on dynamic capabilities (Teece and Pisano 1994; Teece, Pisano, and Shuen, 1997; Winter 1995, 2000), which is central to the modern strategic management literature. The fact that firms may have properties that are not found in their individual members taken severally has major implications for the theory of the firm. As well as the possibility that the transaction costs of contracts between individuals can be reduced within a firm, the firm itself may help enhance the capabilities of the groups and individuals within, and hence the existence of the firm may not be due to the potential reduction of transaction costs alone (Hodgson and Knudsen 2007).

## 1.5. Conclusion

In sum, recent scholarship has provided a rigorous explanation of the mechanisms by which institutional environments can enhance individual cognitive capabilities. There is no institutional mind apart from the minds of individuals, but the relations between individuals provide a structured context in which individual learning and memory capabilities are enhanced. There is nothing mystical about this; it has a robust foundation in philosophy and widespread theoretical and practical implications.

In reviving this conception, the suggestion here is that some advantage can be gained by relating the more recent developments to earlier prefigurations of the idea, including the emergentist philosophy of Lewes and the notion of collective knowledge in the writings of Veblen. In particular, by stressing that an institutional whole is more than its individual parts, and has properties that stem from relations/interactions between individuals, we are pointing to a long tradition of emergentist philosophy, stemming back to Morgan (1923) and others (Blitz 1992), and to recent work in social theory that lies within a broad emergentist tradition (Bhaskar 1979; Kontopoulos 1993; Weissman 2000). Emergentist philosophy is now enjoying a renaissance, bolstered by developments from both the philosophy of biology and the complexity theory (Auyang 1998). Explorations into the history of ideas are not mere idle curiosity, but useful means of giving core ideas more rigour and meaning.

Economists have often been suspicious of terms such as 'organizational learning' and the idea of institutions as repositories of knowledge because of their historic focus on the role of the individual. Whether or not such concepts are compatible with 'methodological individualism' depends on the precise definition of this often-used but typically ill-defined term (Hodgson 2007a, 2007b). The bottom line is that no social analysis is possible without considering *both* individuals *and* relations between individuals. Once such social relations are admitted as real, then the whole is more than the sum of its parts and organizations amount to more than the sum of their individual members. The concept of emergence refers precisely to the additional properties that are unassociated with individuals taken severally. Among these properties, we may include organizational learning, organizational capabilities, and organizational routines, and the general role of institutions as repositories of information.[5]

# References

Allport, F. H. (1924). 'The Group Fallacy in Relation to Social Science', *American Journal of Sociology*, 29: 688–706.

—— (1927). 'The Psychological Nature of Political Structure', *American Political Science Review*, 21: 611–18.

Argyris, C. and Schön, D. A. (1996). *Organizational Learning II: Theory, Method, and Practice*. Reading, MA: Addison-Wesley.

Auyang, S. Y. (1998). *Foundations of Complex-System Theories: In Economics, Evolutionary Biology, and Statistical Physics*. New York and Cambridge: Cambridge University Press.

Becker, M. C. (2004). 'Organizational Routines: A Review of the Literature', *Industrial and Corporate Change*, 13: 643–77.

—— (2005). 'The Concept of Routines: Some Clarifications', *Cambridge Journal of Economics*, 29: 249–62.

Bhaskar, R. (1979). *The Possibility of Naturalism: A Philosophic Critique of the Contemporary Human Sciences*, 1st edn. Brighton, UK: Harvester.

Blitz, D. (1992). *Emergent Evolution: Qualitative Novelty and the Levels of Reality*. Dordrecht: Kluwer.

---

[5] Note that both Douglass North (contrary to a widespread misconception) and myself define organizations as a type of institution. See Hodgson (2006) for evidence and definitions.

Buckle, H. T. (1858). *History of Civilization in England*, 2 vols. London: Longmans Green.

Clark, A. (1997). 'Economic Reason: The Interplay of Individual Learning and External Structure', in J. N. Drobak and J. V. Nye (eds.), *The Frontiers of the New Institutional Economics*. San Diego, CA, and London: Academic Press.

Cohen, M. D. and Bacdayan, P. (1994). 'Organizational Routines are Stored as Procedural Memory—Evidence from a Laboratory Study', *Organization Science*, 5: 554–68.

Commons, J. R. (1925). 'Marx Today: Capitalism and Socialism', *Atlantic Monthly*, 136: 686–7.

Cook, S. D. N. and Yanow, D. (1993). 'Culture and Organizational Learning', *Journal of Management Inquiry*, 2: 373–90.

Cooley, C. H. (1902). *Human Nature and the Social Order*, 1st edn. New York: Scribner's.

—— (1907). 'Social Consciousness', *American Journal of Sociology*, 12: 675–94.

Darwin, C. R. (1859). *On the Origin of Species by Means of Natural Selection, or the Preservation of Favoured Races in the Struggle for Life*, 1st edn. London: Murray.

Dorfman, J. (1934). *Thorstein Veblen and His America*. New York: Viking Press.

Giddings, F. H. (1896). *The Principles of Sociology: An Analysis of the Phenomena of Association and of Social Organization*. New York: Macmillan.

Hodgson, G. M. (2003a). 'The Hidden Persuaders: Institutions and Individuals in Economic Theory', *Cambridge Journal of Economics*, 27: 159–75.

—— (2003b). 'Institutions as Repositories of Knowledge: Some Milestones in the Evolution of an Idea', *Économie Appliquée*, 56: 211–27.

—— (2004). *The Evolution of Institutional Economics: Agency, Structure and Darwinism in American Institutionalism*. London and New York: Routledge.

—— (2006). 'What Are Institutions?', *Journal of Economic Issues*, 40: 1–25.

—— (2007a). 'Institutions and Individuals: Interaction and Evolution', *Organization Studies*, 28: 95–116.

—— (2007b). 'Meanings of Methodological Individualism', *Journal of Economic Methodology*, 14: 211–26.

—— and Knudsen, T. (2007). 'Firm-Specific Learning and the Nature of the Firm: Why Transaction Cost Theory May Provide an Incomplete Explanation', *Revue Économique*, 58: 331–50.

Huxley, T. H. (1894). *Collected Essays*, 9 vols. London: Macmillan.

Kogut, B. (2000). 'The Network as Knowledge: Generative Rules and the Emergence of Structure', *Strategic Management Journal*, 21: 405–25.

Kontopoulos, K. M. (1993). *The Logics of Social Structure*. Cambridge: Cambridge University Press.

Lane, D., Malerba, F., Maxfield, R., and Orsenigo, L. (1996). 'Choice and Action', *Journal of Evolutionary Economics*, 6: 43–76.

Langlois, R. N. (2001). 'Knowledge, Consumption, and Endogenous Growth', *Journal of Evolutionary Economics*, 11: 77–93.

Lazaric, N. (2000). 'The Role of Routines, Rules and Habits in Collective Learning: Some Epistemological and Ontological Considerations', *European Journal of Economic and Social Systems*, 14: 157–71.

Levitt, B. and March, J. G. (1988). 'Organizational Learning', *Annual Review of Sociology*, 14: 319–40.

Lewes, G. H. (1874). *Problems of Life and Mind: First Series: The Foundations of a Creed*, vol. 1. London: Trübner.

—— (1875). *Problems of Life and Mind: First Series: The Foundations of a Creed*, vol. 2. London: Trübner.

—— (1877). *Problems of Life and Mind: Second Series: The Physical Basis of Mind*, vol. 3. London: Trübner.

—— (1879). *Problems of Life and Mind: Third Series*, 2 vols. London: Trübner.

Marengo, L. (1992). 'Coordination and Organizational Learning in the Firm', *Journal of Evolutionary Economics*, 2: 313–26.

Marx, K. (1981). *Capital*, vol. 3, trans. by David Fernbach from the German edition of 1894. Harmondsworth: Pelican.

Mead, G. H. (1934). *Mind, Self and Society—From the Standpoint of a Social Behaviorist*. Chicago, IL: University of Chicago Press.

Morgan, C. L. (1896). *Habit and Instinct*. London and New York: Edward Arnold.

—— (1923). *Emergent Evolution*, 1st edn. London: Williams and Norgate.

Nelson, R. R. and Winter, S. G. (1982). *An Evolutionary Theory of Economic Change*. Cambridge, MA: Harvard University Press.

Teece, D. J. and Pisano, G. (1994). 'The Dynamic Capabilities of Firms: An Introduction', *Industrial and Corporate Change*, 3: 537–56.

—— —— and Shuen, A. (1997). 'Dynamic Capabilities and Strategic Management', *Strategic Management Journal*, 18: 509–33.

Veblen, T. B. (1898). 'The Beginnings of Ownership', *American Journal of Sociology*, 4: 352–65. Reprinted in T. B. Veblen (1934). *Essays on Our Changing Order*. edited by Leon Ardzrooni. New York: Viking Press.

—— (1899). *The Theory of the Leisure Class: An Economic Study in the Evolution of Institutions*. New York: Macmillan.

—— (1906). 'The Place of Science in Modern Civilisation', *American Journal of Sociology*, 11: 585–609. Reprinted in T. Veblen (1919).

—— (1908a). 'Professor Clark's Economics', *Quarterly Journal of Economics*, 22: 147–95. Reprinted in T. Veblen (1919).

—— (1908b). 'On the Nature of Capital I', *Quarterly Journal of Economics*, 22: 517–42. Reprinted in T. Veblen (1919).

—— (1908c). 'On the Nature of Capital II: Investment, Intangible Assets, and the Pecuniary Magnate', *Quarterly Journal of Economics*, 23: 104–36. Reprinted in T. Veblen (1919).

—— (1914). *The Instinct of Workmanship, and the State of the Industrial Arts*. New York: Macmillan.

—— (1919). *The Place of Science in Modern Civilization and Other Essays*. New York: Huebsch.

—— (1921). *The Engineers and the Price System*. New York: Harcourt Brace and World.

Wallace, A. R. (1870). *Contributions to the Theory of Natural Selection: A Series of Essays*. London: Macmillan.

Weismann, A. (1893). *The Germ-Plasm: A Theory of Heredity*, trans. by W. Newton Parker and H. R. Ronnfeldt. London and New York: Walter Scott and Scribner's.

—— (2000). *A Social Ontology*. New Haven, CT: Yale University Press.

Winter, S. G. (1995). 'Four Rs of Profitability: Rents, Resources, Routines, and Replication', in C. A. Montgomery (ed.), *Resource-Based and Evolutionary Theories of the Firm: Towards a Synthesis*. Boston, MA: Kluwer.

—— (2000). 'The Satisficing Principle in Capability Learning', *Strategic Management Journal*, 21: 981–96.

# 2

# Dynamic Capability as a Source of Change

*Sidney G. Winter*

## 2.1. Introduction

For over a decade, researchers in the field of strategic management have been devoting substantial attention to the dynamic capabilities of business firms.[1] As proposed by Teece, Pisano, and Shuen (1997), dynamic capability confers upon a firm the ability to cope with change—where successful 'coping' involves, in particular, the maintenance of high profitability. Needless to say, the suggestion that there is a reliable method for achieving such a widely shared objective is the sort of thing that evokes not only considerable interest but also some scepticism. The nature of dynamic capability, its sources, and its links to profitability have been somewhat controversial; there is a variety of perspectives that many regard as healthy, while some others are led to suspect an underlying state of confusion.

Most of these perspectives have in common, however, the idea that dynamic capability is a form of learned competence, akin to the ordinary capabilities by which firms and other organizations carry out their typical activities—and akin also, at the individual level, to skill. It has previously been argued that there is an essential, theoretically significant

[1] I am indebted to Paul Adler, Gautam Ahuja, David Collis, Anuja Gupta, Connie Helfat (and her other co-authors of Helfat et al. 2007), Tammy Madsen, and Maurizio Zollo for discussions that substantially improved this chapter. The flaws are my own responsibility. At some points, this chapter draws directly on prior work, particularly Winter (2003) and Knudsen and Winter (2007).

unity in this broad family (Nelson and Winter 1982) and that this kinship provides an effective key to the concept of dynamic capability (Winter 2003). The term 'kinship' correctly suggests the existence not only of contemporary relatives but also of ancestors. Indeed, the recent discussion of dynamic capability was prefigured historically, with a variety of terminology, in a number of sources. Perhaps the most directly relevant example among these earlier contributions is Schumpeter's discussion of the 'routinization of innovation' (Schumpeter 1950). Schumpeter's argument presented, however, an issue that remains central in contemporary discussion of dynamic capability—the possibly problematic character of the claim that there is such a thing as 'learned competence' for doing *new things*.

In the present chapter, I review and explicate the concept of dynamic capability as it has developed in the strategic management field, taking primarily the 'learned competence' perspective and emphasizing the proactive uses of dynamic capabilities by business firms. I seek in particular to elucidate the issue just referred to, attempting to clarify how apparent opposites—novelty and familiarity, creativity, and learned routine—come into a pragmatic synthesis in the context of dynamic capability. Also, I seek to place the discussion in a broader frame than the usual profit-oriented one of strategic management, giving more emphasis to both causes and consequences at levels of analysis above that of the individual firm. For the business participants in the broader drama, profit is necessarily a central concern—but covering costs is even more obviously necessary, and dynamic capability does not come for free. Can a firm afford to make costly preparations to facilitate adjustment to contingencies that are now remote in time or improbable? In this chapter, this question motivates a substantial analysis of the 'hierarchy of change' proposal, the suggestion that higher-order dynamic capabilities might exist—for example, capabilities for learning to change.

In structuring this chapter, I have made the judgement that motivation deserves (temporal) priority over precision. Thus, I begin with a review of the intellectual background, linking the dynamic capability idea to Schumpeter's 'routinization of innovation' and to the analysis of routines in evolutionary economics. I then sketch two examples of dynamic capabilities—product development in semiconductors and retail outlet replication. Only after the dynamic capability concept is thus motivated and illustrated do I proceed to more careful definitions and economic analysis of the hierarchy of change.

## 2.2. Background

### 2.2.1. Schumpeter

The writings of Joseph Schumpeter contributed an essential part of the broad conceptual framework that now embraces the discussion of dynamic capabilities. In his early work, Schumpeter (1934) portrayed the economy as a system not only involving strong tendencies towards an equilibrium in which continuing activity would have a routine, repetitive character but also involving repeated episodes in which innovations, large and small, disrupt the equilibria the system has achieved and temporarily suspend its equilibrium tendencies. Innovations are carried out by entrepreneurs, and this activity is both the essential calling of the entrepreneur and the essential driver of the long-term historical development of capitalism. Although this entrepreneurial activity repeatedly introduces novelty to the system, it must itself be understood as an essential *feature* of the system it transforms—not an 'exogenous shock' appearing for extra-economic reasons, such as a series of bad harvests.

Towards the end of his life, Schumpeter re-painted his picture of capitalist development on an even broader canvas. In *Capitalism, Socialism and Democracy* (Schumpeter 1950), he offered a complex, multifaceted argument that the type of capitalism he had earlier described might be passing from the historical scene, morphing by small degrees into some variety of socialism. An important element of this argument concerned the 'obsolescence of the entrepreneurial function'. One conceivable cause of such obsolescence would be an approach to 'an approximately complete satisfaction of wants or . . . absolute technological perfection' (Schumpeter 1950: 131), which would mean that society no longer needed entrepreneurs. More probable and more imminent, however, was the possibility that

Progress itself may be mechanized as well as the management of a stationary economy, and this mechanization of progress may affect entrepreneurship and capitalist development nearly as much as the cessation of economic progress would (Schumpeter 1950: 131).

What historical change might account for the fact that 'mechanization' is becoming feasible in a role where heroic leadership was once required? In Schumpeter's rather brief development of his proposition, the answer is that the task is becoming easier:

. . . it is much easier now than it has been in the past to do things that lie outside familiar routine—innovation itself is being reduced to routine. Technological progress is increasingly becoming the business of teams of trained specialists who turn out what is required and make it work in predictable ways....

many more things can be strictly calculated that had of old to be visualized in a flash of genius...

personality and will power must count for less in environments which have become accustomed to economic change—best instanced by an incessant stream of new consumers' and producers' goods....

...the resistance...of consumers and producers to a new kind of thing because it is new has well-nigh vanished already...

Thus, economic progress tends to become depersonalized and automatized. Bureau and committee work tends to replace individual action.

(Schumpeter 1950: 132–3)

To interpret these propositions correctly, it is necessary to keep in mind the basic Schumpeterian distinction between innovation and *invention*—one might legitimately write 'mere invention', because in Schumpeter's view it is innovation that presents the main challenges and that is the crucial phenomenon of capitalist development. The entrepreneurial function 'does not consist essentially in either inventing anything or otherwise creating the conditions which the enterprise exploits. It consists in getting things done' (Schumpeter 1950: 132). In this regard, the above reference to 'teams of trained specialists' creating 'technological progress' could be considered somewhat inept, since that sounds more like routinization of invention than of innovation.[2] Schumpeter's overall argument becomes stronger, however, if one considers the contribution of other specialists, such as those involved with manufacturing, and with marketing and distribution. Expertise in these functions, and the managerial competence to exploit new inventions by turning that expertise in new directions, surely does help to create a smooth and profitable path for the large corporate innovator. Since Schumpeter's time, the importance of the capabilities and 'complementary assets' under these headings has received increasing emphasis, in respect of both corporate strength in continuing operations (Chandler 1977, 1990) and the appropriation of gains from innovation (Teece 1986).

---

[2] Although, with respect to invention, one could put the emphasis on the knowledge of 'what is required' contributed by market research and the predictability conferred by systematic development, prototyping, and test marketing. These tend to diminish the hazards of false starts that attend attempted innovation. Hence, the detailed character of the invention process does have implications for the prospects of 'getting things done' in the marketplace.

## 2.2.2. *Evolutionary Economics*

Drawing inspiration from Schumpeter and other sources, Nelson and Winter (1982) proposed a view of economic change as an evolutionary process, in which the contrast between routine and innovation is a central feature. In that system, the routines of an organization are its actual patterns of repetitive behaviour, including the patterns of response to familiar types of managerial decision as well as to commonly encountered forms of change in its environment—new orders from customers, competitive moves of rivals, turnover of employees, and so forth. While many such patterns are strongly shaped by the deliberate decisions of managers, including decisions expressed as codified prescriptions of processes, it is clearly impossible for deliberate decisions to shape all the myriad details of a complex organizational performance. It is not surprising, therefore, that the stabilized patterns are sometimes significantly at odds with the official or 'nominal' version of how the organization is supposedly behaving. Furthermore, strong patterning of organizational behaviour can also arise without there being an identifiable stimulus in the form of deliberate decisions, and even in the absence of any awareness that such patterns have come to prevail. Organizations, like individuals, acquire habits without intending to do so, and performance can be either enhanced or degraded by these habits—or at times enhanced and at other times degraded, depending on the environment. These habits are also subsumed under the concept of organizational routine.[3]

The term 'routine' is used flexibly across scales, that is, with respect to the size of the bundle of activities referred to. The typical overall picture is a nested, hierarchical structure (an inclusion hierarchy), with lower-level routines characterizing the performance of specific elements of the higher-level routines. Thus, we might consider an individual airline flight as a high-level unit of routinized activity; its subroutines include fuelling and safety checks of the aircraft, boarding procedures, in-flight refreshments, communications between cockpit and tower, interactions with air traffic control, and so on—including, of course, the activity of the pilot in actually flying the aircraft. At high levels—perhaps the level of 'operations of a low-cost commercial passenger airline'—the terminology of *routine* gives way to that of *organizational capability*, as the following definition indicates.

---

[3] Recent work by Michael Cohen (2006) emphasizes the connections of the routines literature to John Dewey's conception of habit as an aspect of human behaviour.

*An organizational capability is a high-level routine (or collection of routines) that, together with its implementing input flows, confers upon an organization's management a set of decision options for producing significant outputs of a particular type* (Winter 2000). For present purposes, the points deserving emphasis here are the connotations of 'routine'—behaviour that is learned, highly patterned, repetitious or quasi-repetitious, founded in part on tacit knowledge—the deployability or 'option' aspect, and the specificity of objectives. Brilliant improvization is not a routine, and there is no such thing as a general-purpose routine. The phrase 'implementing input flows' refers to the normal requisites of the activity that are not simply learned patterns of coordination, for example, the services of the pilot and aircraft. Coordination does not live in abstractions; organizational capabilities exist only in actual instantiation.

That organizational routines resist change is a proposition validated by common experience as well as by systematic research. This internal resistance in the organization itself is one of the several forms of resistance that innovative effort must surmount. It has multiple sources, with roles that often are intertwined and mutually reinforcing. Some accounts give much weight to individual attitudes, or to the shaping of these attitudes by organizational cultures. Others emphasize incentive issues, otherwise known as vested interests, which may affect the attitudes of individuals or units towards lines of change that might diminish their importance, earnings, and future prospects.

While these accounts capture some of the truth, and in particular cases may capture most of it, there is a danger of misplaced emphasis here. By definition, the routines of an organization characterize the scope of learned coordination among its many actors, determining the range of situations where they know what to do and can find reinforcement in the complementary actions of others. Outside of that scope, actors do not know what to do; rarely indeed will their independent improvizations chance to fall together immediately in the form of an effective performance.[4] New learning is required to achieve new routines, and the necessary learning 'trials' inevitably involve errors, delays, and other costs—regardless of attitudes and incentives.

---

[4] It is taken for granted here that a significant degree of independent improvization is always necessary in the development of new routines, regardless of any deliberate efforts to structure the search by means of plans and directives. This premise derives from the unavoidable reliance on tacit skill, and the related fact that speed is a requisite of effective performance in competitive contexts. The classic experimental study by Cohen and Bacdayan (1994) illuminates these issues extremely well. See also Cohen (2006).

This general line of argument was, in fact, quite plain to Schumpeter from the start, as the following passage indicates:

While in the accustomed circular flow every individual can act promptly and rationally because he is sure of his ground and is supported by the conduct, as adjusted to this circular flow, of all other individuals, who in turn expect the accustomed activity from him, he cannot simply do this when he is confronted by a new task.

(Schumpeter 1934: 79)

In organizations, not only is it the case that an effective new path is hard to find, but the valuable learning investment enshrined in the old path is typically defended by a variety of formal and informal arrangements for monitoring and control. The sort of exploration that new learning requires is thereby forestalled (March 1991).

It is a serious (though commonplace) mistake to extrapolate from the familiar stability of routines to the proposition that routinization and innovation are inherently and diametrically opposed. What is crucial here is to recognize the key causal role played by *the scope of the existing routines*. When that scope is very narrow, an organization may find it challenging to cope even with quite familiar types of fluctuations in the environment. Given that the airline industry has already served as an illustration here, it is natural to cite the example of the crisis experienced by the US carrier JetBlue Airways, when confronted by a spate of particularly bad winter weather in February 2007 (Bailey 2007). The details of this episode make it clear as an example of overly narrow routines, and consequent flawed, uncoordinated improvisation, as one could imagine—yet severe winter weather is hardly unprecedented in the northern USA, and other carriers showed themselves to be better prepared for it.[5] Mounting an effective response involves, for the unprepared organization, the challenges and hazards of innovation, even though other organizations may see the same events as part of 'business as usual'.

While the notion of a learned and practised response to a 'familiar' phenomenon provides a helpful starting point, it does not have the power to illuminate adequately the relations of routinization and innovation. Since history never repeats itself in a literal sense, no new situation is totally familiar (even when perceived to be so). Every specific routinized response therefore involves either ignoring the distinctive features of the

[5] The interesting question of *why* organizations are so often unprepared to face familiar challenges is a large one, at least partially illuminated by the analysis below of the economic logic of dynamic capability.

instant case or making an adaptation to them.[6] It is therefore necessary to distinguish degrees of familiarity and, more productively, to notice that the 'degree' question can often be parsed into a series of questions about how the specific new situation matches up to the scope of prevailing subroutines. When much relevant competence is available in those subroutines, the task of adapting the high-level routine is reduced to gap-filling and reconnecting.[7] In the assessment of such questions, account must be taken of the fact that in the typical hierarchical structure of complex routines there are often established mid-level arrangements to handle 'exception' conditions at lower levels; this means that the actual scope is broader—in the sense that the range of potentially problematic novelty is narrower—than might appear from the inspection of the low-level routines alone. Finally, it is also noteworthy here that innovation itself is often characterized as the carrying out of 'new combinations' (Schumpeter 1934)—with the implication that the things combined are familiar, though the combination itself is not. Creation is facilitated when not everything has to be created from scratch, and more specifically, when the elements recombined are themselves reliable and broad in scope (Nelson and Winter 1982).

### 2.2.3. Routines and Dynamic Capability

As suggested in the introduction, the claim that there can be a learned competence at organizational change—or that innovation can be routinized—is seen by many as problematic. Not only is there much conventional wisdom expressing doubt about this claim but also there is a long tradition in organizational theory that sees creativity as essential to innovation and bureaucratic organization (routinized procedures) as inimical to creativity, hence to innovation (Adler 2007). The framework reviewed above helps in sorting this problem out. There is, however, a price to be paid for the clarification. Additional complexity appears when we look past the broad-brush terminology and ask how much 'creativity' is required and where in the 'innovation' it is located, and then ask the corresponding questions about the possibly constructive role of 'routines' or 'bureaucratization' in creating innovation. The quotation marks point implicitly to further complications, for we must ultimately ask the

---

[6] The philosophical depths and empirical complexities of this issue are strikingly illuminated in a recent paper by Birnholtz, Cohen, and Hoch (2007).

[7] This line of thinking has been developed by Bryce, Dyer, and Furr (2006) for the case of a firm acquiring new capabilities.

operational question of how we propose to identify and measure these things. This is clearly very difficult territory, especially if the attempt aims at measures that can be claimed to be comparable across broad domains— say, how much creativity is required to create a new drug as compared to a new mobile phone, Internet connection, camera, or entertainment device.[8] These complexities of measurement are related to those arising from the nature of innovation as recombination: the smaller the fraction of truly novel elements in the package, the greater the temptation to say that little creativity is involved—but of course that conclusion might be invalid if the novel elements are really very novel indeed.[9]

Given these difficulties, it is fortunate that we can progress in our understanding of dynamic capability and its role in economic change without relying on any absolute, cross-domain assessments of creativity and innovation. The subsequent analysis in this chapter rests on a 'relativistic' approach, where the relativity in question involves the comparison of the novelty of the performance to the scope of (previously) prevailing routines. To be securely anchored, such a comparison must generally involve the identification of the specific organization that is the home of those 'prevailing routines'. For while the routines of organizations doing similar things often display strong surface similarities, close examination typically reveals substantial differences—and the consequences of these tend to be magnified when the organizations are coping with change (Nelson 1991).

In short, we reaffirm here in the context of organizational innovation— and even 'creativity'—a point that is highly familiar in the context of individual skills. The skilled performer, drawing on years of practice, 'makes it look easy'. When assessing the extent to which a particular performance transcends 'easy', relativistic standards are helpful—both the longitudinal standard (the 'personal best') and the cross-sectional, competitive one prevailing at a given time (gold, silver, or bronze?). By contrast, questions of absolute comparison across domains and across wide spans of time can spawn interesting conversations, but are very hard to resolve.

---

[8] Within domains, expert judgement can provide considerable help in assessing creativity or innovation, at least in terms of ordinal or qualitative comparisons. This does not work well across domains, however, for there is not enough real cross-domain expertise to support it.

[9] Analogous complexities are familiar in patent law, specifically in relation to the way the examiners in the patent office interpret 'novelty' when applying the 'novelty test' for patentability. Nothing in that rich fund of experience is reassuring with respect to the feasibility of objective assessments that have a comparable basis across domains. In recent years, particularly intense controversy arose with respect to 'business methods' patents such as the 'One-click' ordering system of Amazon.com. For discussion, see Jaffe and Lerner (2004).

The implications of dynamic capability for system change do not much depend on the degree to which learning and practice may actually have supplanted creativity as the source of the core dynamic, or whether on the other hand the stable aspect of the capability is merely a framework to support and exploit the highly creative individuals and teams who generate the isolated elements of true novelty in the overall performance.[10] A new bridge across a major river may or may not be a highly innovative bridge, in terms of its design and construction, and the bridge-building community may debate just how innovative it is. Regardless of that debate, the completed bridge will change traffic patterns in the area in a semi-permanent way, thus transforming both the problems and the opportunities facing many other actors. Furthermore, the construction of such a bridge expresses a capability that surely cannot be quickly developed by a randomly chosen large organization, nor would the contract be awarded to such an organization. Thus, while the role of 'creativity' in the construction of the bridge may be disputable, the contribution of learned competence—organizational capability—is not surely. The stance taken here is that it is the system consequences and the role of learned competence in producing those consequences that demand our attention.

In the following section, I adopt this viewpoint in brief descriptions of two important examples of dynamic capability.

## 2.3. Two Examples[11]

### 2.3.1. *New Semiconductor Products: The Miniaturization Trajectory*

The price of computers in the USA has been falling at an average annual rate of about 20–5 per cent for about half a century now (Bresnahan and Malerba 1999). The 'price' referred to here is the real price (adjusted for inflation) and quality-adjusted. That is, the quoted rate of price decrease relates to computers of constant quality, priced in dollars of constant purchasing power.[12]

---

[10] The availability of these rival interpretations is nicely illustrated by Hargadon and Sutton (1997) who report a detailed study of the design firm IDEO. They describe elaborate organizational arrangements to promote the creation of novel designs (via recombination), but of course there are also individual design engineers on the scene, and they may perhaps be contributing 'true creativity'. Or perhaps not; in the end the etiology of those novel designs remains mysterious.

[11] For a richer collection of examples, see Helfat et al. (2007).

[12] The measurement problems involved in both the inflation adjustment and the quality adjustment are substantial, but the methods used do have a well-considered and plausible

If we take the 20 per cent estimated rate of change seriously and compute the result of compounding it for fifty years, a striking implication is revealed. The amount of computing power that cost $10,000 in 1957 now costs a bit over $1. At the 25 per cent rate change, it costs about 14 cents.

What are the sources of this dramatic change, whose extended implications have greatly shaped the world we now live in? While the design of computer hardware involves many features and components, and while effective use of a computer for a given class of problems requires appropriate software, it is quite clear that it is the improvement in one class of components that has been the key driver of overall progress in computers, as well as in other technologies where rapid computation is useful, but where the relevant devices are not typically labelled 'computers'—such as electronic games, mobile phones, or ignition systems for automobiles. These key components are the semiconductor devices that do the actual computation. Since the invention of the microprocessor in 1970, it has become the case that it is the improvement of that single component, the 'computer on a chip' that has driven progress in the personal computing applications with which most of us are familiar. Those same microprocessors, organized in vast arrays, do much of the heavy lifting in large-scale computing applications such as the support of Google's search service, and in many supercomputers.

The leading firm of the world 'merchant' semiconductor industry is Intel Corporation. Intel was founded in 1968 by Gordon Moore and Robert Noyce, two employees of the industry leader of c.1960, Fairchild Semiconductor. Similar lines of descent are shared by virtually all firms of the world industry, and in particular by the approximately 450 semiconductor firms founded by former employees of Fairchild (Barnett, Starbuck, and Pant 2003).

In 1965, when director of R&D at Fairchild, Gordon Moore published a short article (Moore 1965) pointing out a trend: the number of transistors that could be placed on a silicon chip had been doubling annually since about 1959. He predicted that the trend would continue at least to 1975. It did indeed continue, and in 1975 Moore produced an update of his analysis. Noting the emergence of technological considerations that would tend to slow the pace, he now predicted a doubling time of approximately two years—and again the prediction proved remarkably

conceptual basis. The quality adjustment technique relies on the 'hedonic index' technique to sidestep the obvious difficulty that actual computers exemplifying a specific quality level are available in the market for only a fraction of the total time span considered.

accurate. The predicted pace of progress became known as 'Moore's law' and it became increasingly evident that this had become an enacted law rather than a purely descriptive one.

In other words, the law became a focal point for the creation of plans, the execution of which sustained the validity of the law (Barnett, Starbuck, and Pant 2003). This point could hardly be made more explicit than it is following statements from Intel's website in 2002: 'The mission of Intel's technology development team is to continue to break down barriers to Moore's Law' (quoted in Barnett, Starbuck, and Pant 2003). Intel has clearly been the key actor in the 'orchestration' of Moore's law—and for the period 1975–87, Moore himself was directing the orchestra in his capacity as CEO of Intel.

The proposition offered here is that the dynamic capabilities of Intel have in recent decades been the most important single factor behind Moore's law, and in that sense also the principal source of the continuing change in semiconductor technology. As the following discussion indicates, this does not deny the importance of several other considerations or the high degree of complementarity among them.

The diversity, complexity, and scale of the surrounding structures are remarkable. There is, first, an overall knowledge structure that has remained relatively constant over decades of change. A central organizing feature of this structure is the set of high-level heuristic principles that define the 'technological paradigm' guiding the search for faster devices (Dosi 1982). In its most elementary and overly concise form, the leading heuristic is 'smaller is better'. As Moore put it:

By making things smaller, everything gets better simultaneously. There is little need for trade-offs. The speed of our products goes up, the power consumption goes down, system reliability, as we put more of the system on a chip, improves by leaps and bounds, but especially the cost of doing things electronically drops as a result of the technology.

(Moore 1995)

Note that the 'smaller is better' paradigm offers a ready-made answer to an important question that in general has to be addressed by creative thinking, namely, What is the question? The answer–question offered by the paradigm is: How can we make things smaller? More specifically, the smaller the tiny lines that are the image of a circuit on a silicon chip, the more circuits can be drawn in a single chip. In this paradigm, therefore, line width—meaning, in practice, the line widths achievable in the efficient manufacturing of devices—is one of the critical parameters.

The achievement of continuing line-width reduction has been a major challenge in the enactment of Moore's law, because the basic physics pushes back. As Henderson (1995) describes in detail for the period up to the early 1990s, there were recurrent predictions of an early end to the era of reliance on optical techniques in semiconductor lithography, because achieved line widths were approaching limits determined by the wavelength of the radiation. Actually, however, the predictions did not rely directly on the physical limits, but presumed that other engineering constraints would continue to apply, such as those relating to feasible lens sizes. As device generations passed, the economic incentives changed, new problem-solving efforts occurred that relaxed the constraints, and the predictions proved false—for the time being. Much the same pattern seems to have characterized the past decade. Today again, the question of how progress can be sustained in next-generation lithography is under active discussion, with the use of radiation in the extreme ultraviolet range being a leading candidate for the answer—but with many specific problems still awaiting solution.

Overall, the story of the continuing quest for line-width reduction provides an excellent illustration of some basic issues introduced above. It is clear that the novelties encountered in the course of time are significant novelties; substantial technological challenges are encountered for which no ready-made solution exists. Thus, the dynamic capabilities of the principal actors involved—particularly the equipment manufacturers and other device producers as well as Intel—are not reasonably regarded as illustrating literally repetitive behaviour or 'dead routine'. On the other hand, the creative achievements that occur are produced in an elaborately evolved context that is simultaneously very supportive of change and highly continuous in time. As suggested above, the contribution of the paradigm—the stable and relatively operational framing of the *questions and solution heuristics*—should not be underestimated. Given the many strongly facilitating factors and the scale of the resources involved, it may be reasonable to view individual problem-solvers as interchangeable parts relating to one of the many requisites of the overall system performance. The capability to *manage* such 'parts' effectively is certainly another requisite, and a particularly critical one—but not necessarily one that itself requires continuing improvement as lower-level change continues (Adler 2007).

This brief sketch barely begins to suggest the overall complexity of this key dynamic of our changing world. In the extensive literature of the subject—the management and social science literature is distinguished

from the technical literature and the historical or biographical literature—
a large fraction of the picture is at least partially illuminated. To cite only
a few examples, there is first of all Nelson's account of the beginnings—
the invention of the transistor by Shockley and his associates at Bell
Telephone Laboratories (Nelson 1962).[13] The management and strategy
of Intel have been the object of much close-in observation and analysis
(see Burgelman 1994, 2002; Gawer and Cusumano 2002).

On the whole, this picture seems highly supportive of Schumpeter's
observation that 'progress itself can be routinized'. A symbolic representative for this general observation is Burgelman's account of how Intel
made the critically important transition from being primarily a memory
device manufacturer to being primarily a microprocessor manufacturer—
a strategic shift that it accomplished primarily by simply adhering to
its established routines, particularly a medium-level routine known as
the 'wafer starts' routine (Burgelman 1994). But it is clear that much
more than firm-level capability has been involved, and in particular that
there has been a major role for highly structured, continuing interactions
among actors of different types. On this record, it seems Schumpeter
might better have said that 'progress itself can be routinized *and institutionalized*'.


### 2.3.2. Replication[14]

For a second broad example of dynamic capabilities in action, I turn to the
activities of replicator organizations. These are organizations that pursue,
as a primary growth strategy, the creation of large numbers of substantially similar operating units. The dynamic capabilities in question are
those of replication itself, that is, the capabilities that support the creation
of new units, thereby extending the geographic scope of the activities
of the replicator. For a business firm that has achieved a significant and
distinctive but *local* form of economic success, there are large pecuniary
incentives to attempt to identify the 'secret' of that success and then to
attempt to replicate it on a broad geographic scale. Although often dep-
recated in uninformed discussion, successful replication is a significant
accomplishment—first, because no 'secret' is actually known, and second

---

[13] On the substantial role of government policy and of industry structure, see Levin (1982)
Langlois and Steinmuller (1999).

[14] The discussion here is substantially informed by the work of Gabriel Szulanski and
others—jointly with me, independently, and in various combinations. There is too much
to cite here, but see Winter et al. (2007) for a recent example and references to earlier work.

for the simple reason that space-time is far from homogeneous, and this often matters (Knudsen and Winter 2007). Replication is a particularly powerful and visible source of change in the for-profit sector, but it is familiar enough in public and non-profit settings as well.

Replicator organizations are particularly common in retail settings, such as fast food, restaurants, hotels and motels, banks, brokers, coffee shops, office supplies, home improvements, book stores, low-priced furniture, and clothing shops.[15] The prevalence of replicators in such settings presumably reflects the selective advantages of a transferable reputation in contexts where a small increase in the probability that customers choose one store over another has, in the aggregate and in the long run, enormous consequences. Since a transferable reputation can only be sustained for the long run if it is based in real uniformity, there is substantial pressure to assure that replication is accomplished in fact, and not merely in appearance—the more so in those cases where the customer base is in fact highly mobile.

The more challenging the task of creating the requisite uniformity, the more significant are the dynamic capabilities required to accomplish it. In such settings, mature replicator organizations typically have substantial central functions that are concerned with the replication process itself. Such central functions address a range of issues, including property acquisition, zoning and regulation, design and decor, manager (or franchisee) selection and training, codification and improvement of operating rules, identification of preferred suppliers, procurement of centrally supplied inputs, control of signage and advertising, promulgation of system-wide literature, and special promotions—all for the purpose of assuring that the actual productive operations directly valued by customers take place in a desirable and *highly uniform* way across a large and increasing number of local outlets. The most substantial challenges, and hence the greatest theoretical interest, arise in examples where significant local production takes place, such as the fast food industry. In these cases, replication must involve particularly substantial efforts to *replicate organizational routines*, to assure that similar results are achieved by similar-to-identical means

---

[15] For the sake of simplicity in this sketch, the discussion is confined to the retailers. Following are some examples of replicator companies that are prominent in the US context, and in many cases in the global context as well (arranged by categories mentioned above): McDonalds, Burger King, Pizza Hut, Kentucky Fried Chicken, Denny's, Outback Steakhouse, Holiday Inn, Hilton (various brands), Marriott (various brands), Bank of America, Wachovia, HSBC, Merrill Lynch, Starbucks, Cosi, Office Depot, Staples, Home Depot, Loew's, Borders, Barnes and Noble, Ikea, The Bombay Company, Benetton, The Gap.

at all of the local outlets.[16] Cases where standardized, centrally produced finished goods are retailed in commonplace ways, using widely available skills, are not so interesting. In practice, however, closer inspection often reveals that prominent replicator–retailers of externally procured goods are actually handling those goods in decidedly distinctive, non-commonplace ways.[17]

McDonald's Corporation is probably the world's most widely recognized, loved, and hated replicator organization. The origins of its local business model are readily traced to a few hamburger stands operated by the McDonald brothers in San Bernardino, CA; the first of the type opened in 1948. The replicator organization was built by Ray Kroc, who bought out the brothers in 1961, and it currently claims over 32,000 outlets worldwide. The system Kroc created is legendary for its multifaceted investment in uniformity—the training of managers at Hamburger University, the large and detailed operating manual for a unit, the monitoring regime that seeks among other things to assure that enough food is thrown away (i.e. don't keep it around too long). Somewhere in all this is, presumably, the secret of the mysterious appeal of the French fries—long a target for attempted imitation, by Burger King in particular. Perhaps it depends in part with the rule for the correct cooking time (cook until the oil temperature rises by 3°)—but that particular piece of the puzzle, at least, is in the public domain.[18]

The dynamic capabilities in the semiconductor example live far upstream in the value chain, in the development of semiconductor products and the processes, including the equipment with which they are manufactured. The products themselves are components inputs for a wide range of both producer and consumer goods. In the replication case, the dynamic capabilities are far downstream; establishing the operating capabilities of new outlets that then deal directly with the consumer. Since the operating capabilities themselves seem fairly mundane—what after all is so challenging about a hamburger stand or a coffee shop?—it may seem strange to bracket this example with the high technological drama of Moore's law. But the dynamic capabilities are not serving the hamburgers and coffee, they are creating functioning hamburger stands and coffee shops, often at the rate of one or two a day, and with minimal

---

[16] See Baden-Fuller and Winter (2007) for discussion of the puzzling question of what 'replication' means, and of the contingencies affecting success.

[17] Border's books are an interesting case in point, see Raff (2000) for an historical account of the methods of Borders and of Barnes and Noble.

[18] Or was, perhaps the rule has changed; see Hayes, Pisano, and Upton (1996: 54).

variation in key attributes. As previously suggested, such a performance rests so heavily on accumulated learning and specialized investments that it is difficult to assess, in the end, whether it should be considered 'easy' or 'hard' for the experienced performer—but very clear what it would be for the inexperienced performer. And clear also, that cross-domain comparisons, to semiconductors or anything else, are hazardous.

Manifestly, the types of dynamic capabilities that have served as the examples here are transforming the world we live in, albeit in quite different ways.

## 2.4. Higher-Order Capabilities: An Endless Hierarchy?

While a definition of 'organizational capability' has been offered, the nature of the distinction between 'ordinary' and 'dynamic' capabilities has been left largely implicit, invoked but not explained. The word 'dynamic' connotes change, but the degree of familiarity of a situation to an organization must (it has been argued) be assessed relative to the scope of prevailing routines. This assessment is most effectively made at the level of the individual organization, and the flow of this thinking carries us along to the conclusion that the meanings of 'dynamic' and 'change' are themselves best thought of as organization-specific. There are possible objections to this conclusion, of course, but the discussion below seeks out the gains from taking it seriously.

### 2.4.1. The Hierarchy of Change

The image of a hierarchy of routines, in which 'exception' cases are passed to higher levels, has already been evoked. In the straightforward interpretation of that picture, the exceptions constitute a small fraction of total cases—for example, a small fraction of customer orders—and they arrive sporadically and more or less independently. A related but different picture appears if the 'exception' is a quasi-permanent shift in the environment: it is not just *this customer* who wants something different from what we usually offer, but *most customers in the foreseeable future* are likely to take a similar view. On that interpretation, what the firm needs is not a good response for a single customer with idiosyncratic needs, but an adjustment of the prevailing operating routines governing 'what we usually offer'. If adjustments of this kind are needed fairly frequently, the process of making them may itself become routinized. If so, it might be reasonable to repeat the questions for this higher-level routine: Does it too require occasional adjustment? Is that adjustment made routinely? The idea that this might be the case emerges quite easily from the image of the hierarchical structure (with available analogies to the structure of computer programs), and has close parallels elsewhere.

In the strategic management literature, a particularly explicit and formal proposal along this line was put forward by Collis (1994). Beginning from the proposition that the first-order dynamic capabilities govern the rate of change of ordinary capabilities, he followed the example of the differential calculus and pointed to the existence of second-order, third-order, etc., dynamic capabilities—and explicitly proposed the extension 'ad infinitum'. This terminological approach is adopted here, but with an important caveat as to whether higher-order capabilities 'exist' in an interesting sense. From a logical point of view, the 'existence' of higher-order rates of change is in question only in the mathematical sense that some derivatives might not exist; and from a computational point of view, a time sequence of $N + 1$ values of a variable suffices to compute one value of the $N$th order rate of change. But if dynamic capabilities are similar to ordinary capabilities in that they involve *highly patterned* activity oriented to relatively specific objectives, then there is no guarantee that the organizational processes governing high-order change are highly patterned, and substantial reason to think otherwise. In this important substantive sense, high-order dynamic capabilities are always a logical possibility, but they do not necessarily exist. This point lies close to the heart of the economics of dynamic capability, because capability is costly and this gives good reason to expect that high-order capabilities might exist very rarely.

### 2.4.2. The 'Zero Level' in the Hierarchy of Change

To anchor the concept of a hierarchy of capabilities or rates of change, we need a convention to identify the 'zero level' of the hierarchy, the analogue of position for objects moving in space. Because capabilities are complex, structured, and multi-dimensional, this question may not have an answer that seems both clear and compelling in all cases. There is, however, a heuristic guide available that conforms to common sense and existing practice, at least for the capabilities of firms competing in markets.

Consider a hypothetical firm 'in equilibrium', or equivalently, in Schumpeter's 'circular flow'. This is an organization that keeps earning its living by producing and selling the same product, on the same scale and to the same customer population over time. The capabilities exercised in that stationary process are the operating or zero level capabilities, the 'how we earn a living now' capabilities. Deprived of them, the firm could not collect the revenue from its customers that allows it to buy more inputs and do the whole thing over again. By contrast, capabilities that would change the product, the production process, the scale, or the customers (markets) served are not at the zero level. Capabilities that enable Intel to bring out a new, faster chip in two years are not at the zero level; neither are the capabilities that enable replicator organizations to rapidly gain new customers in new geographic areas. These examples are prototypical (first-order) dynamic capabilities because they unquestionably involve first-order change, given the definition of the zero level, and it is equally beyond question that they are highly patterned and 'routine' in many respects. Given the terminological framework under construction here, these examples are a conclusive answer to anyone who doubts the 'existence' of dynamic capabilities. (Of course, their doubts may relate to a different understanding of 'dynamic capability'.)

This way of defining the 'zero level' involves the acceptance of the 'relativistic' perspective introduced above. We abstain from the attempt at a global definition of change; the 'zero level' is only locally defined. For example, the IDEO design firm makes a living producing new product designs (Hargadon and Sutton 1997); this is their *operating* capability. Were an IDEO customer to stop outsourcing the design task and perform it in-house, the customer would be developing a first-order dynamic capability. Should this be considered a drawback of the relativistic approach, on the ground that it is objectionable to assign different labels to the 'same thing'? No, because it is not at all the same thing. The dynamic capability cannot possibly be highly similar to IDEO's operating capability, because the multiplicity and diversity of IDEO's customers, and its 'technology brokering' among them, is of the essence of what IDEO does for a living (Hargadon and Sutton 1997). Also, it is easy to see that the status of a design engineer would differ greatly between the two contexts, and this can clearly matter. Arguably, this example illustrates the strength of the relativistic approach rather than its limitations.

### 2.4.3. *Many Ways to Change*

Of course, it is quite possible for an organization to change its routines without having a dynamic capability. To begin with, change often occurs by *force majeure* from the environment, predictably or not, for better or worse. Whether it is because such an external challenge arrives or because an autonomous decision to change is made at a high level, organizations often have to cope with problems they are not well prepared for. They may be pushed into 'firefighting' mode, a high-paced, contingent, opportunistic, and perhaps creative search for satisfactory alternative behaviours. It is useful to have a name for the category of such change behaviours that do *not* depend on dynamic capabilities—behaviours that are largely non-repetitive and at least 'intendedly rational' and not merely reactive or passive. I propose the term 'ad hoc problem-solving'. Ad hoc problem-solving is not routine; in particular, not highly patterned and not repetitious. As suggested above, it often appears as a response to novel challenges from the environment or other relatively unpredictable events. Thus, ad hoc problem-solving and the exercise of dynamic capabilities are two different ways to change—or two categories comprising numerous different ways to change.

Of course, close study of a series of 'fires' may well reveal that there is pattern even in 'firefighting'. Some of the pattern may be learned and contribute positively to effectiveness, and in that sense be akin to a skill or routine. In organizational improvization, as in jazz, creative achievement typically rises from a foundation of patterned and practised performance, a rich fund of micro-patterns that are recombined and sequenced in creative ways. Responses to highly dynamic environments may also be patterned at a higher level, guided by adherence to relatively simple rules and structural principles (Eisenhardt and Martin 2000; Miner, Bassoff, and Moorman 2001). Finally, it is quite common for top management to initiate a *project* when it perceives a need to design and/or implement a significant change in the organization (Adler and Obstfeld 2007). At least for an organization that is experienced in doing projects, such an effort is quite far from the 'firefighting' end of the spectrum of change modes. There are nevertheless important commonalities with other 'ad hoc' modes, in particular the indeterminacy of the outcomes initially anticipated, and the way the costs are typically borne.

At the other end of the spectrum, even the most incremental effort at product modification can run into unexpected snags that are beyond the scope of the dynamic capability, and require a complementary dose of ad hoc problem-solving. To acknowledge these various points is not, however, to concede that there is no difference between dynamic capabilities and ad hoc problem-solving; to say that would be to indulge in the 'shades of grey' fallacy. For the concepts and the contrast to be useful aids to understanding, it is not necessary that the pure forms exist in the

59

world, or even that we have high 'inter-rater reliability' in sorting real cases into only two conceptual boxes.

### 2.4.4. *Contrasting Cost Structures*

Dynamic capabilities typically involve long-term commitments to specialized resources. The more pervasive and detailed the patterning of the activity involved, the higher the costs of the commitments tend to be. The ability to sustain a particular patterned approach to new product development, for example, depends to some extent on continuity in the engineering personnel involved; there may be substantial continuity in facilities and equipment as well. Similarly, an established replicator organization has a central staff that combines the various functions required in the creation of a new outlet. For these sorts of commitments to be economically sound, the capability must be exercised. To have a dynamic capability and find no occasion to exercise it is merely to carry an overhead cost burden. On the other hand, an aggressive search for such occasions may also be a mistake. Attempting too much change— perhaps in a deliberate effort to exercise the dynamic capability—can impose additional costs when the frequent disruption of the underlying capability outweighs the competitive value of the novelty achieved. There is an ecological demand for balance between the costs of the capability and the use that is actually made of it.

By contrast, the costs of ad hoc problem-solving largely disappear if there is no problem to solve. Many of those costs take the form of opportunity costs of personnel who have alternative productive roles in the operating capability. True, it is at least conceivable that a similar pattern could obtain in an organization that had dynamic capabilities. This would mean that people could step out of their zero-level roles and into their dynamic capability roles—their learned, patterned change roles—and then step back again when change was completed. Something like this does happen in organizations that have frequent recourse to projects when coping with change. Where, however, the recurring problems are of a similar type, the plausibility of this image is undercut by the 'rustiness' problem: successful maintenance of a skill or routine typically requires frequent exercise by much the same personnel, which would again imply a continuing cost burden. Regardless of whether that objection is decisive in itself, it seems that, in practice, prominent examples of dynamic capabilities generally involve a lot of specialized personnel who are committed full time to their change roles, and other types of investments as well. The contrast with the lighter cost burdens of ad hoc problem-solving is clear.

### 2.4.5. *Dynamic Capability Is Not a 'Rule for Riches'*

It should now be apparent that it is not necessarily advantageous for a firm to invest in (first-order) dynamic capabilities. Rivals who rely on ad hoc problem-solving to accomplish change when needed are carrying a lower-cost burden. If opportunities for competitively significant change are sparse enough or expensive enough to realize, then the added cost of dynamic capabilities will not be matched by corresponding benefits on the average—even if an occasional notable success might suggest the contrary. Also, if the change environment does sustain dynamic capabilities relative to ordinary capabilities (plus ad hoc problem-solving), competition among many firms pursuing a similar dynamic capabilities strategy may compete away the rents, because (e.g.) product markets are saturated with rival innovations or because the salaries of scientists and engineers are bid up. A related and long-familiar example of a disadvantageous dynamic capability is innovative R&D that does not pay off in the presence of strong rivals who invest only in imitative R&D (see, e.g. Nelson and Winter 1982).

The (descriptive) rule for riches is to occupy a favoured and relatively uncontested place in the ecology of behaviours—for example, by having a strong R&D unit when others in the industry lack both innovative and imitative capabilities. While an individual actor can exert some influence on that ecology, it may well have difficulty in identifying the favoured and uncontested niches, or in forestalling unfavourable change after such a niche has been exploited for a while. Hence, the descriptive rule is of little prescriptive value.

### 2.4.6. *Higher-Order Capabilities*

If exogenous change is 'competence destroying' at the level of first-order dynamic capabilities (Tushman and Anderson 1986), those who invest in routinizing the response to familiar types of change may find themselves disadvantaged relative to more flexible players who have invested in higher-order capabilities. Deliberate investments in organizational learning may, for example, facilitate the creation and improvement of dynamic capabilities for the management of acquisitions or alliances (Zollo and Winter 2002). Collis (1994) argues that the existence of higher-order capabilities provides a rebuttal to any claim that there is generally advantage to be had from strength at any particular level of dynamic capability: there is always a higher level, and in his view superiority at the higher level always 'trumps' superiority at a lower level. Here, the same sceptical conclusion about advantage rests on the alternative argument that ad hoc problem-solving is always a substitute for dynamic capability and may be economically superior. Collis also makes, however, the related interesting suggestion that there is a historical tendency for the locus of competitive action to rise in the capability hierarchy. Strategic innovation often involves 'changing the game' in a way that 'takes it to a higher level'—a phrase that often connotes a focus on strengthening higher-order change capabilities. This notion appeals at the descriptive level, and there is clearly some logic to it. The argument for such upward progression seems to depend, however, on a missing assumption that restricts the character of exogenous change in such a way as to assure that the investment in higher-order capabilities becomes increasingly attractive relative to the cost-cutting move in the opposite direction. Just how such an assumption might be framed is unclear, but the logic is incomplete without it.

## 2.5. Conclusion

Large organizations are often capable of bringing about significant, continuing change by acting in a highly systematic, patterned way—'routinizing innovation' by the proactive application of 'dynamic capability'. Undoubtedly, efforts of this kind always involve meeting some technological and organizational challenges, and quite often these challenges are significant. Particularly in the latter cases, the organization's ability to mobilize the creative problem-solving efforts of individuals may be a key element of its dynamic capability. An accurate assessment of the importance of that element would, however, have to take full account of the fact that 'practice makes perfect'—and a dynamically capable organization has typically been engaged for many years in some quasi-repetitive undertaking that *brings about change in the world*—while not necessarily changing that much itself. Thus, the assessment would need to recognize the potentially very large difference between 'inside' and 'outside' perspectives on the same events. Similarly, it would confront great difficulties if it sought to make meaningful comparisons across domains, given the facts of great complexity and manifestly large contextual differences.

It has been argued here that, in any case, such an assessment should have a lower priority than deepening our understanding of how dynamic capabilities are actively reshaping our world—which they are surely doing, regardless of how much creativity we might find 'inside'. This process will likely continue in the future, but its grand themes as well as its narrow specifics will inevitably change. Any quasi-repetitive procedure depends for its success on the persistence of certain features in the environment, and such constancy cannot be expected to prevail indefinitely. For example, there is in the end a finite niche available in the world for faster semiconductor chips—let alone for fast-food restaurants of a given type. As these contextually determined limits are approached, further improvement in operating capabilities will no longer provide returns that cover the costs of the first-order dynamic capability. For a time, some of the necessary adjustments may be accomplished in smooth, well-practised ways, that is, by invoking higher-order capabilities. However, the economic fundamentals of the matter, to say nothing of the epistemology, seem to rule out the possibility that higher-order capabilities could provide a full solution. In such a context of multi-level frustration, it is quite possible that the entire organizational heritage of practised change methods becomes a deeply rooted cognitive barrier to the discovery of new solutions (Leonard-Barton 1992; Tripsas and Gavetti 2000). Thus, organizations (and the human species) will doubtless have to rely in the long run on creative solutions to unprecedented problems. Dynamic capability itself has intrinsic limits.

## References

Adler, P. (2007). 'The Bureaucratization of Innovation: A Marxist Analysis. Los Angeles', Working Paper, Marshall School of Business, University of Southern California.

——and Obstfeld, D. (2007). 'The Role of Affect in Creative Projects and Exploratory Search', *Industrial and Corporate Change*, 16: 19–50.

Baden-Fuller, C. and Winter, S. G. (2007). 'Replicating Organizational Knowledge: Principles or Templates?', Working Paper, Cass Business School, London.

Bailey, J. (2007). 'Chief "Mortified" by JetBlue Crisis', *The New York Times*, New York, NY.

Barnett, M. L., Starbuck, W. H., and Pant, P. N. (2003). 'Which Dreams Come True? Endogeneity, Industry Structure and Forecasting Accuracy', *Industrial and Corporate Change*, 12: 653–72.

Birnholtz, J. P., Cohen, M., and Hoch, S. V. (2007). 'Organizational Character: On the Regeneration of Camp Poplar Grove', *Organization Science*, 18: 315–32.

Bresnahan, T. and Malerba, F. (1999). 'Industrial Dynamics and the Evolution of Firms' and Nations' Capabilities in the World Computer Industry', in D. Mowery and R. Nelson (eds.), *The Sources of Industrial Leadership*. Cambridge: Cambridge University Press.

Bryce, D. J., Dyer, J. H., and Furr, N. R. (2006). 'Bootstrapping New Capabilities: Long Leaps and the Performance Consequences of Core Strategic Change', Working Paper, Brigham Young University, Provo, UT.

Burgelman, R. A. (1994). 'Fading Memories: A Process Theory of Strategic Business Exit in Dynamic Environments', *Administrative Science Quarterly*, 39: 24–56.

—— (2002). *Strategy is Destiny: How Strategy-Making Shapes a Company's Future*. New York: Free Press.

Chandler, A. D. (1977). *The Visible Hand: The Managerial Revolution in American Business*. Cambridge, MA: Belknap Press.

—— (1990). *Scale and Scope: The Dynamics of Industrial Competition*. Cambridge, MA: Harvard University Press.

Cohen, M. and Bacdayan, P. (1994). 'Organizational Routines are Stored as Procedural Memory', *Organization Science*, 5: 554–68.

—— (2006). 'What's Different is Routine', *Industrial and Corporate Change*, 15: 387–90.

Collis, D. J. (1994). 'Research Note: How Valuable are Organizational Capabilities?', *Strategic Management Journal*, 15: 143–52.

Dosi, G. (1982). 'Technological Paradigms and Technological Trajectories: A Suggested Interpretation of the Determinants and Directions of Technical Change', *Research Policy*, 11: 147–62.

Eisenhardt, K. M. and Martin, J. (2000). 'Dynamic Capabilities: What Are They?', *Strategic Management Journal*, 21: 1105–21.

Gawer, A. and Cusumano, M. A. (2002). *Platform Leadership: How Intel, Microsoft, and Cisco Drive Industry Innovation*. Boston, MA: Harvard Business School Press.

Hargadon, A. and Sutton, R. I. (1997). 'Technology Brokering and Innovation in a Product Development Firm', *Administrative Science Quarterly*, 42: 716–49.

Hayes, R. H., Pisano, G. P., and Upton, D. M. (1996). *Strategic Operations: Competing Through Capabilities*. New York: Free Press.

Helfat, C. E., Finkelstein, S., Mitchell, W., Peteraf, M. A., Singh, H., Teece, D. J., and Winter, S. G. (2007). *Dynamic Capabilities: Understanding Strategic Change in Organizations*. Oxford: Blackwell.

Henderson, R. (1995). 'Of Life Cycles Real and Imaginary: The Unexpectedly Long Old Age of Optical Photolithography', *Research Policy*, 24: 631–43.

Jaffe, A. B. and Lerner, J. (2004). *Innovation and Its Discontents: How Our Broken Patent System is Endangering Innovation and Progress, and What To Do About It*. Princeton, NJ: Princeton University Press.

Knudsen, T. and Winter, S. G. (2007). 'An Evolutionary Model of Spatial Competition', Working Paper, University of Southern Denmark, Odense.

Langlois, R. N. and Steinmuller, W. E. (1999). 'The Evolution of Competitive Advantage in the Worldwide Semiconductor Industry, 1947–1996', in D. C.

Mowery and R. R. Nelson (eds.), *Sources of Industrial Leadership: Studies of Seven Industries*. New York: Cambridge University Press.

Leonard-Barton, D. (1992). 'Core Capabilities and Core Rigidities: A Paradox in Managing New Product Development', *Strategic Management Journal*, 13: 111–25.

Levin, R. C. (1982). 'The Semiconductor Industry', in R. R. Nelson (ed.), *Government and Technical Progress: A Cross-Industry Analysis*. New York: Pergamon Press.

March, J. G. (1991). 'Exploration and Exploitation in Organizational Learning', *Organization Science*, 2: 71–87.

Miner, A. S., Bassoff, P., and Moorman, C. (2001). 'Organizational Improvisation and Learning: A Field Study', *Administrative Science Quarterly*, 46: 304–37.

Moore, G. (1965). 'Cramming More Components onto Integrated Circuits', *Electronics Magazine*, 38, 19 April.

—— (1995). 'Lithography and the Future of Moore's Law', *Proceedings of the SPIE*, 2438: 2–17.

Nelson, R. R. (1962). 'The Link between Science and Invention: The Case of the Transistor', in R. R. Nelson (ed.), *The Rate and Direction of Inventive Activity*. Princeton, NJ: Princeton University Press.

—— (1991). 'Why Do Firms Differ, and How Does It Matter?', *Strategic Management Journal*, 12: 61–74.

—— and Winter, S. G. (1982). *An Evolutionary Theory of Economic Change*. Cambridge, MA: Harvard University Press.

Raff, D. M. G. (2000). 'Superstores and the Evolution of Firm Capabilities in American Bookselling', *Strategic Management Journal*, 21: 1043–59.

Schumpeter, J. (1934). *The Theory of Economic Development*. Cambridge, MA: Harvard University Press.

—— (1950). *Capitalism, Socialism and Democracy*. New York: Harper and Row.

Teece, D. (1986). 'Profiting from Technological Innovation', *Research Policy*, 15: 285–305.

—— Pisano, G., and Shuen, A. (1997). 'Dynamic Capabilities and Strategic Management', *Strategic Management Journal*, 18: 509–33.

Tripsas, M. and Gavetti, G. (2000). 'Capabilities, Cognition, and Inertia: Evidence from Digital Imaging', *Strategic Management Journal*, 21: 1147–61.

Tushman, M. and Anderson, P. (1986). 'Technological Discontinuities and Organization Environments', *Administrative Science Quarterly*, 31: 439–65.

Winter, S. G. (2000). 'The Satisficing Principle in Capability Learning', *Strategic Management Journal*, 21: 981–96.

—— (2003). 'Understanding Dynamic Capabilities', *Strategic Management Journal*, 24: 991–5.

—— Szulanski, G., Ringov, D., and Jensen, R. J. (2007). 'Reproducing Knowledge: Inaccurate Replication and Failure in Franchise Organizations', Working Paper, INSEAD, Singapore.

Zollo, M. and Winter, S. G. (2002). 'Deliberate Learning and the Evolution of Dynamic Capabilities', *Organization Science*, 13: 339–51.

# 3
# Rules, Routines, and Learning in Organizations

*Alfred Kieser*

## 3.1. Rules, Routines, and Related Constructs

Organizational routine is often used as a generic term for all kinds of interdependent actions in organizations like rules, standard operating procedures, practices, etc. (Cohen et al. 1996; Cohen and Bacadayan 1994; Feldman and Pentland 2003; Grant 1991; Nelson and Winter 1982). This dominance of the term organizational routine seems unfortunate since, as already observed by Weber, formal rules predominantly distinguish formal organizations from other institutions:

> Originally there was a complete absence of the notion that rules of conduct possessing the character of 'law', i.e., rules which are guaranteed by 'legal coercion', could be intentionally created as 'norms'.... But where there had emerged the conception that norms were 'valid' for behavior and binding in the resolution of disputes, they were at first not conceived as the products, or even the possible subject matter, of human enactment.
>
> (Weber 1978: 760)

The word 'to organize' or 'organizer' originated in the French Revolution and designated the formation of governmental institutions according to the needs of the population. In a book that became highly influential, Sieyès (1988: 126) formulated: 'Il est impossible de créer un corps pour une fin sans lui donner une organisation, des formes et des lois propres à lui fair remplir les functions auxquelles on a voulu le destiner' (It is impossible to create a body for a specific purpose without giving it organization, forms, and laws that enable it to the fulfilment of the functions for which it has been created (my translation)).

Foundations of organizations as well as major organizational changes usually are initiated on the basis of formal rules. Since rules rarely prescribe actions in sufficient detail and clarity, routines regularly supplement formal organizational rules. Routines come into existence, for example, when organizational members agree, more or less implicitly, to follow a sequence of activities when implementing a rule. Without routines, rules would not work efficiently as exemplified by the example of a pit-stop team. A well-rehearsed team manages a pit stop in less than ten seconds since every member knows exactly what to do and how to do it. A team in which every member has been given rules about his specific task but that has never practised together will never achieve such a performance. Thus, routines encompass tacit personal and interpersonal knowledge (Becker 2004; Cohen et al. 1996; Cohendet and Llerena 2003; Hodgson 1997, 1998; Howard-Grenville 2005; Knott 2003; Lazaric 2000; Narduzzo, Rocco, and Warglien 2000; Teece, Pisano, and Schuen 1997; Teece and Pisano 1994). However, routines can also develop without being initiated by a formal rule, for example, when teams define tasks or follow their own, unofficial rules.

Routines develop out of trial-and-error processes. Organizational members experiment with sequences of activities in order to apply formal or self-defined tasks and rules. They agree to adopt a specific sequence that appears appropriate or, contingent on different clues, alternative sequences to implement the rule or to complete the task: 'Through repetition and recognition, organizational routines are created' (Feldman and Pentland 2003: 101). Feldman and Pentland call the rough description of a task that leads to a routine the ostensive aspect: 'the ostensive aspect is the ideal or schematic form of a routine. It is the abstract, generalized idea of the routine, or the routine in principle.' It is not necessary that the organizational members involved share the same perception of the task or the aim of the routine: '[T]he ostensive incorporates the subjective understandings of diverse participants' (2003: 101) However, it can be assumed that these subjective understandings do not conflict with each other: 'The network of connections a routine produces can be thought of as the web of perspectives maintained by routine participants. This set of perspectives is likely to lead to collectively shared understandings among routine (and therefore organizational) participants' (Feldman and Rafaeli 2002: 315). Feldman and Pentland (2003) call the implementation aspect of a routine the performative aspect.

Organizational routines not only refer to formal rules, be they formulated in written form or just orally prescribed, they can also integrate societal as well as group norms, or laws and jurisdiction. In most cases, routines integrate several of these elements. For example, rules for hiring and the accompanying routines may include elements that are derived from anti-discrimination laws, from societal norms concerning respectful dealings with applicants, and from practices that have been established in the profession of human relation managers or in the specific industry. Some authors emphasize the interplay between formal rules and routines (Feldman and Pentland 2003; Lazaric 2000; Reynaud 2005).

Routines are not automatic mindless responses, as assumed by Ashforth and Fried (1988). They usually imply considerable variety that requires reflectivity from those who apply them (Espedal 2006; Feldman and Pentland 2003, 2005; Pentland and Rueter 1994).

To a certain extent, routines can be modified to adapt to new conditions. Such a modification need not necessarily lead to a change of the ostensive aspect:

When people do new things, whether in response to external changes or in response to reflexive self-monitoring, they alter the potential repertoire of activities that creates and recreates the ostensive aspect of the routine. Variations . . . may or may not get accepted as legitimate alternatives to existing practice.

(Feldman and Pentland 2003: 108–9)

Zollo and Winter (2002: 341) distinguish between higher-order routines that 'bring about desirable changes in the existing set of routines'. The higher-order routines are seen as contributing to an organization's dynamic capabilities (Eisenhardt and Martin 2000; Levinthal 2000; Narduzzo, Rocco, and Warglien 2000; Zollo and Winter 2002).

## 3.2. Rules and Routines as Repositories of Organizational Knowledge

Rules and routines, and this is important with regard to organizational learning, serve as organizational memories and repositories of organizational knowledge (Argote and Darr 2000; Cyert and March 1963; March, Schulz, and Zhou 2000; Nelson and Winter 1982). If a rule specifies a course of action, organizational members do not have to develop a new solution each time a specific problem emerges. In a certain way, the organization has learned the problem solution that is contained in the routine, the organizational members do not have to remember the specifics of the solution and can focus on non-routine events. A rule as such may be abstract but the routines that develop around it concretize the repetitious problem solution. Sometimes, routines that develop around rules provide the basis for flexible reactions even though changes of the underlying rule are not possible (e.g. for political reasons, see Lukka 2007). Thus, rules and routines help to economize on the limited information processing and decision-making capabilities of organizational members (Becker 2004; Simon 1958).

By providing guidance for information analysis and identification of solutions, rules and routines also reduce uncertainty (Becker and Knudsen 2005; Heiner 1983). The rule appliers need not permanently question the appropriateness of the solution that is built into the routines.

There is wide consensus in organizational studies that rules and routines provide stability—a stability that eventually extends to undesirable inertia (Benner and Tushman 2003; Gilbert 2005; Hannan and Freeman 1977; Teece, Pisano, and Schuen 1997). Rigidity can also be the result of resistance. Organizational members who have learned to apply routines, including its tacit elements, tend to unfold resistance against new rules that necessitate them to acquire new knowledge. As Crozier (1964) shows, organizational members exposed to critique of their performance often tend to follow rules more rigidly than before when adaptations are called for in order to demonstrate that it was not their fault that caused the problem but a fault of the rule designers. A related problem is that organizational members may tend to confound precision in applying rules with quality of problem solution. In the words of Sims, Fineman, and Gabriel (1993: 31): '[r]ules can become the opium of bureaucratic officials. Without the rules, they are lost, paralyzed'.

Feldman and Pentland (2003), Lukka (2007), and Howard-Grenville (2005) argue that routines simultaneously provide stability and flexibility. The embeddedness of rules and routines in organizational and technical structures as well as in social expectations is a source of stability. However, organizational members develop subroutines that they conditionally apply in response to context conditions and thus they increase flexibility (McKeown 2001). Thus formal rules with their routines are, simultaneously, reducing organizational flexibility and facilitating it. Which one of these aspects prevails is dependent on *the way in which rules are getting established* (Adler and Borys 1996). The enabling characteristics of formal rules come to the foreground if the implementation process exhibits the following traits: (*a*) *Providing information on repair*: It is important that rules not only prescribe a sequence of activities but also provide information on how to deal with the occurrence of typical problems, so that the organizational members can help themselves while encountering these problems. (*b*) *Providing transparency*: Enabling rules provide organizational members with a wide range of contextual information, which helps them to interact creatively with the broader organization and environment. Procedures are designed to convey to organizational members an understanding of how their own tasks fit into the whole. (*c*) *Providing flexibility*: Enabling procedures have built in flexibility. Rules not only allow for different courses of action, they are also embedded into an organizational culture in which deviations from formalized rules are predominantly regarded as learning opportunities. An analysis of the reasons for deviations can point to necessary improvements or changes in rules, or to the need for a complete renewal of formalized rules. (*d*) *Participation*: Organizational members have the opportunity to participate in the design of rules. Participation not only improves acceptance and motivation but also increases the effectiveness of the rules, since the organizational members regularly have to contribute valuable experience. A formalized procedure that is designed in cooperation with experts or even completely by the organizational members themselves is not perceived as coercive.

## 3.3. How Norms Support Learning in Societies

Rule-based learning in organizations can be compared with learning in societies through norms. Societies learn faster when the learning of individuals is supported by rules or norms (Boyd and Richerson 2005; Richerson and Boyd 2005). When individuals have to learn isolated for themselves, that is, when norms that provide useful knowledge are not available, learning is very slow. When individuals are capable of imitating others by learning rules or norms that govern the behaviour of others they can learn selectively. They can learn when individual learning is cheap and accurate and imitate when learning is likely to be costly or inaccurate. For example, individuals could use a rule such as 'Try out the two techniques and if one is clearly better than the other one, adopt this technique, otherwise, use the technique that has become customary in the society'. The use of such a rule enables individuals to make fewer errors than individuals who have to depend exclusively on individual learning. Thus, by following rules or norms people can behave sensibly without having to understand why they do what they do. Boyd and Richerson (2005) show that a small amount of individual learning, when coupled with cultural transmission and a tendency to conform to the behaviour of others, can lead to adaptive norms, even though most people simply do what everyone else is doing. Beneficial norms spread if individuals register that those who follow the rules are better off in conditions to which the rules apply than those who do not. Societies learn to adapt to changes in the environment if there is a mix between individual learning and learning by establishing and following rules. Individuals must have the chance to behave unconventionally, that is, to replace rule following by individual learning. Through organizational rules, similar learning processes are established on the organizational level. Organizational rules that build on societal norms accelerate societal learning overall.

## 3.4. Rule Change and Rule Evolution as Organizational Learning

Recognition that rule-following characterizes much of the behaviour in organizations has directed attention to the processes by which rules support organizational learning (March 1981). The behavioural theory emphasizes organizational learning through rule adaptation on the basis of experience. Organizational rules emerge and are further modified incrementally on the basis of feedback from the environment either through the organization's own experience or through imitation of other organizations. This view is in accordance with the concept of organizational rules and routines as repositories of organizational knowledge (partly tacit). Learning is achieved by scrutinizing the existing rules with the aim of identifying opportunities for improvement.

According to Nelson and Winter (1982), imitation of effective routines within the organization can be seen as a powerful mechanism which accomplishes that effective routines spread faster in a given organization than less effective ones. New routines come about when management researchers, engineers, or managers apply problem-solving creativity. In the end, whether attempts of this kind prove successful is decided by environmental selection.

Schulz (1993) analyses which factors induce organizational members to change rules or to introduce new ones in a university. He concentrates on the question of whether organizational members' knowledge acquired in the application of rules has positive or negative effects on rule changes.

Thereby he assumes that the use of a rule results in an increase of competence with regard to the use of this rule. The development of alternative rules would devalue this knowledge and, therefore, the motivation of organizational members to change rules reduces with the age of these rules.

In addition, Schulz assumes that rules become institutionalized over time. New rules are perceived as preliminary attempts to solve certain problems. This perception invites changes. The longer a rule exists, the more members get used to it and the less they are inclined to change it—they develop routines around the rule. However, Schulz also presents a contradictory hypothesis: the older a rule gets the higher the probability that environmental changes necessitate changes to this rule, because the rule no longer fits the changed conditions, because it becomes obsolete. Schulz's data show that the probability of rule change decreases with rule age. However, the age of a rule *version*—the time that has elapsed since the last modification of the rule—has a positive effect on the probability of further rule changes. In his explanation of these results, Schulz points out that rules have stable and unstable elements. The unstable elements become obsolete after a modification. Other elements of rules remain stable because they mean security and an accumulation of competences for the members of the organization. Overall these effects result in a negative relationship between rule age and the probability of rule change.

Schulz (1998) also found that an increasing density of rules has a negative effect on the creation rate. He explains this result with the absorptive capacity of rules. Once problems and their solutions are codified into rules, the impetus for change—in terms of founding new rules—is reduced.

In another project about rule histories and organizational learning, the concept of age dependence of rule changes and suspensions was extended by taking environmental and organizational changes into account. By analysing the development of a German bank's personnel rules, Beck and Kieser (2003) found that the processes of rule change and rule suspension follow rather different patterns. While it could be shown that with increasing age of rule versions the rate of rule change strongly decreased—a finding that supports Schulz's results—the rate of rule suspension increased, which could be due to a process of obsolescence. One conclusion from this finding is that because changes of the rules' content grew less likely with increasing version age this content became obsolete. The two processes seem to be complementary: the growing reluctance to change a rule the older a rule version gets necessitates an increased pressure to suspend that rule, because an additional change might no longer be the appropriate measure to adapt the rule to the changed situation. These complementary yet different patterns of influence underline the necessity to differentiate between the events of rule change and rule suspension, when processes of organizational learning are analysed on the basis of the life cycles of organizational rules. Another important result is that organizational learning not only depends on cumulated experience in dealing with rules but also depends on experience in creating rules. The longer the history of the rule founding process the less likely it becomes that a version of a newly founded rule will be changed or suspended. Especially rule suspension is reduced with each additional year between the introduction of the rule book and the founding of a rule. The stronger reduction of the rule suspension risk might also lead to a situation in which this rule—as a consequence of the reduced suspension risk—has to be changed. However, in contrast to the influence of version age, this complementary pattern does not lead to antagonistic influences of the founding cohorts for rule change and suspension.

## 3.5. Behavioural Theory Models of Rule-Based Organizational Learning

In the first of a row of highly influential models of organizational learning, Cyert and March (1963) assume that search the for better problem solutions is stimulated as soon as existing programmes no longer guarantee the achievement of the organization's goals that are formulated as aspiration levels. Search itself is also controlled by programmes or rules. At first, organizational search proceeds on the basis of simple models of causality. Increasingly complex models are developed if this initial search is not successful. Problem solutions that are identified during this search and appear adequate are stored in new rules that replace old rules. However, organizations not only learn by exchanging problem-solving rules in the described pattern but also learn by adapting goals and attention rules. Two forms of adaptation of attention rules are conceptualized: over time, organizations learn to define more appropriate performance criteria, and they also learn to identify those parts of the environment that are important for them. The basic assumption in this concept of organizational learning is that a rule, be it a decision rule, an attention rule, or a rule that controls goal formulation, that leads to a preferred state at one point is more likely to be used in the future than it was in the past, and a rule that leads to a non-preferred state at some point is less likely to be used in the future than it was in the past.

A fundamental problem of this model is that it defines whole organizations or organizational subunits as the units of analysis which means that the link between individual and organizational learning is neglected. In a later model, March and Olsen (1975) explicitly include the roles of individuals in processes of organizational learning. They conceptualize a complete cycle of learning events in organizations and identify barriers that can interrupt learning at different points in this cycle. The complete cycle consists of four stages: (*a*) Individuals take actions of which they are convinced that they improve performance. (*b*) These individual actions lead to organizational actions that produce certain outcomes. (*c*) These outcomes are interpreted in a meaningful way, that is, success is distinguished from failure and links are drawn between actions and perceived outcomes. (*d*) This reasoning leads to changes in individuals' beliefs.

The creation or modifications of rules that lead to organizational actions are results of experimentation (examples of rule creation can be found in Costello 2000). Thus, rule-based organizational learning consists of three steps: variation of existing rules through experimentation, selection by drawing inferences from experiments, and retention through formulating rules that produce successful actions.

A first possible interruption of the complete learning cycle occurs when individuals are prevented by certain organizational conditions—especially by prevailing role definitions or standard operating procedures—from adapting their behaviour to their beliefs. March and Olsen (1975) call this impediment *role constrained learning*. Organizational members are convinced that new actions have to be initialized because environmental conditions have changed, but they are unable to change their actions because their roles within the organization are so fixed by the organizational structure that there is no possibility for them to act in the way they think they should. The second interruption of the learning cycle is labelled *audience learning*. It occurs when individuals are able to change their own behaviour but cannot affect rule-guided actions of others (Tyler and Balder 2005). A third interruption of the learning cycle is caused by a misinterpretation of the consequences of rule-based organizational actions. Organizational members cannot evaluate correctly which impact the organizational actions that have been induced through new rules have on the environment and on the organization's performance. They tend to interpret data so that the actions taken in response to certain problems that were identified are retrospectively legitimated, that is, *superstitious learning* takes place. The last interruption is called *learning under ambiguity* and occurs when changes in the environment cannot be correctly identified. The organizational members are not able to make sense of the environment or to explain why certain changes took place at all (Denrell and March 2001).

A few examples may serve to illustrate these interruptions of organizational learning. Let us assume that an accountant of a company's profit centre comes to the conclusion that the existing transfer price system is severely flawed. She asks herself whether she can at least modify the respective rules for the profit centre she is working in. On the one hand, this would mean that she could provide better data for the manager of this profit centre, on the other hand, she would run the risk of her 'correction' being detected and disapproved by the headquarter's accountants. If she decides not to implement what she thinks is a necessary correction of the rules of the transfer price system she gives in to *role constraint learning*.

Now let us assume that she manages to implement a new transfer price system in her profit centre and that she tries to convince the central controlling department to change the system of transfer pricing for the whole company. In doing this, she has to realize that an organizational member who points out weak spots risks loosing some reputation in the organization, especially when those criticized belong to other departments or to higher hierarchical levels. She cannot be sure that she will be able to convince others with her arguments. If she fails her career might suffer. It is therefore possible that our accountant decides to keep what she has learned to herself. This would then be an example of *audience learning*. As we have seen in our analysis of the dysfunctions of organizational rules it is often difficult to change existing standard operating procedures.

Let us finally assume that our controller was successful in convincing the people in the central accounting department to change the transfer price system for the whole company. Now everybody is eager to find out whether this was a good idea or not. However, it is extremely difficult to establish the effects of changes in the transfer price system on the performance of the company. Have results improved *because of the changes in the transfer price system*? If they deteriorated: Was this a consequence of the change or would things even be worse without it? The proponents of the change are generally in favour of an optimistic interpretation, while the opponents try to get agreement on a negative interpretation of the new transfer price system's influence on the performance of the company. Thus, there is always the danger that the interpretations are biased, that is, that they reflect *superstitious learning*.

If the organizational members are uncertain how to interpret environmental changes at all, apart from the question how they were influenced by the action of the organization, they face the situation of *learning under ambiguity* (Greve 2003).

Summarizing the development of concepts within the group around March, we can state that at the beginning there was an approach that took organizations as units of analysis which adapted to experience in reaction to environmental changes. The question of how this adaptation is brought about was neglected at first. Then, the theory was extended by analysing interaction processes. Organizations can benefit from their members' identification of problems under the assumption that they manage to transfer their individual knowledge to the organizational level. It can be considered an important result that this organizational learning has pointed out that deviant behaviour of members can substantially contribute to organizational welfare because through divergent interpretations of reality the chances of exploring new possibilities of action are increased.

## 3.6. Recombining Knowledge for Rule Changes

In this section, the processes through which organizational rules are created and modified in order to foster organizational learning will be analysed with an emphasis on rules that extend across several departments.

### 3.6.1. *Is Inter-Specialist Learning Necessary when Creating or Modifying Inter-Departmental Rules?*

Integrating knowledge of different specialists is, in general, a difficult task since specialists refer to different paradigms, they speak different languages—they live in different thought words (Brown and Duguid 1991; Carlile 2002). Different approaches for overcoming these difficulties in attempts to recombine specialists' knowledge have been suggested. There are approaches that assume that knowledge-sharing between specialists in the form of cross-learning is the most effective way of recombining their knowledge (Argyris and Schön 1978; Nonaka 1991, 1994). Other approaches emphasize the need for support mechanisms in interspecialist learning processes. For example, Brown and Duguid (1991: 99–100) argue that knowledge exchange between specialists requires an 'enabling architecture' that encompasses 'translators' between groups of specialists and 'brokers' who participate in several specialized fields as well as 'boundary objects' such as physical objects or technologies (see also Leonard-Barton 1998). The authors who assume cross-learning to be the basic integration mechanism for specialized knowledge imply that the recombination of knowledge takes place in the brains of specialized organizational members. Thus, Hoopes and Postrel (1999: 844), for example, argue that '[a]t some point, knowledge from different specialists must be combined in the brain of one or more individuals who have the authority to make design decisions'.

A third group of authors doubt whether translators or brokers or mediating devices such as boundary objects prove to be mechanisms that efficiently support knowledge sharing in the face of the organizational members' limited cognitive capacities. They argue that there must be mechanisms that bring about recombination of knowledge that do not strongly depend on cross-learning and on the limited cognitive abilities of the human brain. For example, Demsetz (1991) holds that the idea of organizational members intensively learning from each other calls into question the advantages of division of work in organizations:

Although knowledge can be learned more effectively in a specialized fashion, its use to achieve high living standards requires that a specialist somehow uses the knowledge of other specialists. This cannot be done only by learning what others know, for that would undermine gains from specialized learning.

For these authors, the basic research question for cooperation between specialists is *not how* specialists within an organization can learn as much as possible from each other. It should be reformulated into: *How can cooperation between specialists be arranged in such a way that cross-learning is reduced to a level that does not overstretch human cognitive abilities?*

A possible answer to this question could be that in designing and redesigning organizational rules inter-specialist learning is replaced by specialists largely independently revising drafts of new rules or new rule versions in prototyping processes. Rules are, as Grant (1996b: 115) has observed, media that enable specialists to integrate their knowledge without having to intensively learn from each other. He identifies two basic conditions that reduce the need for knowledge exchange (Grant 1996b). First, some kind of *common knowledge*—that should not be confused with *knowledge transfer*—is required to facilitate the interaction between the specialists. This common knowledge encompasses, for example, a common language and other symbolic systems such as computer software or accounting systems. Grant (1996*b*: 116) contends that this common knowledge also encompasses some overlap of specialists' knowledge—some inter-specialist learning. As a second condition specialists develop routines (that include written rules) and 'the essence of routines is that individuals develop sequential patterns of interaction which permit the integration of their specialized knowledge without the need for communicating that knowledge' (Grant 1996*a*), since 'efficiency in organizations tends to be associated with maximizing the use of rules, routines and other integration mechanisms that economize on communication and knowledge transfer, and reserve problem solving and decision making by teams to unusual, complex and important tasks' (Grant 1996*b*).

This leads to a question that Grant does not deal with: How do rules and routines that bring about integration of specialists' knowledge come into existence?

### 3.6.2. *Simulation of Trial-and-Error: Prototyping*

Kieser and Koch (2008) hold that *prototyping* represents a mechanism that enables actors with limited cognitive capacities to bring about changes in rules without having to engage in intensive cross-learning. Prototypes are familiar in product development. Their general logic, however, also applies to organizational rules. Applied to rule changes, prototyping is present in its simplest form as soon as a specialist presents a draft for a rule change to other specialists for feedback. If one or several of these other specialists accept the draft or demand a modification, cooperation for the creation of a new rule has occurred without necessitating intensive cross-learning. The specialist who came up with the proposal need neither understand in detail why colleagues demand changes nor learn the knowledge that enabled these colleagues to make these demands. It is sufficient to understand what kind of modifications the colleagues demand and to trust their expertise. Thus the knowledge of different specialists becomes manifest in a concept of a rule or in a rule.

A later stage of prototyping might consist of testing formulated rules in the 'real world', and waiting for problems to occur that necessitate modifications. Through prototyping, it can be tested whether the different parts of a rule interact properly or whether the changed rule can be expected to interact properly with other rules. Modifications can be discussed among specialists in terms of modifying interfaces between parts of the rule or between rules. Intensive cross-learning between specialists is not required.

### 3.6.3. *Directory Knowledge for the Identification of Organizational Members with Relevant Knowledge*

How can organizational members who are considering a rule change know who is in possession of relevant knowledge when there is no individual member who knows in detail what all other organizational members know? *Directory knowledge*, that is, knowledge of a directory of people who may have knowledge relevant for changing certain rules, is the answer to this problem.

According to the concept of transactive memory, groups, with the help of directory knowledge, can simulate a common memory and thus achieve a higher degree of memorizing capacity than members acting individually (Liang, Moreland, and Argote 1995; Wegner 1995; Wegner, Raymond, and Erber 1991). 'Our directories for memories held by others can be thought of as meta memories. That is, they are memories about memories' (Wegner 1995).

### 3.6.4. *The Concept of Transactive Organizational Learning*

The above analysis has provided all the basic elements that are needed for a concept that explains knowledge sharing between specialists that does not rely on cross-learning. Rules can, in principle, serve as knowledge repositories. Rules are identified as being in need of change as soon as organizational members are confronted with problems of some significance in applying extant rules. The next step is the identification, with the help of *transactive memory*, of the organizational members who possess relevant knowledge. Then drafts for new rule versions are formulated. These concepts are *prototypes* that are presented to other specialists. The feedback of these specialists results in improved drafts. This process of designing trials that are subject to review by experts is repeated until all specialists concerned get the impression that the rule or the rule system will function properly (see Figure 3.1).

### 3.6.5. *An Empirical Test*

The organizational learning mechanisms outlined above were tested on the basis of case studies in two organizations (Kieser and Koch 2008). The usual procedure for rule changes is as follows: once the necessity

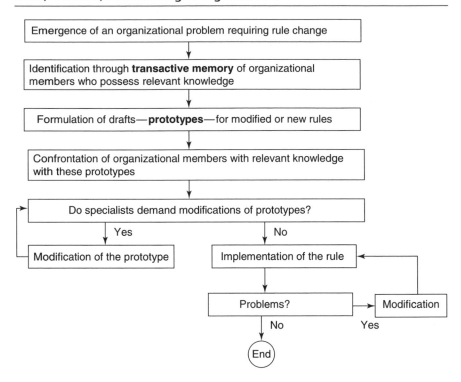

**Figure 3.1.** A concept of transactive organizational learning

of a rule change has been established one or several organizational members who are seen as specialists in areas possibly affected by the rule change have to produce a draft of a new rule version and send it to a number of organizational members for evaluation and comments. To the extent that these comments lead to revisions of the draft, the knowledge of the commentators is transferred into the developing rule.

Organizational members who are involved in processes of rule changes are experts in their respective areas, but do not know much about other areas. However, the members who are involved in a process of rule change share a certain basic understanding about the tasks that the rule awaiting change has to perform.

The results of Kieser and Koch's research (2008) on organizational learning through rule changes show that rules are media in which different specialists' knowledge can be stored as well as recombined in the process of change. In spite of their bad reputation in popular discourse, formal rules provide the basis for organizational efficiency. It was also shown how *prototyping* allows specialists to input specialized knowledge elements into a rule in ways that do not conflict with their limited cognitive capacities. In the light of these findings, it is surprising that the majority of extant concepts of organizational learning place so much weight on inter-specialist learning (Grunwald and Kieser 2007).

It should be pointed out that exploration, that is, the infusion of radical new knowledge, into rules can lead to misadaptation. On the basis of new ideas, specialists may come up with suggestions for rule changes that are inappropriate. Prototyping does not guarantee detection of inappropriate changes. Since each specialist evaluates drafts predominantly from the perspective of the interface—'How does the change affect processes for which I am responsible?'—the effects on the overall performance of the rule do not come into sight, at least not before the rule change gets effective. Even then, it may happen that the specialists who are deeply convinced that the rule changes reflect superior knowledge lack sensitivity for negative feedback from the environment. If there are actors in the environment who strongly believe in the competence of the rule designers and therefore provide encouragement, perhaps even in the form of capital, rules that result in disastrous solutions may result from organizational learning processes. Stein (2003) reports an impressive case of this sort. Organizational narcissism prevented rule designers who had implemented rules based on a sophisticated theoretical model from appropriately interpreting adverse feedback from the environment.

Another question is *to what extent can incremental adaptation through rule changes replace fundamental organizational change*. The concept of punctuated equilibrium (Gersick 1991; Sastry 1997; Tushman and Romanelli 1985) holds that two kinds of organizational change have to be distinguished: fundamental and incremental or evolutionary change. Phases between fundamental changes are predominantly conceptualized as consolidations of the structures that result from fundamental change. The phases are characterized by improvements of existing processes and exploitation of existing knowledge—an approach that eventually might lead into a competency trap (Espedal 2006; Levinthal and March 1993). However, a fundamental change of knowledge and routines can result in a failure trap. A concept that integrates both approaches—incremental and fundamental change—could be based on the idea that rule changes are not only triggered by environmental changes but also by fundamental structural redesigns. In their study, Kieser and Koch (2008) found indications that this is the case.

## 3.7. Conclusion

Rules and routines provide media of organizational learning. Organizational learning based on rules and routines comes about only when there are organizational members who actively pursue changes in rules and routines, when these members overcome the learning barriers and thus complete the learning cycle (March and Olsen 1975) and when the organization succeeds in correctly interpreting feedback from the environment. These are, as we have seen, processes that are ridden with prerequisites.

## References

Adler, P. S. and Borys, B. (1996). 'Two Types of Bureaucracy: Enabling and Coercive', *Administrative Science Quarterly*, 41: 61–89.

Argote, L. and Darr, E. (2000). 'Repositories of Knowledge in Franchise Organizations: Individual, Structural, and Technological', in G. Dosi, R. R. Nelson, and S. G. Winter (eds.), *The Nature and Dynamics of Organizational Capabilities*. New York: Oxford University Press.

Argyris, C. and Schön, D. A. (1978). *Organizational Learning: A Theory of Action Perspective*. Reading, MA: Addison-Wesley.

Ashforth, B. E. and Fried, Y. (1988). 'The Mindlessness of Organizational Behaviors', *Human Relations*, 41: 305–29.

Beck, N. and Kieser, A. (2003). 'The Complexity of Rule Systems, Experience, and Organizational Learning', *Organization Studies*, 24: 793–814.

Becker, M. C. (2004). 'Organizational Routines: A Review of the Literature', *Industrial and Corporate Change*, 13: 643–77.

—— and Knudsen, T. (2005). 'The Role of Routines in Reducing Pervasive Uncertainty', *Journal of Business Research*, 58: 746–57.

Benner, M. J. and Tushman, M. L. (2003). 'Exploitation, Exploration, and Process Management: The Productivity Dilemma Revisited', *Academy of Management Review*, 28: 238–56.

Boyd, R. and Richerson, P. J. (2005). *The Origin and Evolution of Cultures*. Oxford: Oxford University Press.

Brown, J. S. and Duguid, P. (1991). 'Organizational Learning and Communities-of-Practice: Toward a Unified View of Working, Learning, and Innovation', *Organization Science*, 2: 40–57.

Carlile, P. R. (2002). 'A Pragmatic View of Knowledge and Boundaries: Boundary Objects in New Product Development', *Organization Science*, 13: 442–53.

Cohen, M. D. and Bacadayan, P. (1994). 'Organizational Routines Are Stored in Organizational Memory: Evidence from a Laboratory Study', *Organization Science*, 5: 554–68.

——Burkhart, R., Dosi, G., Egidi, M., Marengo, L., Warglien, M., and Winter, S. (1996). 'Routines and Other Recurring Action Patterns of Organizations: Contemporary Research Issues', *Industrial and Corporate Change*, 5: 653–98.

Cohendet, P. and Llerena, P. (2003). 'Routines and Incentives: The Role of Communities in the Firm', *Industrial and Corporate Change*, 12: 271–97.

Costello, N. (2000). *Stability and Change in High-Tech Enterprises: Organizational Practices and Routines.* London: Routledge.

Crozier, M. (1964). *The Bureaucratic Phenomenon.* London: Tavistock.

Cyert, R. M. and March, J. G. (1963). *A Behavioral Theory of the Firm.* Englewood Cliffs, NJ: Prentice-Hall.

Demsetz, H. (1991). 'The Theory of the Firm Revisited', in O. E. Williamson and S. G. Winter (eds.), *The Nature of the Firm.* Oxford: Oxford University Press.

Denrell, J. and March, J. G. (2001). 'Adaption as Information Restriction: The Hot Stove Effect', *Organization Science*, 12: 523–38.

Eisenhardt, K. M. and Martin, J. A. (2000). 'Dynamic Capabilities: What Are They?', *Strategic Management Journal*, 21: 1105–22.

Espedal, B. (2006). 'Do Organizational Routines Change as Experience Changes?', *Journal of Applied Behavioral Science*, 42: 468–90.

Feldman, M. S. and Pentland, B. T. (2003). 'Reconceptualizing Organizational Routines as a Source of Flexibility and Change', *Administrative Science Quarterly*, 48: 94–118.

——and Rafaeli, A. (2002). 'Organizational Routines as Sources of Connections and Understandings', *Journal of Management Studies*, 39: 309–32.

Gersick, C. J. G. (1991). 'Revolutionary Change Theories: A Multilevel Exploration of the Punctuated Equilibrium Paradigm', *Academy of Management Review*, 16: 10–36.

Gilbert, C. G. (2005). 'Unbundling the Structure of Inertia: Resource versus Routine Rigidity', *Academy of Management Journal*, 48: 741–63.

Grant, R. M. (1991). 'The Resource-Based Theory of Competitive Advantage: Implications for Strategy Formulation', *California Management Review*, 33: 114–35.

——(1996a). 'Prospering in Dynamically-Competitive Environments: Organizational Capability as Knowledge Integration', *Organization Science*, 7: 375–87.

——(1996b). 'Toward a Knowledge-Based Theory of the Firm', *Strategic Management Journal*, 17: 109–22.

Greve, H. R. (2003). *Organizational Learning from Performance Feedback.* Cambridge: Cambridge University Press.

Grunwald, R. and Kieser, A. (2007). 'Learning to Reduce Inter-Organizational Learning: An Analysis of Architectural Product Innovation in Strategic Alliances', *Journal of Product Innovation Management*, 24: 369–91.

Hannan, M. T. and Freeman, J. (1977). 'The Population Ecology of Organizations', *American Journal of Sociology*, 82: 929–64.

Heiner, R. A. (1983). 'The Origin of Predictable Behavior', *American Economic Review*, 73: 560–95.

Hodgson, G. M. (1997). 'The Ubiquity of Habits and Rules', *Cambridge Journal of Economics*, 21: 663–84.

——(1998). 'Hayek, Evolution, and Spontaneous Order', in P. Mirowski (ed.), *Natural Images in Economic Thought*. Cambridge: Cambridge University Press.

Hoopes, D. G. and Postrel, S. (1999). 'Shared Knowledge, "Glitches", and Product Development Performance', *Strategic Management Journal*, 20: 837–65.

Howard-Grenville, J. (2005). 'The Persistence of Flexible Organizational Routines: The Role of Agency and Organizational Context', *Organization Science*, 16: 618–36.

Kieser, A. and Koch, U. (2008). 'Bounded Rationality and Organizational Learning Based On Rule Changes', *Management Learning*, 39 (forthcoming).

Knott, A. M. (2003). 'The Organizational Routine Factor Market Paradox', *Strategic Management Journal*, 24: 929–43.

Lazaric, N. (2000). 'The Role of Routines, Rules and Habits in Collective Learning: Some Epistemological and Ontological Considerations', *European Journal of Economic and Social Systems*, 14: 157–71.

Leonard-Barton, D. (1998). *Wellsprings of Knowledge: Building and Sustaining the Sources of Innovation*. Boston, MA: Harvard Business School Press.

Levinthal, D. A. (2000). 'Organizational Capabilities in Complex Worlds', in G. Dosi, R. R. Nelson, and S. G. Winter (eds.), *The Nature and Dynamics of Organizational Capabilities*. New York: Oxford University Press.

——and March, J. G. (1993). 'The Myopia of Learning', *Strategic Management Journal*, 14: 95–112.

Liang, D. W., Moreland, R., and Argote, L. (1995). 'Group versus Individual Training and Group Performance: The Mediating Role of Transactive Memory', *Personality and Social Psychology Bulletin*, 21: 384–93.

Lukka, K. (2007). 'Management Accounting Change and Stability: Loosely Coupled Rules and Routines in Action', *Management Accounting Research*, 18: 76–101.

McKeown, T. (2001). 'Plans and Routines, Bureaucratic Bargaining and the Cuban Missile Crisis', *The Journal of Politics*, 63: 1163–90.

March, J. G. (1981). 'Footnotes to Organizational Change', *Administrative Science Quarterly*, 26: 563–77.

——and Olsen, J. P. (1975). 'The Uncertainty of the Past: Organizational Learning under Ambiguity', *European Journal of Political Research*, 3: 147–71.

——Schulz, M., and Zhou, X. (2000). *The Dynamics of Rules: Change in Written Organizational Codes*. Stanford, CA: Stanford University Press.

Narduzzo, A., Rocco, E., and Warglien, M. (2000). 'Talking About Routines in the Field: The Emergence of Organizational Capabilities in a New Cellular Phone Network Company', in G. Dosi, R. R. Nelson, and S. G. Winter (eds.), *The Nature and Dynamics of Organizational Capabilities*. New York: Oxford University Press.

Nelson, R. R. and Winter, S. G. (1982). *An Evolutionary Theory of Economic Change*. Cambridge, MA: Harvard University Press.

Nonaka, I. (1991). 'The Knowledge-Creating Company', *Harvard Business Review*, 69: 96–104.

—— (1994). 'A Dynamic Theory of Organizational Knowledge Creation', *Organization Science*, 5: 15–37.

Pentland, B. T. and Feldman, M. S. (2005). 'Organizational Routines as a Unit of Analysis', *Industrial and Corporate Change*, 14: 793–815.

—— and Rueter, H. H. (1994). 'Organizational Routines as Grammars of Action', *Administrative Science Quarterly*, 39: 484–510.

Reynaud, B. (2005). 'The Void at the Heart of Rules: Routines in the Context of Rule-Following. The Case of the Paris Metro Workshop', *Industrial and Corporate Change*, 14: 847–71.

Richerson, P. J. and Boyd, R. (2005). *Not by Genes alone: How Culture Transformed Human Evolution*. Chicago, IL: University of Chicago Press.

Sastry, M. A. (1997). 'Problems and Paradoxes in a Model of Punctuated Organizational Change', *Administrative Science Quarterly*, 42: 237–75.

Schulz, M. (1993). *Learning, Institutionalization and Obsolescence in Organizational Rule Histories*. Dissertation Thesis. Stanford: Stanford University.

—— (1998). 'Limits to Bureaucratic Growth: The Density Dependence of Organizational Rule Births', *Administrative Science Quarterly*, 43: 845–76.

Sieyès, E. (1988). *Qu'est-ce que le Tiers État?* Paris: Flammarion.

Simon, H. A. (1958). *Administrative Behavior*, 2nd edn. New York: Schuster and Schuster.

Sims, D., Fineman, S., and Gabriel, Y. (1993). *Organizations and Organizing. An Introduction*. London: Sage.

Stein, M. (2003). 'Unbounded Irrationality: Risk and Organizational Narcissism at Long Term Capital Management', *Human Relations*, 56: 523–40.

Teece, D. J. and Pisano, G. (1994). 'The Dynamic Capabilities of Firms', *Industrial and Corporate Change*, 3: 537–56.

—————— and Schuen, A. (1997). 'Dynamic Capabilities and Strategic Management', *Strategic Management Journal*, 18: 509–33.

Tushman, M. L. and Romanelli, E. (1985). 'Organizational Evolution: A Metamorphosis Model of Convergence and Reorientation', in L. L. Cummings and B. M. Staw (eds.), *Research in Organizational Behavior*, vol. 7. Greenwich, CT: JAI Press.

Tyler, T. R. and Balder, S. L. (2005). 'Can Businesses Effectively Regulate Employee Conduct? The Antecedents of Rule Following in Work Settings', *Academy of Management Journal*, 48: 1143–58.

Weber, M. (1978). *Economy and Society: An Outline of Interpretive Sociology*, edited by G. Roth and C. Wittich. Berkeley, CA: University of California Press.

Wegner, D. M. (1995). 'A Computer Network Model of Human Transactive Memory', *Social Cognition*, 13: 319–39.

——Raymond, P., and Erber, R. (1991). 'Transactive Memory in Close Relationships', *Journal of Personality and Social Psychology*, 61: 923–29.

Zollo, M. and Winter, S. G. (2002). 'Deliberate Learning and the Evolution of Dynamic Capabilities', *Organization Science*, 13: 339–51.

# 4

# Problemistic Search and (Inter-)Organizational Learning

*Henrich R. Greve*

## 4.1. Introduction

How is the institutional environment connected to organizational learning? Levitt and March define learning as follows: 'organizations are seen as learning by encoding inferences from history into routines' (Levitt and March 1988: 320). Learning theory uses organizational experience to explain the creation or change of routines, with a particular focus on problem-solving activities in the organization (Cyert and March 1963). It sees organizational behaviour as goal directed and potentially adaptive, but whether specific forms of learning help the organization or not is addressed empirically rather than posited as an assumption (e.g. Sorenson and Sørensen 2001). Institutions are regulatory, normative, and cognitive structures that create expectations for organizational structures and behaviours and rewards for fulfilling these expectations (Scott 1995). Institutions are argued to constrain organizational behaviour (DiMaggio and Powell 1983), and thus restrict the domain of organizational learning to areas of activity in which institutional constraints are weak or difficult to enforce (Meyer and Rowan 1977).

At the outset, there appears to be a potential conflict between the theory of organizational learning and a view of institutions as constraints. Nevertheless, the same writers who discuss institutional effects on organizations have also argued that institutions are tools for building organizations and hence have an enabling role (Meyer and Rowan 1977). Whether institutions circumscribe learning or, alternatively, direct learning is a question that touches on classic divides in organizational theory.

Theories differ in the extent to which they posit environmental constraints or organizational choice and in the extent to which they address the rational–technical or socially constructed aspects of organizations (Astley and Van de Ven 1983; Hrebiniak and Joyce 1985). Debates about the relative usefulness of these opposing perspectives periodically occur in organizational theory in general and its subfields (DiMaggio and Powell 1991; Selznick 1996), and often contain calls for integration of the opposing views (Greenwood and Hinings 1996; Levinthal 1991).

A sceptic might look at these bursts of meta-theoretical activity and ask whether the integration of these polar perspectives occurs, and whether it is useful for advancing organizational theory. In the following, I will discuss work that integrates organizational learning with effects of environmental characteristics such as institutions. This work adds up to a significant theoretical and empirical contribution, but the extent of progress is easy to underestimate because it has taken place in distinct areas of learning research. I will discuss two areas separately before showing that their theory and findings converge to such an extent that they appear to form a 'new synthesis' in learning research. They have not attracted much attention in institutional theory yet, but have potentially important implications for this theory as well.

The following areas of work form the foundation of the integration between organizational learning and institutional environments. First, the learning process of problemistic search (Cyert and March 1963) has proven to be not just an intra-organizational phenomenon, but also to be affected by social influence from other organizations. The main mechanism here is that social comparison is used to create social aspiration levels for goal variables, and thus to determine whether problemistic search is initiated (Greve 2003a). Social aspiration levels act jointly with historical aspiration levels to determine whether a given performance level is viewed as satisfactory or not, and subsequently to guide organizational actions such as research and development, innovation launch, resource acquisition, and change of market niches. The common theme of these outcomes is that problemistic search is required to identify potential organizational changes, and risk taking is required to implement them.

Second, the classical tradition on inter-organizational diffusion is still very active and is an important area of work for institutional theorists, who examine the spread of institutions to demonstrate mimetic isomorphism (DiMaggio and Powell 1983; Tolbert and Zucker 1983). It has progressed from an initial emphasis on showing that diffusion occurs to more detailed investigation of the sources of heterogeneity in the timing of adoptions (Greve 2005; Strang and Soule 1998). Now the emphasis is on investigating how the social structure determines which organizations have greater influence on a focal organization, and the main theoretical mechanism is information transfer through observation of similar organizations and network contact with organizations. Although networks are important for channelling decision-maker attention, their effects are well described in other work (e.g. Brass et al. 2004) and will not be discussed here. Instead I focus on how similar organizations imitate each other as a result of observation and social comparison.

These two research traditions have different intellectual origins and empirical focus. Despite these differences in history and viewpoint, they have grown closer as a result of theory positing a similar set of influences from managerial cognitions about other organizations as well as from findings indicating interplay between problemistic search and adoption of innovations. This rapprochement opens up areas for significant new research, and is a rare case of theoretical integration across levels of analysis. The organizational process investigated by the theory of problemistic search turns out to match well with the inter-organizational influences examined by institutional theory and other inter-organizational theories, and the new synthesis of these theories promises to significantly advance our understanding of how new behaviours are adopted by organizations and organizational fields.

## 4.2. Problemistic Search with Social Aspiration Levels

The workhorse model of organizational learning is problemistic search, which is an important part of the behavioural theory of the firm (Cyert and March 1963: 114–27). A number of extensions to the original theory exist, and the most important may be the integration with risk-taking concerns from prospect theory (Bromiley 1991; Kahneman and Tversky 1979; Lopes 1987; March 1994: 35–49; Shapira 1994). According to this model, organizational change is a result of the following steps. First, decision-makers compare the organizational performance with an aspiration level that specifies what level of performance is viewed as satisfactory. The aspiration level is determined by the past performance of the focal organization and the performance of its competitors, and is used to interpret the performance through distinguishing success from failure with the aspiration level as the dividing line (March and Simon 1958). Performance below the aspiration level triggers problemistic search, which is directed by heuristics like proximity to the symptom and current organizational practice (Cyert and March 1963). Solutions generated by problemistic search are evaluated for their risk and fit to the organization, with decision-makers accepting greater risk the further the performance is below the aspiration level (Kahneman and Tversky 1979; March and Shapira 1992).

In the basic model of problemistic search, the organization is seen as interacting with the environment through the inspection of the performance, which is affected by its environmental fit relative to that of its competitors. Viewed as an organizational routine for adaptation, problemistic search lets the organization improve features such as market niche and technology, but it does not ensure that the organization can find a globally best solution (Herriott, Levinthal, and March 1985; Levinthal and March 1981). When combined with adjustment of risk taking and elimination of poorly adapted organizations, problemistic search produces robust organizations that forego some profits to avoid risk levels that would increase the rate of failure (Greve 2002). Problemistic search makes organizations sensitive to the reward structures of the environment through their responsiveness to performance levels.

There is a solid record of evidence supporting problemistic search as a source of organizational risk taking and change. Research and development expenditures and innovation launches increase when the performance is below the aspiration level (Antonelli 1989; Audia and Sorenson 2001; Bolton 1993; Greve 2003b; Mullins, Forlani, and Walker 1999), as one would expect given their role in organizational adaptation to the environment. Investment in production facilities is also a key adaptive activity guided by problemistic search (Audia and Greve 2006; Greve 2003c), as is acquisition of other firms (Haleblian, Kim, and Rajagopalan 2005). Market niche changes are more likely following performance below the aspiration level (Greve 1998a), and so are changes in organizational networks (Baum et al. 2005). These findings suggest that organizations engage in a variety of changes in response to performance below the aspiration level, which fits the theoretical emphasis on low performance as an initiator of search, leaving the exact form of change to be determined by the experience and routines of the focal organization (Cyert and March 1963). It follows that broader measures of organizational change that aggregate a number of different behaviours should also show an increase when the performance is below the aspiration level, and this prediction has been supported (Audia, Locke, and Smith 2000; Boeker 1997; Grinyer and McKiernan 1990; Lant, Milliken, and Batra 1992; Miller and Chen 1994). Hence, problemistic search is a well-supported model of how organizations learn from their own experience.

The theory of problemistic search contains an evaluation of performance through comparison with historical and social aspiration levels. The social aspiration level can be viewed as a form of social comparison (Bandura and Jourden 1991; Festinger 1954; Wood 1989) in which managers judge their organization by examining its performance relative to that of a reference group of other organizations (Fiegenbaum and Thomas 1995; Greve 1998a). Social aspiration levels are a direct influence from the environment on the organizational process of identifying problems. They are an interesting contrast to mimetic behaviours because the comparison with others is the same, but decision-makers compare performance levels instead of behaviours and structures, and react by searching for solutions rather than adoption of the same behaviours.

Cyert and March (1963) originally specified the aspiration level as a weighted sum of the past aspirations, the past performance, and the performance of other organizations, and hence did not specify the social aspiration level as an independent influence on managers. However, much of the later work on organizational risk taking and change has examined either the effect of past performance or the average performance of other organizations in the industry, but has not modelled these jointly (Nickel and Rodriguez 2002). Some work has modelled both aspiration levels, however, and showed that they jointly affected decision-making (Greve 1998a; Mezias, Chen, and Murphy 2002), while other work has integrated social and historical influences on the aspiration level and found that the social influence was greater (Greve 2003b). Some risk researchers have arrived at a similar conclusion: although prospect theory specifies that decision-makers compare with the status quo, suggesting a comparison with their own past performance, they have shown that a social aspiration level made as an industry average of the performance yields results consistent with the predictions (Fiegenbaum and Thomas 1988; but see Miller and Chen 2004).

Although it is interesting that managers are responsive to comparisons of their own performance with an industry average, this finding is less precise than what the theory of reference groups would predict. An important element of this theory is that individual cognition about organizations involves intra-industry distinctions based on salient characteristics such as size, location, resource allocation, and market presence (Clark and Montgomery 1999; Fiegenbaum and Thomas 1995; Porac and Rosa 1996; Porac et al. 1995). For example, knitwear producers in Scotland not only focused more on other Scottish producers than on foreign producers but also identified several distinct subgroups of Scottish knitwear firms and were more likely to compare themselves with same-group members than with members from other groups (Porac et al. 1995). Similar findings of narrowly defined reference groups have been found for grocery stores in a town (Gripsrud and Grønhaug 1985) and hotels in Manhattan (Lant and Baum 1995).

If managers let such firm reference groups guide their attention and competitive actions, as evidence suggests (Baum and Lant 2003; Fiegenbaum and Thomas 1995), then it is likely that they also use them when constructing social aspiration levels for firm performance. This suggests a model of social aspiration levels as weighted averages of the performance of other firms, with the weights based on the perceived social similarity of the origin and target firm (Greve 2003*a*). There is still little work on weighted aspiration levels, but recent studies have found that they predict organizational behaviours more accurately than social aspiration levels formed as averages of all competitors (Baum et al. 2005; Greve 2008). Thus, problemistic search is sensitive to inter-firm comparisons of performance and to similarity judgements of firms, giving it a significant social component.

## 4.3. Institutions and Learning in Diffusion Processes

Organizational learning research views the behaviours of others as a form of organizational experience available through observation (Levitt and March 1988). Imitation is one possible response to the observation that other organizations adopt new practices, but the theory does not assume that imitation is the only response or that intended imitation results in an accurate transfer of the practice across organizations (March 1981). Hence, in learning theory, diffusion models belong to a larger class of models on inter-organizational learning that also includes work on deliberate transfer of practices among organizations (Argote, Beckman, and Epple 1990) and non-mimetic responses to innovation adoption (Greve and Taylor 2000). What distinguishes work on diffusion processes in learning theory is that it emphasizes the availability of a solution and judgements on its efficacy as the causal mechanisms, whereas work on problemistic search examines the conditions that give rise to an organizational problem.

Diffusion processes have also been central to institutional theory. Inter-organizational diffusion of structures and procedures through imitation provides direct evidence of social influence on organizational actions. This fact has been used to support the process of mimetic isomorphism, which posits that managers resolve environmental uncertainty by imitating other organizations (DiMaggio and Powell 1983). Thus, evidence on the diffusion of institutions through inter-organizational imitation is an important part of the evidence that cognitive legitimacy of institutions is produced by prevalence (Fligstein 1991; Han 1994; Tolbert and Zucker 1983). Learning theory sees imitation as a way for boundedly rational decision-makers to learn from the behaviour of others, so both theories have a cognitive focus (Levitt and March 1988). What makes a diffusion process distinctively institutional, then, is that a social institution (rather than a technology, for example) is the practice that diffuses and that the diffusion process causes organizations to become isomorphic through the adoption of the same institutions.

Some theory and evidence has pointed towards uniform environmental pressures in diffusion processes that leave little room for organizational diversity. The common theme of such theory is that organizational attention is drawn towards a small set of homogeneous and influential actors, and this set of imitation targets leads to isomorphism. One version of status theory posits that organizations seek status by adopting the practices of the most prominent and respected organizations in their field (Haveman 1993). Consistent with such theory, studies have found that large organizations attract attention and are imitated more often (Baum, Li, and Usher 2000; Greve 2000; Haunschild and Miner 1997; Haveman 1993). More direct measures of status have also yielded evidence of the disproportionate influence of high-status actors (Kraatz 1998; Soule 1997).

Against these findings, however, is evidence that organizations selectively pay attention to the parts of the environment that are judged as most relevant to their problem-solving activities. The attention is still influenced by cognitive structures and judgements of appropriateness that correspond to cognitive and normative institutions, but these structures are used to select organizations that are judged to be similar to the focal organization, and hence can be assumed to provide the most relevant information for learning which practices are beneficial. For example, an alternative version of the status theory posits that imitation occurs most frequently among organizations of intermediate status, because such organizations are more prone to have their legitimacy questioned (Phillips and Zuckerman 2002). More generally, status rankings are associated with different expectations for the attributes of actors at different status levels (Benjamin and Podolny 1999; Podolny 2005). Status similarity is thus a way to pick which other organizations to learn from (Haveman 1993; Lounsbury 2001; Soule 1997).

Attention is guided by comparisons of organizational characteristics, suggesting that the search for solutions also takes into account judgements of whether an organization has sufficiently similar operational characteristics to the focal one that it is a useful reference. A broad range of organizational characteristics appears to influence mimetic behaviours such that organizations selectively adopt the practices of the organizations that are most similar to themselves (Barreto and Baden-Fuller 2006; Baum, Li, and Usher 2000; Davis and Greve 1997; Haunschild and Beckman 1998; Kraatz 1998; Lee and Pennings 2002). For example, Portuguese bank managers made reference groups based on banks' national origin, specialization, and state ownership, and imitated branch location decisions of banks in their group even when this was harmful for their performance (Barreto and Baden-Fuller 2006). Dutch accounting firms imitated a new organizational form adopted by firms of similar size (Lee and Pennings 2002). Organizations also imitate other organizations in similar environments (D'Aunno, Succi, and Alexander 2000; Greve 1998b; Martin, Swaminathan, and Mitchell 1998; McKendrick 2001). For example, niche entry choices by radio broadcasters were more likely to be imitated in same-size markets (Greve 1998b), and hospitals adopted innovative behaviours when organizations facing similar market constraints had done so (D'Aunno, Succi, and Alexander 2000). These findings suggest that learning from others is used to respond to competitive and institutional environments.

The case for learning is strengthened by evidence on the abandonment of behaviours. Abandonment can be treated as a deinstitutionalization process when the behaviour is an institution (Oliver 1992), and shows mimetic influences just as adoption does. However, studies that show mimetic abandonment also produce evidence that these are motivated by pragmatic concerns. A major driver of mimetic abandonment is doubt about the efficacy of the behaviour (Anderson 1999; Burns and Wholey 1993; Greve 1995; Rao, Greve, and Davis 2001), though a wish to avoid sanctions when the abandoned behaviour is highly institutionalized is also a factor (Ahmadjian and Robinson 2001). It may seem strange that abandonment is mimetic when the organization has direct experience with the behaviour, and thus seems capable of judging its efficacy without social influences. However, the attribution of general performance problems to specific practices is complex, and so is prediction of the future performance of practices, so it is reasonable that boundedly rational managers would learn abandonment by observing other organizations.

## 4.4. Integrating Problemistic Search and Diffusion Processes

Problemistic search is often integrated with other theories to produce new predictions, and diffusion research is a major area of integration. Search conducted to find solutions of low performance produce either internal generation of unique solutions or external discovery of solutions applied by others to similar problems. Diffusion processes reach organizations seeking to solve problems addressed by the focal innovation more readily than other organizations. These two observations suggest a match between a view of organizational learning as spurred by internal problems and one of learning as inspired by external opportunities (Levitt and March 1988). Indeed, studies often conclude that a match between the organization and the innovation speeds adoption (Mansfield 1961; Mezias 1990). Organizations are quick to adopt new practices if they have low performance (Greve 1998a; Kraatz 1998; Westphal and Zajac 1994) or if they are simultaneously abandoning an alternative practice (Greve 1995). Hence, one outcome predicted by problemistic search is mimetic adoption of new practices.

The integration of problemistic search and diffusion processes does not end here, however, because more advances can be made by considering imitation to be a result of problemistic search. Problemistic search processes are guided by heuristic judgements of the relevance and efficacy of the practice under consideration. Because organizational decision-making involves sequential consideration of a small set of alternatives (Cyert and March 1963; March and Simon 1958), the order by which alternatives come to the decision-maker's attention matters, which complicates the prediction. Despite this complication, a learning view of search and diffusion is a productive approach for producing new theoretical predictions.

Uncertainty in the evaluation of untested practices is a deterrent against their adoption because uncertain value means that the adoption is risky, so a risk-averse manager needs to have a high mean evaluation of the practice in order to accept the variance in potential outcomes. Learning theory offers two suggestions for how this barrier is overcome. First, a given level of risk is more acceptable when low performance introduces risk seeking, so performance below the aspiration level is associated with mimetic adoption of risky actions such as innovation adoption (Greve 1998a; Kraatz 1998). Second, even risky practices are adopted if the estimated value is sufficiently high. This could lead genuinely valuable practices to be adopted if their value is correctly estimated and less valuable practices to be adopted if their value is overestimated. Uncertainty in the evaluation increases the probability of overestimation, and thus can spur some organizations to adopt (Harrison and March 1984), and overestimation also becomes more likely as a result of observing others adopt (Rao, Greve, and Davis 2001). Thus, not only is uncertainty a threshold condition that triggers imitation (DiMaggio and Powell 1983), but more uncertainty also makes mimetic adoption of risky behaviours more likely (Haunschild 1994).

The linking of problems and solutions to produce mimetic adoption is not the only connection between the theories of problemistic search and diffusion. A more general link is seen in their reliance on managerial attention to the environment as a source of predictions on which organizations will be more influential. Investigation of similarity judgements in forming social aspiration levels and adopting innovations relies on the same model of managerial cognition and posit effects that are nearly the same. Consistent with this, the weighted social aspiration level proposed by Greve (2003a: 47) is very similar to the heterogeneous diffusion model proposed by Strang and Tuma (1993). These theories and the reference group theory that links them can be seen as forming the start of a new synthesis of theories of intra-organizational and inter-organizational influences on organizational behaviours and outcomes.

The new synthesis also contains other theories that integrate problemistic search with inter-organizational influences. The combination of problemistic search and competitive rivalry is an important part of Red Queen theory (Barnett and Hansen 1996). According to this theory, problemistic search causes low-performing organizations to attempt risky changes in order to improve their competitive position. The result is increased failure rates, but also stronger capabilities in the survivors, which in turn puts pressure on their competitors to improve. Two consequences of this process of escalating competition are greater capabilities in organizations with higher competitive experience and specialization towards withstanding the competitive attacks of the same cohort of competitors (Barnett 1997; Barnett, Greve, and Park 1994; Barnett and Hansen 1996; Barnett and Sorenson 2002).

The problem-solving emphasized in the theory of problemistic search is also an assumption in the theory of learning curves in production.

This theory posits that production experience leads to increased efficiency and fewer errors through a process of routine development through trial and error, and has led to a rich tradition of work on the development and transfer of experience in production (Argote 1999; Argote, Beckman, and Epple 1990; Benkard 1999; Darr, Argote, and Epple 1995; Epple, Argote, and Devadas 1991; Levin 2001). Despite the similarity of assumptions of these theories, the specific hypotheses differed so much that work integrating them has been rare. However, recent work in this tradition has shown that organizations use performance levels to determine whether to focus on learning from own experience or from the observed experience of other organizations (Baum and Dahlin 2007), suggesting a greater role of performance in learning curves than originally thought.

The same theme of switching between different forms of learning is seen in work examining the effect of environmental uncertainty on learning patterns. Although this work is in an early phase, it has already produced evidence that organizations rely more on problemistic search in stable institutional environments and more on mimetic change in unstable institutional environments (Wezel and Saka-Helmhout 2006). Likewise, firms put in place structure to facilitate inter-organizational learning under conditions of high environmental uncertainty (Beckman, Haunschild, and Phillips 2004). The impression given by these studies is that organizational learning is flexible and opportunistic, as the learning routines and sources of experience shift depending on the context.

## 4.5. Discussion

Organizational learning theory has increasingly examined environmental influences on the results of problemistic search while maintaining its focus on organizational change as an activity that occurs in response to problem-solving activities. The result has been to connect organizational learning theory with theory of managerial cognition and construction of reference groups, and to show joint influence of these mechanisms on the construction of social aspiration levels and the retrieval of solutions through observation of firms in the organizational reference group. The result is a theory that crosses the organizational and inter-organizational levels of analysis and that provides valuable stimuli for developing organizational learning theory further as well as for developing institutional theory and other theories' positive effects on organizational environments.

An important insight from this theory is that the adoption of new practices leads to localized isomorphism, as it occurs within a social space of organizational reference groups and a temporal space bounded by organizational problem-solving. This insight is a good reason for renewed examination of the diffusion of organizational institutions. The questions of when organizations will imitate each other and which others they will imitate continue to be interesting because they are now seen as providing insights into how organizational attention patterns are directed towards specific problems and solutions.

Another important insight is that organizations engaged in problem-solving have a highly eclectic set of responses. A broad range of organizational behaviours are changed as a result of problemistic search, and the changes can be in the form of imitation of others, internal development of own solutions, or abandonment of practices judged to be of low value. There may be limits to how finely we can model the choices among so many alternative actions, but there is good potential for additional theory and empirical work on how the organizational context and experience provide ideas when managers are solving problems. It is likely that further progress can be made by considering how organizational attention paths and decision-making routines are primed by recent experience with similar problems (March, Sproull, and Tamuz 1991; Ocasio 1997).

It also seems likely that further progress can be made by incorporating problemistic search into institutional theory. Performance differences among organizations have often been observed to influence institutionalization of new practices (Leblebici et al. 1991), and seems important for predicting which organizations will be early adopters of new institutions. Problemistic search can also be used to understand partial institutionalization, as it is likely to make the highest performing organizations less susceptible to mimetic isomorphism, and could be an important driver of deinstitutionalization processes. Institutional theory stands to gain much from the new synthesis of organizational and inter-organizational theory.

The new synthesis of organizational learning theory with the theory of inter-organizational influences is a strong platform for understanding organizational adaptation to the environment and field-level diversity in the responses to new institutions and innovations. It has already contributed to an increased interest in problemistic search, and has led to a number of important theoretical and empirical advances. More progress is possible by incorporating these insights into work on mimetic effects on institutionalization, where they still have seen limited use.

# References

Ahmadjian, C. L. and Robinson, P. (2001). 'Safety in Numbers: Downsizing and the Deinstitutionalization of Permanent Employment in Japan', *Administrative Science Quarterly*, 46: 622–54.

Anderson, P. (1999). 'How Does the Mix of Routines in a Population Change? Technology Choice in the American Cement Industry', in A. Miner and P. Anderson (eds.), *Advances in Strategic Management*. Greenwich, CT: JAI Press.

Antonelli, C. (1989). 'A Failure-inducement Model of Research and Development Expenditure: Italian Evidence from the Early 1980s', *Journal of Economic Behavior and Organization*, 12: 159–80.

Argote, L. (1999). *Organizational Learning: Creating, Retaining, and Transferring Knowledge*. Boston, MA: Kluwer.

——Beckman, S. L., and Epple, D. (1990). 'The Persistence and Transfer of Learning in Industrial Settings', *Management Science*, 36: 140–54.

Astley, W. G. and Van de Ven, A. H. (1983). 'Central Perspectives and Debates in Organization Theory', *Administrative Science Quarterly*, 28: 245–73.

Audia, P. G. and Greve, H. R. (2006). 'Less Likely to Fail? Low Performance, Firm Size, and Factory Expansion in the Shipbuilding Industry', *Management Science*, 52: 83–94.

——and Sorenson, O. (2001). *A Multilevel Analysis of Organizational Success and Inertia*. Manuscript, London School of Business.

——Locke, E. A., and Smith, K. G. (2000). 'The Paradox of Success: An Archival and a Laboratory Study of Strategic Persistence Following a Radical Environmental Change', *Academy of Management Journal*, 43: 837–53.

Bandura, A. and Jourden, F. J. (1991). 'Self-Regulatory Mechanisms Governing the Impact of Social Comparison on Complex Decision Making', *Journal of Personality and Social Psychology*, 60: 941–51.

Barnett, W. P. (1997). 'The Dynamics of Competitive Intensity', *Administrative Science Quarterly*, 42: 128–60.

——and Hansen, M. T. (1996). 'The Red Queen in Organizational Evolution', *Strategic Management Journal*, 17: 139–57.

——and Sorenson, O. (2002). 'The Red Queen in Organizational Creation and Development', *Industrial and Corporate Change*, 11: 289–325.

——Greve, H. R., and Park, D. Y. (1994). 'An Evolutionary Model of Organizational Performance', *Strategic Management Journal*, 15: 11–28.

Barreto, I. and Baden-Fuller, C. (2006). 'To Conform or to Perform? Mimetic Behaviour, Legitimacy-based Groups and Performance Consequences', *Journal of Management Studies*, 43: 1559–80.

Baum, J. A. C. and Dahlin, K. B. (2007). 'Aspiration Performance and Railroads' Patterns of Learning from Train Wrecks and Crashes', *Organization Science*, 18: 368–85.

Baum, J. A. C. and Lant, T. K. (2003). 'Hits and Misses: Managers' (Mis)-categorization of Competitors in the Manhattan Hotel Industry', in J. A. C. Baum and O. Sorenson (eds.), *Geography and Strategy: Advances in Strategic Management*, vol. 20. Oxford: JAI Press and Elsevier.

—— Li, S. X., and Usher, J. M. (2000). 'Making the Next Move: How Experiential and Vicarious Learning Shape the Locations of Chains' Acquisitions', *Administrative Science Quarterly*, 45: 766–801.

—— Rowley, T. J., Shipilov, A. V., and Chuang, Y. T. (2005). 'Dancing with Strangers: Aspiration Performance and the Search for Underwriting Syndicate Partners', *Administrative Science Quarterly*, 50: 536–75.

Beckman, C. M., Haunschild, P. R., and Phillips, D. J. (2004). 'Friends or Strangers? Firm-specific Uncertainty, Market Uncertainty, and Network Partner Selection', *Organization Science*, 15: 259–75.

Benjamin, B. A. and Podolny, J. M. (1999). 'Status, Quality, and Social Order in the California Wine Industry', *Administrative Science Quarterly*, 44: 563–89.

Benkard, C. L. (1999). *Learning and Forgetting: The Dynamics of Aircraft Production*, NBER Rep. No. 7127, Cambridge, MA: NBER.

Boeker, W. (1997). 'Strategic Change: The Influence of Managerial Characteristics and Organizational Growth', *Academy of Management Journal*, 40: 152–70.

Bolton, M. K. (1993). 'Organizational Innovation and Substandard Performance: When Is Necessity the Mother of Innovation', *Organization Science*, 4: 57–75.

Brass, D. J., Galaskiewicz, J., Greve, H. R., and Tsai, W. (2004). 'Taking Stock of Networks and Organizations: A Multi-level Perspective', *Academy of Management Journal*, 47: 795–814.

Bromiley, P. (1991). 'Testing a Causal Model of Corporate Risk Taking and Performance', *Academy of Management Journal*, 34: 37–59.

Burns, L. R. and Wholey, D. R. (1993). 'Adoption and Abandonment of Matrix Management Programs: Effects of Organizational Characteristics and Interorganizational Networks', *Academy of Management Journal*, 36: 106–38.

Clark, B. H. and Montgomery, D. B. (1999). 'Managerial Identification of Competitors', *Journal of Marketing*, 63: 67–83.

Cyert, R. M. and March, J. G. (1963). *A Behavioral Theory of the Firm*. Englewood Cliffs, NJ: Prentice-Hall.

D'Aunno, T., Succi, M., and Alexander, J. A. (2000). 'The Role of Institutional and Market Forces in Divergent Organizational Change', *Administrative Science Quarterly*, 45: 679–703.

Darr, E. D., Argote, L., and Epple, D. (1995). 'The Acquisition, Transfer, and Depreciation of Knowledge in Service Organizations', *Management Science*, 41: 1750–62.

Davis, G. F. and Greve, H. R. (1997). 'Corporate Elite Networks and Governance Changes in the 1980s', *American Journal of Sociology*, 103: 1–37.

DiMaggio, P. J. and Powell, W. W. (1983). 'The Iron Cage Revisited: Institutional Isomorphism and Collective Rationality in Organizational Fields', *American Sociological Review*, 48: 147–60.

——(1991). 'Introduction', in W. W. Powell and P. J. DiMaggio (eds.), *The New Institutionalism in Organizational Analysis*. Chicago, IL: University of Chicago Press.

Epple, D., Argote, L., and Devadas, R. (1991). 'Organizational Learning Curves: A Method for Investigating Intra-plant Transfer of Knowledge Acquired Through Learning By Doing', *Organization Science*, 2: 58–70.

Festinger, L. (1954). 'A Theory of Social Comparison Processes', *Human Relations*, 7: 117–40.

Fiegenbaum, A. and Thomas, H. (1988). 'Attitudes Towards Risk and the Risk Return Paradox: Prospect Theory Explanations', *Academy of Management Journal*, 31: 395–407.

——(1995). 'Strategic Groups as Reference Groups: Theory, Modeling and Empirical Examination of Industry and Competitive Strategy', *Strategic Management Journal*, 16: 461–76.

Fligstein, N. (1991). 'The Structural Transformation of American Industry: An Institutional Account of the Causes of Diversification in the Largest Firms 1919–1979', in W. W. Powell and P. J. DiMaggio (eds.), *The New Institutionalism in Organizational Analysis*. Chicago, IL: University of Chicago Press.

Greenwood, R. and Hinings, C. R. (1996). 'Understanding Radical Organizational Change: Bringing Together the Old and the New Institutionalism', *Academy of Management Review*, 21: 1022–54.

Greve, H. R. (1995). 'Jumping Ship: The Diffusion of Strategy Abandonment', *Administrative Science Quarterly*, 40: 444–73.

——(1998a). 'Performance, Aspirations, and Risky Organizational Change', *Administrative Science Quarterly*, 44: 58–86.

——(1998b). 'Managerial Cognition and the Mimetic Adoption of Market Positions: What You See Is What You Do', *Strategic Management Journal*, 19: 967–88.

——(2000). 'Market Niche Entry Decisions: Competition, Learning, and Strategy in Tokyo Banking 1894–1936', *Academy of Management Journal*, 43: 816–36.

——(2002). 'Sticky Aspirations: Organizational Time Perspective and Competitiveness', *Organization Science*, 13: 1–17.

——(2003a). *Organizational Learning from Performance Feedback: A Behavioral Perspective on Innovation and Change*. Cambridge: Cambridge University Press.

——(2003b). 'A Behavioral Theory of R&D Expenditures and Innovation: Evidence from Shipbuilding', *Academy of Management Journal*, 46: 685–702.

——(2003c). 'Investment and the Behavioral Theory of the Firm: Evidence from Shipbuilding', *Industrial and Corporate Change*, 12: 1051–76.

——(2005). 'Inter-organizational Learning and Heterogeneous Social Structure', *Organization Studies*, 26: 1025–47.

Greve, H. R. (2008). 'A Behavioral Theory of Firm Growth: Sequential Attention to Size and Performance Goals', *Academy of Management Journal*, 51, forthcoming.

—— and Taylor, A. (2000). 'Innovations as Catalysts for Organizational Change: Shifts in Organizational Cognition and Search, *Administrative Science Quarterly*, 45: 54–80.

Grinyer, P. and McKiernan, P. (1990). 'Generating Major Change in Stagnating Companies', *Strategic Management Journal*, 11: 131–46.

Gripsrud, G. and Grønhaug, K. (1985). 'Structure and Strategy in Grocery Retailing: A Sociometric Approach', *The Journal of Industrial Economics*, 33: 339–47.

Haleblian, J., Kim, J. Y. J., and Rajagopalan, N. (2005). 'The Influence of Acquisition Experience and Performance on Acquisition Behavior: Evidence from the U.S. Commercial Banking Industry', *Academy of Management Journal*, 49: 357–70.

Han, S. K. (1994). 'Mimetic Isomorphism and its Effect on the Audit Services Market', *Social Forces*, 73: 637–63.

Harrison, J. R. and March, J. G. (1984). 'Decision Making and Postdecision Surprises', *Administrative Science Quarterly*, 29: 26–42.

Haunschild, P. R. (1994). 'How Much is that Company Worth? Interorganizational Relationships, Uncertainty, and Acquisition Premiums', *Administrative Science Quarterly*, 39: 391–411.

—— and Beckman, C. M. (1998). 'When Do Interlocks Matter? Alternate Sources of Information and Interlock Influence', *Administrative Science Quarterly*, 43: 815–44.

—— and Miner, A. S. (1997). 'Modes of Interorganizational Imitation: The Effects of Outcome Salience and Uncertainty', *Administrative Science Quarterly*, 42: 472–500.

Haveman, H. A. (1993). 'Follow the Leader: Mimetic Isomorphism and Entry Into New Markets', *Administrative Science Quarterly*, 38: 593–627.

Herriott, S. R., Levinthal, D., and March, J. G. (1985). 'Learning From Experience in Organizations', *American Economic Review*, 75: 298–302.

Hrebiniak, L. G. and Joyce, W. F. (1985). 'Organizational Adaptation: Strategic Choice and Environmental Determinism', *Administrative Science Quarterly*, 30: 336–49.

Kahneman, D. and Tversky, A. (1979). 'Prospect Theory: An Analysis of Decision Under Risk', *Econometrica*, 47: 263–91.

Kraatz, M. S. (1998). 'Learning by Association? Interorganizational Networks and Adaptation to Environmental Change', *Academy of Management Journal*, 41: 621–43.

Lant, T. K. and Baum, J. A. C. (1995). 'Cognitive Sources of Socially Constructed Competitive Groups: Examples from the Manhattan Hotel Industry', in W. R. Scott and S. Christensen (eds.), *The Institutional Construction of Organizations: International and Longitudinal Studies*. Thousand Oaks, CA: Sage.

——Milliken, F. J., and Batra, B. (1992). 'The Role of Managerial Learning and Interpretation in Strategic Persistence and Reorientation: An Empirical Exploration', *Strategic Management Journal*, 13: 585–608.

Leblebici, H., Salancik, G. R., Copay, A., and King, T. (1991). 'Institutional Change and the Transformation of Interorganizational Fields: An Organizational History of the U.S. Radio Broadcasting Industry', *Administrative Science Quarterly*, 36: 333–63.

Lee, K. and Pennings, J. M. (2002). 'Mimicry and the Market: Adoption of a New Organizational Form', *Academy of Management Journal*, 45: 144–62.

Levin, D. Z. (2001). 'Organizational Learning and the Transfer of Knowledge: An Investigation of Quality Improvement', *Organization Science*, 11: 630–47.

Levinthal, D. A. (1991). 'Organizational Adaptation and Environmental Selection: Interrelated Processes of Change', *Organization Science*, 2: 140–5.

——and March, J. G. (1981). 'A Model of Adaptive Organizational Search', *Journal of Economic Behavior and Organization*, 2: 307–33.

Levitt, B. and March, J. G. (1988). 'Organizational Learning', in W. R. Scott and J. Blake (eds.), *Annual Review of Sociology*, 14: 319–40.

Lopes, L. L. (1987). 'Between Hope and Fear: The Psychology of Risk', *Advances in Experimental Social Psychology*, 20: 255–95.

Lounsbury, M. (2001). 'Institutional Sources of Practice Variation: Staffing College and University Recycling Programs', *Administrative Science Quarterly*, 46: 29–56.

Mansfield, E. (1961). 'Technical Change and the Rate of Imitation', *Econometrica*, 29: 741–66.

March, J. G. (1981). 'Footnotes to Organizational Change', *Administrative Science Quarterly*, 26: 563–77.

——(1994). *A Primer on Decision Making: How Decisions Happen*. New York: Free Press.

——and Shapira, Z. (1992). 'Variable Risk Preferences and the Focus of Attention', *Psychological Review*, 99: 172–83.

——and Simon, H. (1958). *Organizations*. New York: Wiley.

——Sproull, L. S., and Tamuz, M. (1991). 'Learning from Samples of One or Fewer', *Organization Science*, 2: 1–13.

McKendrick, D. G. (2001). 'Global Strategy and Population-level Learning: The Case of Hard Disk Drives', *Strategic Management Journal*, 22: 307–34.

Martin, X., Swaminathan, A., and Mitchell, W. (1998). 'Organizational Evolution in the Interorganizational Environment: Incentives and Constraints on International Expansion Strategy', *Administrative Science Quarterly*, 43: 566–601.

Meyer, J. W. and Rowan, B. (1977). 'Institutionalized Organizations: Formal Structure as Myth and Ceremony', *American Journal of Sociology*, 83: 340–63.

Mezias, S. J. (1990). 'An Institutional Model of Organizational Practice: Financial Reporting at the Fortune 200', *Administrative Science Quarterly*, 35: 431–57.

Mezias, S. J., Chen, Y. R., and Murphy, P. R. (2002). 'Aspiration-level Adaptation in an American Financial Services Organization: A Field Study', *Management Science*, 48: 1285–300.

Miller, D. and Chen, M. J. (1994). 'Sources and Consequences of Competitive Inertia: A Study of the U.S. Airline Industry', *Administrative Science Quarterly*, 39: 1–23.

Miller, K. D. and Chen, W. R. (2004). 'Variable Organizational Risk Preferences: Tests of the March–Shapira Model', *Academy of Management Journal*, 47: 105–15.

Mullins, J. W., Forlani, D., and Walker, O. C. (1999). 'Effects of Organizational and Decision-maker Factors on new Product Risk Taking', *Journal of Product Innovation Management*, 16: 282–94.

Nickel, M. N. and Rodriguez, M. C. (2002). 'A Review of Research on the Negative Accounting Relationship Between Risk and Return: Bowman's Paradox', *Omega*, 30: 1–18.

Ocasio, W. (1997). 'Towards an Attention-based Theory of the Firm', *Strategic Management Journal*, 18: 187–206.

Oliver, C. (1992). 'The Antecedents of Deinstitutionalization', *Organization Studies*, 13: 568–88.

Phillips, D. J. and Zuckerman, E. W. (2002). 'Middle-status Conformity: Theoretical Restatement and Empirical Demonstration in Two Markets', *American Journal of Sociology*, 107: 379–429.

Podolny, J. M. (2005). *Status Signals: A Sociological Theory of Market Competition*. Princeton, NJ: Princeton University Press.

Porac, J. F. and Rosa, J. A. (1996). 'Rivalry, Industry Models, and the Cognitive Embeddedness of the Comparable Firm', *Advances in Strategic Management*, 13: 363–88.

——Thomas, H., Wilson, F., Paton, D., and Kanfer, A. (1995). 'Rivalry and the Industry Model of Scottish Knitwear Producers', *Administrative Science Quarterly*, 40: 203–27.

Rao, H., Greve, H. R., and Davis, G. F. (2001). 'Fool's Gold: Social Proof in the Initiation and Abandonment of Coverage by Wall Street Analysts', *Administrative Science Quarterly*, 46: 502–26.

Scott, W. R. (1995). *Institutions and Organizations*. Thousand Oaks, CA: Sage.

Selznick, P. (1996). 'Institutionalism "Old" and "New" ', *Administrative Science Quarterly*, 41: 270–7.

Shapira, Z. (1994). *Risk Taking*. New York: Russell Sage.

Sorenson, O. and Sørensen, J. B. (2001). 'Finding the Right Mix: Franchising, Organizational Learning, and Chain Performance', *Strategic Management Journal*, 22: 713–24.

Soule, S. A. (1997). 'The Student Divestment Movement in the United States and Tactical Diffusion: The Shantytown Protest', *Social Forces*, 75: 855–83.

Strang, D. and Soule, S. A. (1998). 'Diffusion in Organizations and Social Move-ments: From Hybrid Corn to Poison Pills', *Annual Review of Sociology*, 24: 265–90.

——and Tuma, N. B. (1993). 'Spatial and Temporal Heterogeneity in Diffusion', *American Journal of Sociology*, 99: 614–39.

Tolbert, P. S. and Zucker, L. G. (1983). 'Institutional Sources of Change in the Formal Structure of Organizations: The Diffusion of Civil Service Reform 1880–1935', *Administrative Science Quarterly*, 28: 22–39.

Westphal, J. D. and Zajac, E. J. (1994). 'Substance and Symbolism in CEO's Long-term Incentive Plans', *Administrative Science Quarterly*, 39: 367–90.

Wezel, F. C. and Saka-Helmhout, A. (2006). 'Antecedents and Consequences of Organizational Change: "Institutionalizing" the Behavioral Theory of the Firm', *Organization Studies*, 27: 265–86.

Wood, J. V. (1989). 'Theory and Research Concerning Social Comparisons of Personal Attributes', *Psychological Bulletin*, 106: 213–48.

# 5

# Change in Institutional Fields

*C. R. Hinings and Namrata Malhotra*

## 5.1. Introduction

This chapter examines institutional change at the field level of analysis. In doing this, we provide an overview of the work on archetypes and institutional change that has been developed theoretically and empirically through work on municipalities, accounting, law, architecture and management consulting firms, health care organizations, and sport organizations. There have been three elements to this work:

1. The derivation and development of the concept of institutional archetypes as a way of understanding radical organizational change within a field.

2. An examination of the processes by which individual organizations and groups within them respond to institutional change, utilizing the concepts of contextual pressures, value commitments, interests, power, and capacity for action.

3. The development of a process model of institutional change consisting of five stages: (*a*) pressures for change, (*b*) the sources of new practices from institutional entrepreneurs, (*c*) the processes of deinstitutionalization and re-institutionalization, (*d*) the dynamics of deinstitutionalization and re-institutionalization, and (*e*) re-institutionalization and stability.

The aim is to provide a coherent and consistent account of the dynamics of change in an institutional field, one that involves inter-organizational relations, and also the reactions of individual organizations and groups within organizations. Change in institutionalized fields can be understood only as constant interactions between these various levels. Causality is reciprocal, involving structure and agency. Reflexive agents are involved in all change at any level of analysis, whether these be entrepreneurs bringing in new ideas from outside the field, innovators seeing opportunities within the field to move in new directions, or even well-established, powerful actors who see their interests being served by pushing for the adoption of new beliefs and practices. We will elaborate the elements of the theory and conclude with a research agenda.

## 5.2. The Concept of an Institutional Archetype

Greenwood and Hinings (1993: 1052) defined an archetype as 'a set of structures and systems that reflects a single interpretive scheme'. The interpretive scheme is key (Bartunek 1984) because structures and systems are infused with meanings, values, and preferences. Ranson, Hinings, and Greenwood (1980) suggested that organizational structures should be seen as embodiments of ideas, beliefs, and values that constitute an overarching and prevailing 'province of meaning' or 'interpretive scheme'. As Greenwood and Hinings (1988: 295) said, 'the classification and identification of organizational design archetypes becomes a function of the clusters of ideas, values and beliefs coupled with associated patterns of organization design'. In elaborating the idea of an archetype, they drew on the idea of organizational configurations (Meyer, Tsui, and Hinings 1993) elaborating the holistic and coherent nature of organizational structures and systems, but arguing that 'coherence comes from the relationships between provinces of meaning *and* structure *and* processes' (Greenwood and Hinings 1988: 298). As a result, the starting point for the identification and classification of archetypes is the interpretive scheme and then showing how this scheme relates to structural attributes and processes.

There have been three major developments of the original formulations of the 1980s. First, that archetypes are firmly located in institutional fields; it is these fields that are the producers of legitimated archetypes. As a result, the initial theoretical ideas have become more and more firmly located in institutional theory. Second, there has been an empirical elaboration of different archetypes, particularly in professional service firms, health care, and sport organizations. Most of this work has suggested that fields have two conflicting archetypes and that there are major processes of change from one to another. And third, there has been a concern with the processes of change from one archetype to another that has been labelled 'neo-institutionalism'.

### 5.2.1. *The Institutional Specificity of Archetypes*

Archetypes are institutionally specific; archetypes are firmly located in institutional fields and are produced as legitimated archetypes by these fields. The work of Ranson, Hinings, and Greenwood (1980), Hinings and Greenwood (1988*a*), and Greenwood and Hinings (1988) was not set initially in institutional theory; rather, it was concerned with the dynamics of organizational change and structuration. By the 1990s, the work had become firmly located in institutional theory as ideas were developed about the ways in which archetypes are legitimated by institutional fields (Greenwood and Hinings 1993, 1996; Greenwood, Hinings, and Brown 1990; Greenwood and Suddaby 2006; Greenwood, Suddaby, and Hinings 2002; Hinings and Greenwood 1988*b*; Hinings et al. 2003; Kikulis, Slack, and Hinings 1995*a*, 1995*b*; Reay and Hinings 2005; Slack and Hinings 1994). The work of the past fifteen or so years has become more and more firmly located in institutional theory.

Institutional theory argues that archetypes originate outside an organization. There is an institutional field within which organizations are located and such fields are an important environment. As DiMaggio and Powell (1991: 278) put it:

Organizational environments are composed of cultural elements, that is, taken for granted beliefs and widely promulgated rules that serve as templates for organizing. Institutional reproduction has been associated with the demands of powerful central actors, such as the state, the professions, or the dominant agents with organizational fields. This emphasis has highlighted the constraints imposed by institutions and stressed the ubiquity of rules that guide behavior.

In Hinings and Greenwood (1988*b*) and Hinings et al. (2003), it was argued that organizations receive pressures from the institutional content to organize in prescribed ways (and not to organize in proscribed ways). It is these prescriptions that constitute archetypes—or as DiMaggio and Powell (1991) put it, 'templates for organizing'. This position is consistent with the initial theorizing of Meyer and Rowan (1977) who argued that organizations conform to sectoral rules and requirements for reasons of legitimacy and resource flows. Scott (1987: 497) wrote that 'institutionalized belief systems constitute a distinctive class of elements that can account for the existence and/or elaboration of organizational structure'.

Baum and Oliver (1992) showed that organizations increase their survival capabilities by conforming to institutional norms. Greenwood, Suddaby, and Hinings (2002), following DiMaggio and Powell (1983), show how the collective beliefs that are the interpretive schemes or institutional logics (Thornton and Ocasio 1999), giving archetypes their meanings, are reinforced by state agencies and professional bodies as legitimate. Thus, the search for archetypes starts within an institutional sphere, for it is there that institutional prescriptions for organizing will be found; generally, institutional theory has argued that in a stable, mature field there will be a dominant archetype (cf. Greenwood and Hinings 1993; Scott et al. 2000).

## 5.2.2. Different Archetypes

Our second point about archetypes is that there has been an empirical elaboration of different archetypes, particularly in local government, professional service firms, sport organizations, and health. Most of this work has centred on elaborating two alternative archetypes and examining the processes of change from one to another.

Hinings and Greenwood (1988a), in their original empirical work, elaborated two archetypes in local government in England and Wales. They named these the *heteronomous professional bureaucracy* (Scott 1965) and the *corporate bureaucracy* (Greenwood and Stewart 1973). They argued that the first of these represented traditional administration based on differentiated sets of responsibilities of professional groups; autonomy of service provision was emphasized. However, this structure was increasingly defined as inappropriate during the 1960s, resulting in external validation for a new corporate design archetype that was connected to a significantly different conception of the purpose and domain of the local authority. The aim was to have an organizational form based on an integrated structure that operated on the basis of more managerially rational analysis of objectives, activities, outcomes, and performance. The rest of this particular study elaborated the nature of the change process from the HPB to the CB.

With regard to professional service firms, Brock, Powell, and Hinings (2007) have argued that the archetype approach is dominant in spite of criticisms. Greenwood, Hinings, and Brown (1990) identified the $P^2$ archetype as the traditionally dominant form. The structure, systems, and underlying values are embedded in notions of *partnership* and *professionalism* (Malhotra, Morris, and Hinings 2006). Partnership as a governance form embodies three beliefs: the fusion of ownership and control, a form of representative democracy for purposes of strategic and operational decision-making, and the non-separation of professional and managerial tasks (Greenwood, Hinings, and Brown 1990; Nelson 1988). The $P^2$ archetype is professionally and partnership focused and tends to discourage any emphasis on management.

However, in response to changing client demands, globalization, and regulatory changes, an emphasis on efficiency, marketing, and growth strategies became increasingly important (Brock, Powell, and Hinings 1999; Cooper et al. 1996). There was pressure to separate professional and management roles producing a new emerging archetype, the *Managerial Professional Business*. The underlying interpretive scheme or logic of this archetype is to see the organization as a business within which professionalism is a particular skill. 'Productivity', 'client service', and 'marketing' represent the importation of the language and style of business over and above 'professionalism'. Strategic and operational control of activities becomes important along with more structural integration between services.

These two archetypes are well documented for professional service firms, and have been applied to accounting firms (Greenwood, Hinings, and Brown 1990; Greenwood, Suddaby, and Hinings 2002; Hinings, Greenwood, and Cooper 1999; Malhotra, Morris, and Hinings 2006), law firms (Cooper et al. 1996; Gray 1999; Malhotra, Morris, and Hinings 2006; Morris and Pinnington 1999; Pinnington and Morris 2002), and architectural practices (Pinnington and Morris 2002). More detail on the institutional logics, structures, and systems of these archetypes can be found in the cited contributions.

With regard to sport organizations, Kikulis, Slack, and Hinings (1992), Slack and Hinings (1994), Kikulis, Slack, and Hinings (1995*a*, 1995*b*), and Amis, Slack, and Hinings (2004) have elaborated the institutionally specific archetypes to be found in Canadian national sport organizations. As with previous studies using the archetype concept, the context was that of a changing institutional field with a historically legitimated archetype and emerging new archetypes. However, these studies found three extant archetypes that they named *Kitchen Table*, *Boardroom*, and *Executive Office*. Kikulis, Slack, and Hinings (1995*a*, 1995*b*) suggested that the *Kitchen Table* archetype has been the institutionally approved mode of organization for many decades. Dedicated volunteers ran the organization in their spare time, often from the kitchen tables of their homes. However, with increased public-sector involvement in national sport organizations in the 1970s, the *Boardroom* became the institutionally approved archetype with an emphasis on professional staff assisting volunteers. The pressure was for these organizations to become more businesslike in their operations. With further government involvement and a specific attempt to introduce planning organized around the Olympic cycle, the *Executive Office* archetype emerged. Here control was shifted from volunteers to professional staff.

Thus, the notion of archetypes has been utilized in a number of arenas, something that supports the usefulness of the concept. Also, this work clearly sees archetype change as originating at the field level.

### 5.2.3. *The Dynamics of Archetype Change*

The whole purpose for the development of the archetype concept was to use it as a way of dealing with radical organizational change within an institutional setting; this is the third major development. For Greenwood and Hinings (1993, 1996), radical change is defined as the movement from one archetype to another. Starting with Ranson, Hinings, and Greenwood (1980), the concern is to show how the dynamics of archetype change involved both the normative embeddedness of an organization within its institutional field and internal organizational dynamics. The most complete statements of this are in Hinings and Greenwood (1988*a*), Greenwood and Hinings (1988, 1996), and Hinings, Greenwood, and Cooper (1999). Central to the arguments are the processes by which individual organizations retain, adopt, and discard templates for organizing, given the institutionalized nature of organizational fields.

Historically, institutional theory has been seen as an explanation of the similarity and stability of organizational arrangements, of why organizations exhibit 'such startling homogeneity, not variation' (DiMaggio and Powell 1991: 64). However, this has changed significantly in the past decade (Dacin, Goodstein, and Scott 2002; Greenwood and Hinings 1996; Oliver 1992). Actually, institutional theory has always incorporated an account of change, such as the two-stage dissemination model (Baron, Dobbin, and Jennings 1986; Tolbert and Zucker 1983), in which, during the initial development of an organizational field, technical performance requirements are more important than in later stages of the field's development, when institutional pressures rise in salience. Another approach to understanding change focuses on the structure of the institutional field. Fligstein, for example, concludes that 'innovative behaviour is more likely to occur within "ill-formed" fields' (1991: 316). D'Aunno, Sutton,

111

and Price (1991), DiMaggio and Powell (1991), Oliver (1991), Powell (1991), and Scott (1994) argue that institutional fields may have multiple pressures providing inconsistent cues or signals, opening the possibility for idiosyncratic interpretation and subsequent variation in practices.

Both of these approaches emphasize contextual pressures as the primary drivers of both stability and change. Even though early contributions may have emphasized inertia, institutional theory also deals with broad, sweeping change within an organizational field (Reay and Hinings 2005; Scott et al. 2000). However, there is no doubt that institutional theory is weak in explaining why particular organizations respond in particular ways to the same sets of field-level pressures for change. The theory has been relatively silent on why some organizations change and others do not, which is where the articulation of the dynamics of change is relevant (Greenwood and Hinings 1996; Hinings and Greenwood 1988a).

When radical change comes to a field, the result will be 'deinstitutionalization' (Oliver 1992). Such change involves the delegitimation of existing archetypes, accompanied by a search for new ways of organizing (Greenwood, Suddaby, and Hinings 2002). But when faced with change, how quickly an organization moves from one archetype to another will depend on intra-organizational dynamics (Greenwood and Hinings 1996). The response of an organization to changing institutional and other contextual circumstances will be a function of the extent of *differentiation* within the organization, whether groups are dissatisfied with the realization of their *interests*, the *value orientations of* the major groups within the organization, the distribution *of power* between groups, and the existence of a *capacity for action*. Understanding why organizations respond differently to institutional pressures involves the *interaction of* contextual and intra-organizational dynamics.

An important idea underlying the dynamics of field-level institutional change at the organizational level is that of tracks (Amis, Slack, and Hinings 2004; Greenwood and Hinings 1988, 1993; Hinings and Greenwood 1988a; Kikulis, Slack, and Hinings 1995a, 1995b). At the field level, institutional theory suggests that over some relatively lengthy time period, all organizations eventually conform to the new archetype(s). However, research on local government organizations, professional organizations, and sport organizations over periods as long as fifteen years suggests that some organizations change relatively rapidly in a straightforward way, others never take on all the elements of the new archetype, while others remain suspended between the old and new archetypes. That is, organizations follow different tracks of change. For example, in their work on local government organizations, Hinings and Greenwood (1988*a*) distinguished four tracks:

1. *Reorientation*: when an organization moves relatively smoothly from an old to a new archetype.
2. *Unresolved excursions*: when an organization moves away from the old archetype but, over the period of observation of the change, fails to complete the process of adopting the new archetype.
3. *Discontinued excursions*: when an organization begins the process of moving away from the old archetype but eventually moves back to it.
4. *Inertia*: when an organization does not move away from the old archetype.

The idea of tracks derives from two important considerations for institutional theory. The first is that the actual process of institutionalization is uneven between organizations. Yet so much of institutional theory since DiMaggio and Powell (1983) has been intent on showing that there is homogeneity in the process. Fortunately, since the *Academy of Management Journal* special issue (Dacin, Goodstein, and Scott 2002), there has been much more focus on change and the unevenness of institutional diffusion. Much more research is needed on the ways in which such diffusion actually occurs and the extent to which there is difference between organizations. The emphasis needs to be on variation rather than homogeneity.

The second consideration, which is the heart of the concern with dynamics, is that these tracks of institutional change are different because of the role of different groups within an organization. There are three elements to be considered.

First, there is the extent of differentiation within an organization. As Greenwood and Hinings (1996: 1996) put it, 'it is necessary to take seriously the internal complexity of organizations (i.e., every organization is a mosaic of groups structured by functional tasks and employment status)'. Organizational differentiation creates groups whose interests and values may collide. The greater the extent of differentiation, the greater the possibility that differences in beliefs and interpretations of events will produce debate and discussion for change. Work on differentiation in organizations (Lawrence and Lorsch 1967; Nystrom 1986) shows how technical boundaries between departments are reinforced by cognitive boundaries. Through internal differentiation, all organizations have within them alternative ways of viewing goals, design, and performance assessment. This is a view consistent with the 'old' institutionalism of Selznick (1949).

Second, there are *precipitating dynamics*, in particular, whether groups are dissatisfied with the realization of their *interests*, and the *value orientations* of these groups within the organization. Groups seek to translate their interests into favourable allocations of scarce and valued organizational resources. A pressure for inertia or change is the extent to which groups are satisfied, *or not*, with how their interests are met. However, dissatisfaction, per se, does not provide a direction for change that comes from the value commitments of the various actors and their groups. Dissatisfied groups have to recognize the relationship between the prevailing institutional archetype, which shapes the distribution of privilege and their own position of disadvantage. It is the pattern of value commitments that becomes the driver of archetype change or inertia. Hinings and Greenwood (1988a) and Greenwood and Hinings (1996) identify four generic patterns:

1. *Status quo commitment*: where all organizational groups are committed to the prevailing institutional archetype.
2. *Indifferent commitment*: where groups are neither committed nor opposed to the prevailing archetype.
3. *Competitive commitment*: where some groups support the prevailing archetype and others put forward an alternative archetype.
4. *Reformative commitment*: where all groups prefer an alternative archetype to the currently prevailing archetype.

Thus, the argument is that there will be external pressures in a field that are both market and institutional to which organizational actors have to respond. The first aspect of that response derives from interest dissatisfaction and the pattern of value commitments, the precipitating dynamics. But change will occur only in conjunction with a *capacity for action* and *supportive power dependencies* that are the *enabling dynamics* of change or inertia.

Organizational groups have differential power; as a result some groups are listened to more keenly than others. The relations of power and domination enable some members to constitute and recreate the organization according to their preferences (Pettigrew 1985; Ranson, Hinings, and Greenwood 1980; Walsh et al. 1981). Again, to quote Greenwood and Hinings (1996: 1038), 'the operation of values and interests can be conceptualized and understood only in relation to the differential power of groups'. It is when the dominant coalition recognizes the weaknesses of the prevailing archetype, *and is aware of an alternative archetype*, that change will occur. So, change occurs where the enabling pattern of power dependencies combines with a pattern of value commitments that is reformative or competitive.

There is a further enabling dynamic, namely, *capacity for action*. This is the ability to manage the transition process from one institutionally derived archetype to another. There are three aspects of capability:

1. Having an understanding of the new destination, that is, of the alternative archetype, how it is structured, what systems support it and what the underpinning interpretive scheme is.

2. Having the skills and competencies that are needed to operate in the new archetype.

3. Having the abilities to manage the process of moving from the prevailing to the new archetype.

Of course, a capacity for action will not, in and of itself, enable archetype change; there has to be a motivation for change driven by the enabling dynamics of dissatisfaction with interests coupled with a reformative or competitive pattern of value commitments.

Understanding why organizations respond differently to institutional pressures involves the *interaction of* contextual and intra-organizational dynamics. Hinings and Greenwood (1988*a*) suggested that movement away from a prevailing archetype to a new one requires the existence of an articulated alternative archetype and a power structure that allows that alternative to be expressed in important arenas. Movement requires a high degree of organizational capacity, and initial movement is consolidated through both a spreading of commitment to the new archetype and a tightening of the power structure. This is just one possible interaction from many possibilities that require further research.

## 5.3. A Process Model of Institutional Change

The next step in this approach to institutional theory is to present an overall model of institutional inertia and change at the field, organizational, and intra-organizational levels. Accounts of change in institutional theory focus on organizational fields and the institutional logics that pre-scribe appropriate behaviour. Within this, we have emphasized archetypes that have achieved institutional legitimacy. The starting question is not whether organizations can or cannot move between archetypal forms, but with the social processes that construct the *choice-set* of acceptable archetypes. Exploring these processes focuses attention on values, mean-ings, and language, and to the role of the professions, regulators, and the state. A second, consequential question is how and why organiza-tions in the same field respond differently to institutional processes. An initial version of a model to put all of this together was in Greenwood, Suddaby, and Hinings (2002) where stages of institutional change were presented in the context of an organizational field. This model was further refined in Hinings et al. (2003). This process model of institu-tional change consists of six stages: (*a*) pressures for change, (*b*) dein-stitutionalization, (*c*) pre-institutionalization, (*d*) theorization, (*e*) diffu-sion, and (*f*) institutionalization. This overall model is presented in Figure 5.1.

### 5.3.1. *Pressures for Change*

Work in institutional theory suggests that the pressures and precipitators for field-level change arise from outside the field and the organizations within it as destabilizing 'jolts' (Meyer 1982; Meyer, Brooks, and Goes 1990). These can take the form of social upheaval, technological disrup-tions, competitive discontinuities, or regulatory change (Fox-Wolfgramm, Boal, and Hunt 1998; Lounsbury 1999). Their effect is to disturb the socially constructed field-level consensus.

However, it is possible for change to arise *endogenously*. Seo and Creed (2002) point to 'contradictions' within organizational fields, such as mutually inconsistent values, and a further possibility is differences in interests (Reay and Hinings 2005). An important point is that, with maturity, the internal contradictions of fields become amplified and thus more potent precipitators of change. Such contradictions set the stage for 'praxis', that is, reflection by actors concerning the reconstruction of insti-tutional arrangements. Hoffman (1999) describes fields as populations of organizations that, though connected and influenced by overarching logics, nevertheless subscribe to different values and beliefs. Thus, fields contain tensions between dominant and latent logics 'that may lie within the individual populations (or constituencies) that inhabit the field' (Hoff-man 1999: 365; see also, Reay and Hinings 2005).

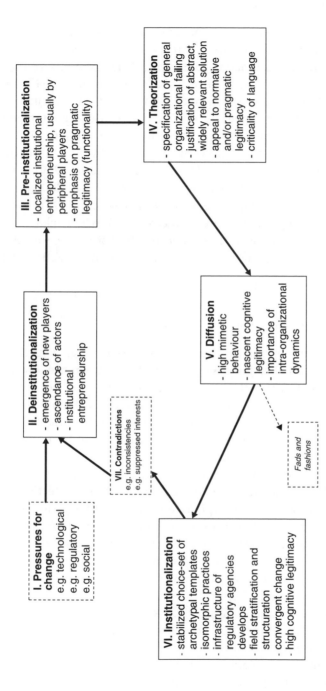

**Figure 5.1.** A neo-institutional model of change

*Source:* Based on Tolbert and Zucker (1996); Greenwood, Suddaby, and Hinings (2002); and Hinings et al. (2003).

### 5.3.2. Deinstitutionalization

The impact of these pressures for change is to deinstitutionalize a field, that is, the dominant logics and their associated archetypes are challenged and new logics are openly put forward. The stability of the field that is central to institutional theory frays. According to Greenwood and Hinings (1996), there is 'normative fragmentation'. Change, thus, occurs 'in the wake of triggering events that cause a reconfiguration of field membership and/or interaction patterns' (Hoffman 1999: 351). These events allow and even encourage the entry of new actors (Kraatz and Moore 2002; Thornton 1995; Thornton and Ocasio 1999), enable a change in the legitimation of existing actors (Scott et al. 2000), encourage local entrepreneurship (DiMaggio 1988; Lawrence 1999; Leblebici et al. 1991), and change the climate of ideas (e.g. Davis, Diekmann, and Tinsley 1994). The effect of all these actions is to disturb the socially constructed field-level consensus by allowing new ideas and practices to be in play.

### 5.3.3. Pre-institutionalization

When fields deinstitutionalize there are actions through which a new process of institutionalization begins (Oliver 1992). Lawrence, Hardy, and Phillips (2002: 281) write of 'proto-institutions' that are 'new practices, rules, and technologies that transcend a particular collaborative relationship and may become new institutions if they diffuse sufficiently'. The key issue is where does innovation and diffusion come from and which organizations are more likely to innovate and why? A more recent view in institutional theory is that, even in a relatively stable and mature field, logics and archetypes are not hegemonic, but always imperfectly diffused (Greenwood et al. 2008). One explanation suggests that peripheral organizations are more likely to innovate because they are less embedded. Organizations at the field's centre, on the other hand, are more socialized, better advantaged, and thus more resistant to change (e.g. D'Aunno, Succi, and Alexander 2000; Hirsch 1986; Kraatz and Zajac 1996; Leblebici et al. 1991; Palmer and Barber 2001). However, this is not absolute (e.g. Greenwood, Suddaby, and Hinings 2002; Rao, Monin, and Durand 2003; Sherer and Lee 2002). It may be in the interest of powerful field members to push for change.

A central point is that fields are never static and because of this they are open to ideas and practices entering from other fields and also to the entrepreneurial motivations of imperfectly embedded organizations (Lawrence, Hardy, and Phillips 2002). However, the likelihood of change will vary from field to field. Fields vary in the extent to which their boundaries are 'permeable' (Greenwood and Hinings 1996). They also vary in the degree to which they have clearly legitimated organizational templates combined with 'highly articulated mechanisms (the state, professional associations, regulatory agencies...) for transmitting those templates to organizations...' (Greenwood and Hinings 1996: 1029). The more elaborated these templates and the stronger the mechanisms for their deployment, the more resistant the field will be to change.

### 5.3.4. Theorization

Strang and Meyer (1993) define theorization as the rendering of ideas into compelling formats. It is critical for new organizational forms to gain legitimacy. In a situation of field-level change, theorization involves two activities: specification of a general organizational failing that allows challenges to the adequacy of the prevailing archetype; and justification of a new archetype as an appropriate solution to those failings (Tolbert and Zucker 1996). Critical here is the use of cultural symbols and language as those for and against prevailing and new archetypes contest their appropriateness (Covaleski, Dirsmith, and Rittenberg 2003; Greenwood, Suddaby, and Hinings 2002, 2003; Maguire, Hardy, and Lawrence 2004; Suddaby and Greenwood 2005).

Theorization is the stage where competing arguments become fully articulated and struggle for supremacy. Institutional theory, through its attention to socio-cultural processes, emphasizes how social approval is attached to novelty. The rhetoric of these claims seeks efficiency, effectiveness, and moral acceptability for the new archetype (Suddaby and Greenwood 2005). This stage is about articulating and legitimizing a new institutional archetype.

### 5.3.5. Diffusion

Diffusion follows successful theorization and until recently much work in institutional theory has been on demonstrating diffusion, through showing the role of mimetic, coercive, and normative mechanisms, and the occurrence of isomorphism (DiMaggio and Powell 1983; Mizruchi and Fein 1999). However, as much of this chapter has argued, organizations do not blindly follow institutional prescriptions. It is here that the intra-organizational dynamics of precipitating (interests and values) and enabling (power dependencies and capacity for action) come into play. The inference is that institutional values 'enter' organizations filtered through the value-sets of occupational groups. Thornton (2004) provides a similar analysis of tensions in the publishing industry.

Of course, diffusion studies repeatedly show organizations adopting new organizational strategies and structures, essentially through mimetic processes (Mizruchi and Fein 1999). Indeed, institutional theory began as an explanation of the similarity and stability of organizational forms in a given population of organizations. Yet it has always been implicit in the theory that organizations *can* and *will* change, if institutional forces shift the choice-set of archetypes. Studies of attempted shifts between archetypes, however, indicate that less than one in four are successful (Amis, Slack, and Hinings 2004; Hinings and Greenwood 1988*a*, 1998*b*; Kikulis, Slack, and Hinings 1995*a*, 1995*b*; Morris and Pinnington 1999). Thus the diffusion stage is fraught with difficulty and certainly requires further detailed studies of the micro-process of institutional work.

### 5.3.6. *Institutionalization*

In spite of the diffusion stage illustrating uneven take-up of a new institutionally approved archetype, the model proposes that a time is reached when there is a stabilized choice-set of legitimated archetypes. There is a process of structuration leading to convergent change. As Scott (1994: 207–8) put it, 'the notion of a field connotes the existence of a community of organizations that partakes of a common meaning system and whose participants interact more frequently and fatefully with one another than with actors outside of the field'. So, institutionalization has taken place when new archetypes are accepted as part of the common meaning system and any new actors are now interacting within field boundaries. Of course, it is the case that there is always the potential for instability and change within a field and that institutionalization is never complete.

## 5.4. Further Research Agendas

This chapter has outlined the centrality of the concept of institutional archetypes as a way of understanding radical organizational change within a field. Also, the processes by which individual organizations and groups within them respond to institutional change have been outlined. This approach has culminated in the development of an overall process model of institutional change, consisting of five stages that covers deinstitutionalization to re-institutionalization. The aim is to provide a consistent account of the dynamics of change in an institutional field that involves inter-organizational relations, and the reactions of individual organizations and groups within organizations to those field-level change pressures. We have stressed the social processes, whereby archetypal forms are constructed and sustained. We have particularly addressed why some organizations change whereas others do not, pointing to intra-organizational dynamics that link organizations to the field and direct their responses to it.

Crucially, institutional fields are the producers of archetypes. A first research agenda, therefore, is to continue to unearth archetypes in different fields and to examine how far the generic model of movement from one archetype to another actually occurs. Essentially, as institutional theory has become more concerned with change, so the emphasis has been on what here we call radical change; in our terms, the replacement of one archetype by another. However, there are two things in particular that require further theorization and empirical work. One is to examine whether fields contain several archetypes at any particular time. The other is to examine the possibility of fields exhibiting radical, incremental, and no change. This is where the idea of tracks is important. It suggests that the actual process of institutionalization is uneven between organizations. Much more research is needed on the ways in which diffusion actually occurs and the extent of institutionalization that occurs. The emphasis needs to start from the possibility of variation rather than homogeneity.

Second, institutional change needs to be understood through the *iterative* action of processes and dynamics. Research should be less focused on how a particular institutional template is transformed into an alternative template, and more on the processes by which that happens and *how those processes are constant, ongoing, and evolutionary*. This concern with social dynamics and social processes is becoming somewhat more common and is brought together in the variety of papers in the edited volume by Greenwood et al. (2008). Understanding why organizations respond differently to institutional pressures involves the *interaction of* field-level and intra-organizational dynamics. Hinings and Greenwood (1988a) and Greenwood and Hinings (1996) suggested a number of ways in which these dynamics operated. However, there are many possibilities that require further research. Because of the interactive dynamics of field-level pressures, the differentiated structure of groups in any particular orga-nization and the particular patterning of interests, value commitments, power and capacity for action, more detailed studies of the micro-process of institutional work are required.

Third, it is important to emphasize the multilevel interactions between the field level and the organizational level, and within organizations. Institutional innovations can occur within individual organizations or clusters of organizations, and these have implications for the field level of analysis. Similarly, innovations may occur at a field level, and these impact individual organizations and inter-organizational relations. This point links to the first as it is the iterative relationship between field level, individual organizations, occupational groups, regulatory organizations, and the state that becomes important. Such an approach also requires that the notion of field as explicated by DiMaggio and Powell (1983) and Scott (1994) be taken seriously as a set of actors interacting within a common meaning system. Most studies of fields centre on the main providers of products and services and neglect the effect of other field-level actors, though there has been some work done on professional associations and regulatory organizations (Galvin 2002; Greenwood, Suddaby, and Hinings 2002; Lounsbury 2001).

A fourth point is that the role of power in institutional change requires further exploration. Institutional change is a highly political process at both field and organizational levels. Research should focus on the instru-mental nature of power in allowing the achievement of both deinstitu-tionalization and re-institutionalization, the extent to which the sources of new practices are evaluated in power terms, and the role of power in both the processes and dynamics of institutional change. A start has been made on this by Lawrence, Winn, and Jennings (2001) with their typology of power, but there have been few attempts to utilize the extant literature on power (cf. Clegg and Hardy 2006) to understand institutional change and inertia. There is a great deal of room for work that attempts to integrate approaches to power into institutional theory. Given the model of organizational diffusion proposed here a particular emphasis is needed on the relationship between differentiation and power at both field and organizational levels.

Fifth, there are strong methodological implications from the questions being raised here. The kind of attention to internal organizational dynam-ics, the interactive and iterative nature of field-level and organizational-level actions that are essential to the ideas put forward here are unlikely to be able to be studied through large-scale, quantitative studies. Issues of relationships between levels, of the reflexive roles of actors, of processes and dynamics require detailed work with archival documents, interviews with current and past actors, surveys of practices, and observations of activities. Thus, carrying out research on these topics represents a major challenge both theoretically and methodologically. Indeed, it calls for multilevel- and micro-process-oriented research that requires painstaking detailed data collection over extended periods. The combination of multi-level analysis and extended periods calls for a multi-method and multiple case study approach, that is, time consuming and labour intensive.

Thus, we see a major research agenda here. Indeed, perhaps the closing point is that dealing with change in institutional fields requires programmatic research that attempts to deal with multiple concepts, multiple levels of analysis, and multiple methods of data sources, collection, and analysis. A great challenge indeed!

## References

Amis, J., Slack, T., and Hinings, C. R. (2004). 'The Pace, Sequence and Linearity of Radical Change', *Academy of Management Journal*, 47: 15–39.

Baron, J., Dobbin, F., and Jennings, D. (1986). 'War and Peace: The Evolution of Modern Personnel Administration in U.S. Industry', *American Journal of Sociology*, 92: 250–83.

Bartunek, J. (1984). 'Changing Interpretive Schemes and Organizational Restructuring: The Example of a Religious Order', *Administrative Science Quarterly*, 29: 355–72.

Baum, J. and Oliver, C. (1992). 'Institutional Embeddedness and the Dynamics of Organizational Populations', *American Sociological Review*, 57: 540–59.

Brock, D., Powell, M., and Hinings, C. R. (eds.) (1999). *Restructuring the Professional Organization: Accounting, Healthcare and Law*. London: Routledge.

————— (2007). 'Archetypal Change and the Professional Service Firm', in W. Passmore and R. Goodman (eds.), *Research in Organizational Change and Development*, 16: 221–52.

Clegg, S. and Hardy, C. (2006). 'Some Call it Power', in S. Clegg, C. Hardy, T. Lawrence, and W. Nord (eds.), *Handbook of Organization Studies*. London: Sage.

Cooper, D. J., Hinings, C. R., Greenwood, R., and Brown, J. (1996). 'Sedimentation and Transformation in Organizational Change: The Case of Canadian Law Firms', *Organization Studies*, 17: 623–47.

Covaleski, M., Dirsmith, M. W., and Rittenberg, L. (2003). 'Jurisdictional Disputes Over Professional Work: The Institutionalization of the Global Knowledge Expert', *Accounting Organizations and Society*, 28: 325–55.

D'Aunno, T., Sutton, R., and Price, R. (1991). 'Isomorphism and External Support in Conflicting Institutional Environments: A Study of Drug Abuse Treatment Units', *Academy of Management Journal*, 34: 636–81.

—— T., Succi, M., and Alexander, J. A. (2000). 'The Role of Institutional and Market Forces in Divergent Organizational Change', *Administrative Science Quarterly*, 45: 679–703.

Dacin, M. T., Goodstein, J., and Scott, W. R. (2002). 'Institutional Theory and Institutional Change: Introduction to the Special Research Forum', *Academy of Management Journal*, 45: 45–57.

Davis, G. F., Diekmann, K. A., and Tinsley, C. H. (1994). 'The Decline and Fall of the Conglomerate Firm in the 1980s: The Deinstitutionalization of an Organizational Form', *American Sociological Review*, 59: 547–70.

DiMaggio, P. J. (1988). 'Interest and Agency in Institutional Theory', in L. G. Zucker (ed.), *Institutional Patterns and Organizations: Culture and Environment*. Cambridge, MA: Ballinger.

—— and Powell, W. W. (1983). 'The Iron Cage Revisited: Institutional Isomorphism and Collective Rationality in Organizational Fields', *American Sociological Review*, 48: 147–60.

—— —— (1991). 'Introduction', in P. J. DiMaggio and W. W. Powell (eds.), *The New Institutionalism in Organizational Analysis*. Chicago, IL: Chicago University Press.

Fligstein, N. (1991). 'The Structural Transformation of American Industry: An Institutional Account of the Causes of Diversification in the Largest Firms 1919–79', in P. J. DiMaggio and W. W. Powell (eds.), *The New Institutionalism in Organizational Analysis*. Chicago, IL: Chicago University Press.

Fox-Wolfgramm, S. J., Boal, K., and Hunt, J. G. (1998). 'Organizational Adaptation to Institutional Change: A Comparative Study of First-Order Change in Prospector and Defender Banks', *Administrative Science Quarterly*, 43: 87–126.

Galvin, T. L. (2002). 'Examining Institutional Change: Evidence From the Founding Dynamics of U.S. Health Care Interest Associations', *Academy of Management Journal*, 45: 673–96.

Gray, J. (1999). 'Restructuring Law Firms: Reflexivity and Emerging Forms', in D. Brock, M. Powell, and C. R. Hinings (eds.), *Restructuring the Professional Organization: Accounting, Healthcare and Law*. London: Routledge.

Greenwood, R. and Hinings, C. R. (1988). 'Design Types, Tracks and the Dynamics of Strategic Change', *Organization Studies*, 9: 293–316.

—— —— (1993). 'Understanding Strategic Change: The Contribution of Archetype', *Academy of Management Journal*, 36: 1052–82.

—— —— (1996). 'Understanding Radical Organizational Change: Bringing Together the Old and the New Institutionalism', *Academy of Management Review*, 21: 1022–55.

—— Stewart, J. (1973). 'Towards a Typology of English Local Authorities', *Political Studies* 21: 64–9.

—— Suddaby, R. (2006). 'Institutional Entrepreneurship in Mature Fields: The Big Five Accounting Firms', *Academy of Management Journal*, 49: 27–48.

—— Hinings, C. R., and Brown, J. (1990). 'The P2-Form of Strategic Management: Corporate Practices in the Professional Partnership', *Academy of Management Journal*, 33: 725–55.

—— Suddaby, R., and Hinings, C. R. (2002). 'Theorizing Change: The Role of Professional Associations in the Transformation of Institutional Fields', *Academy of Management Journal*, 45: 58–80.

—— Oliver, C., Suddaby, R., and Sahlin-Andersson, K. (2008). *The Handbook of Organizational Institutionalism*. London: Sage.

Hinings, C. R. and Greenwood, R. (1988a). *The Dynamics of Strategic Change*. Oxford: Basil Blackwell.

—— —— (1988b). 'The Normative Prescription of Organizations', in L. Zucker (ed.), *Institutional Patterns and Organizations*. New York: Ballinger.

—— —— and Cooper, D. J. (1999). 'The Dynamics of Change in Large Accounting Firms', in D. Brock, M. Powell, and C. R. Hinings (eds.), *Restructuring the Professional Organization: Accounting, Healthcare and Law*. London: Routledge.

—— —— Reay, T., and Suddaby, R. (2003). 'Dynamics in Institutional Fields', in M. S. Poole and A. H. Van de Ven (eds.), *Handbook of Organizational Change*. New York: Oxford University Press.

Hirsch, P. (1986). 'From Ambushes to Golden Parachutes: Corporate Takeovers as an Instance of Cultural Framing and Institutional Integration', *American Journal of Sociology*, 91: 800–37.

Hoffman, A. J. (1999). 'Institutional Evolution and Change: Environmentalism and the US Chemical Industry', *Academy of Management Journal*, 42: 351–71.

Kikulis, L., Slack, T., and Hinings, C. R. (1992). 'Institutionally Specific Design Archetypes: A Framework for Understanding Change in National Sport Organizations', *International Review for the Sociology of Sport*, 27: 343–70.

—— —— —— (1995a). 'Sector-specific Patterns of Organizational Design Change', *Journal of Management Studies*, 32: 67–100.

—— —— —— (1995b). 'Towards an Understanding of the Role of Agency and Choice in the Changing Structure of Canada's National Sport Organizations', *Journal of Sport Management*, 9: 135–52.

Kraatz, M. S. and Moore, J. H. (2002). 'Executive Migration and Institutional Change', *Academy of Management Journal*, 45: 120–43.

—— Zajac, E. J. (1996). 'Exploring the Limits of the New Institutionalism: The Causes and Consequences of Illegitimate Organizational Change', *American Sociological Review*, 61: 812–36.

Lawrence, P., and Lorsch, J. (1967). *Organization and Environment: Managing Differentiation and Integration*. Boston, MA: Graduate School of Businesss Administration, Harvard University.

Lawrence, T. (1999). 'Institutional Strategy', *Journal of Management*, 25: 161–87.

125

Lawrence, T., Hardy, C., and Phillips, N. (2002). 'Institutional Effects of Inter-organizational Collaboration: The Emergence of Proto-Institutions', *Academy of Management Journal*, 45: 281–91.

——Winn, M. I., and Jennings, P. D. (2001). 'The Temporal Dynamics of Institutionalization', *Academy of Management Review*, 26: 624–44.

Leblebici, H., Salancik, G., Copay, A., and King, T. (1991). 'Institutional Change and the Transformation of the US Radio Broadcasting Industry', *Administrative Science Quarterly*, 36: 333–63.

Lounsbury, M. (1999). 'From Heresy to Dogma: An Institutional History of Corporate Environmentalism', *Administrative Science Quarterly*, 44: 193–6.

——(2001). 'Institutional Sources of Practice Variation: Staffing College and University Recycling Programs', *Administrative Science Quarterly*, 46: 29–56.

Maguire, S., Hardy, C., and Lawrence, T. G. (2004). 'Institutional Entrepreneurship in Emerging Fields: HIV/AIDS Treatment Advocacy in Canada', *Academy of Management Journal*, 47: 657–79.

Malhotra, N., Morris, T., and Hinings, C. R. (2006). 'Variation in Organizational Form Among Professional Service Organizations', in R. Greenwood and R. Suddaby (eds.), *Research in the Sociology of Organizations: Professional Service Firms*, 4: 171–202.

Meyer, A. D. (1982). 'How Ideologies Supplant Formal Structures and Shape Responses to Environments', *Journal of Management Studies*, 29: 45–61.

——Brooks, G. R., and Goes, J. B. (1990). 'Environmental Jolts and Industry Revolutions: Organizational Responses to Discontinuous Change', *Strategic Management Journal*, 11: 93–110.

——Tsui, A., and Hinings, C. R. (1993). 'Configurational Approaches to Organizational Analysis', *Academy of Management Journal*, 36: 1175–95.

Meyer, J. W. and Rowan, B. (1977). 'Institutionalized Organizations: Formal Structure as Myth and Ceremony', *American Journal of Sociology*, 83: 440–63.

Mizruchi, M. and Fein, L. (1999). 'The Social Constitution of Organizational Knowledge: A Study of the Uses of Coercive, Mimetic and Normative Assumptions', *Administrative Science Quarterly*, 44: 653–83.

Morris, T. and Pinnington, A. (1999). 'Continuity and Change in Professional Organizations: The Evidence from Law Firms', in D. Brock, M. Powell, and C. R. Hinings (eds.), *Restructuring the Professional Organization: Accounting, Health Care and Law*. London: Routledge.

Nelson, R. (1988). *Partners with Power: The Social Transformation of the Large Law Firm*. Berkeley, CA: University of California Press.

Nystrom, P. (1986). 'Comparing Beliefs of Line and Technostructure Managers', *Academy of Management Journal*, 29: 812–19.

Oliver, C. (1991). 'Strategic Responses to Institutional Processes', *Academy of Management Review*, 16: 145–79.

—— (1992). 'The Antecedents of Deinstitutionalization', *Organization Studies*, 13: 563–88.

Palmer, D. and Barber, M. (2001). 'Challengers, Elites and Owning Families: A Social Class Theory of Corporate Acquisitions in the 1960s', *Administrative Science Quarterly*, 46: 87–120.

Pettigrew, A. M. (1985). *The Awakening Giant: Continuity and Change in Imperial Chemical Industries*. Oxford, UK: Blackwell.

Pinnington, A. and Morris, T. (2002). 'Transforming the Architect: Ownership Form and Archetype Change', *Organization Studies*, 23: 189–210.

Powell, W. W. (1991). 'Expanding the Scope of Institutional Analysis', in P. J. DiMaggio and W. W. Powell (eds.), *The New Institutionalism in Organizational Analysis*. Chicago, IL: Chicago University Press.

Ranson, S., Hinings, C. R., and Greenwood, R. (1980). 'The Structuring of Organizational Structures', *Administrative Science Quarterly*, 25: 1–17.

Rao, H., Monin, P., and Durand, R. (2003). 'Institutional Change in Toque Ville: Nouvelle Cuisine as an Identity Movement in French Gastronomy', *American Journal of Sociology*, 108: 795–843.

Reay, T. and Hinings, C. R. (2005). 'The Recomposition of an Organizational Field: Health Care in Alberta', *Organization Studies*, 26: 351–84.

Scott, W. R. (1965). Reactions to Supervision in a Heteronomous Professional Organization', *Administrative Science Quarterly*, 10: 65–81.

—— (1987). 'The Adolescence of Institutional Theory', *Administrative Science Quarterly*, 32: 493–511.

—— (1994). 'Conceptualizing Organizational Fields: Linking Organizations and Societal Systems', in H. Derlien, U. Gerhardt, and F. Scharpf (eds.), *Systemrationalität und Partialinteresse*. Baden-Baden: Nomos.

—— Ruef, M., Mendel, P. J., and Caronn, C. A. A. (2000). *Institutional Change and Healthcare Organizations: From Professional Dominance to Managed Care*. Chicago, IL: University of Chicago Press.

Selznick, P. (1949). *TVA and the Grass Roots*. Berkeley: University of California Press.

Seo, M.-G. and Creed, W. E. D. (2002). 'Institutional Contradictions, Praxis, and Institutional Change: A Dialectic Perspective', *Academy of Management Review*, 27: 222–47.

Sherer, P. D. and Lee, K. (2002). 'Institutional Change in Large Law Firms: A Resource Dependency and Institutional Perspective', *Academy of Management Journal*, 45: 102–19.

Slack, T. and Hinings, C. R. (1994). 'Isomorphism and Organizational Change', *Organization Studies*, 15: 803–28.

Strang, D. and Meyer, J. W. (1993). 'Institutional Conditions for Diffusion', *Theory and Society*, 22: 487–511.

Suddaby, R. and Greenwood, R. (2005). 'Rhetorical Strategies of Legitimacy', *Administrative Science Quarterly*, 50: 35–67.

Thornton, P. H. (1995). 'Accounting for Acquisition Waves: Evidence from the US College Publishing Industry', in W. R. Scott and S. Christensen (eds.), *The Institutional Construction of Organizations: International and Longitudinal Studies*. Thousand Oaks, CA: Sage.

—— (2004). *Markets from Culture*. Stanford, CA: Stanford University Press.

—— and Ocasio, W. (1999). 'Institutional Logics and the Historical Contingency of Power in Organizations: Executive Succession in the Higher Education Publishing Industry 1958–1990', *American Journal of Sociology*, 105: 801–43.

Tolbert, P. S. and Zucker, L. G. (1983). 'Institutional Sources of Change in the Formal Structure of Organizations: The Diffusion of Civil Service Reform 1880–1935', *Administrative Science Quarterly*, 30: 22–39.

—— —— (1996). 'The Institutionalization of Institutional Theory', in S. R. Clegg, C. Hardy, and W. R. Nord (eds.), *Handbook of Organizational Studies*. Thousand Oaks, CA: Sage.

Walsh, K., Hinings, C. R., Greenwood, R., and Ranson, S. (1981). 'Power and Advantage in Organizations', *Organization Studies*, 2: 131–52.

Part II

# Market Process: Rules, Norms, and the Social System of Market Competition

# 6

# Myths of the Market

*Neil Fligstein*

## 6.1. Introduction

The US economy is often held up as the model of the 'free enterprise' system where competition produces firm efficiency and dynamism. It is this dynamism which is supposed to produce economic growth. The role of the state in these processes is viewed in normative terms. States should stay out of the way of market actors, not try to pick firms or technologies as winners and losers, and if they intervene, it is only to enforce competition and contracts. In reality, understanding this dynamism is more complex. The American state and federal governments have been intimately involved in the functioning of the economy from the very beginning (for discussions of the history of this involvement, see Roy 1998 and Fligstein 1990; for a defence of the role of the state in the economy, see Block 1996; and for a theoretical elaboration, see Fligstein 2001). Moreover, the growth and nurturing of new markets are not left entirely to the devices of entrepreneurs. They are helped by a whole array of institutions that are both public and private. My purpose here is not to deny that entrepreneurship and competition matter for the creation of new markets and industry. Instead, it is to supplement our understanding of those activities by demonstrating that they cannot occur without governments and stable social structures to support them.

Two primary forces shape firms' strategic actions: the behaviour of their competitors and the actions of the government to define what is competitive and anti-competitive behaviour between firms. My key argument is that managers and owners in firms search for stable patterns of interactions with their largest competitors. If firms are able to set up stable patterns of interaction that prove to be both legal and profitable, they work to reproduce those patterns. These stable patterns of interaction are based on a set of strategies about what works to make money. Managers and owners across firms develop expectations of one another's behaviour and that increases the reproducibility of their positions in the market (Fligstein 2001: ch. 4). So, for example, in the American market for soft drinks, two firms, Pepsi Cola and Coca Cola, have dominated since the 1950s. Their basic strategy of competition has been to compete over market share through the use of advertising and taking turns discounting their products every week or two. When challengers have arisen, the firms have frequently bought them out. Their domination of that market has remained stable for the past forty years.

There are three main ways that the US government has directly affected market activities in particular markets.[1] First, the government makes laws and rules that determine tax policies, govern the use of equity and debt by corporations, regulate employment relations, the enforcement of patents and property rights, and regulate competition or antitrust policy. Second, the government can act as a buyer of products and a provider of research and development funds to firms. In the USA, the Defense Department has always played an important role in this regard. Governments fund research in universities and provide support for developing technologies. They also encourage the commercialization of useful products. Third, they also make rules that directly can favour certain firms in particular industries often at the behest of the most powerful actors in those industries.[2] The main kind of market intervention that the US government has shied away from in the past thirty years is the direct ownership of firms. Although even here, there has been and continues to be government ownership of utilities. It is useful to show how these types of market interventions by the US state and federal governments help provide the backdrop for economic growth. Governments build up public and private infrastructure that give the impetus for the possibility for new firms and industries to emerge.

---

[1] Of course, governments do many other things that directly and indirectly help entrepreneurs. They provide for infrastructure like roads, other forms of transportation, utilities, and public safety (including national defence). They also provide for the enforcement of contracts more generally and ensure the stability of the financial system. Finally, governments provide social welfare functions.

[2] So, for example, the federal government has agreed not to charge sales tax on purchases over the Internet. This policy is supposed to allow the Internet to 'mature' as a medium of exchange. But obviously giving electronic sellers a 5–7% price advantage over firms that are 'bricks and mortar' is a policy that reflects the interests of one set of sellers over another.

In this chapter, I consider two major developments in the American economy that have been typically hailed as emblematic of the working out of free markets: the emergence of the 'shareholder value' conception of the firm and the rise and growth of Silicon Valley, the home to successive waves of innovation in the computer industry. My purpose is to show how these phenomena were not just caused by entrepreneurial activity. Instead, both were embedded in pre-existing social relations and in both cases, the government played a pivotal role in pushing forward the conditions for 'entrepreneurial activity'.

After considering the role of government in these cases, I discuss more generally why governments sometimes do not figure in either economic or some economic sociological arguments about markets and economic growth. I critique these views by noting that there is ample theory and evidence from both economists and sociologists that governments play important roles in economic development. Finally, I suggest how an economic sociology with a view of embeddedness that includes governments, law, and supporting institutions offers a more complete picture of market evolution. This more complete picture helps us understand why a particular market structure came into existence. It also gives us tools to evaluate how the firms that dominate a particular industry came to occupy that position. So, for example, we would expect to be able to tell if firms have used government connections to help them control competition or if they attain a stable market by virtue of market-oriented strategies. This view of economic sociology can be used to analyse when and what kinds of government interventions are likely to produce more or less economic growth.

## 6.2. The Case of Shareholder Value

In order to apply this general understanding about the link between governments and markets to the case of shareholder value, it is important to understand what shareholder value is, the nature of the market order that it implies, what existed before 'shareholder value', why the idea of 'shareholder value' emerged, and the role of government in aiding the reorganization of firms under the rubric of 'maximizing shareholder value'. The shareholder value conception of the firm refers to a set of understandings about the relationships between the top managers of publicly held corporations, boards of directors, and the equities markets, where the owners of firms buy and sell shares (Fama and Jensen 1983; Jensen 1989).

The main idea is that the job of top managers is to ensure the highest possible profits for their shareholders. The relationships between managers, boards of directors, and equities markets involve monitoring, rewarding, and sanctioning managers in order to get them to maximize profits. Boards of directors are supposed to monitor managers by tying their pay to performance and if performance-based incentives fail to produce high profits, to change management teams. If boards of directors fail to monitor managers closely enough, then the equity markets will punish firms when owners begin to sell stock and the share price of the firm drops. If managers and boards of directors continue to ignore taking actions to increase profits, the final source of discipline for recalcitrant firms is the hostile takeover. Here, a new team of owners and managers will take over the assets by buying them at the depressed price and use them more fruitfully in the pursuit of maximizing shareholder value.

The market that the shareholder value conception of the firm describes is the market for corporate control. The market for corporate control concerns how teams of owners and managers seek out opportunities to use assets to make profits. The shareholder value conception of the firm is an idealized version of how this market is supposed to work. Owners and managers who are effective at making profits retain the rights over assets. Other owners will want to purchase the stock of such a firm (which is a claim over the profit produced by the assets). The current share price reflects the current and future prospects of the management team in exploiting those assets to produce profits. When managers fail to produce sufficient profit, their share price begins to fall as owners sell stock. If the price falls sufficiently, then a new group of owners and managers will appear to take control over those assets and try and raise the profits of the firm.

The shareholder value conception of the firm requires several institutional features. First, of course, there have to be in place the 'right' kinds of laws and rules to allow boards of directors and equity markets to function in this way. This includes rules about protecting shareholder rights, rules governing accounting practices, and rules allowing hostile takeovers. Second, stock ownership has to be sufficiently defused so that it is possible for teams of owners and managers to be able to make bids for all the shares of firms. If firms are tightly controlled by a family, a bank, a government, or cross-holding of various corporations, then it will be difficult if not impossible to make a takeover bid without cooperation from these groups.

The USA is unlike most industrialized societies in that ownership of the stock of the largest corporations is highly diffused (Blair and Roe 1999; Roe 1994). The history of the diffusion begins in the Depression of the 1930s. The banking crisis of the 1930s forced most banks into bankruptcy. Laws were passed to try and restore confidence in banks. Banks were forced to choose which part of the business they wanted to be in and submit to close government scrutiny. Investment banks were separated from commercial and wholesale banks. Commercial and wholesale banks and insurance companies were prevented from holding stock in firms (Roe 1994). After the Second World War, stocks became available to a wider public and stock ownership became more diffused. As a result, banks, which previously had owned stock and lent money to firms they controlled, were forced to be only in the business of lending money. Firms became less dependent on banks and began to raise money from other sources. This resulted in the expansion of the corporate bond market in the post-war era where firms would directly sell bonds to investors. Commercial banks', wholesale banks', and insurance companies' role in directly influencing corporate managers has been decreasing ever since 1950. Now, huge amounts of stock are publicly bought and sold on the equities markets and it is possible, if you have enough money to buy majority stakes in almost all the largest corporations.

Societies that might be interested in creating a market for corporate control in order to force firms to maximize shareholder value would have to undertake a series of political reforms for such a market to emerge. This market would not emerge 'naturally', but would require active interventions by governments. In Europe and much of the rest of the world, families, banks, and to some degree governments, continue to control much of the stock of corporations (see the chapters in Blair and Roe 1999). There are also various forms of share cross-holding such that firms own shares of their important suppliers or customers. These long-term relationships imply that firms' stock is unavailable in the wider market and, therefore, cannot be purchased in a hostile takeover. Banks in Germany and Japan, for example, are both owners of equity and often provide loans to their largest customers (Albert 1991; Aoki 1988). Existing systems of property rights tend to favour currently existing economic elites who certainly would try and prevent governments from undermining their economic power. These elites do not want to give up their control over firms. As a result, it is easy to see why most governments have not put American style corporate governance systems into place. Great Britain, which had laws in place similar to the USA, is the only major government to have created a market for corporate control in the past twenty years (Blair and Roe 1999).

It is useful to ask how and why the shareholder value conception of the firm came to dominate the market for corporate control in the USA. Obviously, the managerial elite of large corporations are an entrenched economic interest who would appeal to the state to protect their position. In order to understand the vulnerability of these managers and the rise of shareholder value, one must understand what existed before shareholder value.

The finance conception of the firm emerged during the merger movement of the 1960s to govern the market for corporate control (Fligstein 1990: ch. 7). At this time, the firm was first conceived of as a bundle of assets that managers would deploy and re-deploy by the buying and selling of firms in order to maximize profits. During the 1960s, diversified portfolios of product lines would be manipulated to maximize profits. The idea had three parts. First, firms could smooth out business cycles by investing in businesses that performed differently as the economy expanded and contracted. Second, financial-oriented managers would have closer control over assets and, thus, be able to use them to make more money than either passive investors in stock portfolios, or as they might make as free standing firms. Finally, financially oriented executives would be able to make investments in firms and evaluate the likelihood that their investments would succeed.

There were two conditions that produced the finance conception. First, large firms in the post-war era were already fairly diversified in their product lines. The problem of internally controlling a large number of products opened an opportunity for executives who could claim to evaluate the profit potential of each product line. Financial executives reduced the information problem to the rate of return earned by product lines and thereby made the large diversified corporation manageable. Second, the federal government was strictly enforcing the antitrust laws in the early post-war era and had passed an anti-merger law that made it difficult to merge with direct competitors or suppliers. This had the unintended consequence of encouraging firms to engage in mergers with firms which produced radically different products to produce growth and avoid government intervention. This gave financial executives more legitimacy because they could claim to have the expertise to evaluate the prospects for products outside of a firm's main lines by making these evaluations in financial terms (Fligstein 1990: ch. 6).

The most spectacular organizational examples of the new financial conception came from firms outside the mainstream of American corporate life. The men who pioneered the acquisitive conglomerate (Tex Thornton at Textron, Jim Ling at L-T-V, and Harold Geneen at ITT) showed how financial machinations involving debt could be used to produce rapid growth with little investment of capital. All the financial forms of reorganization, including hostile takeovers, divestitures, leveraged buyouts, the accumulation of debt, and stock re-purchasing, were invented or perfected in this period. The 1960s witnessed a large-scale merger movement, whereby many of the largest corporations substantially increased their size and diversification. As a result of this success, financial executives increasingly became CEOs of large corporations. By 1969, the finance conception of control had come to dominate the market for corporate control and by implication, the strategies and structures of the largest American firms.

The financial conception of control, which dominated the market for corporate control during the 1960s, therefore already viewed the firm in primarily financial terms. The shareholder value conception of control is also a financial set of strategies, but it had a particular critique of the finance conception of the firms as it had evolved during the 1960s and 1970s. It viewed the principal failure of the financial conception of control as the failure to maximize shareholder value by its failure to raise share prices. What caused this critique to evolve?

The large American corporation in the early 1980s was under siege from two exogenous forces: the high inflation and slow economic growth of the 1970s, and increased foreign competition. Foreign competition, particularly with the Japanese, heated up and American firms lost market shares and, in some cases, entire markets, such as in consumer electronics. The inflation of the 1970s had a set of negative effects on large corporations. Their real assets (i.e. land, buildings, and machines) were increasing in value. High interest rates pushed investors towards fixed income securities like government bonds and stock prices drifted downwards over the decade. The main reaction for managers during this crisis was to leave assets undervalued on their books. Because of the high inflation and poor economic conditions, profit margins were squeezed. If firms revalued assets, then their financial performance would even look worse as standard measures of performance (like return on assets) would make poor profits stand out even more. Firms avoided borrowing money because of high interest rates. This meant that firms kept large amounts of cash on hand. With low stock prices, undervalued assets, and lots of cash, by the late 1970s, many large American firms had stock prices that valued them as being worth less than their assets and cash (Friedman 1985). There was a crisis of profitability during the 1970s for managers of large firms. The conditions were right for some form of change in the conception of control governing large corporations. There were three problems: what would the analysis of problems looks like, who would spearhead it, and what role would government play in sparking the new conception of the firm?

During the late 1970s in America, the discourse of deregulation was already taking shape in the political arena. The Carter administration embraced the view that one way out of the economic crisis known as 'stagflation' (high inflation, low economic growth) was to deregulate product and labour markets. The theory suggested that deregulation would stimulate competition, force down wages, and end inflation. Lower prices would result, and this would stimulate consumption and economic growth. The Carter administration began to experiment by deregulating the airlines and trucking industries. The presidential election of 1980 brought Ronald Reagan into power. Reagan embraced a pro-business, anti-government agenda to combat economic hard times (Block 1996).

Reagan's administration did several things that directly encouraged the merger movement of the 1980s. William Baxter, Reagan's attorney general in charge of antitrust, had been an active opponent of the antitrust laws while a lawyer and academician. In 1981, he announced new merger guidelines. These guidelines committed the government to approving almost all mergers except those that led to concentration ratios within particular markets of greater than 80 per cent. This gave the green light to all forms of mergers, large and small, vertical and horizontal. The Reagan administration also substantially reduced corporate income taxes at the same time. Reagan encouraged firms to use this largesse to make new investments in the economy. The kind of investments that most of them made was mergers. From this perspective, the 1980s market for corporate control was driven by the crisis in the already existing financial conception of the firm and the changes in the regulatory environment, which encouraged firms to use the market for corporate control to reorganize their assets.

The question of who came up with the shareholder value conception of the firm and how they related to those who were working with the financial conception of control has been studied extensively (Davis and Stout 1992; Fligstein 2001; Fligstein and Markowitz 1993; Useem 1993:

ch. 7). There were a number of important actors involved, mostly in the financial community. These included investment banks, stock brokerages, insurance companies, as well as financially oriented executives in mainstream firms. Davis and Stout (1992) described what happened as a social movement. These actors came to create the 'shareholder value' framing of what corporations should be. The idea of maximizing shareholder value can be traced to agency theory and financial economics (Jensen and Meckling 1976). Some executives and institutional investors began to realize that some firms had market values that were less than the value of their saleable assets. This caused them to enter the market for corporate control, make hostile takeover bids, and dismantle or absorb existing firms.

Savvy financial analysts began to realize that by breaking firms up, they could make money. Part of the problem for investment bankers and other institutional investors was raising the cash to engage in hostile takeovers. The most important financial invention of the period was the creation of high yield or junk bonds to aid these purchases. These bonds could be used to buy up the shares of the firm and then the new owners could engage in internal reorganization of the firm to pay the debt down. These reorganizations would involve lay-offs and the sale of assets. The shareholder value rhetoric argued that these reorganizations should not worry about workers, consumers, or suppliers, but instead, their aim was to make more money for the owners of the assets.

By touting deregulation as the solution to all economic problems, the American government began the discourse that allowed the 'shareholder value conception of the firm' to blossom. Deregulation of product and labour markets was thought to be the tonic to restore the American economy to its former growth. But deregulation did not mean that the government was going to entirely get out of the business of regulating markets, contracts, taxes, labour, and capital. The federal government also provided the institutional infrastructure for the maximization of shareholder value by producing regulation of equity and bond markets. It provided tax incentives and capital for mergers and told corporations that it would not disapprove of any mergers. It refused to consider passing laws to protect anyone's rights but shareholders. State governments did try and intervene to prevent firms that engaged in mergers from decimating local labour markets by closing down plants (Davis 1991). But they were not entirely successful at this effort. The federal government also encouraged firms to re-write the labour contract to make workers grow more insecure. They refused to protect workers rights and actively undermined unions.

For example, when the Reagan administration came to power, they swiftly decertified the air traffic controllers' union. While the federal government did not invent the idea of 'maximizing shareholder value', it continuously worked to advantage the owners of capital in order to increase their profitability.

The shareholder value conception of the firm was touted as the main corporate governance solution to the problem of making corporations more competitive (Jensen 1989). The empirical literature, however, provides mostly negative evidence for this assertion. The people who benefited the most from the 1980s merger movement were those who sold the shares of stock to firms engaging in mergers. But the new owners of the assets made no higher profits on average than either the firm made previously or firms in their industry were making (Jensen and Ruback 1994). There is an assumption in the theoretical literature that shareholder value style governance will result in the best allocation of a firm's assets and increase profits. But because many of the takeovers involved the use of debt, firms had a hard time showing higher levels of profit given their high levels of debt and their elevated equity prices. Of course, there were other beneficiaries of the merger movement: the investment bankers who made the deals and the sellers equity and debt.

The link between maximizing shareholder value and competitiveness is even more tenuous. The literature on competitiveness shows that the main factors that determine whether or not a firm is competitive have to do with its competencies at organizing production and creating new and useful technologies (Piore and Sabel 1984; Porter 1990, Womack, Jones, and Roos 1991). Having these competencies is strongly related to treating employees fairly or making investments in the future. A narrow focus on shareholders to the exclusion of other constituencies in the firm may result in the exodus of the best people in the firm. It may also result in under investment in the future of the firm. This can undermine the competitiveness of the firm. It should not be surprising that American corporations never regained ground in industries where they lost competitive advantage to the Japanese and the Europeans (i.e. consumer electronics, automobiles, luxury goods, and high end precision machines) by attempting to maximize 'shareholder value'. Instead, the general tactic of American managers when they faced aggressive competition would be to exit product lines where they could not dominate. Instead of trying to make better products, they would divest themselves of the assets.

## 6.3. The Case of Silicon Valley and the Computer Industry

The explosion of information technology that occurred at the end of the twentieth century has created a whole new set of markets. Let me tell the story of these markets from the perspective of those who favour the view that this has occurred as a result of the spontaneous actions of entrepreneurs. Many believe that these new technologies are transforming the world we live in (Castells 1996). This story has captured the attention of journalists, policymakers, and scholars. These markets are supposed to be creating new kinds of firms that are flatter, more networked, and thus, quicker to take advantage of opportunities (Castells 1996; Saxenian 1994). The new firms learn and change constantly, because if they stop, they die. In doing so, they are creating wealth beyond what anyone has ever imagined. They are also transforming work for the people who run them. People enter and exit firms rapidly, and stock options are a huge part of what attracts work teams to put in extremely high hours to push a new product innovation to the market. Silicon Valley and its imitators in Austin, Seattle, Washington, DC, Boston, New York City (Silicon Alley), and Ann Arbor are living proof that the future belongs to quick, constantly learning, small firms that maintain alliances and networks to keep them alive.

In this new world, firms do not form monopolies because technology will not let it happen. Firms that try to create proprietary processes or products will find others inventing new things in order to go around them. So, Apple (with its proprietary computer operating system) and Sony (with its beta VCR system) found themselves on the losing end of markets as consumers preferred open systems that produced more standard products that were cheaper. Intel and Microsoft with the 'open' architecture of their products spawned whole industries of suppliers of hardware and software built on the openness of their systems. The lesson of these firms was that fortunes were not to be made by trying to be proprietary, but instead, by being 'open'. The way to win was to get there first and have your product adopted as the standard because it was the best. To prevent being blown away by the next generation of the technology, one needed to keep one's product developing, and organizational learning was the only answer. Keeping in touch with competitors and customers, and using networks to evolve products was the only way to stay in the game. This closed the virtuous circle by which the best technology won out, and the firm that produced the technology only stayed in place if it continued to evolve as other technologies evolved.

In the 'old' industrial economics, the bigger a firm got, the less product the market could absorb, the lower the price for the product, and the marginal profit on selling an additional unit of the product would eventually drop to zero. A whole new branch of economics claims that this 'law' has been repealed. Information technologies produce 'increasing returns to scale' (Arthur 1994). The cost of making a product like software is high at the beginning. But if the product becomes a standard, the market locks-in around the product. This lock-in occurs because consumers get used to a particular product and because other related producers build their products around it. The marginal cost of producing additional products is very low because the cost of the floppy disk, in the case of software, is so small. If the product becomes an industry standard, the profits go up as each additional unit of output is sold because the cost of producing an additional amount of the product is near zero.

If one reads this literature, all of this change in the 'new economy' was occurring without any input from governments (see Castells 1996; Powell 2001). Governments were not actively regulating these markets, choosing winning and losing technologies, or making investments that promoted one set of firms over another. It is the knowledge-based industries, invented in universities, driven by entrepreneurs that learn from each other, that are creating this new community of firms. Indeed, the decentralized nature of the markets and the open standards of products are often characterized as antithetical to the slow moving, unimportant bureaucracies of governments.

It turns out that there are a great many problems with this story. First and most important, it fails to recognize the pivotal role that the government has played as producer of rules that concern issues relevant to hardware and software manufacturers, as funders of research and development, as buyers of products, and as funders of basic and applied research in and around universities. At the beginning of markets, there is always a social movement-like flow of firms to start out. New entrants proliferate and many conceptions of action seem possible. The small, 'networked, learning' firm is a strategy for new firms to follow as these markets emerge. Firms face an uncertain market and no one knows which products will be hits. The 'networked, learning firm' is a model to deal with these problems. In essence, it makes a virtue out of a vice. If one cannot engage in controlling the competition, one can try and be connected enough to other firms to know what is happening and to try and anticipate where the market is going.

In this section, I want to consider two issues. First, what has been the role of government in the waves of inventions that have created the computer, software, telecommunications, and Internet industries in general and how did the government help nurture Silicon Valley? Second, I am interested in considering the degree to which the image we have of the industry as small and nimble meshes with the ways in which firms appear to have organized themselves to make money. The question is, will these markets settle on these forms because it will be impossible for bigger firms pursuing more stability-oriented tactics to emerge because of the rapid shifts in technology? Or will some grow large by stabilizing technologies and having control whereby their products lock-in a particular market?

There have been four waves of innovation in these industries. The Second World War and the Cold War stimulated the first by providing backing for innovations in products that were related to radio, microwaves, radar, and guided missile systems. The second came in the late 1950s with the invention and commercial production of the integrated circuit, which became the basis of the semiconductor industry. The first and most important use of these circuits was for guided missile systems. The third wave was personal computers beginning in the 1970s. Finally, in the 1990s, the Internet was invented and experienced explosive growth. The government played a part in all these periods of invention. In some, it played a more direct role and in others, more indirect. I review some of the literature here in order to make this role more explicit.

Before the Second World War, there was a small electronics industry in Silicon Valley (Sturgeon 2000). Most of the electronics firms in the USA were operated by large corporations and were located in the east. The first real stimulus to the growth of the modern electronics industry in Silicon Valley was the Second World War. During the Second World War, the electronics industry in Silicon Valley expanded dramatically. For example, Hewlett Packard, the original Silicon Valley firm, expanded from 9 employees and $70,000 in sales in 1939 to over 100 employees and over $1 million in sales by 1943 due entirely to sales to the US military. During the 1950s, the fastest growing firm in Silicon Valley was Varian and Associates, which sold over 90 per cent of its production to the Defense Department. By the late 1950s, Hewlett Packard, Varian, Lockheed, and other firms were selling the bulk of their computer, electronics, and guided missiles/space vehicles to the government (Henton 2000).

The Defense Department was not just a customer for the region during this period. Leslie (2000) argued that the war effort had pushed along a number of related inventions, in particular advances in tube technology, but also in opening up parts of the electromagnetic spectrum. During the early years of the Cold War, the Defense Department became the most important supplier of money for research and development and the purchaser of many early versions of different technologies. Much of this money poured into firms. But the government also underwrote research and education at many universities. Breshahan (1999) estimates that over 70 per cent of the research support in engineering, computer science, and related fields came from the federal government. At least half of the graduate students in these fields were supported by federal funds as well. More than half of the papers published in computer science journals cite federal funding as pivotal to their research.

One of the biggest recipients of this largesse was Stanford University. The Dean of the Stanford Business School during this period, Frederick Terman, was instrumental in making the Stanford Engineering School the leading research site on the West Coast. Terman recognized that the growth of industry in Silicon Valley depended on building research infrastructure in the region. To do this, the Engineering School would need to develop close, intimate ties to the government (Leslie 2000). He was extremely successful in his efforts. Stanford University set up many programmes to exploit the potential linkage between business, government, and students and professors. Terman pioneered the strategy of encouraging professors and students with good ideas to set up shop in Silicon Valley as private firms. His most successful case was Hewlett–Packard. He often worked his connections in government and business to help in these efforts. Stanford University also provided engineers trained in various fields for firms to employ. One of the other features of the Valley that Terman helped promote was the origin of the venture capital industry. He acted as a financial backer of Hewlett–Packard and helped them find funding to expand their activities. During the 1950s, venture capitalists came to Silicon Valley to underwrite both Varian and Associates and Fairchild Semiconductor. All were encouraged to do so because these firms had a natural market for their products in government.

The transistor, semiconductor, and computer industries were all underwritten by the federal government, and in particular by the Defense Department in the years 1945–65 (Lecuyer 2000). The first of the semiconductor firms was Fairchild Semiconductor. It was the first company to produce transistors for semiconductors. The major innovations by the firm during the 1950s allowed the company to gain a large share of military production. By 1960, it was the leading manufacturer of silicon-based components in the USA and its main customer was the US Defense Department. Ultimately, many of the leaders of Fairchild Semiconductor left the firm and went out on their own. They founded many companies in the Valley including Intel. It was these products, which caused the area to become known as Silicon Valley.

The government continued to support research and development and accounted for a substantial amount of the market for high technology goods until the end of the Cold War. They also continued to underwrite most research and development at universities. During the 1970s and 1980s, the product mix of the Valley began to change. The personal computer and later the Internet meant that consumer markets for goods produced in the Valley were growing very quickly while the market for goods for the Defense Department was either growing less quickly or even contracting.

Most of the stories told about Silicon Valley refer to this period when the government was less in the foreground of development, and more in the background. But it should be noted that the main product innovations that went into these new industries had their origins in the post-war Cold War era. Moreover, the reason that Silicon Valley was poised to be such an important player in these new industries during the 1970s was that thousands of engineers were already working there, mainly for firms supplying goods to the defence industry. There has been an explosion of entrepreneurial activity in Silicon Valley over the past twenty years and an equally explosive growth of venture capital to support this activity. But both of these activities have their roots in the government-funded activities of the post-war era.

But in spite of the important roles that entrepreneurs have played in the past twenty years, the government has played a part. The last of these new innovations, the Internet, owes many of its key features to the Defense Department. An agency in the Defense Department called the Advanced Research Project Agency (ARPA) was founded in the 1960s. It funded the 'Arpanet' which was a computer network whose purpose was to create a decentralized network of communication to ensure communication in event of a nuclear war. Scientists and university scholars were given access to the 'Arpanet', and they used it to send messages and files. In order to make it work better, a series of innovations were necessary to allow for the handling of large amounts of data. This brought forth a number of important software innovations. Most of the basic innovations for these information technologies came from research done in universities where government paid to support the research.

Government support for the computer and electronics industry extends beyond the role of the government as customer and the main organization funding basic research. Congress has written laws that serve the interests of firms. Patent law and property rights issues have favoured the holders of patents (Lerner 2000). The state of California, for example, has very well-developed intellectual property rights laws which, not surprisingly, favour programmers. The Telecommunications Act of 1996 produced rules of competition that are generally favourable to the current incumbent phone and cable firms. These laws have not forced competition between telecommunications and cable companies, but have reinforced the positions of incumbents. Silicon Valley firms have got the government to relax immigration laws to provide a stream of engineers, while these same firms simultaneously moved production offshore. As of 2003, commerce on the Internet is not subjected to sales tax, giving electronic retailers a 5–7 per cent price advantage over their bricks and mortar competitors. In sum, government is everywhere. It nurtures technologies, allows private exploitation of them, and provides legal and regulatory structures to make it easier for firms to raise and make money. It also allows firms to define the rules of competition.

This brings me to my second question. Is Silicon Valley really dominated by the networks of actors who are in small firms and cooperate extensively with one another, and does this model produce a stable situation for producers? The main scholarly studies (Castells 1996; Castillo et al. 2000; Saxenian 1994) seem to think that it is this feature of Silicon Valley, which has produced its distinctive competitive advantage. This imagery seems to directly contradict the story I have told about the role of government in supporting innovation and buying products. It also would seem to undermine the idea that large corporations were the primary beneficiary of the government's actions.

I think there are two points of contention here. First, there are many factors that have made Silicon Valley so successful and it is clear that these have changed over time. Thus, it is important to study all the possible factors and to do it over the whole history of Silicon Valley. So, if one has a sixty-year perspective, one can easily see how the Cold War and active entrepreneurs in universities and firms who took advantage of this opportunity formed the core of the industry. It is also important for scholars who study these processes to not ignore all the potential social factors in the formation of industrial agglomerations like Silicon Valley even if their interest is in what is going on right now. If scholars ignore government funding of research and training in universities and do not include it as a cause in Silicon Valley's success, they will not see the government as being important to what is going on. If scholars fixate narrowly on the networks of engineers or the venture capitalists as the engines of success, then they will see them as the only social groups relevant to study. Second, having said this, I am not denying that entrepreneurs have had the vision to create new and innovative products that have created entirely new industries. I am only denying that they did this on their own, without the aid of government or other institutions.

But I think that the 'network approach' ignores some of the most compelling industrial organization facts about Silicon Valley. There are already high levels of concentration in the main products produced in the information technology revolution. Microsoft (software), Sun (work stations that power the Internet), Cisco Systems (the hardware and switches for the Internet), Intel (computer chips), ATT (cable and long distance), and AOL-Time-Warner (Internet service provider and cable) control over 60 per cent of their relevant markets. While some of these firms are clear technological innovators, they are also using familiar tactics to control competition. Microsoft, Intel, and Cisco have all been targets of antitrust lawsuits based on forms of predatory competition. The Microsoft antitrust case provided ample evidence that Microsoft behaved like a predatory competitor. As each of these new markets has emerged, a single firm has come to dominate.

It is useful to speculate on what kinds of markets are really being built in these new technology industries. The incumbent firms observe the innovators of new technologies and either buy up or incorporate the insights of these technologies into their main products. They stay in the game by aggressively buying up winners in markets connected to their main products. Microsoft, for example, is well known for approaching small software firms and offering to buy them out. If smaller firms refuse, then their products were often re-engineered and made part of the next release of the operating system.

If the incumbents in these industries use their market position to buy out or force out competitors, then what do the challengers do? Challenger firms have a potentially profitable niche strategy available to them. Challenger firms are the innovators who take risks. If they are successful, then they face three potential positive futures (at least from the perspective of their owners): they can go 'public' and sell stock, sell out their firm to one of the industry giants, or try and become on of these giants themselves.

This is a conception of control that defines the structure of incumbents and challengers. It means that investors have the ability to reap returns if their products are successful and it provides the largest firms with new innovations to keep their large firms in the centre of new technology markets. Challenger and incumbents have a symbiotic relation to one another whereby they are competitors, but they also have created tacit rules that allow all to survive.

The issue of 'openness' in computer systems and the related problem of creating technical standards for products are complex (Edstrom 1999). The ability to attach a particular piece of hardware or software to an existing structure makes that structure more valuable. Thus, 'openness' benefits the producers of new products and the owners of such standards. The large stable firms update their products and because of the technological lock-in around their standards, they attain stability. 'Openness' is one way to get a stable market. I would argue that 'openness' evolved when the attempt to create proprietary systems failed. If firms could not control technology markets through patents, then the second best solution was to get their product to be an open standard. It creates stability because it allows industry leaders to form and markets to coalesce around stable standards. The core technologies that form the open standard benefit the incumbent firms that control them. Technical standards can operate in a similar way.

If I am correct, then, as the industry develops, we can expect, consolidation into large firms in many of the major products. We can also expect that firms will pursue one of two tactics in the construction of new markets: either be a small, challenger firm prepared to be bought out, or try and become one of the large, diversified firms that offer standards for others to build on and buy up new technology to protect their franchise. This conception of control, if it emerges and stabilizes, is the deep structure by which firms will make money. The incumbents are the large firms. The challengers are the small firms where fortunes can still be made, but only as a means to ends. The owners of challenger firms are in the game to cash out. The small, networked firm is a product of the early days of new markets. As time goes on, more familiar structures of industrial organization have emerged and will continue to emerge.

## 6.4. States, Markets, and Economic Growth

This chapter has taken the view that firms and markets are best viewed as deeply dependent on laws, institutions, and governments for their existence. It is unimaginable that firms could find stable solutions to their problems of competition without extensive social relationships. It is equally unimaginable that many of the products and markets that exist could have existed without the active intervention of governments. The 'shareholder value' conception of the firm was a solution to a particular problem of American firms. They were financially underperforming c.1980 due to the high inflation and slow economic growth of the 1970s. This underperformance was blamed on the managers of firms, and financial tools were invented to analyse and transform this condition. The federal government helped this process along by suspending the antitrust laws and cutting corporate taxes. The Carter and Reagan administrations came to evolve the view that the government intervened too much into both product and labour markets, and they worked to lessen that role. The Reagan administration worked actively to undermine what was left of unions. These actions had the effect of delivering the message that firms should be reorganized along any lines that owners saw fit.

Ironically, the problem of the lack of competitiveness of American firms did not go away. American firms failed to recapture markets they had lost in the 1970s and early 1980s. Financially reorganized firms did not make higher profits than their counterparts, but instead aided in transferring wealth from workers to managers and owners. The shareholder value conception of the firm is not the fix for industrial competitiveness that some have argued it is (Jensen 1989). Instead, it causes firms to focus more narrowly on financial criteria in their decision-making and less on strategic matters. Because of the shareholder value conception of the firm, managers who are having problems with a particular product will not work to become more competitive in that product, but instead will divest themselves of that product.

The computer revolution led by Silicon Valley during the 1980s and 1990s is emblematic of entrepreneurial American capitalism. Yet close examination of the facts shows that the American government has been intimately involved in funding research, education, and buying the products of the industry for the past fifty years. It has also provided for tax incentives and patent laws that favour producers and investors in risky ventures. But even this has not been enough to stabilize volatile markets for technology products. Firms have found their ways to oligopolies or monopolies, whereby innovative firms are selectively absorbed by larger firms. This allows both sides to profit. The founders of small firms are able to take high risks with potentially high returns. The largest firms are able to stabilize their positions by absorbing new technologies.

The lessons typically drawn about the dynamism of the US economy are simple: keep governments and firms apart, make firms compete, and deregulate labour markets. Even sociologists have bought into the view that what happened in Silicon Valley has more to do with the intra-organizational networks between firms, than the whole system of production (Castells 1996; Powell 2001; Saxenian 1994). But, my chapter should make the reader question this view. Governments and firms are intimately linked. The relative success of capitalist economies to produce wealth, income, goods, and services depends on these linkages. Any account of the success or failure of the American economy (or any other economy for that matter) that does not take both into account is likely to be incomplete at best, and misleading at worse.

The negative view of state intervention in the economy comes from a strand of thought in economics that focuses on how either government are rent seekers or firms who seek government help will produce governmental intervention that promotes rent seeking on their behalf (Buchanan, Tollison, and Tullock 1980; Noll 1989; the literature is reviewed in Peltzman 1989). This implies that governmental interventions into markets are always at the very least suspiciously likely to undermine the efficient operation of markets or are entirely illegitimate (see Block, for the evolution of this argument, 1996).

But the idea that all states are predatory is not just a product of rational choice theory. It is related to the scholarly and policy interest in the past fifteen years in trying to assess how nations could attain competitive advantages for their firms in markets. From the point of view of intellectual trends, many scholars became interested in Japan and the 'Asian miracle' in the 1980s (Dore 1997; Hamilton and Biggart 1988; Johnson 1982). This caused them to try and decipher why Japan, Taiwan, and Korea were able to develop so quickly, and the role of governments was part of the focus of attention.

Others saw the German economy to be admired for its neo-corporatist political system, formal cooperation between labour and capital, and its relatively small firms that were oriented towards exporting high-quality manufactured goods (Albert 1991). Still others viewed the future of manufacturing as being about flexible specialization, where small firms in the industrial districts of Italy, Silicon Valley, or Bavaria existed (Piore and Sabel 1984; Powell 2001; Saxenian 1994). These highly networked firms could respond quickly to changes in market demand. Various scholars became convinced that one of these models held the key to industrial competitiveness among nations.

States played an important part in most of these stories. During the 1990s, the resurgence of the US economy meant that it was natural that the relative success of the American economy has propelled scholars to turn back to the USA and extol the virtues of American-style corporate governance and labour relations as the key to economic success. Given the American view that states should play a minimal role, it is not surprising that governments are now out of favour.

But these fads in intellectual thought do not do justice to the difficulty of unravelling what causes economic growth. It assumes that all government policies have negative effects on economic growth by consuming economic resources that would otherwise be put to more productive uses by the private sector. This argument is wrong both theoretically and empirically. Even in economics, there can be an argument for the positive role states play in economic growth. The 'new institutional economics' suggests several mechanisms by which government spending and policies might positively affect growth. Endogenous growth theory argues that spending on education, health, and communications and transportation infrastructure are thought to have positive effects on growth (Ashauer 1990; Barro 1990; Romer 1990). North (1990) and Maddison (1995) have suggested that states also provide political stability, legal institutions, stable monetary systems, and reliable governments, all of which convince entrepreneurs to invest their money and create new markets.

The approach outlined here agrees with this perspective. Without these social institutions, economic actors will refuse to make investments in economies of scale and scope (for evidence on this point, see the essays in the volume edited by Chandler and Tanaka (1997) that concern why different countries did or did not achieve economic growth). Evans and Rauch have shown recently that the 'competence' of bureaucratic officials has a positive effect on economic growth (1999). Some economists are prepared to believe that different forms of industrial policies might be effective by providing investment in research and development, capital for risky ventures, and military spending (Tyson 1992).

At the very least, the choice is not just for or against governments, but for or against policies that might help economic growth (Evans 1996). The comparative capitalisms literature has demonstrated fairly effectively that governments have played positive roles in the development process as well (Campos and Root 1996; Evans 1996; Wade 1990). The literature comparing specific industrial policies and their effectiveness for advanced industrial societies offers both positive and negative evidence for the role of governments (Crouch and Streeck 1997; Herrigel 1996; Johnson 1982; Ziegler 1997; for a review, see Pauly and Reich 1997).

There are theoretical reasons to believe that states continue to matter in producing economic growth by providing public goods, the stable rule of law, and under certain conditions, good industrial policy. Investments in research and development, higher education, and the subsidization of technologies in their early stages of development are all policies that have worked to produce economic growth. Property rights and rules governing competition and exchange facilitate stable market relations between firms. These encourage investment and economic growth.

## 6.5. Conclusions

One task for economic sociology is to theorize what kind of market interventions are more likely to have positive economic consequences and what kind of market interventions are more likely to have negative economic consequences. One of the main contributions economic sociology can make is the careful attempt to empirically analyse particular market situations in order to decide who economic changes help, who they hurt, and what effects they have more generally on economic growth. So, for example, a sober empirical analysis of the positive and negative effects of the rise of shareholder value has never been undertaken. Such an analysis would prove a useful intervention to policymakers engaged in considering how to reform corporate governance practices.

There are many economic sociological analyses that do not situate market structures in larger institutional contexts. Network analysts often ignore factors not associated with conventional network measures in their analyses of firm and market success and failure. This approach works against the grain of most sociologists. Sociologists usually work with more multivariate models of social processes because they will allow analysts to give weight to various causal factors. Economic sociologists who ignore or avoid other types of social embeddedness will miss key variables that explain positive and negative economic effects. As I have tried to show, firms and states are interrelated and their dynamics over time are pivotal to making sense of the direction of changes in firms and markets. Analyses that do not consider such factors will likely misunderstand many economic processes.

Part of this empirical sensitivity is not to prejudge what effects interventions and changes might have on firms, jobs, inequality, and economic growth. While the problem of rent seeking on the part of different actors, be they managers, firms, the government, or workers, is a theoretical possibility, one has to be cautious in trying to assess whether it really occurs and the degree to which it has bad consequences for other social groups. For example, while Microsoft is a convicted monopolist, the overall effect of having a single dominant platform for software may be positive on other sectors of the economy. In this case, economic sociology might recommend regulating the monopoly position of Microsoft along the lines of a public utility rather than attempting to create multiple incompatible platforms for the sake of inducing competition.

One of the main purposes of economic sociological analyses could be to present a total picture of what has happened in a certain case. So, for example, government intervention into product and labour markets in Silicon Valley has certainly paid off handsomely for society. The government's role in training engineers, underwriting innovation, and encouraging the adoption of new technology has created growth and wealth for the entire economy. It is clear that the government is busily trying to reproduce the same effect in the biotechnology industry.

The example of shareholder value is more mixed. Many workers lost jobs and their economic situations suffered for a long time as a result (Bernhardt et al. 2001). Even managers experienced frequent lay-offs and those that remained worked longer hours (Baumol, Blinder, and Wolff 2003; Fligstein and Shin 2003). While a great deal of wealth was created for those who sold stock and those who benefited from that sale, there are less clear results for the overall competitiveness of the American economy. One substantive conclusion that the two cases suggest is that corporate governance is less likely to be a source of competitive advantage and economic growth and more traditional forms of investment (both public and private) are ways to attain economic growth.

Economic sociology is uniquely positioned to help us understand how firms and market processes are situated in larger political and legal contexts. It can also be used to understand the evolution of stable market structures of particular markets. By doing this, economic sociology provides us with theoretical and empirical analyses that can lead to making more sense of the effects of market change on who in society gains and who lose.

# References

Albert, M. (1991). *Capitalisme contre Capitalisme*. Paris: Seuil.

Aoki, M. (1988). *Information, Incentives and Bargaining in the Japanese Economy*. Cambridge: Cambridge University Press.

Arthur, B. (1994). *Increasing Returns and Path Dependence in the Economy*. Ann Arbor: University of Michigan Press.

Ashauer, D. (1990). *Public Investment and Private Sector Growth*. Washington, DC: Economic Policy Institute.

Barro, R. (1990). 'Government Spending in a Simple Model of Endogenous Growth', *Journal of Political Economy*, 98: 103–25.

Baumol, W., Blinder, A., and Wolff, E. (2003). *Downsizing in America*. New York: Russell Sage.

Bernhardt, A., Morris, M., Handcock, M., and Scott, M. (2001). *Divergent Paths*. New York: Russell Sage.

Blair, M. and Roe, M. (1999). *Employees and Corporate Governance*. Washington, DC: Brookings Institution.

Block, F. (1996). *The Vampire State*. New York: Norton.

Breshahan, T. (1999). 'Computing', in D. Mowery (ed.), *U.S. Industry in 2000: Studies in Comparative Performance*. Washington, DC: National Academy Press.

Buchanan, J., Tollison, R., and Tullock, G. (1980). *Towards A Theory of the Rent-Seeking Society*. College Station, TX: Texas A&M Press.

Campos, J. and Root, H. (1996). *The Key to the Asian Miracle: Making Fast Growth Credible*. Washington, DC: Brookings.

Castells, M. (1996). *The Rise of the Network Society*. Oxford: Blackwell.

Castillo, E., Hwang, H., Granovetter, E., and Granovetter, M. (2000). 'Social Networks in Silicon Valley', in C. Lee, W. Miller, M. Hancock, and H. Rowen (eds.), *The Silicon Valley Edge*. Stanford, CA: Stanford University Press.

Chandler, A., Amatori, F., and Hikino, T. (1997). *Big Business and the Wealth of Nations*. Cambridge: Cambridge University Press.

Crouch, C. and Streeck, W. (1997). *The Political Economy of Modern Capitalism*. London: Sage.

Davis, G. (1991). 'Agents without Principles', *Administrative Science Quarterly*, 36: 583–613.

—— and Stout, S. (1992). 'Organization Theory and the Market for Corporate Control: A Dynamic Analysis of the Characteristics of Large Takeover Targets 1980–1990', *Administrative Science Quarterly*, 37: 605–33.

Dore, R. (1997). 'The Distinctiveness of Japan', in C. Crouch and W. Streeck (eds.), *Political Economy of Global Capitalism*. London: Sage.

Edstrom, M. (1999). *Controlling Markets in Silicon Valley: A Case Study of Java*, MA Thesis, Department of Sociology, University of California.

Evans, P. (1996). *Embedded Autonomy*. Princeton, NJ: Princeton University Press.

——and Rauch, J. (1999). 'Bureaucracy and Economic Growth', *American Sociological Review*, 64: 187–214.

Fama, E. and Jensen, M. (1983). 'Separation of Ownership and Control', *Journal of Law and Economics*, 26: 301–25.

Fligstein, N. (1990). *The Transformation of Corporate Control*, Cambridge, MA: Harvard University Press.

——(2001). *The Architecture of Markets*. Princeton, NJ: Princeton University Press.

——and Markowitz, L. (1993). 'The Finance Conception of the Corporation and the Financial Reorganization of Large American Corporations 1979–1988', in W. J. Wilson (ed.), *Sociology and Social Policy*. Beverly Hills, CA: Sage.

——and Shin, T. (2003). 'The Shareholder Value Society', in K. Neckerman (ed.), *The New Inequalities*. New York: Russell Sage.

Friedman, B. (1985). 'The Substitutability of Equity and Debt Securities', in B. Friedman (ed.), *Corporate Capital Structures in the U.S.* Chicago, IL: University of Chicago Press.

Hamilton, G. and Biggart, N. (1988). 'Market Culture and Authority: A Comparative Analysis of Management and Organization in the Far East', *American Journal of Sociology*, 94: 52–94.

Henton, D. (2000). 'A Profile of Silicon Valley's Evolving Structure', in C. Lee, W. Miller, M. Hancock, and H. Rowen (eds.), *The Silicon Valley Edge*. Stanford, CA: Stanford University Press.

Herrigel, G. (1996). *Industrial Constructions*. Cambridge: Cambridge University Press.

Jensen, M. (1989). 'Eclipse of the Public Corporation', *Harvard Business Review*, 67: 61–73.

——and Meckling, W. (1976). 'Theory of the Firm: Managerial Behavior, Agency Costs, and Ownership Structure', *Journal of Financial Economics*, 3: 305–40.

——and Ruback, R. (1994). 'The Market for Corporate Control: The Scientific Evidence', *Journal of Financial Economics*, 11: 5–50.

Johnson, C. (1982). *MITI and the Japanese Miracle*. Stanford, CA: Stanford University Press.

Lecuyer, C. (2000). 'Fairchild Semiconductor and Its Influence', in C. Lee, W. Miller, M. Hancock, and H. Rowen (eds.), *The Silicon Valley Edge*. Stanford, CA: Stanford University Press.

Lerner, J. (2000). 'Small Business, Innovation, and Public Policy in the Information Technology Industry', in E. Brynjolfsson and B. Kahin (eds.), *Understanding the Digital Economy*. Boston, MA: MIT Press.

Leslie, S. (2000). 'The Biggest Angel of Them All: The Military and the Making of Silicon Valley', in M. Kenney (ed.), *Understanding Silicon Valley*. Stanford, CA: Stanford University Press.

Maddison, A. (1995). *Explaining the Economic Performance of Nations*. Aldershot, UK: Edward Elgar.

155

Noll, R. G. (1989). 'Economic Perspectives on the Politics of Regulation', in R. Schmalensee and R. Willig (eds.), *Handbook of Industrial Organization*. New York: Elsevier.

North, D. (1990). *Institutions, Institutional Change, and Economic Performance*. Cambridge: Cambridge University Press.

Pauly, L. and Reich, S. (1997). 'National Structures and Multinational Corporation Behavior', *International Organization*, 51: 1–31.

Peltzman, S. (1989). 'The Economic Theory of Regulation after a Decade of Deregulation', in *Brookings Papers in Microeconomics*. Washington, DC: Brookings Institution, pp. 1–59.

Piore, M. and Sabel, C. (1984). *The Second Industrial Divide: Possibilities for Prosperity*. New York: Basic Books.

Porter, M. (1990). *The Competitive Advantage of Nations*. New York: Free Press.

Powell, W. (2001). 'The Capitalist Firm in the 21st Century: Emerging Patterns in Western Enterprise', in P. DiMaggio (ed.), *The 21st Century Firm*. Princeton, NJ: Princeton University Press.

Roe, M. (1994). *Strong Managers, Weak Owners*. Princeton, NJ: Princeton University Press.

Romer, P. (1990). 'Endogenous Technological Change', *Journal of Political Economy*, 98: 79–102.

Roy, W. (1998). *Socializing Capital*. Princeton, NJ: Princeton University Press.

Saxenian, A. (1994). *Regional Advantage*. Cambridge, MA: Harvard University Press.

Sturgeon, T. (2000). 'How Silicon Valley Came to Be', in M. Kenney (ed.), *Understanding Silicon Valley*. Stanford, CA: Stanford University Press.

Tyson, L. (1992). *Who's Bashing Whom?* Washington, DC: Institute for International Economics.

Useem, M. (1993). *Executive Defense*. Cambridge, MA: Harvard University Press.

Wade, R. (1990). *Governing the Market: Economic Theory and the Role of Government in East Asian Industrialization*. Princeton, NJ: Princeton University Press.

Womack, J., Jones, D., and Roos, D. (1991). *The Machine That Changed the World*. New York: Rawson Associates.

Ziegler, N. (1997). *Governing Ideas: Strategies for Innovation in France and Germany*. Princeton, NJ: Princeton University Press.

# 7

# On the Social Structure of Markets: A Review and Assessment in the Perspective of the New Institutional Economics

*Rudolf Richter*

## 7.1. Introduction[1]

This chapter deals with the claim of sociologists that the social structure of markets matters for their performance. 'Social structure' is understood as 'structure of social relationships between actors'. To understand the meaning of 'social structure', a reasonable starting point is social network analysis. This chapter starts therefore with a brief description of some basic concepts of social network analysis. Next comes a review and assessment of some of the major sociological contributions on the effect of the structure of social relationships between actors on market performance. It is demonstrated that positive market models need to include elements of existing social networks between actors to become 'sufficiently good approximations for the purpose in hand'.

From an institutional economic viewpoint, neoclassical economists think of markets, roughly speaking, in terms of given formal governance structures that steer the behaviour of a plurality of perfectly rational

[1] Final revision of a paper presented originally at the 6th Annual Meeting of the International Society for New Institutional Economics (ISNIE) at MIT in Cambridge, Massachusetts, 27–9 September 2002. I thank Christoph Engel (Max Planck Institute for Research in Collective Goods, Bonn), Eirik G. Furubotn (Texas A&M University), and Henrik Egbert (University of Giessen) for critical comments. Financial support of the *Deutsche Forschungsgemeinschaft* (DFG) is gratefully acknowledged.

trading automatons at no costs towards market equilibrium. Trading automatons entertain no social ties among each other or with the rest of society. Only the given formal governance structure of markets matters. In contrast, economic sociologists view markets as evolving formal and informal governance structures between a plurality of real people—potential buyers and sellers—who act boundedly rational or in some other way. Social ties between traders and the rest of society play a role. Markets do not function in a social vacuum.[2] The informal social structure of markets matters in addition to the evolving governance structures. Finally, representatives of the New Institutional Economics (NIE) think of markets as lying somewhere in between neoclassical and sociological perspectives.[3] Following Williamson (1985), individuals act boundedly rational within both a given formal governance structure (the neoclassical market order) and an evolving formal or informal governance structure that actors designed by mutual agreement. Social relations become an issue. As a result, Williamsonian NIE and economic sociology overlap to a degree—which may explain the somewhat strained atmosphere between representatives of the New Economic Sociology (NES)[4] and Williamsonian NIE.[5] By contrast, the Northian NIE is much wider. It contains the whole range of formal and informal governance structures, including political markets and the systems of cognitive and moral beliefs (North 1990, 2005).

This chapter is a product of curiosity. We wish, first, to get an idea of what new economic sociologists actually understand by 'social structure', second, how they explain its effect on market performance, and third, what institutional economists can learn from market structure sociology.

## 7.2. Market Structure Sociology

The arguments of market structure sociologists are to some degree influenced by the work of Karl Polanyi (1944) who heavily criticized the view of liberal economists that markets or a whole market economy would develop 'spontaneously' as a consequence of individual

---

[2] Hamilton and Feenstra (1995: 61).

[3] For our view, see Furubotn and Richter (2005: ch. 7).

[4] The New Economic Sociology was started in the 1980s at Harvard by former students of Harrison White, among them Robert Eccles (1981), Mark Granovetter (1985), and Michael Schwartz. Independently of the Harvard group, several other sociologists joined the battle, among them Mitchel Abolafia (1984), Susan Shapiro (1984), and Viviana Zelizer (1983).

[5] For a discussion of the relationship between Williamsonian NIE and some representatives of the New Economic Sociology, see Richter (2001).

self-interest (Hayek 1973: 37; Hume 1739–40/1969: Book III, part 2, section 2; Menger 1883/1963: 15). That view would completely disregard the results of modern historic anthropological research according to which 'man's economy, as a rule, is submerged in his social relationships. He does not act so as to safeguard his individual interest in the possession of material goods; he acts so as to safeguard his social standing, his social claims, his social assets. He values material goods only insofar as they serve this end' (Polanyi 1994/2001: 48).

One may doubt that man values material goods only in so far as they serve to 'safeguard his social standing, his social claims, his social assets'. Still, it is appropriate for economists to remind themselves that human economic activity takes place against a backdrop of social relationships— that social structure matters. Actors and institutions are, as Granovetter puts it, 'embedded' in a network of social relations. They 'are so constrained by ongoing socials relations that to construe them as independent is a grievous misunderstanding' (Granovetter 1985: 212). These arguments were put forward not only by Granovetter but also by Coleman (1984) or Burt (1983), Stinchcombe (1990), Abolafia (1984), and other sociologists.

The concept of 'social structure' is used by sociologists in a rather wide-ranging sense. Some authors, like Fligstein, include what may be called the elementary social order of an economy. Thus, Fligstein (2001: 32) speaks of 'four types of social structures' that make markets work: 'property rights, governance structures, rules of exchange, and conceptions of control'. Moreover, 'Each of these types of social structure is directed at different problems. Some are related to the general problem of creating a market in the first place, and others have to do with ensuring the stability of firms in a particular market' (Fligstein 2001: 33).

These are largely formal rules. Other authors use the term in the sense of specific social relationships between pairs of actors and their enduring (formal or informal) patterns given an elementary or even more specific (formal or informal) social order.[6] In this chapter, we discuss 'social structure' only in the second sense, which appears to be best conceptualized by social network analysis.[7] In fact, network analysis is sometimes described as a 'fundamental tool for the study of social structures' (Wellman and Berkowitz 1988: 4). We will therefore start with some of the basic concepts of network analysis.

---

[6] North (2005: 49) regards social structure as a system of norms and conventions, i.e. formal and informal rules.

[7] Rauch and Hamilton (2001: 21).

## 7.3. Some Basic Concepts of Social Network Analysis

A social network consists of actors, relational ties between pairs of actors, and attributes of actors (Wasserman and Faust 1994: 18–20). Actors may be individuals or groups of individuals (like organizations: firms, states, etc.). While the NIE is dominated by the assumption of methodological individualism, the NES remains open in this respect. So is neoclassical microeconomics where we are also used to speak of firms, households, etc., as specific actors.[8] Relational ties between two actors are any kind of 'social relationship' (Weber 1968: 26–8) that establishes 'a linkage between a pair of actors' (Wasserman and Faust 1994: 18). 'Social relationships' have a much wider meaning than the concept of economic 'transactions' between faceless actors does—like the arm's-length ordering of a product or of paying a bill. They are 'social actions' (Weber 1968: 22–3) that are characterized by

at least a minimum of mutual orientation of the action of each to that of the others. Its content may be of the most varied nature: conflict, hostility, sexual attraction, friendship, loyalty, or economic exchange. It may involve fulfilment, the evasion, or violation of the terms of an agreement; economic, erotic, or some other form of 'competition'; common membership in status, national or class groups.

(Weber 1968: 27)

Furthermore, social relationships relate to formal or informal social orders that actors may either observe or violate to varying degrees.[9]

As with regard to informal relations, the notion of 'strength' of an interpersonal tie plays an important role in the NES. Granovetter (1973: 1361) defines it as follows: 'the strength of a tie is a (probably linear) combination of the amount of time, the emotional intensity, the intimacy (mutual confiding), and the reciprocal services which characterize the tie.' Accordingly, he distinguishes between 'strong ties' and 'weak ties'. Put in concrete terms, 'ties' between prospective buyers and sellers may consist, for example, of already well-tried exchange opportunities with other actors[10] or only of hoped for trade relations.

Attributes of actors are, in the social network literature, measurements of the characteristics of actors such as 'age, gender, race, socio-economic status, place of residence, grade in school, and so on' (Wasserman and

---

[8] 'Delimiting the set of relevant nodes is notoriously difficult' (Zuckerman 2003: 547).
[9] '... may be guided by the belief in the existence of a legitimate order' (Weber 1968: 31).
[10] Cook et al. (1983: 377).

Faust 1994: 38). In the economic literature, the attributes of actors are understood in a much wider sense, including also hypotheses regarding actors' given individual preferences (sociologists oppose the neoclassical assumption of given preferences), choice constraints (i.e. their formal and informal property rights in valued resources, their state of information, their contractual or conventional obligations, and their institutional environment—all based on a given set of elementary constitutional rules), and choice behaviour (e.g. perfectly rational maximizing subject to constraints, boundedly rational choice behaviour, or some other kind of behaviour).[11]

In this sense, our economic models can be translated into 'economic network theories' consisting of actors, attributes of actors (including behavioural hypotheses), and relations between pairs of actors (based on a given set of elementary constitutional rules). Thus, a market can be understood as a system of network connections linking exchange relations into a single network structure (specifying the boundaries of a concrete networks).[12] However, the behavioural hypotheses of social network analysis are much wider than economists would assume: 'The network analyst would seek to model these relationships [the ties among actors] to depict the structure of a group [as a pattern of ties]. One could then study the impact of this structure on the functioning of the group and/or the influence of this structure on the individuals within the group' (Wasserman and Faust 1994: 9).

According to this interpretation, the patterns of ties within a social network have causal implications. In comparison to economics, the behavioural attributes of actors are extended by the assumption that actors are able to influence each other's individual preferences as well as their individual choice sets (the latter as in game theory), and that their capacity to do so depends on their location within the social network, their 'strategic position'. In this sense, social structure impinges on transfers between actors. In addition, sociological assumptions on individual choice behaviour are more comprehensive than in economics. In this respect, sociologists have a more ambitious research programme than economists. However, Zuckerman cautions,

---

[11] Based, e.g. on the principles of the classical liberal state: private property, freedom of contract, and individual liability (see e.g. Furubotn and Richter 2005: 15). Fligstein (1996: 657) criticizes the lack of such social institutions in network analysis.

[12] Although, often the actors would not be aware of those boundaries. Thus, participation in a network typically is not based on 'membership status'. Instead, actors can be viewed as relatively autonomous decision-makers occupying 'positions' in a structure which frequently extends beyond their own awareness (Cook et al. 1983: 379).

it bears recalling that, even among sociologists, there is really no such thing as social network theory as much as there is social network analysis—a set of frameworks and tools for analysing social structures. The great promise of social network analysis has been and continues to be its ability to give greater concreteness to sociological concepts that are relational in character.

(Zuckerman 2003: 562)

Still, as we shall see, sociologists want to provide more than a systematic description of what has actually happened. They also try to explain why, that is, they have some theory in the back of their mind.[13]

Social networks are conveniently described by graph theory. In a graph, actors are represented by nodes, relational ties between pairs of actors by (directed or undirected) lines between pairs of nodes (Wasserman and Faust 1994: 95). Directional ties are oriented from one actor to another; they are symbolized by a directional graph or digraph. Such a graphical representation of a social network is called a *sociogram*. It can also be expressed in matrix form, that is, as a *sociomatrix* (Wasserman and Faust 1994: 150–2). A social network without any hypotheses among the attributes of actors is a much less ambitious concept. However, it could be used only for descriptive purposes (or '*ex post* analysis')—like national accounting in economics. In fact, national accounts can be represented in the form of a sociogram or a sociomatrix.[14]

So much for the time being on social network analysis. Further treatment, provided it is required, will be given below together with the presentation of the literature on the social structure of markets.

## 7.4. On the Influence of the Social Structure of Markets on Market Performance: A Brief Survey of Some of the Sociological Literature

How do sociologists explain the effect of the social structure of markets on market performance? What are their key arguments? We content ourselves with a brief review of a selection of contributions on the role of social relationships between market actors which have appeared since

---

[13] Coleman (1984: 86) writes that the central intellectual problem in the social sciences is 'the problem of moving from a model of individual behavior to a system composed of these individuals, taking social organization explicitly into account, rather than assuming it away'.

[14] As a directed valued graph, i.e. as a digraph of which each arc carries a dollar-value (as, e.g. in Richter, Schlieper, and Friedmann 1981: ch. 3) or in form of a sociomatrix in which each entry records the dollar-amount of the respective debit and credit booking.

the 1970s, namely, Granovetter (1974, 1985), Burt (1983, 1992), Abolafia (1984), Baker (1984), and Podolny (1993).[15] All studies relate to a private ownership economy and there again to what we call elsewhere the operational rules of the market (Furubotn and Richter 2005: 295). They concern the market participants' transaction activities of search, inspection, contracting, execution, control, and enforcement. We take these as measures of market performance and indicate at the beginning of each paper's review to which of the above six transaction activities (as measures of market performance) it is addressed.

### 7.4.1. M. Granovetter

Granovetter deals in his empirical study 'Getting a Job' with the transaction activity of search, namely, job search of professional technical and managerial workers. In his sample, personal contact is the predominant method of finding out about jobs. Thus, the relevant factors of finding a job would be social. Job finding behaviour is 'heavily embedded in other social processes that closely constrain and determine its course and results' (1974/1995: 39). Of those people finding a job through contacts, the majority saw their contact only occasionally or rarely, that is, were only weakly tied with their contacts. To Granovetter's surprise, the 'social distance' was rather short between job seeker and prospective employer.[16] In almost 40 per cent of the cases information came directly from the prospective employer, whom the respondent already knew; in about 45 per cent of the cases there was one intermediate, 12.4 per cent reported two; only about 3 per cent more than two ($N = 64$, Granovetter 1973: 1372). Granovetter concedes that many of his findings are easily explained in terms of rational behaviour. The reason is that information is costly (Granovetter 1974/1995: 96–9). But also the quality of the information may explain why employers and employees prefer to make use of personal contacts in securing labour market information: 'They reason, correctly, that personal ties mean better information' (Granovetter 1974/1995: 97). 'Better' meaning, that is, better filtered information. 'Personal contacts narrow the range within this already narrowed group, and so do cost less than other methods' (Granovetter 1974/1995: 98).

[15] We disregard social bargaining issues and, thus, problems of what economists call 'bargaining power'. They are dealt with, i.e. by Cook and Emerson (1978), Cook et al. (1983), and Markovsky, Willer, and Patton (1988).

[16] Granovetter (1973: 1366, n. 10) defines the 'social distance' between two individuals in a network as the number of lines in the shortest path from one to another. This would be the same as the definition of 'distance' between points in graph theory.

It thus pays for both, employee and employer of professional technical and managerial workers, to maintain 'weak ties' with prospective employers directly or through one or two intermediaries. The logic is simple. Had long information paths been involved, large numbers might have found out about any given job, and no particular tie would have been crucial (Granovetter 1973: 1372). However, 'You can't get somethin' for nothin'! To build (weak) connections with the right people requires time and material resources. Personal entry costs may be high, depending on one's social status, which may be inherited or acquired by an expensive education. The real world market is apparently not the great equalizer— at least not for 'professional technical and managerial workers'. Empirical examples would be of interest.

Granovetter's paper on the problem of embeddedness is aimed at the whole set of transaction activities (1985): search, inspection, contracting, execution, control, and enforcement. It concerns basically the problem of the production of *trust*. In contrast to new institutional economists, Granovetter argues that social relations, not institutional arrangements, would be mainly responsible for the production of trust in economic life. His argument is directed against what Williamson (1996: 256–67) later called 'calculative trust'. Malfeasance would be seen by new institutional economists to be averted because clever institutional arrangements or safeguards make it too costly to engage in (Granovetter 1974/1995: 218).

However, this could hardly be called 'trust', because if one thinks this out consequently one comes to a bottomless process of rational individuals ever thinking up new clever ways to evade one institutional safeguard after another. In such a world, everyday economic life would be poisoned 'by ever more ingenious attempts at deceit' (Granovetter 1974/1995: 218). Thus 'some degree of trust *must* be assumed to operate'. Needed would be an explanation of a brake mechanism for evermore ingenious attempts at deceit.[17] Appealed would be sometimes to the existence of a basic or generalized trust.[18] It would be hard to doubt the existence of some such generalized morality. However, it would refer only to situations like leaving a tip at a roadside restaurant far from home.[19]

---

[17] Aside from the braking action of transaction costs.

[18] Granovetter quotes a well-known passage by Arrow (1974: 26).

[19] Or the use of money? Thus Simmel (1978: 178–9) writes, 'Without general trust that people have in each other, society itself would disintegrate, for very few relationships are based entirely upon what is known with certainty about another person, and very few relationships would endure if trust were not as strong as, or stronger than, rational proof of personal observation. In the same way, money transactions without trust would collapse.'

Granovetter's embeddedness suggests another brake mechanism of deceit: 'the role of concrete personal relations and structures (or "networks") of such relations in generating trust and discouraging malfeasance' (1974/1995: 220). Standard economic theory would neglect the identity and past relations of individual transactors, 'but rational individuals know better, relying on their knowledge of these relations. They are less interested in general reputations than in whether a particular other may be expected to deal honestly with them—mainly a function of whether they or their own contacts have had satisfactory past dealings with the other' (Granovetter 1974/1995: 221).

As a solution to the problem of order, the embeddedness position (the assumption of networks of relations) would be less sweeping than the 'institutional arrangement' or the 'general trust' position, '... since networks of social relations penetrate irregularly and in different degrees in different sectors of economic life, thus allowing for what we already know: distrust, opportunism, and disorder are by no means absent' (Granovetter 1974/1995: 221). Social relations are not sufficient to guarantee trust and trustworthy behaviour, 'they may even provide occasion and means for malfeasance and conflict on a scale larger than in their absence'. Examples are 'confidence' rackets, crimes such as embezzling, fraud pursued by teams like schemes for kickbacks. 'Both enormous trust and enormous malfeasance, ... may follow from personal relations' (Granovetter 1974/1995: 222).[20]

To this author's understanding, the problem of *ex ante* safeguards against *ex post* opportunism lurks behind both explanations of the production of trust or trustworthiness related to economic activities: institutional arrangements and social relations. Trust would be calculable in both cases. Both relate to problems of social order (i.e. systems of social rules): the neo-institutional approach assumes in Granovetter's reading *ex ante* agreed-upon explicit rules, viewed as 'the efficient solution to certain economic problems' (Granovetter 1974/1995: 218); the embeddedness approach supposes—in addition to explicit rules—the evolution of implicit rules, namely, 'concrete personal relations and structures of such relations' (Granovetter 1974/1995: 220). In both cases, trust would be calculative, and in both it would be wise to think about *ex ante*

---

[20] For an extension of Granovetter's embeddedness hypothesis, see, e.g. Uzzi (1996) who shows that firms organized in networks have higher survival chances than do firms that maintain arm's-length market relationships.

safeguards against *ex post* opportunism. Basically, Granovetter deals with the same kind of problems as Williamson, though, in a richer and more general way.

Taken at its face value, Granovetter's combative paper reads as an attack on the evolving NIE in general, on Williamson's 'Markets and Hierarchies' book (1975) in particular.[21] Under its surface, however, it is more of a wake-up call for sociologists whom he warns to keep an eye on new economic institutionalists invading sociologists own territory. If sociologists would avoid the analysis of phenomena at the centre of 'standard economic theory', then they would 'have unnecessarily cut themselves off from a large and important aspect of social life and from European tradition—stemming especially from Max Weber—in which economic action is seen only as a special, if important, category of social action' (Granovetter 1974/1995: 237). Granovetter's wake-up call turned out to be quite successful. After decades of neglect, economic sociology came alive again (Smelser and Swedberg 2005: 14–16).

### 7.4.2. R. S. Burt

Burt (1992) deals in his book *Structural Holes: The Social Structure of Competition* with the transaction activities of 'information' comprising in a wider sense what we called 'search and inspection' and 'control' what we would subsume under 'contracting'.[22] He views markets as networks of social contacts between actors and assumes the existence of positive transaction costs. Competition is the struggle of actors for profitable positions within market networks. Competitors profit from 'information benefits' and 'control benefits'. Information benefits result from access to valuable pieces of information and knowing whom to bring it to; from timing in the sense of being informed early; and from referrals to players 'you do not know personally but are aware of you' (Burt 1992: 13–14). Control benefits consist of the advantages of players in negotiating their relationship (Burt 1992: 47) like the 'tertius gaudens' position in a negotiation between two others (Burt 1992: 31).

We interpret Burt's concept of structural holes as follows: assume markets to be clusters of networks of traders. They can be represented in the

---

[21] I deal with sociologists' attack on Williamson's work and his defence elsewhere (Richter 2001).

[22] Including information about new opportunities like 'new institutions and projects that need leadership, new funding initiatives looking for proposals, new jobs for which you know of a good candidate, valuable items entering the market for which you know interested buyers' (Burt 1992: 13).

shape of a disconnected graph of redundant contacts between players (e.g. Burt 1992: 27, fig. 1.6). It follows: 'One cluster, no matter how numerous its members, is only one source of information, because people connected to one another tend to know about the same things at about the same time' (Burt 1992: 23). Assume there exist three of such market clusters. A profit seeking new competitor ('you') would not locate himself 'within' one of the already existing three clusters but instead somewhere in the 'open' space between the clusters and from there try to establish non-redundant contacts with one trader of each cluster. That would enable him to obtain, so to speak, at one stroke all available information of the three market networks (Burt 1992: 22, fig. 1.4).

The information screen provided by multiple clusters of contacts is broader, providing better insurance that you, the player, will be informed of opportunities and impending disasters. . . . you are assured of being the first to see new opportunities created by needs in one group that could be served by skills in another group. You become the person who first brings people together, which gives you the opportunity to coordinate their activities.

(Burt 1992: 23)

In Burt's terminology, structural holes between the above three clusters are 'bridged' by the non-redundant contacts that 'you' (or any other competitor) entertain with at least one actor in each of the clusters. Bridges may consist of strong or weak ties (or anything in between). Information benefits travel over all bridges, strong or weak ones (Burt 1992: 17, fig. 1.6); weak ties may be even more effective in this respect than strong ones as Granovetter (1973) has shown. Control benefits, on the other hand, require strong ties (Burt 1992: 28). In general, the task for a strategic player trying to build an 'efficient-effective' network would be 'to focus resources on the maintenance of bridge ties' (Burt 1992: 30).

Burt defines 'social capital' as consisting of the social relationship between two players (1992: 8–10).[23] Social capital offers actors opportunities to use their financial and human capital profitably and, thus, contributes to their individual wealth (the present value of their expected net-income streams). The formation of social capital—as of any other kind of

---

[23] Social capital is a factor 'as routinely critical as financial and human capital' (Burt 1992: 59). Note the expanding literature on social capital, cf. Sobel (2002), and the definition by Bourdieu (1986), as quoted by Sobel (2002: 139), 'Social capital is an attribute of an individual in a social context. One can acquire social capital through purposeful actions and can transform social capital into conventional economic gains. The ability to do so depends on the nature of the social obligations, connections, and networks available to you.' For an early definition, see also Coleman (1988).

capital—requires the input of real resources (i.e. investments in 'relation-specific assets'). However, in contrast to financial or human capital, social capital is jointly owned by the parties to the relationship. No actor (of the relationship) has the exclusive ownership rights to 'his' social capital (Burt 1992: 58). Thus, who gets how much profits out of his investments in relation-specific assets depends on the social quality of the relationship; in the case of typical business relationships, it would be a matter of contracting between the parties. In any case, however, problems of *ex post* opportunism or freeriding are to be expected and the question is to be asked: Why should I invest in social capital if the fruits of my investments may be reaped by others? Williamson's problem of *ex ante* safeguards against *ex post* opportunism reappears in generalized form, relating to specific investments into all kinds of social relationships, from strong ties to weak personal acquaintances. Burt does not go into the details of related safeguarding issues. However, he confirms that the governance structures of relationships matter by referring to the 'powerful complementarities' between Williamson's transaction cost economic reasoning and his structural hole argument (Burt 1992: 240). Another question Burt does not touch upon is: To what extend is the firm value of an intermediary firm in a two-sided market equivalent to Burt's concept of social capital?[24] How does a merger affect such intermediary firms social welfare?

### 7.4.3. M. Abolafia

Abolafia (1984) addresses in his chapter on 'Structured Anarchy: Formal Organization in the Commodity Futures Market' essentially all major types of transaction activities: search, inspection, contracting, execution, control, and enforcement, however, in particular the activities of search and contracting. Object is the open auction (double auction) of commodity futures held in 'pits' where buyers and sellers stand facing each other in a multi-tiered ring: 'At the opening bell traders begin making offers to buy or sell. They use hand signals and strong voices to offer and accept trades across the pit. These trades are recorded by each party to the trade. Trading does not stop after each transaction. It continues this way . . . until the closing bell rings in the afternoon' (Abolafia 1984: 132–3).

To economists such gatherings of buyers and sellers would be the representation of a perfectly competitive market. While economists are interested only in the resulting equilibrium price(s), sociologists focus on

---

[24] The provider of a dating club, of computer-operating system makers, video game manufacturers, etc. On general economics of two-sided markets Rochet and Tirole (2003).

the context of all this dramatic action. In fact, what seemed to be near anarchy is steered by a coordination and control system whose task is 'to discover problems in the pit (e.g. under-capitalized traders or market concentration) and taking whatever corrective action necessary to protect market efficiency' (Abolafia 1984: 147). Thus, 'commodity exchanges exercise the monopoly power of cartels in the midst of this otherwise classical competitive industry' (Abolafia 1984: 131). Abolafia argues that this paradox is a central feature in the social organization of all markets. Markets are in effect a coalition of economic actors who compete with each other (as buyers and sellers) subject to an agreed-upon system of 'informal norms among traders, formal rules of trade and organizational arrangements to coordinate collective action' (Abolafia 1984: 132). The implication is that 'competitive markets do not emerge and maintain themselves "naturally"'.

Abolafia's paradox that traders are both fiercely competing with each other and mutually dependent is an interesting issue.[25] It plays an important role in all kinds of markets, also in developing markets like those in the field of information technology illustrated by Saxenian in her Silicon Valley study: 'Even under relentless competitive pressure, an underlying loyalty and shared commitment to technological excellence unified members of the industrial community. Local firms both competed for market share and technical leadership and simultaneously relied on the collaborative practices that distinguished the region. The paradox of Silicon Valley was that competition demanded continuous innovation, which in turn required cooperation among firms' (Saxenian (1994: 46). Thus, contrary to a much-quoted remark by Adam Smith,[26] it may be (or in fact is) socially useful that market participants know each other and tend their contacts (Granovetter 1973; Podolny and Page 1998: 59).

### 7.4.4. W. E. Baker

Baker (1984) concerns himself mainly with the two transaction activities of 'search' and 'contracting' in his paper on 'The Social Structure of a National Security Market'. He demonstrates that the social structure of actors matters even in such highly organized markets as security

[25] As Adler and Adler (1984: 197) put it: 'the formal market structure is supplemented and occasionally subverted by an informal social structure or network of roles, relationships and social organization'.

[26] Adam Smith (1776/1976: 27), 'People of the same trade seldom meet together, even for merriment and diversion, but the conversation ends in a conspiracy against the publick, or in some contrivance to raise prices.'

exchanges. It influences price volatility. The type of markets analysed by Baker reminds an economist of the well-known double-auction market experiment described by Vernon Smith (1962). However, it differs in three respects, as follows. Positive transaction costs hamper communication between traders: 'Noise and physical separation of potential trading partners are... major impediments to the efficient communication of offers to buy and sell. Furthermore,... a floor participant is not able to survey all potential partners to the trade. Searching for all alternatives is a costly process' (Baker 1984: 778–9).[27] Traders are allowed to act as speculators (market makers), that is, to buy and sell for their own account during a trading period.[28] Therefore, opportunistic behaviour (like fictitious trading) is possible and has to be allowed for by market makers.

Because of positive transaction costs, even a well-organized stock option market will be socially structured (Baker 1984: 778).[29] The more traders, that is, the greater the 'crowd' size,[30] the more difficult (costly) for traders to search the 'other side' to find the final price.[31] As a consequence, option market performance will be impaired; price volatility and, thus, price uncertainty increase. Opportunism becomes more of a problem (Lebleici and Salanick 1982). Social structure matters. Baker concludes, 'Limiting the size of crowds might be an effective... way to dampen price volatility' (Baker 1984: 807) and, thus, to reduce the risk of holding a position in an underlying stock market (Baker 1984: 808).

We know from market experiments in the style of Vernon Smith's (1962) that we need neither large numbers of traders nor complete information of traders to have the market price converge to its competitive equilibrium level.[32] All traders need to know, besides the quality of their traded good, the prices at which the good is currently exchanged during the trading period. Given the rapid progress of information technology during the past twenty-five years since the publication of Baker's article, traders may now get all the price information they need with the speed

---

[27] Baker avoids this term in the description of his approach, but nevertheless uses it in some connection towards the end of his paper (Baker 1984: 806).

[28] A 'market maker' is a professional speculator, trading for his own account. He is not permitted to act as a broker (Baker 1984: 789).

[29] Even when the high transaction costs of floor trading would be eliminated by replacing it with electronic trading, the latter would also become subject to bounded rationality and opportunism (Baker 1984: 806).

[30] A 'crowd' is the aggregate of buyers and sellers of options on a particular underlying stock (Baker 1984: 776).

[31] The density of ties between traders decreases with increasing crowd size.

[32] Four traders on each side sufficed in an experiment by Holt, Langan, and Villamil (1986).

of light. However, what remains is the opportunism problem faced by market makers. There is no information technical way out; market makers have to trust their trading contacts.[33] The conservative way to cope with this problem is the establishment of personal relationships.

### 7.4.5. J. M. Podolny

Podolny (1993) deals in his article 'A Status-based Model of Market Competition' with the two transaction activities 'search' and 'inspection' given positive transaction costs.[34] His analysis aims at, what economists call, qualitative competition among experience goods.[35] Product quality is signalled by producer's status in the market. Podolny defines 'a producer's status in the market as the perceived quality of that producer's products in relation to the perceived quality of that producer's competitors' products' (Podolny 1993: 830). Different from Weber (1968) or Veblen (1953), status is viewed as a signal of the underlying quality of a firm's product (Podolny 1993: 831). Social relations mediate the link between quality and status. What exists and what is being expected may not correspond. There is only a loose linkage between a signal and that which it is supposed to represent. In other words, quality shifts need not to be realized immediately by consumers.

Lags between quality shifts and its perception by consumers are not only caused by technical impediments but, to a degree, also caused by the affiliations of consumers to social networks of brand users like 'Mercedes drivers' or 'BMW users'. The status position of brand users would be analytically irrelevant if quality shifts were recognized immediately: 'However, the greater the decoupling, the more the status position insulates and circumscribes the producer's action and the more the producer's reputation becomes external to itself. In short, due to the loose linkage of quality and status, a niche emerges as a given constraint that the producer must confront in trying to decide upon an optimal course of action' (Podolny 1993: 835).[36] As a result, high-status firms may have to stop producing, despite marginal costs that are well below market price, because 'status provides severe constraints on production decisions. Recognizing

[33] This is not analysed in the Vernon Smith market experiment. Capital or asset market experiments deal with the problem of informational efficiency of markets (Sunder 1995). They are not dealing with the problem of opportunism in the sense of trading abuses.
[34] Although he mentions the term 'transaction costs' only in passing (Podolny 1993: 838).
[35] Podolny states, 'quality is, by definition, unobservable before the transaction' (Podolny 1993: 834).
[36] For economists, a case of monopolistic competition à la Chamberlin (1933).

that profitability is bound to identity, producers halt production before it reaches a level that threatens that identity' (Podolny 1993: 847). In fact, that is a case of monopolistic competition. Producers charge monopoly prices.

The core of Podolny's model is formed by three assumptions which are coupled with the implicit behavioural assumption that producers are boundedly rational profit maximizers: consumers cannot observe the quality of a product prior to consummation ('experience good'). Market status of a producer is a signal of quality on which consumers can and do rely for their decisions. A producer's relations with others in the market mediate the relationship between status and quality. They create inertial tendencies in the formation of exchange relations (i.e. ties between actors) by biasing evaluation of the products (Podolny 1993: 835).

The economic consequence of a producer's position in the market network is that it affects his gross revenue and costs: 'For a producer of a given level of quality, additional status is most likely to translate into increased revenue, either in form of higher prices or greater market share' (Podolny 1993: 837). Consumers will be more reluctant to enter into a transaction with a low-status producer than they would be with a high-status producer even if both claim to manufacture the same quality good and sell it for the same price. Empirically, this manifests itself in several cost advantages for the high-status producer. Thus, for higher-status producers, advertising costs for attracting a given volume of business are lower (Podolny 1993: 838). The same can be said for 'transaction costs' in the sense of convincing customers of the quality of the product and for credit costs (Podolny 1993: 838). Finally, financial costs are lowered also by an increase in status (Podolny 1993: 839). In short, 'the costs for a given quality output will be lower for the higher-status producer than the lower-status producer' (Podolny 1993: 840). The status of a firm is not fixed. Firms can shift their status position within a market. Further, multi-market identity would be not inconsistent with the dynamics of a status-based model. The incorporation of status processes into the understanding of market competition would provide considerable ground for the development and an extension of a sociological approach to markets (Podolny 1993: 868).

Podolny (1993) has used networks as a cause and consequence of the creation of a market status hierarchy. He supplements Burt's interpretation of competition as a struggle of actors for profitable positions within a market network by adding the advantages of 'status improvements' to Burt's 'information benefits' and 'control benefits'. As a result, Podolny's considerations pour quite a bit of water onto the theory of reputation equilibrium as applied by economists (e.g. Klein and Leffler, 1981; Shapiro 1983). He could have attacked it as following: if status and product quality (of experience goods) are loosely linked and if producers' market status can be cultivated by other means than only costly quality improvements, then producers of a 'status-prone culture' may find it more profitable to invest in the promotion of their market status instead of in quality improvements of their products. But would not producers of high-quality products win in the long run? Not necessarily. In the long term, a reputation equilibrium makes sense only if understood as a moving equilibrium. It may contain a long-term quality growth rate of any size. If status and product quality are only loosely linked, then a moving reputation equilibrium could include a quality growth path with a low growth rate. In a status-prone society, producers may find it more profitable to invest in other means of status improvements than in the development of their product quality.[37] As a consequence, producers' long-term reputation equilibrium may move on a rather low product quality growth path. Producers' cultural beliefs in the role of status, their particular 'status culture', become an issue.[38]

## 7.5. What Institutional Economists Can Learn from Market Structure Sociology

Basically, we learned two things: first, we acquired a wealth of examples of informal norm systems (informal institutions) in addition to the previous state of knowledge of institutional economists (for market theory summarized, e.g. in Furubotn and Richter 2005: ch. 7). Second, we explored the instrument of social network analysis and its application to market issues. All our above described examples relate to network analysis.

To summarize, markets are more than abstract systems of formal norms. Personal relationships, which can be described as networks of informal relational ties between market actors (traders), affect market performance.

---

[37] The family of moving reputation equilibrium paths may be understood as a set of multiple Nash equilibria characterized by different long-term product quality growth rates. Competitors implicitly agree to choose that reputation equilibrium path that contains the focal product quality growth rate ('focal' in the sense of Schelling 1960). Its size depends on cultural beliefs of actors.

[38] Another problem is that each brand may have several status levels. Thus, General Motors sought to establish a hierarchy of brands—Chevrolet, Pontiac, Oldsmobile, Buick, LaSalle, and Cadillac. There was, however, overlapping between brands. For example a high-level Oldsmobile could possess more status than a low-level Buick did.

Traders themselves are more or less heavily embedded in a more general social network, like the local, national, or global society, economy, and the polity. Ties between actors may be anything between strong and weak relationships (e.g. historically developed exchange opportunities on the one side, passing acquaintances on the other). Cultivating weak ties is not without value. They transmit, besides white noise, profitable information, as about better paid or more interesting jobs, promising inventions, scientific insights, etc. On the other hand, a dense network of strong ties facilitates the emergence of mutual trust among members of the network. Generally, long-term network relationships between economic actors ease local and global trade. Finally, exchange networks are both difficult to build and to demolish. To destroy them by war or revolution takes more than ten or fifteen years, as is illustrated by the German *Wirtschaftswunder* since 1948 in comparison with the slow adaptation of the East German economy to West Germany after German reunification of 1990.[39]

Social structure—the pattern of ties among actors—helps ease the burden of personal uncertainty, information complexity, and limited rationality of actors. It influences individual preferences. The density of ties, structural holes, and prestige or status of actors matters. More novel information flows more likely through weak than through strong ties. Additional status is most likely to translate into increased revenue. Competition consists in competing for social positioning, it is less a matter of numbers. A new actor entering an already existing market faces the challenge of positioning himself among already established actors. He enjoys a strategic advantage if he positions himself in a structural hole. Building links with other actors requires sunk investments in social relationships, that is, the formation of social capital.

The apparent anarchy among real life actors, who trade under conditions close to perfect competition, is socially structured. It leads to a market equilibrium provided actors strictly observe their formal market order. Actors are interested in the continued existence of their markets and tend

---

[39] As for the German *Wirtschaftswunder*, much of the pre-1933 global personal and business connections still existed or were easily revived in 1948. Big West German corporations like Mercedes, Siemens, Bosch, and Leitz—as well as West German small- and medium-sized firms and their networks of national and international contacts still existed. On the other hand, East Germany had lost all of its old firms and business contacts by 1990. It had to start virtually from scratch. Rauch (2001) surveys modern sociological literature on business and social networks in international trade, though, without touching upon the causes for the smooth and fast reintegration of the West German economy into international trade after the Second World War.

to establish, administer, and enforce the order of markets themselves. As a result, fierce competition and cooperation of traders go together—a paradox observed not only in an organized exchange but also in developing markets. Traders concentrate their trade among a few counterparties even in a formally well-organized exchange.

To our judgement, 'network imagery and methodology' became the eye-opening insight of market structure sociology.[40] Since the early 1990s, it has been taken up by an increasing number of economists—among them Schmidt-Trenz (1990), Greif (1993), Rauch and Casella (1998), Kranton (1996), and Kali (1999).[41] Forecasting models need to be based on more than formal market orders or formal contractual governance structures. They also need to take into account the social organization of actors, that is, their integration into the prevailing social network, to become 'sufficiently good approximations for the purpose in hand' (Friedman 1953).[42]

As a result, we defined the 'market' in our new edition of Furubotn and Richter (2005: 315) as a social network consisting of (*a*) a set of actors who maintain customer relationships with each other and (*b*) a 'legitimate order' (Weber 1968) or 'governance structure' (Williamson 1985), which controls the transactions between market actors. The common goal of market actors is to lower transaction costs and thus reach a higher level of individual utility. The social relations between actors and their order or governance structures are of economic value to them and make up their 'market-specific social capital'. This is 'produced' by the market participants' input of real resource-specific (sunk) investments into their relationships with other actors.

## References

Adler, P. A. and Adler, P. (1984). 'Toward a Sociology of Financial Markets', in P. A. Adler and P. Adler (eds.), *The Social Dynamics of Financial Markets*. Greenwich, CN: JAI Press.

Abolafia, M. Y. (1984). 'Structural Anarchy: Formal Organization in the Commodity Futures Markets', in P. A. Adler and P. Adler (eds.), *The Social Structure of Financial Markets*. Greenwich, CN: JAI Press.

Arrow, K. J. (1974). *The Limits of Organization*. New York: Norton.

Baker, W. E. (1984). 'The Social Structure of a Securities Market', *American Journal of Sociology*, 89: 775–811.

---

[40] Baron and Hannan (1994: 1142).     [41] See Rauch and Hamilton (2001: 4).
[42] Instead of assuming it away, cf. Coleman (1984: 86).

Baron, J. N. and Hannan, M. T. (1994). 'The Impact of Economics on Contemporary Sociology', *Journal of Economic Literature*, 32: 1111–46.

Bourdieu, P. (1986). 'Forms of Capital', in J. G. Richardson (ed.), *Handbook of Theory and Research for the Sociology of Education*. Westport, CT: Greenwood Press.

Burt, R. S. (1983). *Corporate Profits and Cooptation. Networks of Market Constraints and Directorate Ties in the American Economy*. New York: Academic Press.

——(1992). *Structural Holes: The Social Structure of Competition*. Cambridge, MA: Harvard University Press.

Chamberlin, E. H. (1933). *The Theory of Monopolistic Competition. A Reorientation of the Theory of Value*. Cambridge, MA: Harvard University Press.

Coleman, J. S. (1984). 'Introducing Social Structure into Economic Analysis', *American Economic Review*, Papers and Proceedings, vol. 74, pp. 84–8.

——(1988). 'Social Capital in the Creation of Human Capital', *American Journal of Sociology*, 94: 95–120.

Cook, K. S. and Emerson, R. M. (1978). 'Power, Equity and Commitment in Exchange Networks', *American Sociological Review*, 43: 721–39.

——— Gillmore, M. R., and Yamagishi, T. (1983). 'The Distribution of Power in Exchange Networks: Theory and Experimental Results', *American Journal of Sociology*, 89: 275–305.

Eccles, R. G. (1981). 'The Quasi Firm in the Construction Industry', *Journal of Economic Behavior and Organization*, 2: 335–57.

Fligstein, N. (1996). 'Markets as Politics: A Political Cultural Approach to Market Institutions', *American Sociological Review*, 61: 656–73.

——(2001). *The Architecture of Markets. An Economic Sociology of Twenty-First-Century Capitalist Societies*. Princeton, NJ: Princeton University Press.

Friedman, M. (1953). *Essays in Positive Economics*. Chicago, IL: University of Chicago Press.

Furubotn, E. G. and Richter, R. (2005). *Institutions and Economic Theory: An Introduction to and Assessment of the New Institutional Economics*, 2nd edn. Ann Arbor: University of Michigan Press.

Granovetter, M. (1973). 'The Strength of Weak Ties', *American Journal of Sociology*, 78: 1360–80.

——(1974/1995). *Getting A Job. A Study of Contacts and Careers*, 2nd edn. Chicago, IL: University of Chicago Press.

——(1985). 'Economic Action and Social Structure: The Problem of Embeddedness', *American Journal of Sociology*, 91: 481–510.

Greif, A. (1993). 'Contract Enforceability and Economic Institutions in Early Trade: The Maghribi Traders' Coalition', *American Economic Review*, 83: 525–48.

Hamilton, G. G. and Feenstra, R. C. (1995). 'Varieties of Hierarchies and Markets: An Introduction', *Industrial and Corporate Change*, 4: 51–91.

Hayek, F. A. (1973). *Law, Legislation, and Liberty*, vol. 1. Chicago, IL.: University of Chicago Press.

Holt, C. A., Langan, L., and Villamil, A. (1986). 'Market Power in Oral Double Auctions', *Economic Inquiry*, 24: 107–23.

Hume, D. (1739–40/1969). *A Treatise of Human Nature*. London: Penguin Books.

Kali, R. (1999). 'Endogenous Business Networks', *Journal of Law, Economics and Organization*, 15: 615–36.

Klein, B. and Leffler, K. B. (1981). 'The Role of Market Forces in Assuring Contractual Performance', *Journal of Political Economy*, 89: 615–41.

Kranton, R. E. (1996). 'Reciprocal Exchange: A Self-Sustaining System', *American Economic Review*, 86: 830–51.

Lebleici, H. and Salanick, G. R. (1982). 'Stability in Interorganizational Exchanges: Rulemaking Processes of the Chicago Board of Trade', *Administrative Science Quarterly*, 27: 227–42.

Markovsky, B., Willer, D., and Patton, T. (1988). 'Power Relations in Exchange Networks', *American Sociological Review*, 53: 220–36.

Menger, C. (1883/1963). *Problems of Economics and Sociology*, trans. by F. J. Nock from the German edition of 1883, edited by L. Schneider. Urbana: University of Illinois Press.

North, D. C. (1990). 'A Transaction Cost Theory of Politics', *Journal of Theoretical Politics*, 2: 355–67.

——(2005). *Understanding the Process of Economic Change*. Princeton, NJ: Princeton University Press.

Podolny, J. M. (1993). 'A Status-Based Model of Market Competition', *American Journal of Sociology*, 98: 829–72.

——and Page, K. L. (1998). 'Network Forms of Organization', *Annual Review of Sociology*, 24: 57–76.

Polanyi, K. (1944/2001). *The Great Transformation. The Political and Economic Origins of Our Time*, foreword by Joseph E. Stiglitz, introduction by Fred Block. Boston, MA: Beacon Press.

Rauch, J. E. (2001). 'Business and Social Networks in International Trade', *Journal of Economic Literature*, 39: 1177–203.

——and Casella, A. (1998). 'Overcoming Informational Barriers to International Resource Allocation: Prices and Group Ties', NBER Working Paper 6628. Cambridge, MA: National Bureau of Economic Research.

——and Hamilton, G. (2001). 'Networks and Markets: Concepts for Bridging Disciplines', in J. E. Rauch and A. Casella (eds.), *Networks and Markets*. New York: Russell Sage.

Richter, K. (2005). *Die Geschichte des frühen deutschen Kartellrechts als Rechtswirkungsgeschichte. Ein institutionenökonomischer Ansatz*. Habilitationsschrift, Berlin: Law Faculty of the Humboldt University.

Richter, R. (2001). 'New Economic Sociology and New Institutional Economics', paper presented at the 2001 Conference of the International Society for New Institutional Economics (ISNIE) at Berkeley, CA. http://mpra.ub.uni-muenchen.de/4747/

Richter, R. (2005). 'The New Institutional Economics: Its Start, Its Meaning, Its Prospects', *The European Business Organization Law Review*, 6: 161–200.

—— (2008). 'The Attack of New Economic Sociologists on Oliver Williamson's Transaction Cost Economics', in J. G. March and D. J. Teece (eds.), *Festschrift for Oliver Williamson* (forthcoming).

—— Schlieper, U., and Friedmann, W. (1981). *Makroökonomik. Eine Einführung*, 4th edn. Berlin: Springer.

Rochet, J.-Ch. and Tirole, J. (2003). 'Platform Competition in Two-Sided Markets', *Journal of the European Economic Association*, 14: 990–1029.

Saxenian, A. (1994). *Regional Advantage. Culture and Competition in Silicon Valley and Route 128*. Cambridge, MA: Harvard University Press.

Schelling, T. C. (1960). *The Strategy of Conflict*. Cambridge, MA: Harvard University Press.

Schmidt-Trenz, H.-J. (1990). *Außenhandel und Territorialität des Rechts: Grundlegung einer Neuen Institutionenökonomik des Außenhandels*. Baden-Baden: Nomos.

Shapiro, C. (1983). 'Premiums for High Quality Products as Returns to Reputations', *Quarterly Journal of Economics*, 97: 659–79.

Shapiro, S. P. (1984). *Wayward Capitalists: Target of the Securities and Exchange Commission*. New Haven, CT: Yale University Press.

Simmel, G. (1978). *The Philosophy of Money*, trans. by T. Bottomore and D. Frisby. London: Routledge and Kegan Paul.

Smelser, N. J. and Swedberg, R. (2005). 'Introducing Economic Sociology', in N. J. Smelser and R. Swedberg (eds.), *The Handbook of Economic Sociology*, 2nd edn. Princeton, NJ: Princeton University Press.

Smith, A. (1776/1976). *An Inquiry into the Nature and Causes of the Wealth of Nations*, vol. 1, edited by R. H. Campbell and A. S. Skinner, textual editor W. B. Todd. Oxford: Clarendon Press.

Smith, V. (1962). 'An Experimental Study of Competitive Market Behavior', *Journal of Political Economy*, 70: 111–37.

Sobel, J. (2002). 'Can We Trust Social Capital?', *Journal of Economic Literature*, 40: 139–54.

Stinchcombe, A. (1990). *Information and Organization*. Berkeley: University of California Press.

Sunder, S. (1995). 'Experimental Asset Markets: A Survey', in J. H. Kagel and A. E. Roth (eds.), *The Handbook of Experimental Economics*. Princeton, NJ: Princeton University Press.

Uzzi, B. (1996). 'The Sources and Consequences of Embeddedness for the Economic Performance of Organizations: The Network Effect', *American Sociological Review*, 61: 674–98.

Veblen, T. (1953). *The Theory of Leisure Class*. New York: New American Library.

Wasserman, S. and Faust, K. (1994). *Social Network Analysis: Methods and Applications*. Cambridge: Cambridge University Press.

Weber, M. (1968). *Economy and Society: An Outline of Interpretative Sociology*, ed. by G. Roth and C. Wittich. Berkeley: University of California Press.

Williamson, O. E. (1975). *Markets and Hierarchies*. New York: Free Press.

——(1985). *The Economic Institutions of Capitalism*. New York: Free Press.

——(1996). *The Mechanisms of Governance*. New York: Oxford University Press.

Zelizer, V. A. (1983). *Morals and Markets: The Development of Life Insurance in the United States*. New Brunswick: Springer.

Zuckerman, E. W. (2003). 'On *Networks and Markets* by Rauch and Casella, eds.', *Journal of Economic Literature*, 41: 545–65.

# 8

# Institutional Entrepreneurship and the Structuring of Organizations and Markets

*Peter Walgenbach and Renate E. Meyer*

## 8.1. Introduction

As many critics of organizational institutionalism have argued, the early publications of this approach presented organizations as social entities which adapted without much hesitance to expectations in their institutional environments (DiMaggio and Powell 1983; Meyer and Rowan 1977). Organizations were portrayed as passive social units which reflect rationalized and institutionalized rules of organizing and managing (Oliver 1991). Strategies, such as resistance, opposition, intervention, or manipulation, implemented in order to countervail institutionalization processes or to avoid pressure from external stakeholders to adopt a certain structural element or management practice were not addressed. Similarly, strategies aimed at identifying and institutionalizing alternatives in society, which are beneficial for the organization or a group of organizations, were not discussed (Hirsch and Lounsbury 1997).

A major problem that resulted from this perspective was immediately recognized by several proponents of organizational institutionalism (DiMaggio 1991; Zucker 1987). Powell (1991) admitted that institutional theory offers an over-socialized portrayal of actors which leaves little leeway for recognizing the important role which actors play. DiMaggio (1988: 4) states in his seminal contribution:

[I]nstitutional theory has no explicit or formal theory of the role that interests play in institutionalization and consequently defocalizes, or distracts attention from, the ways in which variation in the strategies and practices of goal-oriented actors may be related to variation in organizational structures, practices, and forms.

Although the theory was regarded as a suitable theoretical framework that could be applied in many areas to address a large number of research questions (DiMaggio 1988), its focus appeared to be too narrow. Two aspects increasingly came to the fore: (*a*) The capacities of individuals and organizations to act or react to institutionalized expectations were seen to be too limited. Options for individuals and organizations other than compliance were hardly addressed (Oliver 1991). (*b*) A more severe limitation was that the neglect of actors, interests, and strategic behaviour implied that organizational institutionalism was unable to adequately explain either the institutionalization of organizational forms, structures, and management practices or their deinstitutionalization (DiMaggio 1988). Thus, no adequate theory of organizational change was provided, as was underscored by DiMaggio (1988: 11):

[W]ithout more explicit attention to interest and agency of the kind that institutional rhetoric has thus far obstructed, institutional theorists will be unable to develop predictive and persuasive accounts of the origins, reproduction, and erosion of institutionalized practices and organizational forms.

In order to solve these problems, a conceptualization of actors and interests was needed that allows for questions such as 'Who has institutionalized the myths (and why)?' and 'Who has the power to "legitimate" a structural element?' (DiMaggio 1988: 10) to be asked without inducing contradictions with the basic assumptions of the approach. That is, it was necessary to take into consideration both the cultural embeddedness of actors and actions and actors' capability to act. The difficulty of trying to meet both demands, however, led to a situation in which 'new institutionalism has shifted uneasily back and forth between, on the one hand, a notion of culturally dominated actors and, on the other hand, a notion of rational actors as constrained in their instrumental course of action by the reality of institutionalized practices in an organizational field' (Beckert 1999: 789).

Despite all criticism, it is important to mention that the decentring of actors, interests, power, and strategic behaviour in institutional theory was not a by-product of other assumptions nor did the proponents of institutional theory 'forget' to address these issues. Moreover, it does not imply that it is impossible to address these phenomena with institutional arguments. Rather, the decentring of actors, interests, and strategic behaviour was intentional and purposive. Thus, the critique—at least in its radical form—does not take the central aims of new institutionalism into consideration. For example, Meyer and Rowan (1977: 348) point out that powerful organizations 'actively seek charter from collective authorities and manage to institutionalize their goals and structures in the rules of such authorities'. They further suggest that '(p)owerful organizations force their immediate relational networks to adapt their structures and relations'. These organizations also create their own markets:

powerful organizations attempt to build their goals and procedures directly into society as institutional rules. Automobile producers, for instance, attempt to create the standards in public opinion defining desirable cars, to influence legal standards defining satisfactory cars, to affect judicial rules defining cars adequate enough to avoid manufacturer liability, and to force agents of the collectivity to purchase only cars.

Notwithstanding these references, the concepts only play a minor role in the early writings and remained largely unelaborated, which is, however, understandable if the core aims of institutional theory are kept in mind. Right from the beginning, institutional theory was developed as an approach 'in reaction to prevailing conceptions of organizations as bounded, relatively autonomous, rational actors' (Scott and Meyer 1994: 1). It was conceptualized as 'an important break with rational-actor models and a promising strategy for modeling and explaining instances of organizational change that are *not* driven by processes of interest mobilization' (DiMaggio 1988: 3; emphasis in original). However, it is less the assumption of rationality in rational-choice models per se which is challenged. On the contrary, rational, goal-oriented behaviour is regarded as a form of agency orientation; however, it is seen as *one possible form* of agency orientation and not as a universal doctrine. Moreover, it is suggested that the economic rationality in terms of expected utility maximization is only one possible, socially constructed and thus historically and culturally contingent form of rationality, albeit one of the most influential myths of modernity, the diffusion of which is at the centre of Meyer's world polity approach (2005). In this sense, theories that build on the economic rationality of actors are part of this myth and not part of its explanation.

In contrast to rational-choice models, the goal of organizational institutionalism is to reverse the conventional and still dominant view in organizational theory that institutions are the products of decisions and choice and to see what can be gained when we conceptualize social actors and their decisions and choices as derivative from institutions, that is, if institutions are regarded as independent variables and social actors as dependent ones. Thus, the goal is to encompass those facets of organizations and the social world which can hardly be grasped by actor-centred approaches (Jepperson 2002). In this respect, institutionalists aim at no less than 'to question the assumed naturalness of organizations, seeing them instead as "(a) connected to and (b) constructed by wide social environments" (Meyer and Scott 1992: 1), as opposed to being prior realities external to the cultural system (Meyer, Boli, and Thomas 1987: 22)' (Jepperson 2002: 234). If the institutionalization of actors and interests is moved to the foreground, the image of modern actors (such as nation states, organizations, and individuals) as specific, integrated, and autonomous actors—as portrayed by most theories in the social sciences—is questioned. Subsequently, these actors appear as open social entities that are penetrated by their institutional environments. Actors and their interests are regarded as the outcome of processes of institutionalization.

The decentring of actors does not imply that actors, interests, power, and strategic behaviours do not matter at all in institutional theory. As Meyer (1977: 75) argues, the institutionalization of organizational structures or the existence of rationalized myths is reflected 'not in the fact that individuals believe them, but in the fact that they "know" everyone else does'. Jepperson (2002: 232; emphasis in original) adds that 'the truly fundamental beliefs for reproducing a social order are people's beliefs about *others'* behavior and beliefs; the basic "myths" of society operate primarily by establishing beliefs about what others think and expectations about how others will behave.' Moreover, in institutional theory actors are regarded neither as imbeciles nor as fools who comply with institutionalized expectations without any reflection. Management does not simply implement institutionalized directives. On the contrary, '[L]eadership (in a university, a hospital, or a business) requires an understanding of changing fashions and governmental programs' (Meyer and Rowan 1977: 352). Finally, actors are not denied their capability to act. New institutionalism is, as Scott (1995: 41) points out, 'not at all inconsistent with an activist view of human actors. Individuals do construct and continuously negotiate social reality in everyday life, but they do so within the context of wider, preexisting cultural systems: symbolic frameworks, perceived to be both objective and external, that provide orientation and guidance.'

Although actors, interests, and strategic behaviours are conceptually integrated into new institutionalism, their conceptualization fundamentally differs from those we find in other organizational theories. The starting point is not a more or less rational actor who makes autonomous decisions. Rather, the cultural definition and embeddedness of social actors, interests, and behaviours is emphasized. In this respect, actors, interests, and strategic behaviours are decentred and regarded as categorizations derived from the institutional environment:

Institutional frameworks define the ends and shape the means by which interests are determined and pursued. Institutional factors determine that actors in one type of setting, called firms, pursue profits; that actors in another setting, called agencies, seek larger budgets; that actors in a third setting, called political parties, seek votes; and that actors in an even stranger setting, research universities, pursue publications.

(Scott 1987: 508)

Thus, although organizational institutionalism has included a conceptualization of actors, their interests, power, and strategic behaviours right from the beginning, the contours have remained blurred until recently.


## 8.2. Agentic Social Actors

According to Meyer and Jepperson (Jepperson 2002; Meyer 1988; Meyer and Jepperson 2000), the actors of modern society are not to be regarded as an ontological given entity, but rather as the result of a cultural construction of social agency. They regard actorhood of individuals, organizations, and nation states as a complex system of social agency, conceiving agency as authorized agency in which the agent acts on behalf of various legitimized principles including the self: in the entirely rationalized and universalized modern culture, which, according to the world polity approach (Meyer 2005), has its origins in the USA and has now spread worldwide, the legitimized actors of modernity are attributed the capability and responsibility (1) to act as a mobilized actor for the self (*agency for the self*); (2) to act in relationship with other actors (*agency for other actors*) as 'other'; and (3) to act as agent for entities, which in and of themselves are not regarded as actors, and to act for the cultural authority, that is, imagined natural and moral laws (*agency for principles*) (Meyer and Jepperson 2000).

(1) Meyer and Jepperson (2000) emphasize that modern culture creates an agentic individual who tries to achieve goals that are thought to reside in its personality or life course. They understand the modern organization and the modern nation state in a similar way, that is, as cultural products. Further, it is argued that modern individuals, organizations, and nation states as well as their goals and activities are highly standardized and scripted, even if (or especially if)—as in the case of individuals—self-actualization is emphasized. For example, with respect to the individual, the perpetual discourse on self-esteem and self-actualization has become transformed over time into standardized conceptions and technologies of the self. Subsequently, with respect to their own course of life, individuals are not only responsible for acting on their self-interests; rather, they also have the obligation to act on those entirely rationalized and institutionalized rules and beliefs that form the basis of their actorhood. These rationalized beliefs also include the assumed capacity of the individual to take initiative and make a difference. Similarly, the cultural conception of modern organizations has been differentiated and refined over time. For example, a large number of different departments and management techniques, which are assumed to increase the capacity of organizations to act rationally, have been introduced. The modern nation state has also become the agent thought to be responsible for an increasing number of areas of society. Today, the formal structure of nation states is much more elaborate than in earlier decades of the last century.

(2) However, at the same time institutionalized conceptions of actorhood and agency are also based on the expectation that they serve the interests of other specific and generalized actors and society. For Meyer and Jepperson (2000), it is a striking feature of modern society that actors are prepared to act as agents of others. It is due to the standardization and stylization of modern actors that they are able and willing to act as employees, consultants, voters, or citizens for other actors. Since modern actors and their activities are supported by standardized external cultural definitions and social structures, actors can easily shift from agency for the self to agency for others.

(3) Moreover, Meyer and Jepperson (2000) mention a third form of agency, namely, agency for 'higher' principles (i.e. agency for a cultural authority) where the actor is assumed to act on behalf of imagined institutionalized moral and natural rules and laws.

This makes clear that institutional theory does contain a concept of the actor, namely, that of an agentic actor for the self, for other actors, or for principles. The roles, interests, and behaviour of the agentic actor are culturally defined and institutionalized:

(W)ho has the right to have interests, what interests are regarded as reasonable or appropriate, and what means can be used to pursue them are all products of socially constructed rules: Institutional rules invent rationality, defining who the actors are and determining the logics that guide their actions. This means that, as the rational choice theorists argue, if actors pursuing interests take actions to create institutional frameworks, this can occur only under particular circumstances in which selected actors are constituted as having those interests and powers. Where social agency is located—who has the right to take self-determined and self-interested actions—is expected to vary over time and place.

(Scott 1995: 140)

However, the concept of the agentic actor does not entirely rebut the critique. Especially, the question of how innovation and change are possible if actors are constituted by their institutional environment has been addressed more recently as a 'paradox of embedded agency' (Seo and Creed 2002). Fligstein (2001: 110) criticizes not only the conception of actors in theories based on the rational-choice model but also the conception of actors in institutional theory:

A sociological theory of action needs to take rational actor views seriously in the sense that actors do pursue interests and aggressively engage in strategic interaction.

Thus, even if the concept of the actor has been clarified by Meyer and Jepperson, strategic and goal-orienting behaviour that can lead to new organizational forms or the institutionalization of new markets is still under-theorized in organizational institutionalism. Such a concept of agency is seen, at least by some proponents of institutional theory, in Giddens's structuration theory (1979, 1984) (see, e.g. Barley and Tolbert 1997; DiMaggio 1997; DiMaggio and Powell 1991; Scott 2001).

## 8.3. Combining Organizational Institutionalism and Structuration Theory

Similar to institutional theory, structuration theory decentres the actor. It focuses on social practices through which social actors, by drawing on social structures, continuously produce and reproduce the very same structures. In structuration theory, the reflexive monitoring of activities is a general feature of everyday action. Knowledgeable and reflexive actors have the capability to act that includes being able to act otherwise, that is, 'being able to intervene in the world, or to refrain from such intervention, with the effect of influencing a specific process or state of affairs' (Giddens 1984: 14). Being an actor and to act, thus, means to be able 'to make a difference'.

According to Giddens (1984), as an inherent aspect of what they do, human agents have the capacity to understand what they do while they do it. They are able to control their activities with respect to their own or given goals. However, the concept of strategic behaviour as found in structuration theory does not imply that the result of this behaviour is intended:

Agency refers not to the intentions people have in doing things but to the capability of doing things in the first place... Agency concerns events of which an individual is the perpetrator, in the sense that the individual could, at any phase in a given sequence of conduct, have acted differently. Whatever happened would not have happened if that individual had not intervened. Action is a continuous process, a flow, in which the reflexive monitoring which the individual maintains is fundamental to the control of the body that actors ordinarily sustain throughout their day-to-day lives. I am the author of many things I do not intend to do, and may not want to bring about, but none the less I *do*.

(Giddens 1984: 9, emphasis in original)

According to Giddens (1984), action is to be understood as a stream, a continuous flow of reflexive action. Action can neither be grasped as a discrete activity nor be separated from the actor or the relationship between the actor and the environment. In daily interaction, the reflexive monitoring of action also implies that actors routinely consider their environment of interaction. Thus, in their actions, social actors also routinely refer to the structural moments, that is, the institutionalized aspects of social systems.

An important argument in Giddens's work (1984) is that structures (i.e. the institutionalized aspects of social life) do not operate as mechanisms that are located outside the actor, but that they are produced

187

and reproduced because they are represented in the 'memory traces' of knowledgeable agents and that these serve as a means of orienting action—also a core argument of the cognitive organizational institutionalism. Scott (1994a: 97) points out that the institutional environment is not 'out there somewhere', but rather exists within the minds of the organizational participants. According to structuration theory, actions are intended and agents (discursively or practically) know about the structural or institutional conditions of their action, and in their action they draw on these conditions. Central to structuration theory is the idea of a duality of structure. This idea addresses the 'essential recursiveness of social life, as constituted in social practices: structure is both medium and outcome of social practices. Structure enters simultaneously into the constitution of the agent and social practices, and "exists" in the generating moments of this constitution' (Giddens 1979: 5). Structure and agency are not regarded as competing theoretical conceptions; instead, they presuppose each other (Sewell 1992). A similar argument can be found, for example, in the writings of Scott (2001: 67): 'Actors in interaction constitute social structures, which, in turn, constitute actors. The products of prior interactions—norms, rules, beliefs, resources—provide the situational elements that enter into individual decision making.' With the focus on *social practices*, structuration aims at bridging the gap between paradigms in social theory and at decentring the acting subject without losing sight of the actor. The overpowering, deterministic influence of institutionalized structures is pushed back without denying the existence and impact of social structures (Clark 1990; Cohen 1989; Craib 1992).

Social structures are seen as rules and resources which stabilize social relationships over time and space (see also Outhwaite 1990; for a critique, see Thompson 1989). However, Giddens (1984) also highlights that rules must be interpreted and that they are open to different interpretations. Thus, structures do not unequivocally specify behaviours (for similar arguments within institutional theory, see Creed, Scully, and Austin 2002; Czarniawska and Sevón 1996; Sahlin-Andersson and Engwall 2002). Resources may also be employed in different ways. The relationship between social structure and action is thus ambiguous and, in general, even in situations that are characterized by extreme dependence leave resources which may be used to defend some autonomy (Giddens 1979), that is, as long as the capacity to act—to make a difference—is retained, change is possible. According to structuration theory, it is possible for fundamentally new practices to be developed which leads to radical institutional change. It is also possible that identical routines are continuously reproduced, which subsequently leads to an extremely durable social system. It is plausible to argue that, in the first case, the rules can be widely interpreted and the resources easily converted. In the second case, it seems likely that the rules are defined more narrowly and the resources are much more difficult to convert (for a similar argumentation from an institutional perspective, see Scott 1994b).

On the one hand, rules are the basis of sense-making (*signification*) and are used as interpretative schemes or typifications to make sense of what actors say or do. This conceptualization of rules is similar to Scott's outline of the cultural–cognitive pillar of institutions (2001). On the other hand, rules refer to rights and obligations (*legitimation*). These rules are linked to the sanctioning of social behaviours. This understanding of rules in structuration theory corresponds with the understanding of the normative and the regulative pillars of institutions in Scott's model. Rules are understood as generalized practices. They should, however, neither be equated with formalized rules and regulations nor be treated in the singular (Giddens 1984). Rules are better grasped as more or less linked sets of rules, which develop their impact in conjunction with one another. Again, the similarity between Giddens's concept and the way Scott (2001) sees the relationship between the three pillars of institutions is evident.

Further, rules should not be conceptualized apart from resources, since it is only then that structural properties express forms of domination and power (Giddens 1984). Giddens distinguishes two kinds of resources that may be combined in one medium: (*a*) Allocative resources refer to capabilities which generate command over objects, goods, or material phenomena. (*b*) Authoritative resources refer to types of transformative capacities generating command over actors (Cohen 1990; Giddens 1984). For example, money as a generalized medium is not only an allocative resource but often also forms the basis of authority and power. What becomes clear is that this use of the term 'resources' makes it seem possible to bring power into institutional theory in a way that is consistent with the founding works of institutionalism (see especially Berger and Luckmann 1967). A combination of institutional and structuration theory, thus, can also contribute to overcome the critique that institutional theory neglects the phenomenon of power (Lounsbury 2003).

Renate Meyer (2004) has recently shown that the distribution of power as well as authority and domination as forms of institutionalized power are central in institutional analyses. Drawing on Berger and Luckmann (1967: 109), she argues that those with 'the bigger stick' have the better chance of imposing their definition of reality, and it is this definition of reality which defines the distribution of the sticks. Thus, it is not so much the theoretical ingenuity that is relevant for the success of an institutionalization project, but rather the degree to which the proponents of a symbolic universe are legitimated and supported by the institutional order. Power helps impose a certain definition of reality because it is also power that defines who has access to the symbolic universe. Further, power includes the power to control processes of socialization and thus to define reality. More recently, Luckmann (2002: 113; translation by authors) has again highlighted the unequal distribution of power and its relevance for processes of institutionalization:

The 'emergence' of institutions primarily presupposes 'initially' direct, and continuously, reciprocal social work, but reciprocity is not based on equality. The specification of what is an important problem is in its nature not a matter of 'democratic rationality'. Solutions are not necessarily contrived by actors with 'equal rights': Institutionalization as a rational and symmetric contract between actors can only be thought of as a historically marginal case. In the 'analysis of the constitution' of institutions it is possible to exclude authority and domination, but not to exclude power.

Similarly, Giddens (1984) stresses that structures of *signification* (symbolic orders, myths, and belief systems), *legitimation* (especially legal institutions), and *domination* (in particular political and economic institutions) can only be distinguished analytically. For example, economics is not adequately described as competition for scarce resources, but is bound up with certain world views and legal institutions, and the enforcement of sanctions is always tied to the factual disposal of resources and linked with certain value systems.

According to Giddens (1984), structures are the reason for the continuous reproduction of social practices over different spans of time and space and the basis for giving social practices a systemic form. The term 'social system' thus denotes continuously reproduced relationships between social actors which can be observed in the form of regular social practices in specific contexts. Social practices that have a great time–space extension—scripts and routines in terms of institutional theory—can be referred to as institutions.

Two trends regarding the integration of structuration theory can be identified in the literature on institutional theory. In some contributions (see, e.g. Barley and Tolbert 1997), the emphasis is on the reproduction of institutionalized structures. These studies are closely related to the traditional arguments of institutional theory. Other contributions (see, e.g., Beckert 1999; Clemens and Cook 1999) highlight that integrating conceptual elements of structuration theory is one promising opportunity to better explain institutional change. Based on the assumption of knowledgeable agents, it seems possible to grasp this phenomenon. 'Knowledge of a rule or schema by definition means the ability to transpose or extend it—that is, to apply it creatively' (Sewell 1992: 18). Institutions can be reflected—that is, exactly what happens in institutional theory. Institutions are thus open to intentional actions that aim at changing institutions in a way that they better serve the (institutionalized) interests of actors. Conscious attention to institutionalized behaviours is the starting point of processes of deinstitutionalization (Berger and Kellner 1984). This, however, by no means implies that strategic actions and institutional entrepreneurship necessarily bring about the intended changes in the institutional frame. Giddens (1984) explicitly points to unintended consequences. Further, structuration theory does not imply that all kinds of institutions can be changed at any time. Institutional structures do sometimes change in intended ways (Lawrence 1999). However, institutional change often appears more as an unintended result, as, for example, Lawrence and Phillips (2004) have nicely shown in their study on 'whale-watching'. These latter changes should, however, not be understood as random mutations that result from inaccurate perception and the adoption of institutionalized expectations. According to structuration theory, these changes are also based on intentional actions. However, the result of these intentional actions, for example, the kind of institutional change, was not intended.

## 8.4. Institutional Entrepreneurship

With the institutional entrepreneur, a specific type of actor has been introduced to institutional theory as an attempt to explain institutional change endogenously and to avoid having to rely on exogenous factors like external shocks or crises. This makes it necessary to trace the emergence of new as well as the persistence of established institutions to the interventions of active agents (DiMaggio 1988; Townley 2002; Zilber 2002). Institutional entrepreneurship, in terms of a continuous support of emerging or already existing institutions, is linked to the material or ideal interests of individual actors or groups of actors and discretion over resources. The emergence of new institutions is conceptualized as the result of a contest of actors with different levels of power. While some are interested in establishing a new institutional order, others try to avoid this institutional change (DiMaggio 1988). Institutional entrepreneurship for existing institutions implies the commitment of resources in order to maintain these institutions. Resources may, for example, be used to suppress latent conflicts with those actors who question the taken-for-grantedness of certain institutions.

Many studies have addressed the question of which characteristics of an actor or a field increase or decrease the probability that an actor will take on the role of an institutional entrepreneur (see, e.g. Battilana 2006; Dorado 2005; Greenwood and Suddaby 2006; Maguire, Hardy, and Lawrence 2004; Rao, Davis, and Ward 2000). Establishing generic new organizational forms such as companies, universities, hospitals, and museums; or specific new organizational forms such as newspaper companies and automobile manufacturers (Carroll and Hannan 1989; Greenwood and Suddaby 2006; Hannan et al. 1995; Munir and Phillips 2005; Rao 1994); or new structural elements, management techniques, and practices (Battilana 2006; Boxenbaum 2006; Déjean, Gond, and Leca 2004; Maguire, Hardy, and Lawrence 2004; Meyer 2004; Walgenbach 2000) requires an institutionalization project driven by strong material and/or ideal interests and considerable investment of resources. The institutionalization of a new organizational form presupposes, for example, the provision of a theorization that contains legitimate justifications and accounts for this new organizational form and makes the new form appear essential. Institutional entrepreneurs thus must have access to sufficient allocative and authoritative resources in order to potentially realize their (institutionalized) interests (DiMaggio 1988; Giddens 1984). In addition, they must draw on resonating frames or interpretive schemes and provide the necessary legitimation for their claims.

The importance of a sufficient endowment with resources as well as the legitimacy of a new organizational form has been demonstrated in many empirical studies. Referring to institutional arguments, for example, organizational ecologists have shown that in the early stages of the development of a new industry, the number of newly founded organizations is low while the mortality rate of these organizations is high (Brüderl and Schüssler 1990; Hannan 1986; Hannan and Carroll 1992; Hannan and Freeman 1989) because the newly founded organizations are not assigned the legitimacy which is required to ensure their survival. In other words, the new organizational form is not sufficiently institutionalized. The argument applies in a similar way to organizations which innovate in a significant way. Meyer and Rowan (1977: 353) highlight that

'Organizations which innovate in important structural ways bear considerable costs in legitimacy.' Because of the lack of legitimacy, newly founded organizations and organizations which innovate in significant ways or which operate with structures and techniques that are not regarded as legitimate have difficulties in gaining access to and attracting resources such as capital, labour, or patronage from other sources (Aldrich and Fiol 1994). Thus, institutional entrepreneurship—like entrepreneurship in general—is often a failure. In case of success, however, institutional entrepreneurship produces small and big heroes who are celebrated for their achievements.

Institutionalization projects benefit if institutional entrepreneurs cooperate with like-minded people, that is, if the entrepreneurs are able to mobilize collective action in order to push an institutionalization project. Fligstein (2001: 106) regards the mobilization of consensus and cooperation to be at the centre of the activities of institutional entrepreneurs: 'These entrepreneurs are skilled strategic actors who find ways to get disparate groups to cooperate precisely by putting themselves into positions of others and creating meanings that appeal to large number of actors.' For Suchman (1995), the creation of an environment in which their own interests can be realized is one of the central challenges institutional entrepreneurs face (see also McCarthy and Zald 1987; Meyer 2004; Tilly 1978, 1984; Walgenbach 2000; Walgenbach and Beck 2002; Zimmerman and Zeitz 2002). An essential actor in this respect is the media (Lounsbury and Glynn 2001; Pollock and Rindova 2003), which themselves often benefit from the institutionalization of a new organizational form, structural element, or management technique and, thus, not only provide a platform or arena, but often act themselves as institutional entrepreneurs.

However, it is important to emphasize that certain resources that may be used in an institutionalization project are freely accessible. Legitimate and shared belief systems such as the idea of the superiority of formal rationality and accountability can, at least in the modern Western world, easily be activated and capitalized for most life spheres. Even change can be used as an institutional resource. In societies based on a belief in progress, those who oppose reforms that are promoted on the basis of rationalized accounts are put under pressure to justify their position. Further, in all modern societies and organizational fields, a multiplicity of institutional rules exists, and entrepreneurs may try to draw on several rules in order to push their institutionalization project. However innovative these projects might appear: it is important to note that no actor—not even the institutional entrepreneur—operates in an institutional vacuum:

'[T]here is no hypothetical moment in which agency actually gets "free" of structure' (Emirbayer and Mische 1998: 1004). They too are institutionally constituted as social actors, and their projects need to be made sense of within the shared interpretive schemes.

New industries, products and services, new organizational structures, and management practices do not emerge out of the blue—'they are shaped by extant social institutions, social trends that create new opportunities, and by entrepreneurs who both open up and cultivate those opportunities' (Jones 2001: 914). Innovations must fit into the existing cultural knowledge in order to gain legitimacy. As has been shown by Hargadon and Douglas (2001) in their study on the institutionalization of electric light and the deinstitutionalization of gas lighting by Thomas A. Edison, the most important task of institutional entrepreneurs is not primarily to highlight the innovativeness of a new solution, but to communicate the innovation in terms of existing and well-established solutions in order to activate associations with the familiar and to avoid feelings of alienation. Thus, if a society lacks the necessary terms to grasp a fundamental innovation, it seems unlikely that this innovation will be adopted. In short, new phenomena make sense only in terms of existing phenomena. This is why innovations such as new products and organizational forms must be presented in ways and terms which both appear familiar and at the same time highlight their newness. Innovations must be linked to established value and meaning systems that are anchored in the institutional environment (see also Meyer and Scott 1983). Similarly, Ruef (2000: 661) states, 'Novel organizational forms are most likely to become legitimated when they fit into the pre-existing cultural beliefs, meanings, and typifications of an organizational community.' This argument finds further support in a study by Jones (2001). She shows that the early producers of successful commercial movies adopted the symbols as well as the format of the well-established and institutionalized Broadway theatres. Further, they recruited prominent actors in order to increase the acceptance of the new product.

Not all institutional structures that gain relevance in an institutionalization project are located at the same level. On the contrary, typically, higher- and lower-level institutions can be distinguished. Meta-institutions exhibit a higher degree of stability and persistence than lower-level institutions do, even if the latter may be taken for granted. Further, it can be argued that societal ends or goals generally have a higher degree of institutionalization than the means regarded as appropriate to reach the ends. By referring to meta-institutions (such as the market) and higher-order ends and goals (such as, e.g. efficiency, technical and/or social progress, or justice) or generally accepted principles, it is possible to legitimate institutional innovations in a society or an organizational field by linking the new concept to the theorization or framing of the established meta-institutions. For example, the concepts of diversity management may be institutionalized with little effort only if their contribution to the realization of human rights has been theorized in a plausible way. Moreover, institutionalized structural elements or management practices may be questioned by institutional entrepreneurs if they use rationalized accounts to point to those characteristics which may reduce the efficiency of organizations and to highlight the efficiency gains that may be realized by breaking institutionalized rules (Beckert 1999). The criterion of efficiency is, however, not as unambiguous as those trying to defend an existing institutional structure or striving for institutional change claim. Efficiency is not only grasped in different ways in different cultures (Friedland and Alford 1991); the term efficiency may also be open to interpretation within a culture. Thus, it is open whether efficiency should be conceived of at the level of the individual, the organization, or the society. Furthermore, it is debatable as to what the goals of individuals, organizations, and societies are. Moreover, the individual, organizational, or societal resources as well as the expected or realized returns are to a large extent subject to subjective evaluations (Zimmerman and Zeitz 2002), thus making institutionalization and deinstitutionalization processes a political endeavour. Therefore, the institutionalized beliefs that certain products, organizational forms, and management techniques are superior to others are increasingly becoming the result of processes of social construction and negotiation in modern societies.

Furthermore, different and sometimes inconsistent institutionalized belief systems often overlap (Scott 1994b, 2001). It is these overlaps that may form the basis for institutional entrepreneurship: '[W]here systems cross-cut and structural properties are diverse, actors need only draw selectively on rules and resources, instantiating some, leaving others in reserve. Rules need not collapse into practice; selective engagement of structural properties provides the critical distance for strategic manipulation' (Whittington 1992: 704; see also Suchman 1995). Finally, institutionalized rules are rarely unambiguous. They have to be interpreted (Creed, Scully, and Austin 2002; Czarniawska and Sevón 1996; Dobbin and Sutton 1998; Sahlin-Andersson and Engwall 2002; Scott 1994b). Because of this requirement, institutional entrepreneurs have the opportunity to change the institutional frame if they are able to successfully institutionalize their specific interpretation of an institutionalized rule (Tempel and Walgenbach 2007).

## 8.5. Conclusion

Institutions produce stability. However, they do not determine action. In general, they define a repertoire of acceptable behaviours that give actors different degrees of leeway in their decisions and actions. Thus, institutions also enable agency and are a precondition for strategic behaviours, and institutional entrepreneurship and thus for the structuring of organizations and markets.

## References

Aldrich, H. E. and Fiol, C. M. (1994). 'Fools Rush In? The Institutional Context of Industry Creation', *Academy of Management Review*, 19: 645–70.

Barley, S. R. and Tolbert, P. S. (1997). 'Institutionalization and Structuration: Studying the Links Between Action and Institution', *Organization Studies*, 18: 93–117.

Battilana, J. (2006). 'Agency and Institutions: The Enabling Role of Agents' Social Position', *Organization*, 13: 653–76.

Beckert, J. (1999). 'Agency, Entrepreneurs, and Institutional Change: The Role of Strategic Choice and Institutionalized Practices in Organizations', *Organization Studies*, 20: 777–99.

Berger, P. L. and Kellner, H. (1984). *Für eine neue Soziologie. Ein Essay über Methode und Profession*. Frankfurt am Main: Fischer.

——and Luckmann, T. (1967). *The Social Construction of Reality*. New York: Anchor.

Boxenbaum, E. (2006). 'Lost In Translation: The Making of Danish Diversity Management', *American Behavioral Scientist*, 49: 939–48.

Brüderl, J. and Schüssler, R. (1990). 'Organizational Mortality: The Liability of Newness and Adolescence', *Administrative Science Quarterly*, 35: 530–47.

Carroll, G. R. and Hannan, M. T. (1989). 'Density Dependence in the Evolution of Populations of Newspaper Organizations', *American Sociological Review*, 54: 524–41.

Clark, J. (1990). 'Anthony Giddens, Sociology and Modern Social Theory', in J. Clark, C. Modgil, and S. Modgil (eds.), *Anthony Giddens: Consensus and Controversy*. London: Falmer Press.

Clemens, E. S. and Cook, J. M. (1999). 'Politics and Institutionalism: Explaining Durability and Change', *American Review of Sociology*, 25: 441–66.

Cohen, I. J. (1989). *Structuration Theory: Anthony Giddens and the Constitution of Social Life*. Basingstoke: MacMillan.

—— (1990). 'Structuration Theory and Social Order: Five Issues In Brief', in J. Clark, C. Modgil, and S. Modgil (eds.), *Anthony Giddens: Consensus and Controversy*. London: Falmer Press.

Craib, I. (1992). *Anthony Giddens*. London: Routledge.

Creed, W. E. D., Scully, M. A., and Austin, J. R. (2002). 'Clothes Make the Person? The Tailoring of Legitimating Accounts and the Social Construction of Identity', *Organization Science*, 13: 475–96.

Czarniawska, B. and Sevón, G. (eds.) (1996). *Translating Organizational Change*. Berlin: De Gruyter.

Déjean, F., Gond, J. P., and Leca, B. (2004). 'Measuring the Unmeasured: An Institutional Entrepreneur Strategy in an Emerging Industry', *Human Relations*, 57: 740–76.

DiMaggio, P. J. (1988). 'Interest and Agency in Institutional Theory', in L. G. Zucker (ed.), *Institutional Patterns and Organizations: Culture and Environment*. Cambridge: Ballinger.

—— (1991). 'Constructing an Organizational Field', in W. W. Powell and P. J. DiMaggio (eds.), *The New Institutionalism in Organizational Analysis*. Chicago, IL: University of Chicago Press.

—— (1997). 'Culture and Cognition', *Annual Review of Sociology*, 23: 263–87.

—— —— (1983). 'The Iron Cage Revisited: Institutional Isomorphism and Collective Rationality in Organizational Fields', *American Sociological Review*, 48: 147–60.

—— —— (1991). 'Introduction', in W. W. Powell and P. J. DiMaggio (eds.), *The New Institutionalism in Organizational Analysis*. Chicago, IL: University of Chicago Press.

Dobbin, F. R. and Sutton, J. R. (1998). 'The Strength of a Weak State: The Rights Revolution and the Rise of Human Resource Management Divisions', *American Journal of Sociology*, 104: 441–76.

Dorado, S. (2005). 'Institutional Entrepreneurship, Partaking, and Convening', *Organization Studies*, 26: 385–414.

Emirbayer, M. and Mische, A. (1998). 'What Is Agency?', *American Journal of Sociology*, 103: 281–317.

Fligstein, N. (2001). 'Social Skill and the Theory of Fields', *Sociological Theory*, 19: 105–25.

Friedland, R. and Alford, R. R. (1991). 'Bringing Society Back In: Symbols, Practices, and Institutional Contradictions', in W. W. Powell and P. J. DiMaggio (eds.), *The New Institutionalism in Organizational Analysis*. Chicago, IL: University of Chicago Press.

Giddens, A. (1979). *Central Problems in Social Theory*. London: MacMillan.

—— (1984). *The Constitution of Society*. Cambridge: Polity Press.

Greenwood, R. and Suddaby, R. (2006). 'Institutional Entrepreneurship in Mature Fields: The Big Five Accounting Firms', *Academy of Management Journal*, 49: 27–48.

Hannan, M. T. (1986). *Competitive and Institutional Processes in Organizational Ecology*, Tech. Rep. 86–13. Ithaca, NY: Cornell University, Department of Sociology.

——and Carroll, G. R. (1992). *Dynamics of Organizational Populations: Density, Legitimation and Competition*. New York: Oxford University Press.

——and Freeman, J. H. (1989). *Organizational Ecology*. Cambridge, MA: Harvard University Press.

——Carroll, G. R., Dundon, E. A., and Torres, J. C. (1995). 'Organizational Evolution in a Multinational Context', *American Sociological Review*, 60: 509–28.

Hargadon, A. B. and Douglas, Y. (2001). 'When Innovations Meet Institutions: Edison and the Design of the Electric Light', *Administrative Science Quarterly*, 46: 476–501.

Hirsch, P. M. and Lounsbury, M. (1997). 'Ending the Family Quarrel—Toward A Reconciliation of "Old" and "New" Institutionalisms', *American Behavioral Scientist*, 40: 406–18.

Jepperson, R. L. (2002). 'The Development and Application of Sociological Neo-institutionalism', in J. Berger and M. Zelditch (eds.), *New Directions in Sociological Theory: The Growth of Contemporary Theories*. Lanham: Rowman and Littlefield.

Jones, C. (2001). 'Co-Evolution of Entrepreneurial Careers, Institutional Rules, and Competitive Dynamics in American Film, 1895–1920', *Organization Studies*, 22: 911–44.

Lawrence, T. B. (1999). 'Institutional Strategy', *Journal of Management*, 25: 161–88.

——and Phillips, N. (2004). 'From Moby Dick to Free Willy: Macro-Cultural Discourse and Institutional Entrepreneurship in Emerging Organizational Fields', *Organization*, 11: 689–711.

Lounsbury, M. (2003). 'The Problem of Order Revisited: Towards a More Critical Institutional Perspective', in R. Westwood and S. Clegg (eds.), *Debating Organization: Point-Counterpoint in Organization Studies*. Oxford: Blackwell.

——and Glynn, M. A. (2001). 'Cultural Entrepreneurship: Stories, Legitimacy, and the Acquisition of Resources', *Strategic Management Journal*, 22: 545–64.

Luckmann, T. (2002). *Wissen und Gesellschaft. Ausgewählte Aufsätze 1981–2002*. Konstanz: UVK.

McCarthy, J. D. and Zald, M. N. (1987). 'Resource Mobilization and Social Movements: A Partial Theory', in M. N. Zald and J. D. McCarthy (eds.), *Social Movements in an Organizational Society—Collected Essays*. New Brunswick, NJ: Transaction.

Maguire, S., Hardy, C., and Lawrence, T. (2004). 'Institutional Entrepreneurship in Emerging Fields: HIV and AIDS Treatment Advocacy in Canada', *Academy of Management Journal*, 47: 657–79.

Meyer, J. W. (1977). 'The Effects of Education as an Institution', *American Journal of Sociology*, 83: 55–77.

——(1988). 'Society Without Culture: A Nineteenth-Century Legacy', in F. O. Ramirez (ed.), *Rethinking the Nineteenth Century*. New York: Greenwood.

——(2005). *Weltkultur: Wie die westlichen Prinzipien die Welt durchdringen*. Frankfurt am Main: Suhrkamp.

——and Jepperson, R. L. (2000). 'The Actors of Modern Society: The Cultural Construction of Social Agency', *Sociological Theory*, 18: 100–20.

——and Rowan, B. (1977). 'Institutionalized Organizations: Formal Structure as Myth and Ceremony', *American Journal of Sociology*, 83: 340–63.

——and Scott, W. R. (1983). 'Centralization and the Legitimacy Problems of the Local Government', in J. W. Meyer and W. R. Scott (eds.), *Organizational Environments: Ritual and Rationality*. Beverly Hills, CA: Sage.

————(1992). 'Preface to the Updated Edition', in J. W. Meyer and W. R. Scott (eds.), *Organizational Environments: Ritual and Rationality*, 2nd edn. Beverly Hills, CA: Sage.

——Boli, J., and Thomas, G. M. (1987). 'Ontology and Rationalization in the Western Cultural Account', in G. M. Thomas, J. W. Meyer, F. O. Ramirez, and J. Boli (eds.), *Institutional Structure: Constituting State, Society, and the Individual*. Newbury Park, CA: Sage.

Meyer, R. E. (2004). *Globale Managementkonzepte und lokaler Kontext. Organisationale Wertorientierung im österreichischen öffentlichen Diskurs*. Wien: WUV.

Munir, K. A. and Phillips, N. (2005). 'The Birth of the "Kodak Moment": Institutional Entrepreneurship and the Adoption of New Technologies', *Organization Studies*, 26: 1665–87.

Oliver, C. (1991). 'Strategic Responses to Institutional Processes', *Academy of Management Review*, 16: 145–79.

Outhwaite, W. (1990). 'Agency and Structure', in J. Clark, C. Modgil, and S. Modgil (eds.), *Anthony Giddens: Consensus and Controversy*. London: Falmer Press.

Pollock, T. G. and Rindova, V. P. (2003). 'Media Legitimation Effects in the Market for Initial Public Offerings', *Academy of Management Journal*, 46: 631–42.

Powell, W. W. (1991). 'Expanding the Scope of Institutional Analysis', in W. W. Powell and P. J. DiMaggio (eds.), *The New Institutionalism in Organizational Analysis*. Chicago, IL: University of Chicago Press.

Rao, H. (1994). 'The Social Construction of Reputation: Certification Contests, Legitimation, and the Survival of Organizations in the American Automobile Industry, 1895–1912', *Strategic Management Journal*, 15: 29–44.

——Davis, G. F., and Ward, A. (2000). 'Embeddedness, Social Identity and Mobility: Why Firms Leave the NASDAQ and Join the New York Stock Exchange', *Administrative Science Quarterly*, 45: 268–92.

Ruef, M. (2000). 'The Emergence of Organizational Forms: A Community Ecology Approach', *American Journal of Sociology*, 106: 658–714.

Sahlin-Andersson, K. and Engwall, L. (eds.) (2002). *The Expansion of Management Knowledge: Carriers, Flows, and Sources*. Stanford, CA: Stanford University Press.

Scott, W. R. (1987). 'The Adolescence of Institutional Theory', *Administrative Science Quarterly*, 32: 493–511.

—— (1994*a*). 'Institutional Analysis: Variance and Process Theory Approaches', in W. R. Scott and J. W. Meyer (eds.), *Institutional Environments and Organizations: Structural Complexity and Individualism*. Thousand Oaks, CA: Sage.

—— (1994*b*). 'Conceptualizing Organizational Fields: Linking Organizations and Societal Systems', in H. U. Derlien, U. Gerhardt, and F. W. Scharpf (eds.), *Systemrationalität und Partialinteresse*. Baden-Baden: Nomos.

—— (1995). *Institutions and Organizations*. Thousand Oaks, CA: Sage.

—— (2001). *Institutions and Organizations*, 2nd edn. Thousand Oaks, CA: Sage.

—— and Meyer, J. W. (1994). 'Developments in Institutional Theory', in W. R. Scott and J. W. Meyer (eds.), *Institutional Environments and Organizations: Structural Complexity and Individualism*. Thousand Oaks, CA: Sage.

Seo, M. G. and Creed, W. E. D. (2002). 'Institutional Contradictions, Praxis, and Institutional Change: A Dialectical Perspective', *Academy of Management Review*, 27: 222–47.

Sewell, W. H. Jr. (1992). 'A Theory of Structure: Duality, Agency, and Transformation', *American Journal of Sociology*, 85: 1–29.

Suchman, M. C. (1995). 'Managing Legitimacy: Strategic and Institutional Approaches', *Academy of Management Review*, 20: 571–610.

Tempel, A. and Walgenbach, P. (2007). 'Global Standardization of Organizational Forms and Management Practices? What New Institutionalism and the Business Systems Approach Can Learn From Each Other', *Journal of Management Studies*, 44: 1–24.

Thompson, J. B. (1989). 'The Theory of Structuration', in D. Held and J. B. Thompson (eds.), *Anthony Giddens and His Critiques*. Cambridge: Cambridge University Press.

Tilly, C. (1978). *From Mobilization to Revolution*. Reading: McGraw-Hill.

—— (1984). 'Social Movements and National Politics', in C. Bright and S. Harding (eds.), *State-Making and Social Movements*. Ann Arbor: University of Michigan Press.

Townley, B. (2002). 'The Role of Competing Rationalities in Institutional Change', *Academy of Management Journal*, 45: 163–79.

Walgenbach, P. (2000). *Die normgerechte Organisation*. Stuttgart: Schäffer-Poeschel.

—— and Beck, N. (2002). 'The Institutionalization of the Quality Management Approach in Germany', in K. Sahlin-Andersson and L. Engwall (eds.), *The Expansion of Management Knowledge: Carriers, Flows, and Sources*. Stanford, CA: Stanford University Press.

Whittington, R. (1992). 'Putting Giddens into Action: Social Systems and Managerial Agency', *Journal of Management Studies*, 29: 693–712.

Zilber, T. B. (2002). 'Institutionalization as an Interplay Between Actions, Meanings, and Actors: The Case of a Rape Crisis Centre in Israel', *Academy of Management Journal*, 45: 234–54.

Zimmerman, M. A. and Zeitz, G. J. (2002). 'Beyond Survival: Achieving New Venture Growth by Building Legitimacy', *Academy of Management Review*, 27: 414–31.

Zucker, L. G. (1987). 'Institutional Theories of Organizations', *Annual Review of Sociology*, 13: 443–64.

# 9

# Organizational Ecology as a Theory of Competition

*Nikolaus Beck*

## 9.1. Introduction

The topic of market formation and competition between organizations forms the core of a theoretical concept that has been one of the most important approaches in economic sociology for thirty years: organizational ecology. Although this approach is also concerned with 'non-market' influences on market processes, namely, with legal, regulatory, or institutional influences of market formation, these factors do not form its centre of interest. It is rather the impact of changes in the composition of competitors and resources that is the focus of ecological studies on market formation.

Organizational ecologists regard market formation as the development of certain, distinguishable populations of organizations, that is, organizations that share certain formal rules and a certain pattern of organizational conduct in a similar market segment (e.g. Hannan and Freeman 1986).

While the enormous impact of the organizational ecology approach on the sociology of markets is documented by a vast amount of highly renowned publications (for overviews, see Amburgey and Rao 1996; Baum 1996; Baum and Amburgey 2002), this approach is far from being undisputed. Since organizational ecologists argue that the formation of organizational populations is based on selection processes in which those organizations survive that have the best fit with the environmental conditions, this approach can obviously be regarded as 'Darwinian'. Consequently, the analogy to a biological concept aiming to explain the development of organic life on earth has caused much criticism in organizational research (e.g. Young 1988), especially in Germany (e.g. von der Oelsnitz 2005). Critics argue that organizations are not comparable to biological species, where development is solely dependent on an uncontrollable natural process, namely, evolution. Since the fate of organizations obviously rests on deliberate actions of more or less rational actors—basically the managers—the transfer of a Darwinian concept to the sphere of organizations seems not to be appropriate: 'Concepts developed for biology are often difficult to apply to organizations, reasoning is sometimes questionable, new hypotheses developed for organizations do not seem to be derived or to benefit from biological theory, and empirical support is lacking' (Young 1988: 1).

However, I think that much of the criticism is not fully justified and relies on some misunderstandings. I want to show that organizational ecology is much more sociological and less biological than many critics of organizational ecology think. I argue that organizational ecology and its theory of competition rests heavily on the seminal work of Emile Durkheim on the division of labour (1933) and on the thoughts of Amos Hawley on human ecology (1950). Thus, I want to set up the (slightly) provocative thesis that the expressions used by the agents of organizational ecology are 'Darwinian' but that the theoretical argumentation is 'Durkheimian'. Therefore I first want to highlight the theoretical foundations of organizational ecology. By doing that I want to underline that competition—and not the biological aspects of evolution—forms the core of the organizational ecology theory.

In a second step, I want to discuss the most important sub-concepts of organizational ecology that deal with competition and market formation, namely, density dependence (Hannan 1989) and resource partitioning (Carroll 1985). The first concept deals with the impact of the number of competitors on the survival and founding chances of organizations. The latter concept is concerned with the influence of market concentration on the vital rates of specialist and generalist organizations. These concepts have stimulated an enormous amount of empirical studies in which they have been given continued development. Especially by incorporating the dimension of geographical location, new insights into the selection processes have been gained (e.g. Greve 2002).

However, I want to show how a more ample consideration of the 'spatial' dimension of organizational ecology, namely, the spatial dimension of customers, has the potential to improve our understanding of market formation and competition.

## 9.2. Competition as the Basic Element of Social Ecological Approaches

From my point of view, the fundamentals of organizational ecology cannot be explained without referring to the most important theoretical predecessors of this approach, namely, the concept of human ecology that was developed by Amos Hawley (1950, 1986) and Durkheim's reasoning (1933) on the development of modern industrial societies presented in his famous 'division of labour'.

Durkheim (1933) argues that the growth of the volume and density of societies, that is, the increase in a society's population and in the social contacts among the society's members, leads to an amplified rivalry among individuals in their struggle for survival. With reference to Darwin, he states that this competition among any living organisms increases with the degree of similarity between these organisms. Living creatures with the same needs and goals compete for the same resources in any aspect of life. Therefore, he concludes that the rivalry among societal members decreases with the degree of differentiation in a society. As a consequence, the division of labour has the ability to attenuate conflicts that have previously occurred because individuals in less differentiated societies have been too similar to each other. Durkheim already mentions examples from economic life to underpin his arguments: enterprises with similar functions for the society will compete with each other and the degree of rivalry increases with the degree of similarity between organizations. Consequently, this competition will either lead to the extinction of inferior competitors or to the transformation of the inferior competitors into different organizations (Durkheim 1933: 328).

Amos Hawley (1950), in modelling a more general theory of societal development, draws heavily on these considerations of Durkheim. He presents an enhanced theory of the relationship between competition and differentiation that includes four different stages. The first stage is characterized by a situation in which the size of a population of individuals with similar demands exceeds the supply of resources.

Hawley then states that the initial consequence of this increased competition for resources is a greater *homogeneity* among competitors. Thus, a foreseeable threat of elimination leads to copying the seemingly most successful strategies of competitors. One example that Hawley presents, in order to explain this competitive situation, is the way grocery stores display goods. Under conditions of increased competition, the displaying strategies become increasingly similar among competitors.

The third stage of competition within Hawley's framework is the one of selection. Competitors who are too weak in one or more of the relevant dimensions of competition are eliminated from the population. This, however, does not mean the simple extinction of those entities or individuals that lose out in the selection process. It can also mean that inferior competitors move to other areas of resources or develop more specialized strategies of survival. Thus, this change of behaviour forms the fourth stage of competition.

A highly important aspect of Hawley's approach is the idea of isomorphism. He argues that each distinguishable set of environmental conditions leads to a certain form of human organization. Thus, all entities that draw on the same kind of resources display a similar form of organization (Hawley 1968). As a consequence, the heterogeneity in the environmental conditions determines the number of different human organizations. Thus, competition and adaptation are the basic processes that lead to a situation of distinguishable human populations that have an optimal fit with their distinct environmental conditions, that is, resources.

In the seminal paper of Hannan and Freeman (1977) that undoubtedly constituted the organizational ecology approach, the ideas of Hawley (1950, 1968) are taken up but are not fully reproduced. Hannan and Freeman combine Hawley's idea of selection with the notion of organizational inertia. They claim that there exist several internal and external barriers to the ability of organizations to adapt to increased competitive pressure due to a change in environmental conditions. Among those barriers to adaptation are, for example, prior investments in production facilities and specialized personnel; the path dependency of organizations, that is, their own history; and legal and fiscal regulations that force organizations to continue what they have previously done.

The emphasis on organizational inertia then constitutes the idea that the adaptive capacity of organizations is strongly constrained. This in turn means that the selection process among organizations very often leads to the death of maladapted organizations. A movement of inferior organizations to other resource areas, suggested by Hawley as a common strategy of those organizations that lose out in the selection process, becomes at the very least an unlikely option, according to this reasoning. Thus, Hannan and Freeman further the view that isomorphism of organizational forms in distinct resource spaces, that is, the evolution of distinct populations of organizations, is brought about by the extermination of unfit organizations in a competition process. The variety of organizational forms, an obvious empirical fact, is then due to founding activities (Freeman 1982). Hence, entrepreneurs discover new fields of resources in which they can start a business. These resources basically consist of customers' and/or organizational stakeholders' preferences and interests (Carroll, Dobrev, and Swaminathan 2002).

It is exactly this reasoning on the inflexibility of existing organizations that has caused the largest opposition among critics of organizational ecology (e.g. Frese 1992). In many practice-oriented management theories (e.g. the learning organization), organizational change is seen as a virtue in itself and it is argued that change, that is, adaptation to new competitive pressures within a given resource space, can be achieved more or less easily, if only rational managers use the appropriate techniques of change management (e.g. Senge 1990).

I think this criticism can be faced with two different arguments: first, if adaptation were unproblematic, as many of the practice-oriented theoreticians suggest, why should these organizations, often led by well-trained managers, fail at all? Second, Hannan and Freeman (1977) and other organizational ecologists do not deny the possibility of adaptation! They rather point to the fact that almost all other organizational theories that existed at the time when they developed the ecological approach concentrated on the adaptation of organizations.[1] Thus, the possibility of organizational failure was widely neglected—against all empirical evidence. Therefore, Hannan and Freeman quite provocatively focus on selection through organizational failure; however, this is primarily as a supplement to adaptation theories rather than as a contradiction to adaptation. 'We argue that in order to deal with the various inertial pressures the adaptation perspective must be *supplemented* with a selection orientation' (Hannan and Freeman 1977: 933, note emphasis). They remain fully aware of the fact that some organizations might have strong adaptive capabilities (Hannan and Freeman 1977: 937). Hannan and Freeman take these strong adaptive capacities of human organizations as well as their ability to expand almost infinitely as a clear example of the departure of human or organizational ecology from biological approaches. Thus, just like Hawley (1968), they suggest that competition between social entities, and not biological aspects of evolution, like the inheritance of genetic material, is the most important aspect of human ecological theories.

---

[1] e.g. the open system approach of Thompson (1967) and the behavioural decision approach of Cyert and March (1963) as typical examples of the adaptive perspective. The new institutionalism of organizational theory (e.g. Meyer and Rowan 1977; see also the chapter of Walgenbach and Meyer in this book) and the resource dependence view (Pfeffer and Salancick 1978) are also examples of adaptive theories that were developed at about the same time as organizational ecology.

Moreover, it is important to note that they assume differences in the way that competition processes are situated. Hence, they concentrate on the extermination of organizations that are not able to face competition, thereby deliberately neglecting those circumstances in which organizations are able to adapt. 'The first order of business is to study selection processes for those situations in which inertial pressures are sufficiently strong that mobility among forms is unlikely' (Hannan and Freeman 1977: 937).

At a later stage in the development of their theory, Hannan and Freeman (1984) explicitly reintroduced adaptation. For instance, they argued, in accordance with Thompson (1967) and Scott (1981), that organizational change at the periphery of the organization can help buffer the core from environmental influences, thereby securing the survival of organizations. They also stated that organizational core change in reaction to environmental shifts disrupts present organizational routines and therefore causes an immediate threat to survival. However, in the long run, when internal and external stakeholders of the organization have adjusted to the new structure of the organization, such a change might have beneficial consequences—provided that it really means an increase in the degree of adaptation to the environment. Moreover, relatively early empirical analyses within the field of organizational ecology have found that there exist situations in which the movement of organizations into other resource areas and not the extermination of organizations is the dominant reaction to increased competitive pressures (Delacroix, Swaminathan, and Solt 1989).

Meanwhile, organizational change, that is, a switch or an extension of an organization's market niche that is tantamount to its idiosyncratic resource area, is an established topic within the field of empirical studies in organizational ecology (e.g. Amburgey, Kelly, and Barnett 1993; Baum and Singh 1996; Dobrev, Kim, and Carroll 2003; Kelly and Amburgey 1991).

Returning to the initial steps in the development of the organizational ecological approach, Hannan and Freeman (1977) identify two ecological situations that should have a strong impact on selection, that is, on the death rates of organizations. The first one is the situation that has already been described by Hawley and Durkheim: the number of competitors exceeds the supply of resources. The second one is the application of different basic strategies—either generalist or specialist strategies—of organizational conduct in different environments. The identification of the first situation led to the research field of density dependence of organizational vital rates. The interest in the second topic initially gave rise to the development of the 'fitness set theory' (Freeman and Hannan 1983). However, while fitness set theory never really got established in organizational ecology, another related concept that is also concerned with the vital rates of generalist and specialist organizations became tremendously influential in ecological research on organizations until the present day: resource partitioning (Carroll 1985). Both theoretical concepts—density dependence and resource partitioning—are presented in more detail in the next paragraph of this chapter.

## 9.3. Forms and Consequences of Competition: Density Dependence and Resource Partitioning

### 9.3.1. Density Dependence

A simple hypothesis with respect to the ideas of social ecology scholars on competition and selection would be that, with increasing numbers of competitors in a given resource space, selection pressures increase and therefore organizational failure becomes increasingly likely and organizational founding increasingly unlikely. However, Hannan (1989) develops a concept in which the increasing number of competitors does not exert such a simple linear influence on the vital rates of focal organizations.

He argues that an increasing number of organizations with the same properties can initially help establish the legitimacy of a certain organizational form before the conditions of competition among organizations of the same type prevail. Thus, under conditions of low density of organizations with a certain organizational form, it is supposed that the failure rate of organizations with this form is quite high and that the founding rate of organizations of this type is quite low, since the new form is still unknown and the institutional environment on which these new organizations depend is not willing to spend many resources on this new form. When the number of organizations of a certain type increases, the legitimacy of this organizational form increases as well. This means that the institutional environment begins to take a certain organizational form for granted once the number of organizations with this form noticeably increases.

However, the gains in legitimacy of an organizational form reduce with an increasing number of organizations of the same type. On the other hand, the forces of competition get ever stronger given an increasing number of organizations of the same type. At low density, competitive pressures among organizations hardly play a role. However, at higher density, when many organizations of the same type exist, each additional increase in the number of these organizations leads to a much stronger increase in the competitive pressures.

Therefore, while the legitimacy effect of increasing density dominates in a situation where only few organizations of the same type exist, competition dominates at higher organizational density. This in turn leads to a non-monotonic effect of density on organizational founding and failure rates; at lower density, an increasing number of organizations of the same type lead to a reduction of the risk of failure and an increase in the founding rate since legitimacy gains of density dominate. However, once the density of organizations of the same type has exceeded the point where competition pressures become stronger than legitimacy gains, a further increase of organizations of the same type leads to an increase of the failure rate and a decrease of the founding rate.

Although this basic model of density dependence of organizational vital rates has found impressive support in most empirical studies, there are also studies in which the described influence pattern of organizational density could not be found (e.g. Delacroix, Swaminathan, and Solt 1989).[2]

Moreover, the whole model of density dependence did not remain undisputed either. While there is almost no disagreement concerning the competition part of the model, the arguments concerning legitimacy gains through an increasing number of organizations of the same type have caused intense debate on the correctness of the original assumptions of the density model. A major question that has been asked in this debate is whether legitimacy gains are achieved by certain processes that are put in force by an increase in numbers of organizations of the same type or whether improved linkages to different resource-providing institutions in the environment of organizations that co-evolve with density are responsible for better survival and founding chances. Thus, the question is asked whether density controls the legitimation processes (Hannan and Carroll 1992) or whether increasing density is a 'proxy' variable that only reflects more complicated processes of building up legitimacy (Baum 1996; Baum and Powell 1995; Zucker 1989).

---

[2] It is however important to note that the model of density dependence always regards density relative to carrying capacity. The carrying capacity of a population is the maximum number of organizations that can exist in a certain resource space under given economic, political, and social conditions that can change over time.

In an attempt to refine and amend the competition argument of the density dependence concept, Barnett and Amburgey (1990) argue that competitive pressures are not exerted by the density, that is, by the *number* of organizations of the same form, but by mass, that is, the number of organizations weighted by their individual sizes. The introduction of mass dependence is explained by the notion that larger organizations, due to their better access to resources, generate stronger competitive pressures than smaller organizations do.

### 9.3.2. Resource Partitioning

While the density dependence concept was originally developed to explain the effects of competition within organizational populations, that is, among organizations with the same organizational form, other concepts explicitly take competition between organizations of different forms into account. A very influential distinction among organizational forms is the one between generalists and specialists—again a classification with strong Darwinistic connotations. Freeman and Hannan (1983) regard generalists as organizations that survive by drawing on a broad range of resources. Thus generalists are organizations that possess a wider niche than specialists. In addition, resources can be regarded as mainly controlled by the customers' preferences (see also Carroll, Dobrev, and Swaminathan 2002). However, it is also important for a generalist to be located in the centre of a market. This means that generalists are serving the interests and preferences of the majority of customers that can be found in a certain market. As a consequence, it is not necessarily the case that generalists offer a greater variety of products than specialists do. It is much more important for a generalist to offer the product that is demanded by the majority of customers.[3] Specialists, on the other hand, have a higher degree of adaptation, however, in a narrower market niche.

Carroll (1985) set up a theoretical model that considered that at any time in a given market there are certain resources available for generalists and other resources for specialists. Moreover, he explicitly defines resources as being provided by customers. He also claims that the amount of resources that are available for either organizational form varies over

---

[3] e.g. Freeman and Hannan (1983) consider, among other things, those restaurants to be generalists that offer a general—i.e. American—menu that is not dominated by any specific ethnic cuisine. As a consequence, it might be the case that a specialist ethnic restaurant offers more dishes than a generalist American restaurant.

time—due to changes in the structure of the overall market in which both generalists and specialists are active.

Carroll (1985) states that generalists compete for resources in the centre of the market. In a situation in which many generalist competitors exist, they have to differentiate themselves from each other. Therefore, generalists also offer somewhat more specialized products. As a consequence, the resource space that is occupied by generalists is large and there is only little 'room' for specialists to exist.

However, in a situation in which there are only few generalists in the market—a highly concentrated market—it is not a rational strategy for these generalists to try to satisfy those more specialized demands that are met by generalists in a less concentrated market, since this would mean the loss of economies of scale that generalist organizations possess. As a consequence, in a more concentrated market there are more resources available for specialists. Therefore, market concentration should generally make a specialist strategy more viable and a generalist strategy more risky.

According to this theoretical model, Carroll (1985) found that the death rate of generalist newspapers—daily newspapers of general interest—grows with increasing concentration in the market, measured either as concentration in circulation or as concentration in newspaper advertising. On the other hand, the death rate for specialist newspapers declined with increasing concentration.

In many empirical studies in a variety of industries, for example, the film industry (Mezias and Mezias (2000), financial auditing firms (Boone, Bröcheler, and Carroll 2000), the banking industry (Freeman and Lomi 1994), the beer brewing industry (Carroll and Swaminathan 1992, 2000), and wineries (Swaminathan 1995, 2001)), this theoretical model received strong empirical support. Moreover, it seems to be a theoretical model that is quite undisputed among organizational researchers.

## 9.4. The Spatial Dimension of Competition

In recent years, another dimension of market segmentation has moved into the focus of scholars of organizational ecology: the geographical (spatial) partitioning of markets. The importance of this dimension for the analysis of organizational vital rates seems obvious since it belongs to everyday knowledge that economic conditions vary over different geographical regions in a given market. Clusters of industrial production as well as the existence of advantaged and disadvantaged local areas of business are visible in many countries. However, in their initial forms, the theoretical concepts of organizational ecology that have been discussed so far do not include a comprehensive discussion of the geographical dimension of markets. Moreover, in the very early phase of empirical studies on density dependence and resource partitioning, the markets that have been taken into account have been (implicitly) considered to be geographically homogeneous.

At a later stage of the theoretical development, but still quite early in the development of empirical studies within population ecology, researchers have recognized that the differences in local conditions might have a considerable impact on the mechanisms of density dependence, resource partitioning, and other factors that are important in the selection process.

In order to form unbiased estimates of the density dependence of Italian rural banks' founding rate, Lomi (1995) controlled for the influence of regional heterogeneity by including regional fixed effects. He also considered region-specific co-variates that covered economic, social, and competitive conditions. Other early considerations of the spatial dimension included analyses in which density was accounted for at different levels of aggregation, for example, at the national, regional, or city level (e.g. Carroll and Wade 1991; Swaminathan and Wiedenmayer 1991). The basic goal of these studies was to find out whether local markets that are predominantly shaped by local interests and affections, for example, the beer and wine markets, are penetrated by national influences or whether these markets are somehow buffered from developments outside the local or regional boundaries (see also Lomi 2000). Generally, in many comparable studies it was found that local density affects vital rates more strongly than non-local or national density (e.g. Cattani, Pennings, and Wezel 2003; Greve 2002; Sorenson and Audia 2000).

The pattern of density dependence *across* national boundaries has also been a subject of research. Hannan et al. (1995) found that the increase of automobile manufacturers in Europe exerted legitimation effects on a broad, supra-national level while the competition effect of density only operates on the national level. Cultural aspects and attitudes towards products seem to penetrate national boundaries while the competition for material resources necessary for survival basically takes place within a certain country.

With respect to resource partitioning, Freeman and Lomi (1994) also used the above-mentioned strategy of including fixed effects for the analysis of national concentration on the founding of Italian rural banks. However, they had to conduct additional region-specific analyses to find that resource partitioning works in some regions but not in other ones. Related to this finding is the study of Boone, Carroll, and van Witteloos-tuijn (2002) who found that resource partitioning of Dutch newspapers predominantly works outside the great urban area of the Netherlands, the 'Randstad'. In the Randstad, national and regional—that is specialist— newspapers do not differ significantly, since local Randstad news is also of non-local, national interest. Therefore, an increasing concentration of national newspapers only leads to a significant increase of the success of non-Randstad specialist newspapers.

Another topic addressed in ecological studies that deal with spatial factors is the effect of regional clusters (e.g. McKendrick et al. 2003; Wezel 2005). These clusters are considered not only as areas that provide particularly good resources for organizations of the same type but also as a breeding ground for commonly shared morals and a community-specific identity of the producers. For example, Wezel (2005) found that the density-dependent legitimation of organizational foundings within a regional industrial cluster (the Coventry–Birmingham–Wolverhampton agglomeration of motorcycle producers) is much stronger than out-side that cluster. On the other hand, density-dependent competition is weaker within the cluster than outside since '[t]he presence of cul-tural homogeneity reinforces consensus and tempers competition' (Wezel 2005: 733).

However, a different view on clusters leads to the notion that geo-graphic concentration facilitates the entry of new firms in a regional cluster due to particularly good opportunities concerning information and recruitment of a qualified labour force, but that otherwise the failure rate in these regionally agglomerated markets is higher because of *stronger* competitive forces between local competitors (Sorenson and Audia 2000). This reasoning leads to another very important spatial dimension in ecological studies: the distance of a focal firm from its competitors. In order to account for stronger influences of competitors that are closer to a focal firm, Sorenson and Audia (2000) weighted local density by the distances between the various firms in the American footwear industry.

In an analysis of the Manhattan hotel industry, Baum and Mezias (1992) found that the failure rate of these hotels decreased in accordance with the average of the distances between a focal hotel and all other hotels. This result was reproduced by a study of Ingram and Inman (1996), who analysed the failure rate of hotels at Niagara Falls. Baum and Mezias (1992) also took into account that there might be geographic boundaries of competition. Thus, they defined a 'window' of competition. Hotels that are too far away from each other fall outside this window and are supposed not to compete with each other.

Baum and Haveman (1997) are interested in the founding process of Manhattan hotels. They look at the tendency of newly founded hotels, either to differentiate themselves with respect to geographic location, size, and price from the hotels that already exist or to try to be similar to them in order to benefit from spillover effects or positive externalities. They have discovered that newly founded hotels locate far away from competitors, again within predefined local boundaries, if the size of the newly founded hotel is similar to the sizes of the existing hotels. On the other hand, if new hotels locate close to existing hotels, they are similar to them as far as prices are concerned.

To summarize ecological studies that include geographical influences, one can state that there is not yet a clear-cut or comprehensive theoretical consideration of this dimension to be found in organizational ecology. Many studies simply claim that local conditions are more important than non-local conditions, especially as far as competition is concerned. However, at least the studies of Wezel (2005) and Baum and Haveman (1997) indicate that there might also be some kind of cooperation within spaces in which organizations of the same type are located closely to each other. What is missing is a clear theoretical concept that explains under which conditions competitive pressures of proximity prevail and under which conditions cooperative effects dominate.

## 9.5. The Spatial Dimension of Customers

Moreover, so far ecological studies have not considered that even in regionally confined markets or within predefined boundaries it is not necessarily the case that each firm competes with every other firm. In other words, although ecological studies have highlighted the spatial dimension of firms, that is, producers, they have—until now—neglected the spatial dimension of *customers*. Firms that produce in a locally confined market often do not have the potential to attract all possible customers for a simple reason: some customers live far away from the producing organization and the organization cannot afford to sell the products everywhere in the market since this would require investments that the organization either cannot afford or is not willing to undertake for other reasons. Of course, firms differ in the radius of the distribution of their goods in a regionally confined market. Some organizations might attract surrounding customers from each regional part of the local market, while others focus only on customers within the immediate surroundings of the firm. This means that firms located in the same regional market differ to a great extent in the number and type of competitors that they have to face. This tendency is magnified if there is heterogeneity in the geographic proximity of firms. Of course, these considerations hold mainly true for specific markets, predominantly markets for handmade products while firms that produce goods for the national automobile market, for example, surely have the potential to attract customers from all parts of the country.

The inclusion of the spatial dimension of customers, that is, the regional distribution of goods, can enhance studies of organizational ecology in several ways. (1) Studies on density dependence can benefit from a more exact formulation of competitive or cooperative structures. Only organizations that have overlaps in the regional distribution of products can be supposed to be in competition with each other. It is also possible to analyse whether cooperative tendencies are more prevalent within a community of organizations that draw on the same regional potential of customers or whether cooperative influences develop between organizations that draw on customers from different areas. (2) Studies on resource partitioning can use a much more subtle distinction between different forms of organizations: instead of simply using the categories 'specialist' or 'generalist' organizations that often refer to a more *locally* or a more *nationally* orientated organization (e.g. newspapers), one can use a continuum of different forms, according to the area of distribution of goods. Studies in which the definition of a specialist does not depend on a locally constrained operation of an organization, but only on the type of the product, for example, speciality brewers (Carroll and Swaminathan 1992, 2000), can be supplemented by taking the local area of distribution into account. Moreover, one can model much more exactly the resources provided by customers on which a focal organization relies by obtaining socio-demographical data for the different areas in which focal firm's products are sold.

Of course, information on the distribution of products is not easily obtained. Archival data, on which most of the empirical studies within organizational ecology are based, do not normally provide this specific information. Therefore, it might be necessary to obtain this information from experts within the industry—for example, business historians or enthusiasts for the handmade products and their producers—or simply to ask the entrepreneurs in the industry themselves.

215

## 9.6. Discussion and Conclusion

It is to be hoped that this chapter has shown that the theoretical basics of the organizational ecology approach cannot be regarded as a simple transfer of Darwin's concept of biological evolution to the situation of the development of organizational populations. It is much more the case that classical sociological concepts concerning the influence of competition among members of society on the formation of distinct societal entities—that is, the development of social differentiation—have built the foundations of organizational ecology. Although these very fundamental sociological considerations, as well as the theoretical basis of organizational ecology, contain certain Darwinistic elements, they surely cannot be considered as 'biological'. Competition among living entities or organizations is an empirical fact that—incidentally—constituted a considerable part of economic theory. Thus, from my point of view, similarities between the Darwinian theory of biological evolution and sociological ecological approaches are due to the simple truth that some aspects of the Darwinian concept do apply for biological as well as sociological situations.

Moreover, it is also important to note that organizational ecology never denied the possibility of organizational adaptation. In its initial stage this theoretical concept simply focused on selection, that is, organizational failure, since this highly important aspect in the development of certain organizational populations has been neglected by other organizational theories. However, even at this stage of the theory's development the possibility of successful organizational change was never excluded from the theoretical framework. With the maturation of the ecological concept, change, that is, adaptation to environmental alterations, became an increasingly important aspect of ecological empirical studies.

Finally, I think that the consideration of the spatial dimension of organizations greatly improved the empirical sub-concepts of density dependence and resource partitioning that are concerned with the empirical analysis of competitive structures among organizations. Currently, however, it is basically the geographical aspects of the producers that are taken into account in ecological studies. In order to get a more realistic picture of the competitive structure I think it is also necessary to introduce 'the spatial dimension of customers' to ecological studies. Only with the consideration of the area of distribution of the firms' products is it possible to model which organizations are really in competition with each other.

This chapter only highlighted some, although very important, aspects of organizational ecology. I think it is especially interesting that this type of thinking about organizations is constantly 'in a state of flux'. Ideas from other theoretical approaches, that is, new institutionalism (Wade, Swaminathan, and Saxon 1998), industrial organization and strategic management (Boone and van Witteloostuijn 1995), behavioural approaches (van Witteloostuijn 1998), or the resource-based view (van Witteloostuijn and Boone 2006), have been incorporated in this approach. Therefore, organizational ecology can be expected to continue to contribute to our understanding of how markets and competitive structures between organizations are formed.

## References

Amburgey, T. L. and Rao, H. (1996). 'Organizational Ecology: Past, Present, and Future Directions', *Academy of Management Journal*, 39: 1265–86.

——Kelly, D., and Barnett, W. P. (1993). 'Resetting the Clock. The Dynamics of Organizational Change and Failure', *Administrative Science Quarterly*, 38: 51–73.

Barnett, W. P. and Amburgey, T. L. (1990). 'Do Larger Organizations Generate Stronger Competition?', in J. Singh (ed.), *Organizational Evolution: New Directions*. Beverly Hills, CA: Sage.

Baum, J. A. C. (1996). 'Organizational Ecology', in S. R. Clegg, C. Hardy, and W. R. Nord (eds.), *Handbook of Organization Studies*. London: Sage.

——and Amburgey, T. L. (2002). 'Organizational Ecology', in J. Baum (ed.), *Blackwell Companion to Organizations*. Malden, MA: Blackwell.

——and Haveman, H. (1997). 'Love Thy Neighbor? Differentiation and Agglomeration in the Manhattan Hotel Industry, 1898–1990', *Adminstrative Science Quarterly*, 42: 304–38.

——and Mezias, S. J. (1992). 'Localized Competition and Organizational Failure in the Manhattan Hotel Industry, 1898–1990', *Administrative Science Quarterly*, 37: 580–604.

——and Powell, W. W. (1995). 'Cultivating an Institutional Ecology of Organizations: Comment on Hannan, Carroll, Dundron, and Torres', *American Sociological Review*, 60: 529–38.

——and Singh, J. V. (1996). 'Dynamics of Organizational Responses to Competition', *Social Forces*, 74: 1261–97.

Boone, C. and van Witteloostuijn, A. (1995). 'Industrial Organization and Organizational Ecology: The Potentials for Cross-Fertilization', *Organization Studies*, 16: 265–98.

——Bröcheler, V., and Carroll, G. R. (2000). 'Custom Service: Application and Tests of Resource Partitioning Theory among Dutch Auditing Firms from 1896 to 1992', *Organization Studies*, 21: 355–81.

Boone, C., Carroll, G. R., and van Witteloostuijn, A. (2002). 'Environmental Resource Distributions and Market Partitioning: Dutch Daily Newspaper Organizations from 1968 to 1994', *American Sociological Review*, 67: 408–31.

Carroll, G. R. (1985). 'Concentration and Specialization: Dynamics of Niche Width in Populations of Organizations', *American Journal of Sociology*, 33: 1262–83.

——and Swaminathan, A. (1992). 'The Organizational Ecology of Strategic Groups in the Brewing Industry from 1975 to 1990', *Industrial and Corporate Change*, 1: 65–97.

——— (2000). 'Why the Microbrewery Movement? Organizational Dynamics of Resource Partitioning in the U.S. Brewing Industry', *American Journal of Sociology*, 106: 715–62.

——and Wade, J. (1991). 'Density Dependence in the Organizational Evolution of the American Brewing Industry Across Different Levels of Analysis', *Social Science Research*, 20: 271–302.

——Dobrev, S. D., and Swaminathan, A. (2002). 'Organizational Processes of Resource Partitioning', *Research in Organizational Behavior*, 24: 1–40.

Cattani, G. J., Pennings, M., and Wezel, F. C. (2003). 'Spatial and Temporal Heterogeneity in Entrepreneurial Activity', *Organization Science*, 14: 670–85.

Cyert, R. M. and March, J. G. (1963). *A Behavioral Theory of the Firm*. Englewood Cliffs, NJ: Prentice-Hall.

Delacroix, J., Swaminathan, A., and Solt, M. E. (1989). 'Density Dependence Versus Population Dynamics: An Ecological Study of Failings in the California Wine Industry', *American Sociological Review*, 54: 245–62.

Dobrev, S. D., Kim, T. Y., and Carroll, G. R. (2003). 'Shifting Gears, Shifting Niches: Organizational Inertia and Change in the Evolution of the U.S. Automobile Industry, 1885–1981', *Organization Science*, 14: 264–82.

Durkheim, E. (1933). *The Division of Labor in Society*. New York: Free Press.

Freeman, J. (1982). 'Organizational Life Cycles and Natural Selection Processes', in B. M. Staw and L. L. Cummings (eds.), *Research in Organizational Behavior*, vol. 4. Greenwich: JAI Press.

——and Hannan, M. T. (1983). 'Niche Width and the Dynamics of Organizational Populations', *American Journal of Sociology*, 88: 1116–45.

——and Lomi, A. (1994). 'Resource Partitioning and Foundings of Banking Cooperatives in Italy', in J. A. C. Baum and J. V. Singh (eds.), *The Evolutionary Dynamics of Organizations*. New York: Oxford University Press.

Frese, E. (1992). *Organisationstheorie. Historische Entwicklung—Ansätze—Perspektiven*, 2nd edn. Wiesbaden: Gabler.

Greve, H. R. (2002). 'An Ecological Theory of Spatial Evolution: Local Density Dependence in Tokyo Banking, 1894–1936', *Social Forces*, 80: 847–79.

Hannan, M. T. (1989). 'Competitive and Institutional Processes in Organizational Ecology', in J. Berger, M. Zelditch, and B. Anderson (eds.), *Sociological Theories in Progress: New Formulations*. Newbury Park, CA: Sage.

——and Carroll, G. R. (1992). *Dynamics of Organizational Populations: Density, Legitimation and Competition*. Oxford: Oxford University Press.

——and Freeman, J. (1977). 'The Population Ecology of Organizations', *American Journal of Sociology*, 82: 929–64.

————(1984). 'Structural Inertia and Organizational Change', *American Sociological Review*, 49: 149–64.

————(1986). 'Where Do Organizational Forms Come From?', *Sociological Forum*, 1: 50–72.

——Carroll, G. R., Dundon, E. A., and Torres, J. C. (1995). 'Organizational Evolution in Multinational Context: Entries of Automobile Manufacturers in Belgium, France, Germany and Italy', *American Sociological Review*, 60: 509–28.

Hawley, A. H. (1950). *Human Ecology: A Theory of Community Structure*. New York: Roland Press.

——(1968). 'Human Ecology', in D. L. Sills (ed.), *International Encyclopedia of the Social Sciences*. New York: Macmillan.

——(1986). *Human Ecology: A Theoretical Essay*. Chicago, IL: University of Chicago Press.

Ingram, P. and Inman, C. (1996). 'Institutions, Intergroup Rivalry, and the Evolution of Hotel Populations around Niagara Falls', *Administrative Science Quarterly*, 41: 629–58.

Kelly, D. and Amburgey, T. L. (1991). 'Organizational Inertia and Momentum. A Dynamic Model of Strategic Change', *Academy of Management Journal*, 34: 591–612.

Lomi, A. (1995). 'The Population Ecology of Organizational Founding: Location Dependence and Unobserved Heterogeneity', *Administrative Science Quarterly*, 40: 111–44.

——(2000). 'Density Dependence and Spatial Duality in Organizational Founding Rates: Danish Commercial Banks, 1846–1989', *Organization Studies*, 21: 433–61.

McKendrick, D. G., Jaffee, J., Carroll, G. R., and Khessina, O. M. (2003). 'In the Bud? Disk Array Producers as a (Possibly) Emergent Organizational Form', *Administrative Science Quarterly*, 48: 60–93.

Meyer, J. W. and Rowan, B. (1977). 'Institutional Organizations: Formal Structure as Myth and Ceremony', *American Journal of Sociology*, 83: 340–63.

Mezias, J. and Mezias, S. (2000). 'Resource Partioning and the Founding of Specialist Firms: The American Feature Film Industry, 1912–1929', *Organization Science*, 11: 306–22.

Pfeffer, J. and Salancick, G. R. (1978). *The External Control of Organizations*. New York: Harper and Row.

Senge, P. M. (1990). 'The Leader's New Work: Building Learning Organizations', *Sloan Management Review*, 32: 7–23.

Sorenson, O. and Audia, P. G. (2000). 'The Social Structure of Entrepreneurial Activity: Geographic Concentration of Footwear Production in the United States, 1940–1989', *American Journal of Sociology*, 106: 424–62.

219

Swaminathan, A. (1995). The Proliferation of Specialist Organizations in the American Wine Industry, 1941–1990', *Adminstrative Science Quarterly*, 40: 653–80.

——(2001). 'Resource Partitioning and the Evolution of Specialist Organizations: The Role of Location and Identity in the U.S. Wine Industry', *Academy of Management Journal*, 44: 1169–85.

——and Wiedenmayer, G. (1991). 'Does the Pattern of Density Dependence in Organizational Mortality Rates Vary across Levels of Analysis? Evidence from the German Brewing Industry', *Social Science Research*, 20: 45–73.

Scott, W. R. (1981). *'Organizations': Rational, Natural, and Open Systems*. Englewood Cliffs: Prentice Hall.

Thompson, J. D. (1967). *Organizations in Action*. New York: Transaction.

van Witteloostuijn, A. (1998). 'Bridging Behavioral and Economic Theories of Decline: Organizational Inertia, Strategic Competition, and Chronic Failure', *Management Science*, 44: 501–19.

——and Boone, C. (2006). 'A Resource-Based Theory of Market Structure and Organizational Form', *Academy of Management Review*, 31: 409–26.

von der Oelsnitz, D. (2005). ' "Orangenbäumchen am Plattensee" Erkenntnistheoretische Überlegungen zum Ideologieproblem in der (Management-) Forschung', *Die Betriebswirtschaft*, 65: 333–49.

Wade, J. B., Swaminathan, A., and Saxon, M. S. (1998). 'Normative and Resource Flow Consequences of Local Regulations in the American Brewing Industry, 1845–1918', *Administrative Science Quarterly*, 43: 905–35.

Wezel, F. C. (2005). 'Location Dependence and Industry Evolution: Founding Rates in the United Kingdom Motorcycle Industry, 1895–1993', *Organization Studies*, 26: 729–54.

Young, R. (1988). 'Is Population Ecology a Useful Paradigm for the Study of Organizations?', *American Journal of Sociology*, 94: 1–24.

Zucker, L. (1989). 'Combining Institutional Theory and Population Ecology: No Legitimacy, No History', *American Sociological Review*, 54: 542–5.

# 10

# Different Paths of Industry Evolution: Timing of Entry, Legitimation, and Competition Spillovers Across Countries

*Filippo Carlo Wezel, Christophe Boone, and Arjen van Witteloostuijn*

## 10.1. Introduction

Organizational ecology (Hannan and Freeman 1977) analyses the patterns of population density evolution and the variations in their composition over time. The original insight of the theory points to the emergence of an S-shaped pattern of evolution deriving from the non-linear impact of density on organizational entry and exit rates. Competitive and legitimacy forces underlie the impact of density on the population's growth rate (Ruef 2004). More recently, however, the original model has been challenged, based on the variety of empirical patterns observed in diverse settings (e.g. Hannan et al. 1995, but see also Baum 1996; Lomi, Larsen, and Freeman 2005). As Carroll and Hannan (2000: 221) have recognized, '[c]omparative analysis of such variations in density dependence across populations and contexts holds great promise for corporate demography.... The ability to make comparisons of this magnitude allows one to understand in a serious way the empirical patterns (and departures from them).... It also allows one to examine extant theoretical claims rigorously and to advance novel nuanced arguments.'

Recent attempts to account for industry-specific *temporal* differences in the intensity of the density-dependent forces of competition and legitimation include temporal heterogeneity (Hannan 1997; Wezel 2005), density delay (Delacroix and Carroll 1983), mass dependence (Winter 1990), and population-level inertia (Lomi, Larsen, and Freeman 2005; Ruef 2004), as well as different forms of weighted density according to resource base overlap or behavioural experience (e.g. Barnett 1997). Other studies have been concerned with *geographical* boundaries, and the way in which their correct detection impinges on the magnitude of density-dependent competition and legitimation (Carroll and Wade 1991; Cattani, Pennings, and Wezel 2003). In this chapter, contrary to most of the existing research in organizational ecology, we will *not* devote our attention to vital rates but rather focus on the forces that regulate the intensity of legitimation and competition *at the population level*—under the assumption that the factors influencing entries and exits in populations are fully symmetrical, and, thus, focusing on compound growth (see Ruef 2004, but also Hannan and Freeman 1977: 941). In so doing, this chapter aims at accomplishing two goals: (*a*) being able to model some of the variety of evolutionary paths of organizational populations empirically observed and (*b*) elaborate on a model refinement that captures the existence of legitimation and competition spillovers *across national populations*. In this respect, we hope to contribute to an emerging branch of organizational ecology concerned with evolutionary processes taking place at the *international level* (see e.g. Barnett and McKendrick 2004; Hannan et al. 1995, 1998). This research may be seen as a special case of community ecology, focusing on different populations of the same industry across space (e.g. the domestic motorcycle industries in countries $x$, $y$, and $z$), rather than on different populations in a bounded geographical area (e.g. automobile and motorcycle industries in a single country $x$).

Indeed, the evolutionary pattern of density of different countries operating in the same industry tends to differ widely. This is clear, for instance, from the reported trajectories of density evolution in the automobile industry in Europe (Hannan et al. 1995, 1998). Another example is the motorcycle industry (Boone, Wezel, and van Witteloostuijn 2007). In Figure 10.1, by way of illustration, we plot the evolution of density of motorcycle producers in Germany, Italy, and the UK.

We claim that the intensity of legitimation and competition forces shaping the evolution of these populations may be related to the timing of entry of the focal population. Moreover, we build on the literature that points to the existence of legitimation spillovers across countries (Hannan et al. 1995). While promising, this avenue of research keeps mapping competition as being localized (or domestic), remaining at odds with the dynamics of many industries in the international arena that were, and are, dominated by cross-country competition (Barnett and McKendrick

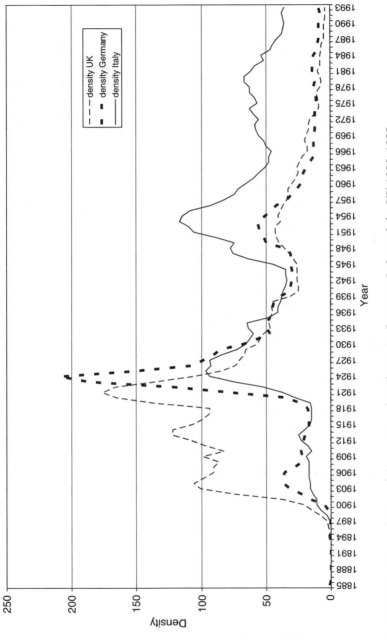

**Figure 10.1.** Density evolution of the motorcycle industry in Germany, Italy, and the UK 1885–1993

2004). Because of this empirical evidence, the impact of competitive spillovers on the strength of density-dependent forces and, ultimately, on local density evolution remains unclear. Our aim in this chapter is *not* to present an empirical test of alternative models (e.g. Ruef 2004), but rather to theoretically introduce a mechanism that may induce the variations in density evolution patterns as observed empirically. In particular, we propose a model that points to *cross-country* differences in timing of entry and development as key drivers of the *country-specific* processes of legitimation and competition. Here, we distinguish pioneer from follower countries, and use this distinction to advance how observable patterns of population evolution—that is, density growth and decline—may be related to and sustained by spillover effects across countries. The model proposed here is largely inspired by that literature in biology (Bernstein 2003; Sæther, Engen, and Matthysen 2002), in which the form and the strength of density-dependent evolution are modelled.

Note that we acknowledge that the interpretation of the biological model presented here, and the related role of the timing of population entry, represents just one of many possible interpretations. This is why this chapter should be considered as a tentative step in the direction of injecting more insights from recent developments in bio-ecology to the world of organizations. Section 10.4 discusses this issue in more detail, pointing to other possible interpretations of the model proposed here. The remaining part of this chapter first introduces the basic model, as 'borrowed' from bio-ecology. Subsequently, we propose a set of propositions that are potentially testable in a variety of empirical settings. Finally, Section 10.4 discusses the contributions, extensions, and implications suggested by our model formulation.

## 10.2. In the Direction of a Few Extensions

### 10.2.1. *The Original Intuition*

Organizational ecologists (Hannan and Freeman 1977: 941) developed a theory that aimed at explaining the density growth of organizational populations along a sigmoid-shaped trajectory. The intuition is that a logistic evolutionary pattern followed by an organizational population stems from a growth rate influenced by density. The source of inspiration for this model was that developed by Verhulst (1838), which speculated about density dependence regulating the growth of biological species. The common model adopted by biologists to predict the growth of biotic populations points to logistic growth in population density. Let $R_0$ indicate the natural growth rate of the population when no constraints on resources apply and $K$ flag the carrying capacity of the system. Equation (10.1) is used to model a logistic model of population density over time, $t$, as indicated from:

$$N_{t+1} = N_t \times \left[1 + R_0\left(1 - \frac{N_t}{K}\right)\right] \text{ or } N_{t+1} = N_t + N_t R_0 - \frac{N_t^2 R_0}{K}, \quad (10.1)$$

where $N_t R_0$ indicates the natural growth of the population under no resource constraints and $\frac{N_t^2 R_0}{K}$ acts as a 'break' to exponential growth because of carrying capacity limitations—that is, $K$. The non-linear effect of density on *population growth* becomes apparent from maximizing equation (10.1) in $N$. Examples of the associated plots are reproduced in Figures 10.2 and 10.3.

According to the transposition of this model to the world of organizations (Hannan 1986), the growth of organizational populations is a bit more complicated and stems from a non-linear relation of density dependence with *organizational vital rates*—that is, entries and exits. This is so because population density is regulated by the two countervailing forces of legitimation and competition. At low values of density, legitimation dominates ($N$), whereas the opposite holds true at high values of density ($N^2$). The focus of the theory has been concentrated on the detection of a non-linear pattern of density dependence in the analysis of vital rates while controlling for the level of resources available—that is, by keeping $K$ (the carrying capacity of the system) constant. In a nutshell, the theory assumes that a new organizational form acquires legitimacy when it displays a template or architecture that is socially recognized as such (Meyer and Rowan 1977). At low values of density, legitimacy will be below par as customers and suppliers need to be taught and educated, and employees to be socialized into new roles. Furthermore, it may take some time before the emergence of a new organizational form becomes apparent to the institutional environment. Increases in density augment the social recognition of the new form/organizational population, with the effect of attracting additional entrepreneurial activity and reducing the risk of mortality. Therefore, the population grows in density of organizations.

However, after triggering a large number of entries and reducing exit rates, organizations affect one another's access to vital resources, such as scarce supply of inputs and demand for outputs—a process usually referred to as competition. Competition intensifies because each

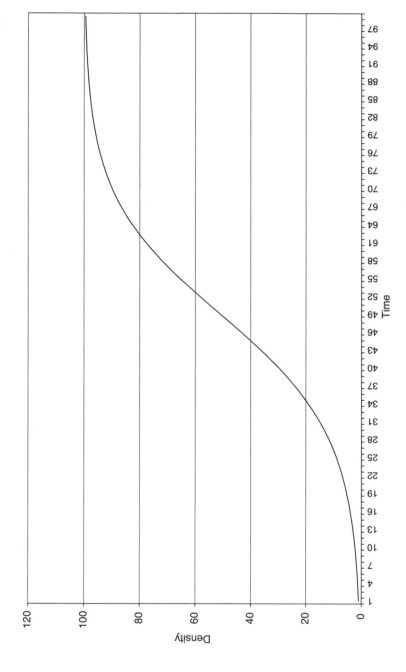

**Figure 10.2.** Logistic pattern of population-density growth with $R_0 = 0.1$ and $K = 100$

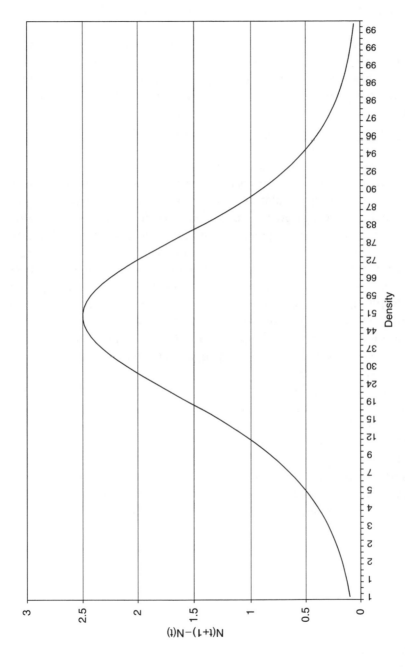

**Figure 10.3.** Population-density growth rate with $R_0 = 0.1$ and $K = 100$

organization within a given population depends on the same pool of increasingly scarce resources (Hannan and Freeman 1977; Hawley 1950). Marginal increments of organizations towards the level of capacity of the system, known as carrying capacity, will slow down population-density growth by triggering competitive pressure. As a consequence, birth rates decrease while death rates increase as populations become crowded. When the carrying capacity ($K$) of the environment (i.e. the maximum number of organizations that can be viably supported by an environment) is reached, density growth stops, and an equilibrium is reached (i.e. births are balanced by deaths).

Organizational ecologists have relied on this model formulation to predict that entry and exit rates are curvilinearly affected by the density of organizations in the population. After two decades of systematic empirical research, we now know how organizational founding and mortality rates are related to specific general population-level processes. Different industries, from labour unions (Hannan and Freeman 1987), newspapers (Hannan and Carroll 1992), and banks (Greve 2002; Lomi 1995, 2000; Ranger-Moore, Banaszak-Hall, and Hannan 1991) to telephone companies (Barnett 1997), beer producers (Carroll et al. 1993; Carroll and Swaminathan 2000), and automobile producers (Bigelow et al. 1997; Hannan 1997; Hannan et al. 1995; Sorenson 2000), have provided empirical evidence on the density dependence of organizational founding (inverted U-shaped) and mortality (U-shaped). Albeit the theory implies a sophisticated logic predicting the impact of density on vital rates, the underlying concepts of legitimation and competition could be seen as properties of the population as a whole. Population growth, in fact, may be conceived as directly proportional to legitimation and inversely related to competition (i.e. $\frac{\partial N}{\partial t} \propto \frac{L_t}{C_t}$)—see also Ruef (2004). This chapter follows this logic and does not aim at contributing to alternative model specifications regulating organizational vital rates, but rather delving into the forces that impinge on the different intensities of legitimation and competition from a population-level standpoint. Before doing that, however, we review the recent findings of the ecological literature regarding the main sources of variation in organizational entries and exits.

## 10.2.2. The Density-Dependence Model in Geographical Space

Despite the robust generality of the empirical results obtained, density-dependence theory has been criticized for its apparent lack of concern for the substantial variations empirically observed. This critique triggered further curiosity that gave an impetus to complementary research into the forces that may accelerate or hamper legitimation and competition. As Carroll and Khessina (2005: 463–4) put it:

Numerous empirical studies on a variety of populations and industries overwhelmingly conclude that the curvilinear predictions of the density-dependence model hold generally (Carroll and Hannan 2000). Yet, differences in the timing and levels of turning points lead Carroll and Hannan (2000) to suggest that as with the demographic transition in human demography, there is ample variation to support further theoretical development via meta-analysis.

Recent research in organizational ecology speaks directly to this concern. Several researchers have focused on the study of founding rates— a genuine population-level process—to understand the origins of such variations. As Hannan and Carroll (1992: 235–6, emphasis in the original) put it, 'Because nonevents cannot be associated with particular organizations, it follows that the unit of analysis cannot be the individual organization. Rather the *organizational population* itself experiences the foundings.' Following this lead, for instance, Carroll and Wade's study of the American brewing industry (1991) has drawn renewed attention to the 'spatial dimension' that is so central in the work of human ecologists (e.g. Hawley 1950). To shed light on the issue of deciding on the spatial boundaries within which density-dependence processes are supposed to operate, some ecologists have followed the geography path by focusing on density dependence in disaggregated geographical areas such as regions or states. Both legitimization and competition are now considered to be subject to geographic variations within nationally defined industries.

In this view, the organizational population itself is the level at which founding events occur (Aldrich and Wiedenmayer 1993). The studies by Lomi (1995) and Greve (2002) address the local nature of these evolutionary phenomena explicitly. Lomi (1995) reveals how different groups of rural cooperative banks in Italy reacted in different ways to national competitive and institutional pressures. While no real 'difference in legitimation was found across models based on local and non-local specification of density, competition is seven times stronger at the regional than at the national level' (Lomi 1995: 137). Bigelow et al. argue that geography and *physical distance* 'account for the different scale of effects of legitimation and competition rather than nation-state political boundaries' (1997: 394). This echoes Lomi's findings (2000) for the core-periphery relationship between commercial banks in Copenhagen and in the rest of Denmark. Greve (2002) shows that local density triggered the evolution of a population within a given geographical area. His findings demonstrate how 'density dependence operated locally within small areas and spilled over from neighboring areas' (Greve 2002: 870).

Another set of studies try to move beyond the intuition of localized processes of legitimation and competition, focusing on boundary-spanning processes across geographically defined populations. Theoretical developments have aimed at reformulating density-dependence theory. Current evidence seems indeed to suggest that legitimation operates at a broader geographical scale than does competition (Bigelow et al. 1997; Hannan et al. 1995). Hannan et al. (1995), for instance, show how legitimation spilled over to other countries, while competition remained largely domestic in the European automobile industry. Empirical support for such a multilevel density-dependence theory of industry evolution, however, still remains scant, being primarily limited to the automobile industry (Hannan 1997; Hannan et al. 1995). An exception to this rule is the study of Wade, Swaminathan, and Saxon (1998) on the US beer industry.

While this literature represents a promising avenue of further research, its logic 'has yet to be thoroughly tested in a wide variety of contexts' (Carroll and Hannan 2000: 234). Moreover, the validity of the main assumption of such a multilevel density-dependence theory is questionable: 'Nation states have frequently succeeded in creating and enforcing laws and regulations that limit competitive threats from outside.... When protectionist sentiment prevails, states attempt to block or reduce the inflow of products and labor and outflows of capital at their borders' (Carroll and Hannan 2000: 255). This assumption is clearly inconsistent with the evidence in many industries, now and in history, that international competition is often the rule rather than the exception, as is witnessed by the impressive history of foreign direct investment (FDI) and international trade flows. This implies that competition spills over across domains and countries. Barnett and McKendrick (2004), for instance, report that in the disk array industry competition became increasingly global over time. This chapter aims at contributing to this unsettled issue in density-dependence theory by nailing down the potential impact of cross-countries competitive spillovers on population-density growth (or decline, for that matter). Below, we will introduce our argument by presenting a revised version of the original model, as 'borrowed' from bio-ecology (Hannan and Freeman 1977; Verhulst 1838). In so doing, we will make abstractions from the processes regulating vital rates and assume that the factors influencing entries and exits operate symmetrically. This assumption renders unnecessary the decomposition of population growth into flows of entries and exits (for a review of these findings, see Carroll and Hannan 2000) and remains coherent with early ecological models aimed at comprehending the pattern of aggregate changes in organizational populations (Carroll 1981; Hannan and Freeman 1977: 941; see Ruef 2004).

### 10.2.3. *A Modified Approach to Population-Density Growth*

When observing organizational populations, consider the different paths to legitimation and competition exhibited by them—see, for example, Figure 10.1. These paths seem to point to different intensities of legitimation and competition processes. How to model such heterogeneity? One possible way to accomplish this goal is to consider a model specification known as '$\theta$ logistic growth'. A parameter, $\theta$, is added into equation (10.1) to model the diverse intensity of the growth curve. This model has been recently adopted by biologists to show how organisms with diverse life histories are heterogeneously regulated by density dependence (e.g. Sæther, Engen, and Matthysen 2002; Sibly et al. 2005). Sæther, Engen, and Matthysen (2002), for instance, modelled the form of density dependence and the strength of density regulation at $K$ (i.e. carrying capacity) by recurring to the $\theta$ logistic model formulation (Gilpin and Ayala 1973). The findings they obtain show that for large values of $\theta$—that is, above 1—the specific population-density growth rate is high with population size at lower densities and a large reduction in the growth rate is observed only when approaching carrying capacity $K$ as the opposite holds true for small values of $\theta$—that is, below 1. This evidence suggests that the value of $\theta$ strongly influences a population's density evolution. In formal terms, and extending equation (10.1),

$$N_{t+1} = N_t \times \left[ 1 + R_0 \left( 1 - \left( \frac{N_t}{K} \right)^{\theta} \right) \right] \tag{10.2}$$

The new element is the $\theta$ parameter. For $\theta = 1$, the model gives the regular logistic growth—that is, equation (10.1). So, the original specification of the density-dependence model is nested into the extended $\theta$ version. If $\theta > 1$, the density growth rate is high at low values of density (i.e. stronger legitimation), but declines rapidly at high-density values (i.e. very strong competition). The opposite holds true for values of $\theta < 1$: then, the growth rate grows slowly at low values of density (relatively slow legitimation), and remains rather flat at high-density values (relatively weak competition). Intuitively, this model formulation impinges on the variation in the general trajectory of the development of organizational populations. This point is illustrated by Figure 10.4.

Finally, note that the key implication of different $\theta$ values is that they affect the timing of reaching the density peak—that is, the density level at which population growth is at its maximum—differently. As Figure 10.4 shows, for $\theta > 1$ the peak of population growth occurs earlier than in the case of $\theta < 1$. So, $\theta$ reflects the *speed* at which the population's carrying capacity $K$ is reached. High-$\theta$ countries quickly converge to $K$, and low-$\theta$ countries do so slowly. In equilibrium terminology, $\theta$ affects the speed and pattern of adjustment to equilibrium—that is, $K$. The interesting question then pertains to the interpretation of this parameter and to the underlying forces influencing its intensity.

## 10.3. Pioneer versus Follower Countries' Population-Density Growth

### 10.3.1. *Legitimation Spillover Effects*

The model reflected in equation (10.2) is flexible by providing a natural weight to population-level legitimation and competition. The key is that $\theta$ acts as an accelerator or decelerator of the impact of density on population-density growth. In the world of organizations, the $\theta$ parameter could be interpreted in multiple ways. It may, for instance, indicate how well-connected or cohesive the population is, either signalling the existence of an influential social movement that sustains its development (i.e. high $\theta$) or how scattered geographically the population is in a context where both legitimacy and competition take place along a geographical gradient. While we consider these and other interpretations to be plausible, and certainly worth exploring in future work, here we interpret the model in light of an international cross-country setting. In attempting to transpose the $\theta$ logistic model to the field of what may be called cross-country ecology, we will make two assumptions. First, in a set of national populations that belong to the same industry (e.g. automobiles or motorcycles) develops at different paces and with different timing patterns (see, for instance, Figure 10.1). For the sake of simplicity, we dichotomize the different patterns of evolution in terms of 'pioneer' and 'follower' countries (see below for more detail). Second,

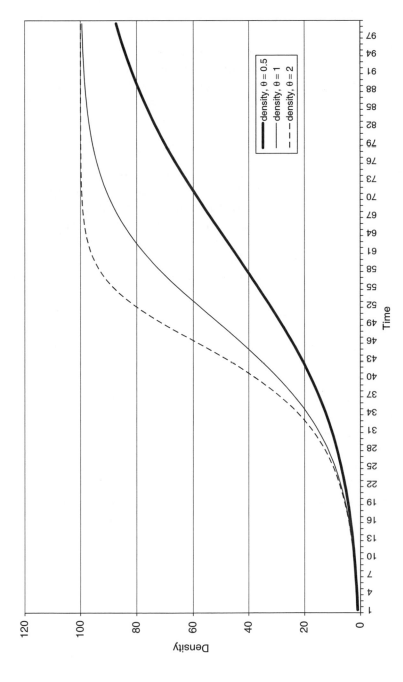

**Figure 10.4.** Patterns of population-density growth with $R_0 = 0.1$, $K = 100$, and $\theta = 0.5$, 1, and 2

the longer a national population takes to enter into an industry, the more the population's (domestic) evolution will rely on outside (foreign) sources of legitimation—that is, legitimacy spillover across countries, as also indicated by Hannan et al. in their study of entries (1995).

Organizational populations in different nations appear on the scene at various velocities, and the spread of a new organizational form takes time to diffuse across national boundaries. The question now is, therefore, how pioneer countries differ from follower ones (provided that they do so at all, of course) in $\theta$ terms. Relating to the patterns of density observed in the automobile and motorcycle industries (cf. Figure 10.1), we would like to offer the following narrative. Early entrants in a pioneer country, albeit confronted with the (costly and risky) need to build up a new industry, may well enjoy fast growth thanks to the emergence of the social actions and physical infrastructures that are often anchored in a limited geographical territory. As Carroll and Hannan (2000: 253) mention, '[e]arly development and refinement of a form usually involve social movement processes, with organizational enthusiasts seeking to define and promulgate a conception of a form. In these cases, the initial accretion of legitimation is highly localized to the birthplace(s). . . . Subsequent proliferation usually involves expansion beyond a form's home ground.' Recent findings concerning the emergence of a new organizational form seem to point to agglomeration in geographical space as an accelerator of legitimacy (McKendrick et al. 2003).

Conversely, the proliferation of the form beyond the home country, albeit benefiting from spillovers from pioneer populations, is unlikely to receive domestic social support to the same extent. They may even— occasionally—face cultural opposition if perceived as inconsistent with local mores and conventions (see e.g. the study of Delmestri and Woywode 2005). Consider also that a new form may emerge from an incremental path of innovation (Levinthal 1998). In the motorcycle sector, the emergence of the UK population in the area of Coventry, Birmingham and Wolverhampton was the natural consequence of the significant presence of bicycle and automobile producers in that area at the end of the nineteenth century (Wezel 2005). Conversely, a late entrant in the automobile industry, such as Italy, had to rely heavily on legitimation spillovers coming from nearby countries like France, for example (Kim, Dobrev, and Solari 2003: 1286). According to this argument, while scarce resources serve as the growth limit of pioneer populations, paradoxically, their follower counterparts will be struggling at even lower densities for the acquisition of resources as they greatly depend on spillovers from other countries. Note that this is not to say that followers will necessarily exhibit slower growth in density, but rather that the pace of their growth will heavily depend on the intensity of the spillover effects (see below). This interpretation thus points to pioneer countries as resembling high-$\theta$ populations—exposed to stronger local population-level legitimation— and followers as low-$\theta$ representatives—with a prolonged path to legitimation.

Empirical evidence offered by Hannan and his colleagues on entries into the European automobile industry suggests that a pioneer country (i.e. France) did indeed exhibit the strongest levels of population-level legiti- mation in the early history of the industry due to very active and robust social movements, whereas the weakest legitimation force was detected in a late mover (i.e. Italy). Other studies have revealed how core countries exhibit stronger population-level legitimation and competition than their peripheral counterparts do in different industries. Take again our motorcy- cle industry example of Figure 10.1. Wezel (2005) reports that the centre of production of motorcycles in the UK (i.e. the core of its development was located in the agglomeration of Coventry–Birmingham–Wolverhampton) was exposed to stronger legitimation forces than the rest of the country. In a cross-country setting, similar density evolution pattern variety can be observed in pioneer versus follower countries (Boone, Wezel, and Wittelooestuijn 2007; see Figure 10.1). That is, the UK, a pioneer country, exhibited much stronger early history population-level legitimation (and also competition when approaching carrying capacity) than a follower counterpart did, like Italy. Building on these arguments, we advance the following twofold proposition:

- *Proposition 1a*: *Ceteris paribus*, pioneer countries exhibit stronger endogenous (i.e. local) population-level legitimation and competi- tion than follower countries do.

- *Proposition 1b*: *Ceteris paribus*, pioneer countries reach their carrying capacity quicker than follower countries do.

The above-mentioned resistance with which early entrants in follower countries are confronted is mitigated by the legitimation spillover effects from pioneer countries. This logic finds empirical support in the work of Hannan et al. (1995), again, who show how legitimation typically oper- ates at a broad geographical scale. In this respect, the constitutive legiti- macy of the focal follower countries ($i$) does depend on the density of its pioneer counterpart ($j$). This tendency reduces the impact of endogenous (i.e. intra-population) legitimacy, supporting our benchmark story of follower countries hosting low-$\theta$ populations. In formal terms, we therefore add a new parameter, $\alpha_i$, to the $\theta$ model of density dependence, which relates to the linear legitimation spillover effects that stem from pioneer countries. The speed of diffusion of these spillover effects depends on density growth in pioneer countries (i.e. on their own $\theta$). This gives:

$$N_{t+1i} - N_{ti} = N_{ti} R_0 \times \left[ 1 - \left( \frac{N_{ti}}{K_i} \right)^{\theta i} \right] + \alpha_i \times \left( \frac{N_{tj}}{K_j} \right) \qquad (10.3)$$

Needless to say, $\alpha_i$ will be equal to zero in pioneer countries, which reduces equation (10.3) for follower countries to equation (10.2) for pioneer countries. Figure 10.5 shows how legitimation spillover effects from pioneer countries contribute to stimulate density growth in populations located in follower countries. This beneficial impact of legitimation spillovers shapes the evolution of follower countries and, depending on its intensity, may trigger diverse evolutionary paths of density, potentially even steeper than those of pioneer countries.

### 10.3.2. Competition Spillover Effects

Population-level legitimation is just one side of the story concerning spillovers, the other one being related to competition. Our further claim therefore is that, besides legitimation, competition may spillover across borders as well. This is immediately clear for modern and more liberal economies: competition is likely to spill over across locales. The continuing debate about the consequences of globalization for domestic economies is fuelled by this very process of international competition (e.g. Hertz 2001; Stiglitz 2002). A case in point is trade, a direct manifestation of competition across countries. However, trade is not a recent invention. In fact, in the decades before the economic crisis of the 1930s, (relative) trade volumes reached an early peak. It took until the 1990s before this early peak could be passed (e.g. Bordo, Taylor, and Williamson 2003; Brakman et al. 2006; O'Rourke and Williamson 1999). A similar story can be told for foreign direct investment (FDI), which reflects direct entry by firms from abroad into domestic populations.

In this respect, we can locate our discussion of cross-country competition into that part of the literature that is concerned with post-peak declines in organizational density. The countervailing forces of legitimation and competition imply that, all other things being equal,

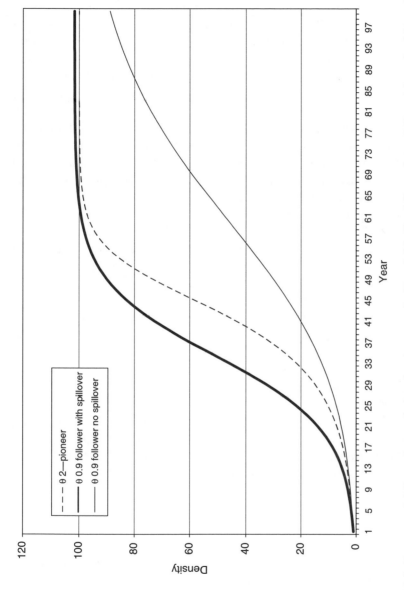

**Figure 10.5.** Patterns of follower's population-density growth ($R_0 = 0.15$, $K = 100$, and $\theta_i = 0.9$)—with and without legitimacy spillovers ($\alpha_i = 0.015$)—compared to a pioneer country with $\theta_j = 2$

organizational populations reach their equilibrium when their density hits carrying capacity (as in Figure 10.2). Simulations of the model show that—while many patterns of density dependence may trigger an S-shaped pattern of evolution—the non-monotonic relationship in vital rates represents an alternative and robust explanation (Hannan and Carroll 1992: ch. 8). As Carroll and Khessina (2005) however pointed out, '[t]he basic formulation of the theory does not fully explain commonly observed late stages of population development, when the industry experiences decline and resurgence'. Different explanations have been proposed to explain the patterns of density decline observed in the late history of industries. Among these, temporal heterogeneity (Hannan 1997; Wezel 2005), density delay (Delacroix and Carroll 1983), mass dependence (Barnett and Amburgey 1990; Winter 1990), and population-level inertia (Lomi, Larsen, and Freeman 2005; Ruef 2004) appear to be the most qualified alternatives.

An equally plausible argument is related to competitive spillover effects across countries. This is especially true when the follower country enters into the industry not only after legitimation has already been established in the pioneer country, but also with such a delay that competition has already kicked in there. Under this scenario, growth opportunities at home for firms in the pioneer country are declining and there may be the need to shift attention to other targets abroad. Following this logic, the magnitude of cross-country competitive spillover effects will critically depend on the speed of development of pioneer countries—that is, on their $\theta$. In the early stages of the industry's history, it is reasonable to assume that such competitive spillover effects are asymmetrical—that is, running from pioneer to follower countries. After all, incumbents in pioneer countries are the ones that will first hit their growth ceiling in their domestic markets, given that carrying capacity will be reached earlier in frontrunner countries. To take this argument on board, a further refinement of the model is needed by adding a new element to equation (10.3):

$$N_{t+1i} - N_{ti} = N_{ti}R_0 \times \left[1 - \left(\frac{N_{ti}}{K_i}\right)^{\theta i}\right] + a_i \times \left(\frac{N_{tj}}{K_j}\right) - \beta_i \times (N_i N_j) \quad (10.4)$$

where $\beta_i \times (N_i N_j)$ refers to competition spillover effects. Intuitively, the intensity of the competitive spillover effect depends on the rate at which pioneer countries' producers will outcompete their follower counterparts, multiplied by the density of them (i.e. the density of 'predators' see

Bernstein 2003). Note that this competitive spillover effect from pioneer country $j$ to follower country $i$ is dependent on the $\theta$ of the pioneer country. Needless to say, the coefficient $\beta_i$ may vary in intensity across populations (and over time), being affected by several factors, such as trade intensity between pioneer and follower countries, and the overlap in product space among populations. While acknowledging the importance of these issues, we will not discuss them here.

Figures 10.6 and 10.7 map the consequences of asymmetric competitive spillover effects from pioneer to follower countries according to their different intensity (Figure 10.7) and depending on the diverse $\theta$ values of the follower population—that is, timing of entry. Of course, the model could be extended to a symmetric scenario too. As for the pioneer population, the plot was obtained by choosing $\theta_j = 2$.

The two figures clearly reveal the effects induced by the follower country's $\theta$ (i.e. the lag in the timing of entry) and the competitive spillover effects from pioneer countries. As Figure 10.6 shows, the domestic populations in follower countries react to competitive spillover effects from pioneer countries in different ways, depending on their own life histories. In particular, $\theta$ ($<1$) seems to be inversely related to the degree of fluctuation triggered by competitive spillover effects. This finding seems to be consistent with the empirically observed density evolution patterns of a wide variety of organizational populations. An example, again, is the motorcycle industry (cf. Figure 10.1). Germany, an early follower, exhibits a sharp decline in density. One rationale for this finding could be related to the fact that similar timing of entry may imply greater homogeneity which may spur legitimation spillovers but also competitive ones. In contrast, Italy, a late entrant, features lower fluctuations and managed to position itself into a more distinct niche (see Boone et al. 2007). Conversely, Figure 10.7 plots the trajectories of a 'typical' follower country (i.e. with theta equal to 0.5) when facing different degrees of competitive spillover from pioneer countries. Intuitively, the weaker the pioneer countries' competitive spillover effect, the higher the peak of the follower population density will be, and the steeper the growth trajectory will be. And conversely, the stronger the competitive spillover effect from abroad, the lower the follower population-density peak, and the earlier the domestic population will be peaking. The reason for this is—according to our logic—related to the intensity of international competition. If competition from abroad is strong, part of domestic carrying capacity will be filled by foreign competitors, either by entry (FDI) or by trade,

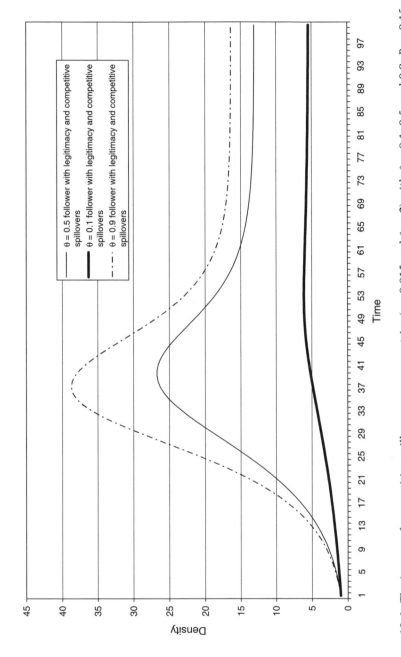

**Figure 10.6.** The impact of competitive spillovers across countries ($a = 0.015$ and $\theta_j = 2$) with $\theta_i = 0.1$, 0.5, and 0.9, $R_0 = 0.15$ and $K = 100$, $\beta = 0.0005$

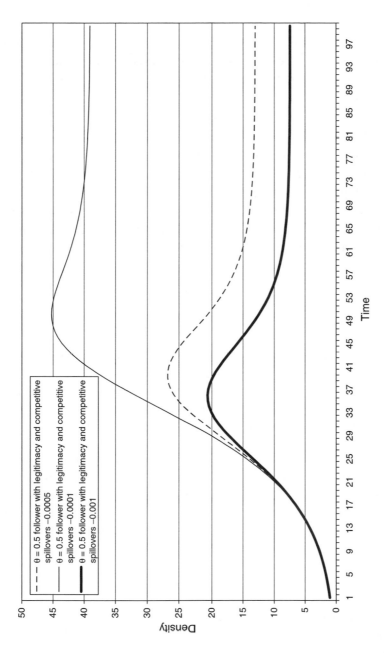

**Figure 10.7.** Patterns of follower's population-density growth in presence of legitimacy and competitive spillovers from pioneer countries ($R_0 = 0.15$, $K = 100$, $\alpha_i = 0.015$) with $\theta_i = 0.5$, $\theta_j = 2$, and $\beta_i = 0.001$, 0.0005, and 0.0001

and quickly so; if international competition is weak, domestic firms will have ample time to fill the follower country's market with home-grown entry or investment. Hence, country $i$'s domestic carrying capacity will be below country $i$'s total carrying capacity if the asymmetric cross-country competitive spillover effect is positive, the former being defined as the peak density of domestic firms and the latter as the peak density of all firms, domestic and foreign ones together.

From these considerations, two further propositions may be advanced, assuming that the competitive spillover effect is asymmetric:

- *Proposition 2*: In presence of competitive spillover effects from pioneer countries, follower countries will exhibit sharper density declines after peaking, the faster their density development has been.

- *Proposition 3*: The stronger the competitive spillover effects from pioneer countries, (*a*) the earlier follower countries will reach their density peak and (*b*) the lower the follower countries' density peak will be.

## 10.4. Conclusion

This chapter aims at presenting an alternative formalization for mapping the different density patterns empirically observed in a wide variety of populations. By way of illustration, we referred to the underlying cross-country legitimation and competition effects in the context of what may be called the international ecology of a single industry in a set of countries. The plots of density evolution patterns in three countries of a domestic motorcycle industry, as pictured in Figure 10.1, offer a case in point; clearly, the original density-dependence model cannot explain the large variance observed here. So, our starting point is the observed variety of evolutionary density patterns in the ecological literature (e.g. Boone et al. 2007; Hannan et al. 1995). We argue that this variation may be the result of differences in the timing of entry and development of national industries. Thus, we decided to advance our overall logic for the specific case of pioneer vis-à-vis follower countries, all with domestic populations of the same industry.

Indeed, our model is able to reproduce some of the empirically observed steep patterns of density growth and adjustment to competition in pioneering countries, as well as the weaker legitimation and competition processes that mark the evolution of density in follower countries. We modelled pioneer countries not only as broadcasters of legitimation for an organizational form, but also as propagators of competition, due to trade and FDI. Under this scenario, different patterns of density fluctuation could be predicted from the interaction of the timing of entry into the industry and the competitive spillover effect from pioneer to follower countries (see Figures 10.6 and 10.7). Some tentative evidence in support of the processes suggested in this chapter is offered by referring to the evolutionary density patterns of populations observed in the existing literature.

This is not to say that our logic is restricted to this specific interpretation—it is not. We believe that the extended density-dependence model proposed here can be applied to all communities of interrelated populations with $\theta$ heterogeneity. To illustrate this general observation, we would like to briefly explore one alternative story, reversing the one advanced above. In this chapter, we assumed that pioneer countries host high-$\theta$ populations, while their follower counterparts are populated with low-$\theta$ ones. Although we offered a rationale for this that fits with the few reported cross-country density evolution patterns in the literature (particularly the automobile and motorcycle industries), we cannot exclude that the opposite holds true in other industries. That is, an equally valid storyline could argue that pioneer countries tend to be populated with low-$\theta$ populations, and follower countries with high-$\theta$ ones. Then, the argument would be that follower countries can benefit from quick legitimation due to spillover effects from pioneer populations, the latter suffering from the slow legitimation that may well be associated with the emergence of new organizational forms. Of course, this would not affect the applicability of the model proposed here; after all, it is still $\theta$ heterogeneity that drives the interrelated-density evolution of populations in a set of countries. In future work, we hope to sharpen our thinking in this respect, theorizing about which narrative is likely to hold true for what type of populations.

By and large, we believe that this chapter provides two contributions to the existing literature, so pointing to different avenues for further development, apart from the one discussed above. First, different fields in macro-organizational theory have been concerned with explaining the patterns of change in organizational populations as related to either endogenous or exogenous mechanisms. A key feature of the organizational ecology tradition is the emphasis on endogenous processes, driven by density-dependent legitimation and competition effects on entry and exit rates. In this respect, the logic of density dependence—albeit applied with several restrictions here, namely with no focus on vital rates—represents a solid and thoroughly investigated framework (for a review, see Carroll and Hannan 2000: ch. 10). This chapter examines the extant theoretical claims, and advances a set of novel arguments. In particular, the novel arguments proposed here represent a theoretical basis for explaining the empirically observed variations in population-level legitimation and competition. Needless to say, our model formulation should be contrasted with other explanations aiming to do the same, such as temporal heterogeneity, density delay, mass dependence, and population-level inertia—as well as applied more rigorously to the prediction of entry and exit rates. A rigorous empirical study is needed to compare the validity of the propositions presented here vis-à-vis that of alternative explanations (e.g. Ruef 2004).

Second, next to or on top of density-regulated mechanisms, the literature points to a series of exogenous events, such as technological innovation, institutional change, and political instability, that systematically shape the decline and renewal of population density. Several studies have provided evidence that technological innovation, for instance, influences organizational turnover within populations (e.g. Tushman and Anderson 1986). Institutional theorists have focused on the destabilization of rules as the key driver of variation in the evolution of organizational fields. According to this view, organizational behaviour is governed by (cultural-)cognitive, normative, and regulative elements that provide stability and meaning to organizations (for a review, see Scott 2001). Such a cognitive and normative stability is challenged by environmental 'jolts'. These 'jolts' can take the form of regulatory change, or shifts in cultural beliefs and practices, introducing new ideas in organizational fields and, together with them, new organizations (Powell 1991). Political instability can also be considered to be another cause of demographic change, as it diminishes the willingness of entrepreneurs to commit resources to uncertain future returns, triggering sharp variations in density trajectories (Delacroix and Carroll 1983). This chapter elaborates on another mechanism that exogenously impinges on the evolutionary density trajectories of populations: competitive spillover effects across countries.

In developing our logic, we implicitly referred to the literature that points to permeable population boundaries and, thus, to communities as the proper unit of analysis of mutualistic and competitive processes (Aldrich 1999; DiMaggio 1994). Relatively recent developments within organizational ecology, such as the work of Hannan et al. (1995), provide an initial investigation into this relatively unexplored domain. This chapter moves further along this path to show how competitive spillover effects (e.g. due to increasing FDI and trade volumes, in the slipstream of economic liberalization) profoundly impact on the evolutionary dynamics of organizational populations in the international arena. While the findings presented here appear to be intuitive, robust empirical validation is needed to provide support for the conjectures advanced above. As a stepping stone, we formulated a few propositions that might be further explored in future empirical work.

Finally, we want to emphasize that multiple applications of the $\theta$ logistic model of population-density growth are imaginable. As already mentioned in Section 10.1 and above, our interpretation of this biological model is tentative, representing only one of the several possible narratives. In fact, the $\theta$ parameter could be easily adopted to map variations in legitimation and competition patterns across other geographical locations than countries (e.g. Cattani, Pennings, and Wezel 2003; Sorenson and Audia 2000). When utilized in this way, the $\theta$ parameter could refer to diverse rules of interactions at low and high levels of density (Lomi and Larsen 1996): low-$\theta$ populations are those marked by immediate competition that leads to the emergence of spatial differentiation over time, whereas their high-$\theta$ counterparts may refer to populations evenly spread across space since the beginning (Hawley 1950). Moreover, different values of $\theta$ could indicate the existence of diverse adjustment elasticities, and hence be associated with different levels of population-level inertia. If so, intuitive predictions concerning the different degrees of resilience of organizational populations when confronted with environmental shocks could be related to this parameter. Whether a high- or a low-$\theta$ population will be more resilient depends on the conceptualization of this parameter as either exogenously (e.g. the timing of entry) or endogenously (e.g. the underlying age structure of the population) determined. A potential application could involve inquiries into population fluctuations due to lagged density effects (e.g. Lomi, Larsen, and Freeman 2005). Then, the prediction may well be that the degree of fluctuation depends on the inherent '$\theta$ nature' of the population under study (e.g. banks vs. motorcycle producers), but also on the underlying demographic structure of the population at the time of manifestation of the effect.

## References

Aldrich, H. E. (1999). *Organizations Evolving*. London: Sage.

—— and Wiedenmayer, G. (1993). 'From Traits to Rates: An Ecological Perspective on Organizational Foundings', in J. Katz and R. Brockhaus (eds.), *Advances in Entrepreneurship, Firm Emergence, and Growth*, vol. I. Greenwich, CT: JAI Press.

Barnett, W. P. (1997). 'The Dynamics of Competitive Intensity', *Administrative Science Quarterly*, 42: 128–60.

—— and Amburgey, T. L. (1990). 'Do Larger Organizations Generate Stronger Competition?', in J. V. Singh (ed.), *Organizational Evolution: New Directions*. Newbury Park, CA: Sage, pp. 246–8.

—— and McKendrick, D. G. (2004). 'Why Are Some Organizations More Competitive than Others? Evidence from a Changing Global Market', *Administrative Science Quarterly*, 49: 535–71.

Baum, J. A. C. (1996). 'Organizational Ecology', in S. R. Clegg, C. Hardy, and W. R. Nord (eds.), *Handbook of Organization Studies*. London: Sage.

Bernstein, R. (2003). *Population Ecology: An Introduction to Computer Simulations*. Hoboken, NJ: John Wiley and Sons.

Bigelow, L. S., Carroll, G. R., Seidel, M. D., and Tsai, L. (1997). 'Legitimation, Geographical Scale, and Organizational Density: Regional Pattern of Foundings of American Automobile Producers 1885–1981', *Social Science Research*, 26: 377–98.

Boone, C., Wezel, F. C., and van Witteloostuijn, A. (2007). 'The Ecology of Intra-Industry Specialization', working paper, University of Lugano, Switzerland.

Bordo, M. D., Taylor, A. M., and Williamson, J. G. (2003). *Globalization in Historical Perspective*. Chicago, IL: University of Chicago Press.

Brakman, S., Garretsen, H., van Marrewijk, C., and van Witteloostuijn, A. (2006). *Nations and Firms in the Global Economy: An Introduction to International Economics and Business*. Cambridge: Cambridge University Press.

Carroll, G. R. (1981). 'Dynamics of Organizational Expansion in National Systems of Education', *American Sociological Review*, 46: 585–99.

—— and Hannan, M. T. (2000). *The Demography of Corporations and Industries*. Princeton, NJ: Princeton University Press.

—— and Khessina, O. M. (2005). 'The Ecology of Entrepreneurship', in R. Agarwal, S. A. Alvarez, and O. Sorenson (eds.), *Handbook of Entrepreneurship: Disciplinary Perspectives*. New York: Kluwer.

—— and Swaminathan, A. (2000). 'Why the Micro-Brewery Movement? Organizational Dynamics of Resource Partitioning in the U.S. Brewing Industry', *American Journal of Sociology*, 106: 715–62.

—— and Wade, J. (1991). 'Density Dependence in the Organizational Evolution of the American Brewing Industry Across Different Levels of Analysis', *Social Science Research*, 20: 217–302.

——Preisendorfer, P., Swaminathan, A., and Wiedenmayer, G. (1993). 'Brewing and Brauerei: The Organizational Ecology of Brewing', *Organization Studies*, 14: 155–88.

Cattani, G., Pennings, J. M., and Wezel, F. C. (2003). 'Spatial and Temporal Heterogeneity in Founding Patterns', *Organization Science*, 14: 670–85.

Delacroix, J. and Carroll, G. R. (1983). 'Organizational Foundings: An Ecological Study of the Newspaper Industries of Argentina and Ireland', *Administrative Science Quarterly*, 28: 274–91.

Delmestri, G. and Woywode, M. (2005). 'Local Struggles and Supranational Legitimation: Diffusion of US-type Multiplex Cinemas in Europe', paper presented at the 21st EGOS Conference.

Dimaggio, P. (1994). 'The Challenge of Community Evolution', in J. A. C. Baum and J. V. Singh (eds.), *Evolutionary Dynamics of Organizations*. New York: Oxford University Press.

Gilpin, M. E. and Ayala, F. J. (1973). Global Models of Growth and Competition', *Proceedings of the National Academy of Science*, 70: 3590–3.

Greve, H. (2002). 'An Ecological Theory of Spatial Evolution: Local Density Dependence in Tokyo Banking 1894–1936', *Social Forces*, 80: 847–79.

Hannan, M. T. (1986). 'Competitive and Institutional Processes in Organizational Ecology', *Technical Report 86–13*. Ithaca, NY: Cornell University.

——(1997). 'Inertia, Density and Structure of Populations of Organizations: Entries in European Automobile Industries 1886–1981', *Organization Studies*, 18: 193–228.

——and Carroll, G. R. (1992). *Dynamics of Populations of Organizations: Density, Legitimation and Competition*. New York: Oxford University Press.

——and Freeman, J. H. (1977). 'The Population Ecology of Organizations', *American Journal of Sociology*, 83: 929–84.

————(1987). 'The Ecology of Organizational Founding: American Labor Unions 1836–1985', *American Journal of Sociology*, 92: 910–43.

——Carroll, G. R., Dundon, E. A., and Torres, J. C. (1995). 'Organizational Evolution in Multinational Context: Entries of Automobile Manufacturers in Belgium, France, Germany and Italy', *American Sociological Review*, 60: 509–28.

————Dobrev, S. D., and Han, J. (1998). 'Organizational Mortality in European and American Motor Industry, Part I: Revisiting the Effect of Age and Size', *European Sociological Review*, 14: 279–302.

Hawley, A. (1950). *Human Ecology: A Theory of Community Structure*. New York: Ronald Press.

Hertz, N. (2001). *The Silent Takeover: Global Capitalism and the Death of Democracy*. New York: Free Press.

Kim, T. Y., Dobrev, S. D., and Solari, L. (2003). 'The Two Sides of the Coin: Core Competence as Capability and Obsolescence', in J. A. C. Baum and A. M. McGahan (eds.), *Advances in Strategic Management*. Oxford: JAI Press and Elsevier.

Levinthal, D. A. (1998). 'The Slow Pace of Rapid Technological Change: Gradualism and Punctuation in Technological Change', *Industrial and Corporate Change*, 7: 217–47.

Lomi, A. (1995). 'The Population Ecology of Organizational Founding: Location Dependence and Unobserved Heterogeneity', *Administrative Science Quarterly*, 40: 111–45.

—— (2000). 'Density Dependence and Spatial Duality in Organizational Founding Rates: Danish Commercial Banks 1846–1989', *Organization Studies*, 21: 433–61.

—— and Larsen, E. R. (1996). 'Interacting Locally and Evolving Globally: A Computational Approach to the Dynamics of Organizational Populations', *Academy of Management Journal*, 39: 1287–321.

—— —— and Freeman, J. H. (2005). 'Things Change: Dynamic Resource Constraints and Systems-Dependent Selection in the Evolution of Organizational Populations', *Management Science*, 51: 882–903.

McKendrick, D. G., Jaffee, J., Carroll, G. R., and Khessina, O. (2003). 'In the Bud? Analysis of Disk Array Producers as a (Possibly) Emergent Organizational Form', *Administrative Science Quarterly*, 48: 60–93.

Meyer, J. W. and Rowan, B. (1977). 'Institutionalized Organizations: Formal Structure as Myth and Ceremony', *American Journal of Sociology*, 83: 340–63.

O'Rourke, K. H. and Williamson, J. G. (1999). *Globalization and History: The Evolution of a Nineteenth-Century Atlantic Economy*. Cambridge, MA: MIT Press.

Powell, W. W. (1991). 'Expanding the Scope of Institutional Analysis', in W. W. Powell and P. J. DiMaggio (eds.), *The New Institutionalism in Organizational Analysis*. Chicago, IL: University of Chicago Press.

Ranger-Moore, J., Banaszak-Holl, J., and Hannan, M. T. (1991). 'Density Dependence in Regulated Industries: Founding Rates of Banks and Life Insurance Companies', *Administrative Science Quarterly*, 36: 36–65.

Ruef, M. (2004). 'For Whom the Bell Tolls: Ecological Perspectives on Industrial Decline and Resurgence', *Industrial and Corporate Change*, 13: 61–89.

Sæther, B. E., Engen, S., and Matthysen, E. (2002). 'Demographic Characteristics and Population Dynamical Patterns of Solitary Birds', *Science*, 295: 2070–2.

Scott, W. R. (2001). *Institutions and Organizations*, 2nd edn. Thousand Oaks, CA: Sage.

Sibly, R. M., Barker, D., Denham, M. C., Hone, J., and Pagel, M. (2005). 'On the Regulation of Populations of Mammals, Birds, Fish and Insects', *Science*, 309: 607–10.

Sorenson, O. (2000). 'The Effect of Population Level Learning on Market Entry: The American Automobile Industry', *Social Science Research*, 29: 307–26.

—— and Audia, P. (2000). 'The Social Structure of Entrepreneurial Activity: Geographic Concentration of Footwear Production in the U.S. 1940–1989', *American Journal of Sociology*, 106: 324–62.

Stiglitz, J. (2002). *Globalization and Its Discontents*. London: Macmillan.

Tushman, M. L. and Anderson, P. (1986). 'Technological Discontinuities and Organizational Environments', *Administrative Science Quarterly*, 31: 439–65.

Verhulst, P. F. (1838). 'Notice sur la Loi que la Population Pursuit dans Son Accroissement', *Correspondance Mathématique et Physique*, 10: 113–21.

Wade, J. B., Swaminathan, A., and Saxon, M. S. (1998). 'Normative and Resource Flow Consequences of Local Regulations in the American Brewing Industry 1845–1918', *Administrative Science Quarterly*, 43: 905–35.

Wezel, F. C. (2005). 'Location-dependence and Industry Evolution: Founding Rates in the United Kingdom Motorcycle Industry 1895–1993', *Organization Studies*, 26: 729–54.

Winter, S. G. (1990). 'Survival, Selection, and Inheritance in Evolutionary Theories of Organization', in J. V. Singh (ed.), *Organizational Evolution: New Directions*. Newbury Park, CA: Sage.

Part III

**Market Governance: Regulation, Coordination, and Public Policy**

# 11

# Co-evolution of Technologies and Institutions in Market Economies*

*Richard R. Nelson*

## 11.1. Introduction

Today these questions are among the most challenging facing professional economists, and are also at the heart of political and ideological controversy. They come up in several different contexts. The central challenge of development economics clearly is to illuminate the causal differences between the countries that were desperately poor in the 1950s, but which have since that time achieved quite productive and progressive economies, and those that have progressed hardly at all. Many of the economies that used to be organized under a communist mode, but abandoned that system largely because of poor economic performance, still are floundering, and searching for whatever it is that lends productivity and progressiveness to at least some capitalist economies. After a period of very rapid growth, in which the productivity and income gaps with the USA were largely closed, the economies of Western Europe and Japan recently have been progressing much more haltingly. Various proposals regarding the reasons, and the reforms that might work, are the subject of hot political debates in these countries. In the USA, after the doldrums of the 1970s and 1980s, the growth surge of the late 1990s rekindled an earlier strong self-confidence that Americans knew the secret of economic progress. However, the last several years have renewed some doubts about that matter.

* An earlier version of parts of this chapter was published as 'What Enables Rapid Economic Progress: What are the Needed Institutions', *Research Policy* (2008), 37: 1–11.

The current vogue, both among professional economists and in the public argument, is to see 'the right institutions' as the basic answer to the first question. This contemporary focus on institutions comes as the result of a long intellectual journey through which modern economists, interested in understanding the sources of productivity differences across nations, and the processes of economic growth, gradually have broadened and deepened their analysis (see Nelson 1998 and Abramovitz 1989 for details on this intellectual history).

Thus in the early years after the Second World War, the gap between high income, high productivity economies, and poor ones was seen as largely the consequence of differences in the stocks of physical and human capital, and investment was seen as the key to advancing economic performance. There were obvious differences between advanced and less-developed countries in terms of their command over modern technologies, but the problem of 'technology transfer' was seen as not particularly difficult, if the needed investments were made. However, it soon became clear that command over technologies was not that easy to achieve, and involved much more than simply investments in physical and human capital. Thus while the communist block countries were marked by high rates of investment in both physical and human capital, by the late 1970s it was clear that productivity in most of their industries was low, and that they lacked abilities to produce high-quality products. Attention began to focus on the features of national economies that seemed to underlie technological capabilities, particularly the incentives and competences of the organizations responsible for production. With the rapid rise of Japan as an economic and technological power, economists and other scholars began to look more closely at differences across countries in the way that business organizations were structured and managed, and at the financial and labour market systems supporting them, and these variables came to be added to the list of factors viewed as influencing economic productivity and progressiveness. As Japan stumbled in the early 1990s, and as biotech and IT firms boomed in the USA, the attention of economists shifted from large stable firms to start-ups and connections between firms and universities, from patent finance to venture capital, and from employment regimes that involved long run mutual commitments to more fluid labour market arrangements. During this same period, an extensive literature grew up focused on 'National Innovation Systems' (see e.g. Nelson 1993), which further broadened the focus, with firms viewed as being embedded in and supported by a variety of non-market organizations and programmes, for example, universities funded by government to undertake research and training in fields relevant to an industry.

Each of these developments shows economists trying to broaden or deepen their analysis of the factors influencing economic productivity and progressiveness, by looking into matters of economic organization and other forces shaping the capabilities and behaviour of economic actors. During the 1980s and 1990s, many economists began to generalize this quest for more basic understanding, and 'institutions' came to be used as the term to characterize the fundamental factors shaping economic productivity and progressiveness. North (1990) was perhaps the most forceful contemporary spokesman for the new interest in institutions, but there were many others.

In a very real sense, the renewed interest of economists in institutions is a coming home to old traditions. Economic institutions, or entities that modern economists might call that, were a central interest of Adam Smith, and the classical tradition that followed him. Indeed, it was only in the second half of the twentieth century that the main line of economics began to take a position that the science of economics ought to be as 'institutions free' as possible, or at least to focus on general market systems without getting tangled up in particular institutional details. It is good that we now are again talking seriously about institutions. But it is less clear we really understand what we are talking about.

Getting at the second question, 'What are the needed institutions?', is a tough task. It is important to recognize that the analytical problem of even making sense of institutions involves a somewhat different kind of theorizing than that contained in standard growth theory. Many years ago, Moses Abramovitz (1952) called attention to the difference between what he called the 'immediate' sources of growth, and causation at a deeper level. Using his language, the advance of physical and human capital and total factor productivity, more generally the variables in a growth accounting, are the 'immediate' sources of economic growth. The deeper question is what lies behind these variables. It is clear that 'institutions' presently is the name many economists give to these deeper causes.

The position I want to argue in this chapter is that the current consensus that 'institutions' are the key is a bit like the recognition, half a century ago, that the 'growth of total factor productivity' was the principal 'immediate' source of economic growth. At that time, while some economists interpreted this variable as a measure of technological advance, it seemed likely to other economists that a number of factors were involved. Abramovitz (1956) called it 'a measure of our ignorance'. In any case, it was clear that the variables that economists felt they understood pretty well that were included in neoclassical growth theory simply were not up to the task of explaining most of growth, or differences across nations in productivity levels. Calling the residual 'growth of total factor productivity' gave it a name. But it has taken many years and much research for economists to get a decent grip on technological advance and other significant components of total factor productivity. And the factors behind the 'immediate' sources of growth still are not well understood.

Indeed, this is an important part of the reason for the current focus on institutions. But we have not made much headway yet on making the term a useful analytical concept.

There are three kinds of questions about 'institutions', and their roles in determining economic productivity and progressiveness, that in my view are wide open.

There is, first of all, the question: What are institutions? These days many scholars of institutions propose that institutions should be understood as 'the basic rules of the game', the broad legal regime and the way it is enforced, widely held norms that constrain behaviour, etc. (North 1990). But other scholars associate institutions with particular governing structures moulding aspects of economic activity, like a nation's financial 'institutions', or the way firms tend to be organized and managed (see e.g. Williamson 1975, 1985). While this conception is not radically inconsistent with the notion that institutions are the rules of the game, it is not quite the same. Still other social scientists associate the term institutions with customs, standard and expected patterns of behaviour in particular contexts, like the acceptance of money in exchange for goods and services.[1] The conception here is with the ways things are done, rather than broad rules or governing structures that constrain behaviour; although these things are connected, they are somewhat different. Also, while many authors use the term 'institution' to refer to somewhat abstract variables, like the consistency and justice of the rule of law in a society, or the general use of money in exchange, other scholars associate the term with particular concrete entities, as the Supreme Court of the USA, or the Federal Reserve System.

This is a very heterogeneous bag of things that are being called institutions. It is apparent, it seems to me, that presently many economist

---

[1] Veblen (1899, 1915, 1958) is the canonical reference here. Among contemporary economists, Hodgson (1988, 2006) is the strongest advocate for a Veblenian perspective.

are using the term 'institutions' largely as a 'place holder', just as we used 'total factor productivity' as a place holder some years ago. And just as in the earlier case progress in understanding required the explicit recognition of several different variables and processes, my bet is that the same will be required before we get a useful grip on the 'institutions' bestiary.

Then there are, second, questions about the relationships between institutions and economic productivity and progressiveness. In much of the contemporary writing by economists, it is almost taken for granted that modern economies need to be largely structured through markets, and that good institutions support the effective operation of such an economy.

But it is not clear that economists presently have a good conception of what 'effective operation' of a 'market economy' involves, particularly if the performance we are trying to understand involves economic growth, which virtually all scholars recognize as being largely driven by innovation. As Schumpeter (1934, 1942) argued long ago, the standard neoclassical theory of market organization and behaviour is not capable of dealing with the phenomenon of innovation. It is also clear that, once one pays attention to the activities that support innovation, a number of non-market organizations (like universities, and government-sponsored R&D support programmes) are involved, as well as market organizations. There is the task, therefore, of developing a theory of innovation-driven economic growth, and the activities involved, that recognizes the key roles played by non-market structures as well as those conventionally seen as market ones.

And finally, there is the question about how institutional change comes about, and how the society that would benefit from a different set of institutions can manage to put these in place. There are a variety of different theories of institutional change, some proposing that institutions 'evolve' in some sense, and some proposing that institutions are consciously chosen in some way. But in any case, it is clear that, even if we knew just what kind of institutions were needed to enhance economic productivity and progressiveness, building and sustaining those institutions is a real challenge.

These big questions will be the topics explored in the following three sections of this chapter. My argument in Section 11.2 is that the conglomerate of things different economists have called institutions largely reflects the fact that many different kinds of structures and forces mould the way individuals and organizations interact to get things done, what Sampat and I (Nelson and Sampat 2001) have called 'social technologies'. Some institutions and the social technologies they support have broad and pervasive influence, and others are sector or activity specific. From this point of view, it is a mistake to search for a small set of institutions that are necessary and sufficient for economic productivity and progress. Many different institutions are needed, and the institutions that are effective are very context dependent.

Section 11.3 develops the argument that economic growth involves the co-evolution of technologies and the institutions needed for their effective operation and advancement. Some institutions provide the broad background conditions under which technologies can proceed, and others come into existence and develop to support the important new technologies that are driving growth. Section 11.4 is concerned with the processes of institutional change. A principal argument is that institutional change, and its influence on economic activity, is much more difficult to direct and control than technological change, and hence prevailing institutions are often drags on economic productivity and progressiveness.

In Section 11.5, I consider the evolution of technology and institutions in pharmaceutical biotech, a case that illustrates nicely in concrete form many of the general arguments I have developed. I conclude with a summing up and a looking forward.

## 11.2. Unpacking the Concept of Institutions

Above I remarked on the wide variety of meanings that different economists, and other social scientists, have given to the term 'institutions', from the rules of the game that influence behaviour, to governing structures that make or enforce rules, to customary behaviour patterns themselves. Writers on institutions also differ in the extent to which they use the term to refer to broad, somewhat abstract things, like legal and moral protection of private property rights, or more concrete things, like the details of patent law in a country. Some writers on institutions see these as variables whose influence on economic activity is pervasive. Others use the term to refer to things that are specific to particular economic sectors; thus, the publicly financed agricultural experimentation station system has been identified as a key institution behind the high-productivity of American agriculture (see e.g. Ruttan and Hayami 1984).

Certainly, we have a wide range of 'things' here. This diversity of meanings, and analytical foci, makes coherent discussion about the nature and role of institutions difficult. Indeed, it can lead to some rather bizarre arguments. Thus in 2004, two articles on institutions and economic development were published in the *Journal of Economic Growth*, one by Rodrik, Subramamian, and Trebbi, and the other by Glaeser, Porta, Lopez-de-Silames, and Shleifer. The first of these articles proposed that differences in the 'quality of institutions' is the primary variable behind the very significant differences in gross domestic product per worker that one finds in the modern world. The authors take a broad macro view of what institutions are, tying these to the clarity and strength of property rights and the rule of law. The 'measures' of the quality of institutions used in their cross-country regression purport to give indicators of this. In contrast, the second article proposes that it is investment in human capital, rather than 'institutions', that is the principal explanation behind cross-country differences in per capital income, and the extent to which economies, initially far behind the frontier, have closed the gap over the last forty years. The authors propose that while government policies had a lot to do with investments made in human capital, the policies were relatively independent of a nation's basic institutions, which they defined in terms of whether the political regimes were democratic or autocratic. There are several striking things about this argument. First, both sets of authors see institutions as broad structures with pervasive impacts on economic activity. Their perspective is that of macroeconomics. But on the other hand, while Rodrik and colleagues focus on property rights and the rule of law, Glaeser and colleagues take a view that the term institutions refers to the form of government. It would seem that the authors of the articles in question are talking past each other.

The recent book 'Imperfect Institutions', written by Thrainn Eggertsson (2005), stands in sharp contrast to both of these macro-oriented analyses. Eggertsson is interested in the same broad question as the authors of the two articles cited above: the determinants of economic development. He is also focused on 'institutions' as the key variable. In his general discussion of what institutions are and how they mould economic behaviour Eggertson considers both rules and norms, and political processes and machinery, an eclectic position I too will espouse. However, and here too my position is similar to his, Eggertsson clearly believes that, to be useful, analysis of how institutions affect economic growth and productivity needs to get into the details of how institutions affect behaviour. He develops this part of his analysis largely in analysis of how 'institutions' affected the development of the fishing industry in Iceland, in the earlier era strongly constraining it, and then later changing to encourage and support it. A reader cannot help but come away from reading Eggertsson's fascinating analysis with an understanding that broad definitions of what institutions are and general statements about what they do cannot carry us very far.

If the research by individual economists and other social scientists on the nature and role of institutions in long run economic development is to go forward in a way that is coherent and cumulative, there clearly needs to be more shared agreement regarding just what the term 'institutions' is presumed to mean, and how they affect economic activity. The position I want to espouse here is that the most useful conception of what institutions are would encompass a wide range of somewhat different things, but with different ones relevant in different analytical contexts. The unity and focus of the research programme would be provided by agreement on what institutions broadly do.

Bhaven Sampat and I have proposed (Nelson and Sampat 2001) that, despite the diversity in the literature regarding how institutions are defined, a large share of the writing is intended to illuminate the factors moulding the goal-oriented behaviours of economic agents in contexts where the actions of several parties determine what is achieved. The authors generally take the position that the simple lean theory contained in standard microeconomics of the forces determining modes of transacting, economic interacting more generally, leaves out important constraints, pressures, and mechanisms, and introduces the concept of 'institutions' to fill in the gaps they see, or in some cases to provide a quite different theory of the determinants of behaviour. The objective of virtually all of the authors is to use the concept of institutions to provide a better explanation of why models of interactive behaviour of economic agents differ across countries and over time in ways that profoundly affect the effectiveness of economic activity. The different concepts of institutions that one finds in the literature partly reflect the particular economic phenomena the authors are focusing on, including whether the phenomena are broad and pervasive or more specific to particular sectors and activities, partly the particular 'institution' they are analysing, and partly where they choose to apply the 'institutions' term in the chain of logic they are proposing.

Sampat and I proposed that the concept of a 'social technology' was a useful one for making more coherent the writings about institutions. Our social technologies concept involved a broadening of the way economists think about an economic 'activity'.

In its standard use in economics, an activity is thought of as a way of producing something, or more generally doing something useful; Sampat and I take a broad view of what the term encompasses. Undertaking an activity or a set of them—producing a radio, growing rice, performing a surgery, baking a cake, procuring a needed item, starting a new business—involves a set of actions or procedures that need to be done, for example, as specified in a recipe for the preparation of a cake. These steps or procedures may require particular inputs (like flour and sugar for the cake, cash or a credit card to procure the ingredients for the cake), and perhaps some equipment (something to stir, a stove, a vehicle to go to the store). Economists are prone to use the term 'technology' to denote the procedures that need to be done to get the desired result.

However, a recipe characterization of what needs to be done represses the fact that many economic activities involve multiple actors, and require some kind of a coordinating mechanism to assure that the various aspects of the recipe are performed in the relationships to each other needed to make the recipe work. The standard notion of a recipe is mute about how this is done. Sampat and I proposed that it might be useful to call the recipe aspect of an activity its 'physical' technology, and the way work is divided and coordinated its 'social' technology. From this perspective, virtually all economic activities involve the use of both physical technologies and social technologies. The productivity or effectiveness of an activity is determined by both aspects.

The social technologies concept does not include all kinds of behaviour that at least some of the writings on institutions appear to want to encompass, but I propose that it does include a large part of the spectrum most relevant to the analysis of economic productivity and progressiveness. The 'technology' part of the term denotes behaviours that are intended to get something accomplished; the 'social' part denotes that these behaviours involve or are responsive to the actions or expected actions of multiple agents.

I would include under the social technologies umbrella both behaviours associated with getting things done within an organization, and actions to get things done involving two or more separate individuals or organizations. Behaviours associated with market activity—for example, individuals or individual organizations acting to achieve their ends through buying from or selling to sometimes anonymous others—would be included. A practice of only transacting with people you know well because only they can be trusted, or of not doing any transacting involving money on holy days because of the force of public opinion, would under my proposed umbrella concept be considered as an aspect of the social technologies employed in a society. More generally, the social technologies concept is meant to encompass those aspects of goal-oriented ways of doing things, where the behaviour of agents is tailored to or intended to influence the expected actions or reactions of other agents.

From this point of view, the social technologies that are employed in an economy are enabled and constrained by things like laws, norms, expectations, governing structures and mechanisms, and customary modes of transacting and interacting. All these tend to support and standardize certain social technologies, and make others difficult or infeasible in a society. Sampat and I suggested that, where these exist, standardized social technologies, the prevalent modes of interacting for getting done particular things in a society, are what much of the writing on institutions is about.

As I have noted, some economists use the term institutions to refer to what they regard as the major influences shaping such social technologies, while others use the term to refer to prevalent social technologies themselves. While the linguistic distinction is clear, and one might think that in practice there ought to be clean lines between these two conceptions of what institutions are, in practice the two conceptions sometimes shade into each other. Some ways of doing things have the support and coercion of strong custom. A good example is the use of money for procuring various kinds of things, which would seem to be at once a social technology when viewed as a goal-oriented behaviour, and an institution when viewed as a custom. At the same time, behind the social technology and custom of using money to acquire things lie a body of law, and a structure of financial institutions, that in many societies make this practice not only possible but easy and safe to employ. In turn, these institutions are supported by prevalent beliefs and norms in a society regarding the appropriateness of market transactions, the importance of honesty, and the like.

More generally, I want to argue that the institutions moulding and supporting social technologies come in layers or concentric circles. Some are tied so closely to the practices in question that one cannot be considered without the other. Others are more removed. An important difference between economists who consider institutions as macroeconomic factors, and those who study behaviour at a more detailed level, is that the former generally do not see the institutions that are 'close in', as it were, to particular ways of doing things, while the latter often do.

It is not surprising, therefore, that economists who take a macroeconomic approach tend to think of institutions as factors that influence the social technologies that are operative in a society, but do not strictly determine them. Societies clearly have a degree of control over institutions like the formal structure of laws, and formal organizational designs and designated authority relationships. However, these kinds of institutions may determine only relatively broadly the social technologies that actually are employed. There remains considerable room for variation in the prevalent habits of action and thought that scholars like Veblen defined as institutions. And it is these patterns of actual behaviour, the social technologies that are prevalent, that directly influence economic performance.

I propose that explicit recognition of the concept of a social technology, together with understanding that a variety of different factors influence which social technologies customarily are employed in a particular context, helps to illuminate why the term 'institution' has been used to cover so many apparently disparate things. My proposed approach is to focus on the prevalent social technologies and be eclectic and inclusive about the 'institutions' that support them. As I have suggested, and will show in the examples developed in the following sections, there generally will be a number of different 'institutions' that support and constrain particular social technologies, and they operate in different ways. Some institutions have a broad and somewhat diffuse effect on the social technologies that are used or not used. Thus the influence of 'respect for the rule of law' is largely atmospheric, affecting broadly a wide range of economic activities and the social technologies used in them. Other institutions are more specific to the particular social technologies under study. Thus each of the cases considered later involves particular governing structures and particular laws. Some institutions provide the background context within which the particular social technologies under study evolve. Others change as an essential part of the evolutionary process.

My proposed eclectic approach is somewhat at tension with the gravitation in recent years of economists writing about institutions to go along with the 'rules of the game' definition, broadly defined. I find the rules of the game notion about what institutions are attractive in that it avoids suggesting that institutions determine behaviours strictly. However, I resist that pull because the range of particular 'things' that reasonably are called institutions under my proposed definition contains many that can be characterized only very partially in terms of a set of rules, for example, the form of government, or the operative financial system, or (to give some examples I will discuss in detail in the following section) the modern corporate organizational form, or the industrial research laboratory. Of course if one adopts a broad enough definition of what can be considered a 'rule', as Hodgson (2006) does in a recent article, I have no trouble with the notion that all institutions define rules. But I question then whether this language usage is particularly helpful.

I have similar remarks on the apparent broad acceptance of the notion that institutions, as the rules of the game, form constraints on behaviour. In many cases, new institutions would seem to open up productive new ways of doing things. While the pathways they make possible are usually limited in some respects, to see the new institutions only as constraints takes attention away from the fact that they support the use of new social technologies. Thus the emergence of the modern corporate form, and the industrial research laboratory, permitted things to be done productively that were impossible or badly hindered under the older set of institutions.

Some writers want to make a clean distinction between institutions and organizations. However, under the conception I propose, broadly accepted organizing principles, to use a term employed by Bruce Kogut (1993, 2000; Kogut and Zander 1992) would definitely be considered a part of the institutional environment, even if particular extant organizations embodying those principles might not (but then what about the Bank of England?). I note that Kogut makes a distinction between organizing principles which, in my language, may be close in to particular social technologies, and institutions that influence what organizational principles are accepted as legitimate within a society, and which are not. This is quite consistent with my proposition that institutions come in layers.

Some institutions, for example, laws bearing on particular activities are, in a sense, external to social technologies, and mould them. However, social technologies can also be self-institutionalized, if I may use that term. This is an important reason why the lines are often blurred between a prevalent practice and the 'institutional' supports for that practice.

Social technologies can be self-institutionalized in several ways. First, customary behaviours, modes of interacting, organizing, tend to be self-reinforcing because they are expected, and familiar, and doing something different may require going against the grain. Second, social technologies tend to exist in systems, with one tuned to another, and self-supporting. This may make going against the grain in one social technology especially difficult, because it involves losing touch with complementary social technologies. Third, social technologies, like physical technologies, tend to progress over time, as experience is accumulated, and shared deliberately or inadvertently. Trying a new social technology, like pioneering a new physical technology, is risky, and involves abandoning the fruits of what may be considerable prior experience. I note that these forces of self-institutionalization are important reasons why a society's ability to control the social technologies in use through conscious designing of institutions may be limited.

Institutions clearly have a certain stability. Yet economic growth, as we have experienced it, clearly has seen old social technologies fade away, sometimes abruptly sometimes slowly, and replaced by new ones. It is time to explore more deeply the role of institutions and institutional change in the process of economic growth.

## 11.3. Institutions and Economic Growth

Before getting into the roles of institutions and institutional change in economic growth, I need to characterize the economic growth process more broadly. I want to begin by baldly asserting that economic growth must be understood as an evolutionary process driven by innovation. Hardly any contemporary economist would have trouble with the second part of this proposition, about innovation being the key driving force in economic growth. The first part is somewhat more controversial, and many contemporary economic growth models assume something close to a moving general equilibrium. However, as Schumpeter (1934, 1942) argued long ago, one simply cannot comprehend innovation within an analytical framework that assumes that economic actors have a good understanding of the consequences of innovating, or not innovating for that matter, and that the system as a whole is in continuing equilibrium.

Schumpeter's discussion of innovation, of course, took off from his base discussion of a circular flow of economic activity, wherein each economic agent did the customary thing, supported in his or her actions by the customary actions of other economic agents. Schumpeter's discussion of the circular flow was his way of articulating what was going on in a Walrasian general equilibrium, though his stress was on the customary patterns of behaviour in such a context, rather than that the actions of each agent were optimal for that agent, given what the others were doing. But in any case, in such a general equilibrium, while economic agents may face some risk in taking the action they deem appropriate in the context, in the sense that they do not know for sure if it will rain or not, there is no Knightian uncertainty regarding what can happen or what is, on average, best to do.

For Schumpeter, such a pattern of activity was exactly what was not going on in an economy where innovation was proceeding at a reasonable clip. Innovators are trying something new, and the consequences of their actions will depend on how effectively they do something they have not done before, and also on how others react. In such a context, there is no empirically rational basis for assigning probabilities to possible outcomes, much less being able even to conceive all the possibilities. If considerable innovation is going on, the non-innovators also face real uncertainty, regarding how they will fare, or even regarding whether their traditional actions will be viable, in the face of the innovation of others. What actually happens will benefit some, and punish others; those who are hurt may need to rethink what they should be doing. Economic growth driven by innovation thus involves essentially the 'creative destruction' of older ways of doing things, and, often, of economic agents who were good at those older ways but cannot or are slow to adopt the new. If innovation stops, the pattern of economic activity may settle down into a new general equilibrium. But if innovation is continuing, which it is under virtually all theories of economic growth, the economy in motion is always at least somewhat out of equilibrium.

Innovators, in competition with each other, and with prevailing practice, cannot know *ex ante* whether they will be winners or losers, nor can those who choose to stay with prevailing practice. Winners and losers, both ways of doing things, and economic agents will be determined *ex post* by the competition. This is exactly the position of modern evolutionary growth theory (Nelson and Winter 1982).

The question that obviously needs to be considered next, given the objectives of this chapter is: 'Where are institutions in the above story?' One can see institutions, if implicitly, in Schumpeter's theory of customary behaviour in the circular flow. In his writings, Schumpeter highlighted that behaviours in the circular flow were mutually supporting and constraining. Under the conception of institutions as forces holding patterns of interactive behaviours in place, these expectations, norms, and hazards of deviating from the established pattern of activity that Schumpeter associated with equilibrium are certainly institutions. And it would not be hard to enrich Schumpeter's analysis to include as shaping factors things like laws, the way the financial system worked, etc. Indeed, much of the current writings about institutions are exactly oriented to identifying the forces moulding equilibrium behaviour.

I want to propose, however, that Schumpeter draws the distinction between behaviour in a static equilibrium and in a dynamic disequilibrium too sharply. Continuing innovation in a field often has its own regularities, and behaviour can be tuned to these. Indeed, for progress to be sustained, there probably must be such tuning. Put in the context of this chapter, particular institutions are often needed to support the kind of continuing fruitful interaction that sustains innovation in a field and makes it productive.

But while stable institutions may be possible, in some cases even necessary, in a regime where physical technologies are advancing briskly, a look at the historical record clearly shows that institutional change is an integral aspect of the processes of long run economic development. New forms of business organization arise, businesses take on board new activities, and some old forms and activities fade away. New markets get developed, and some old ones disappear. I note that Schumpeter's conception of innovation was broad, including new 'social technologies' like the above, as well as technological innovation more narrowly defined. Economic development as we have experienced it also has seen the emergence and development of new non-market organizations, new professions, and new laws. All of this is institutional change, as I have broadly defined the term.

These observations of course lead to the question of just how institutional change is connected with other aspects of the economic development. Several economists, Vernon Ruttan (2001; Ruttan and Hayami 1984) and Douglass North (1990, 1999) prominent among them, have argued that changes in economic conditions associated with development often make established ways of transacting, interacting, organizing, and social technologies in the language I am using, more costly and less advantageous, and call for new social technologies. In turn, these often require the development of new institutions. Ruttan in particular has argued for a theory of induced institutional innovation.

Following the lines I have proposed earlier, I want to argue that, while sometimes the coupling is tight and sometimes looser, changed social technologies and changed physical technologies generally go together. Sometimes change in both is induced by changed economic conditions. However, as Schumpeter had argued, in modern economies efforts at innovation have a drive of their own. In any case, the argument I want to develop in the remainder of this section is that innovation-driven economic growth needs to be understood as involving the co-evolution of physical and social technologies, and that the dynamics of institutional change should be seen from that point of view.

Of course, the notion that physical and social technologies are tied together is an old one in social science. Karl Marx proposed a very tight linkage, with the causal structure running cleanly from physical technologies to the social technologies of production. There is an extensive literature in sociology on how changes in physical technologies affect the organization and social order of economic activity. Below, I briefly describe two historical episodes that nicely illustrate the dynamic connections: the rise of mass production in the USA in the last part of the nineteenth century, and the development of the first science-based industry—synthetic dyestuffs—in Germany during roughly the same period.

Alfred Chandler's work (1962, 1977) is central to my telling of the first story. Under his analysis, the processes that led to mass production in a range of industries were initiated by the development of the telegraph and the railroad, which made it possible for business firms to market their products over a much larger geographical area. At the same time, advances were being made in the ability to design and build highly productive machinery. Together, these developments opened the possibility for significant economies of scale and scope.

However, to exploit these opportunities, firms had to be much larger than had been the norm, and large size posed significant problems of both organization and management. The organizational problem was partly solved by the emergence of the modern hierarchically organized company, and later by the multi-divisional form of organization (the M-form). But to manage these huge companies required many more high-level managers than an owner could garner by canvassing family and friends, which had been the usual practice. The notion of professional management came into being, and shortly after business schools emerged as the institutional mechanism for training professional managers. The financial needs of the giant companies were beyond what could be met through existing financial institutions, and both modern investment banks and modern stock markets emerged to meet the needs.

All these developments raised complicated issues of corporate, labour, and financial law. Gradually these were worked out. At the same time, the market power of the new large firms and their tendency to collude with each other gave rise to new regulatory law and antitrust. Peter Murmann

(2003) provides the most detailed and analytical account of the rise of the industry producing synthetic dyestuffs. Here the initiating event was a breakthrough in the science of organic chemistry. As a result, persons with advanced training in the theory and techniques of chemistry had a special capability for developing synthetic dyestuffs. In order to take advantage of this new capability, business firms had to develop the concept and structure of the industrial research laboratory, as a place where university-trained scientists could work with their peers in discovering and developing new products. German patent law was tightened up better enabling German firms to protect the new dyestuffs they created. Also, in the new regime involving hired scientists, new law also had to be developed to establish who had patent rights on products coming out of the laboratories. And the German university system had to gear itself up to train significant numbers of chemists inclined to work for industry. The various German governments provided significant funding to enable this latter development to happen.

In both of these cases, one can see clearly the intertwining of the development of new physical technologies and the emergence and development of new social technologies. The former required significant investments in new physical capital, and in the case of dyestuffs, human capital. Employment of the new social technologies involved new expectations and norms, new ways of organizing and governing work, in some cases new laws, and new government programmes, more generally new institutions.

Various aspects of the broad institutional environment were clearly necessary for the innovations that drove developments in these two cases to proceed effectively. First of all, the economic and social cultures had to encourage entrepreneurship, and the risk taking that is inevitable when new activities are launched. The relevant 'institutions' here probably mostly involved norms, and expectations, though the legal system had evolved to such an extent that potential entrepreneurs could expect to get rich if they succeeded. Second, in both cases developments involved sharp breaks from the 'circular flow' of economic activity, and finance needed to be available to support new firms doing new things. It would appear that in both of these cases, a lot of that early money came from rich individuals. As large-scale industry became more common, in both countries investment banks became more prominent, and in the USA the modern stock market began to develop. Again, the supporting institutions involved a mix of norms and expectations, laws providing some security for investors, and appropriate organizational structures.

And labour market institutions had to be compatible with new firms being able to attract workers with suitable skills. In both of these cases, the development of the new industry saw demand for people with high levels of training, and the emergence of new professions, professional managers in the one case, and industrial chemists in the other. For rapid development of these industries to proceed, the universities in the countries had to be, and were, responsive to these new demands. In the German case, this involved as well a significant increase in government funding of universities. Many of the institutional changes that were made occurred largely as a result of private actions, but a number required collective action, generally involving government and the political process. I have just mentioned the increases in public monies that went to support chemistry at German universities. Earlier I mentioned several other areas where old law was modified, or new law created.

Note that institutions enter these stories in two ways. First, as background preconditions that enable the developments to arise in the first place and take the shape they did. Here the relevant institutions tend to be associated with broad economy-wide context conditions, like a legal system that defines and enforces contracts, a financial system capable of funding new enterprises, flexible labour markets, and in the dyestuffs case, a strong university research system. Economists doing macroeconomic analysis tend to focus on institutions like these. But second, as the case studies show, the dynamics of development often require old institutions to change or new ones to emerge. Here the institutions in our stories are more technology or industry specific, like bodies of law tailored to a technology or industry, or the development of university research and training in particular fields. These are the kinds of institutions that economists analysing the dynamics of particular sectors or activities tend to focus on.

As I have written up these two case studies, an advance in a physical technology or a science is treated as the initiating cause of a process in which physical and social technologies co-evolve. But if I had started my accounts earlier in time, a developing social technology might have appeared to be the instigator. Thus the great size of the US market that made the installation of railroads and telephone lines so attractive to investors and public officials was the result of the customs built into the expanding American population to move on to new open land, and of the political structure and processes built into the American political system that led to policies that encouraged and supported such movement. German universities were the site of the development of organic chemistry as a powerful new science as a result of earlier German policies, and a supporting philosophy, which encouraged the rise of the research university, a development that occurred earlier in German than in other countries. It is at least as much the case that the institutional background moulds the development of physical technologies, as it is the case that the development of new physical technologies causes institutions to change.

Earlier I noted that many contemporary writers attempting to describe effective institutions have proposed that economies are productive and progressive when institutions support market mechanisms. In both of the cases sketched above, one can see the central role market organization of economic activity plays in fostering productivity and progressiveness. However, the advantages of market organization, and the disadvantages of trying to plan and control economic development from a central author-ity, are not those highlighted by the neoclassical theory of market orga-nization and its virtues. It is the fundamental uncertainties involved in innovation, the inability of economic actors to see clearly the best things to be doing, that make the pluralism, the competition, that is, associated with market organization of economic activity so important. Competition also often tends to keep prices from getting completely out of line with costs. But as Schumpeter argued, by far the principal benefit that society gets from market organization of economic activity, and competition, is innovation and economic progress. Also, non-market institutions play key roles in both of these case studies. As I argued earlier, it is a mistake to see the advance of physical technologies as being influenced only by market institutions and mechanisms. Many important social technologies involve essential non-market elements.

My discussion above has focused on particular technologies and indus-tries, rather than the economy as a whole. However, as Schumpeter sug-gested, economic growth cannot be understood adequately as an undif-ferentiated aggregated phenomenon. Rather, one needs to understand an economy as consisting of many different sectors, each with its own dynamics. Schumpeter also argued that the history of economic growth tends to divide into different eras, and that within any particular era there is a relatively small set of technologies and industries that are driving economic growth. From this point of view, the Chandler and Murmann stories are particularly interesting because mass production undertaken by large hierarchical firms and industrial R&D tied to firms engaged in production and marketing are the hallmarks (sometimes combined and sometimes not) of the industries that drove economic growth in the advanced industrial nations during the first two-thirds of the twentieth century.

Christopher Freeman and Carlotta Perez (1988, see also Freeman and Louça 2001) have proposed that the key technologies and institutions of different eras generally require different sets of supporting institutions. The countries that are successful are those that have the basis of these institutions already in place when they are needed, or which manage to build the appropriate new institutions quickly and well. The large internal market of the USA clearly provided a very favourable environment for the rise of mass production, but the prevailing institutional environment and the rapid development of new institutions tailored to the needs of mass production certainly were also a force behind US leadership in this area. Murmann and others have argued persuasively that the existing strong university research system in Germany, and the ability to support its expansion in chemistry, was a principal reason why German industry led the world in dyestuffs, and later in organic chemical products more generally, at least up until the Second World War.

The argument that rapid economic progress in different eras requires different sets of particular supporting institutions is not to deny the broader point of view, associated with an evolutionary or Schumpeterian view of the general nature of economic progress, that to support innovation and take advantage of its potential fruits the institutions of an economy need to be supportive of entrepreneurship, broadly defined, and enable resources to be shifted from rising economic sectors and firms to declining ones. But it does suggest strongly that those generalizations cannot carry the analysis very far. Rather, the analysis of the institutions required for economic productivity and progress must get into the details, which inevitably are going to differ from sector to sector and era to era.

## 11.4. The Processes of Institutional Change

How do a country's institutions come to be what they are? To what extent can salutary institutional reform be subject to deliberate analysis, planning, and implementation? There is a longstanding divide about these issues in the writings of institutional economists. In the early part of the twentieth century, John R. Commons (1924, 1934), focusing on the evolution of the law, staked out a position that to a considerable extent the institutions that a society had were the ones it had deliberately put in place, wisely or not. Friedrich Hayek's theory (1967, 1973) of why societies had the institutions that they had was different, stressing 'private orders' that changed over time through a relatively blind evolutionary process. There is a similar divide among the 'new institutional economists' regarding this matter. Indeed, Douglass North himself has taken both views, starting from a position that institutions were the result of deliberate, rational choice processes (Davis and North 1971), and later moving to a position very similar to Hayek's (North 1990, 1999), that institutions could not be effectively planned, and that the societies that had good ones should regard themselves as fortunate. Thrainn Eggertsson (1999, 2005) has followed a similar intellectual traverse.

Partly the difference here relates to the assumed influence and effectiveness of human purpose, intelligence, and forward looking planning versus more or less random change and *ex post* selection. Partly the difference is in regards to whether institutional change is seen as occurring largely through collective, generally governmental, action, or whether the process is seen as being largely decentralized, involving many actors. The position I espouse here is that on both counts the contrast often is drawn too sharply. I want to agree strongly with the economists and other social scientists who argue that institutions evolve rather than being largely planned. However, I also want to argue that beliefs about what is feasible, and what is appropriate, often play a major role in the evolution of institutions. Human purpose and human beliefs play an important role both in the generation of the institutional alternatives on which selection works, and in determining what survives and what does not. And in many cases, the process involves both decentralized and collective action.

The mix of course depends on the kind of institution one is analysing. The development of formal law obviously involves deliberate governmental action. Generally, there is debate about what the law should be, and some kind of a formal decision process. On the other hand, the evolution of custom generally is highly decentralized and whatever conscious deliberation there is tends to be myopic. But it may be a mistake to see the processes here as completely separated. Thus Commons noted explicitly that, particularly in common-law countries, the development of formal bodies of law tended to be strongly influenced by the customs of the land that were broadly deemed appropriate. And Hayek too recognized that formal law often was developed to support custom, while warning of the dangers of putting in place formal law, or public policies more generally, that were not based on the wisdom of custom.

In the cases described earlier, the development of new organizational forms was an important part of the story. While Chandler's account of the emergence and development of the organizational structure of the modern corporation highlights innovation by individual companies, a body of corporate and financial law developed along with, responsive to, and supporting and constraining these private developments. Murmann's account of the development of the modern industrial laboratory involves a mix of private experimentation and decision-making, and the formation of laws and public programmes responsive to the emergence of industrial research.

While both of these cases show an evolutionary process that is sensitive to changing needs and conditions, I now want to argue that the process of evolution of social technologies and their supporting institutions is erratic, compared with the way physical technologies evolve. The ability to design institutions that work as planned is much more limited than the ability to design new physical technologies. Selection forces, including the ability of the human agents involved to learn from experience what works well and what does not, usually are significantly weaker for institutions and social technologies than for physical technologies. And usually there is much less ability to compare alternative institutions analytically.

One important reason is that physical technologies are more amenable to sharp specification and control, and are easier to replicate and imitate more or less exactly, than are social technologies. The performance of physical technologies, including the nature of the output they produce, tends to be relatively tightly constrained by the physical inputs and processing equipment used in their operation. On the other hand, social technologies are much more open to the vagaries of human motivations and understandings regarding what is to be done, which seldom can be controlled tightly. Granovetter (1985) has argued against the 'over-socialization' of theories of human behaviour.

Certainly, the institutions that can be consciously designed tend to mould behaviours only relatively loosely, and themselves are often difficult to specify and control tightly. Thus, it is clear from Chandler's discussion of the multi-divisional form (the M-form) of business organization, that arose in the early twentieth century and became 'standard' among companies producing a range of products and selling them in different areas, that there was very considerable variation among firms. The variation involved both formal structure and the actual division of decision-making between the central office and the branches, which were only partly a matter of managerial choice. Indeed, there was a certain fuzziness to the general concept, and even individuals in the companies who were nominally in charge seem not to have known in any detail just how the system they had actually worked.

A second important difference is that in most cases, not always, it is far more difficult to get reliable evidence on the efficacy of a new institution or social technology than for a new physical technology. In part, this is a consequence of the phenomena just discussed. For a company contemplating adoption, the problem of estimating the efficacy of the M-form of organization was surely made more difficult by the fact that what the M-form actually was and how it actually worked differed significantly from firm to firm, and within a particular firm tended to change over time. But even without this complication, it tends to be very difficult to sort out the effects of a particular institution or social technology from the influences of a wide variety of other variables that bear on the profitability of a firm, or to estimate reliably the benefits and costs reaped by society from a complex of strongly interacting policies and laws. In contrast, it is much easier to gain a reliable assessment of the efficacy of a new pharmaceutical, or the performance of a new aircraft design.

Both of these differences are related to the fact that a lot can be learned about physical technologies, product designs, or modes of production, by building prototypes and doing controlled experimentation 'offline' as it were, in research and development. It is much harder to do this for institutions. Thomke (2003) provides a convincing and detailed analysis of the role of deliberate experimentation in the design and development of physical technologies. If a physical technology can be made to work in a controlled setting, it is often possible to routinize and embed it in physical hardware, and in this and other ways shield it from environmental influences that could be different online from experimental conditions. The looser coupling of institutions that can be designed and the behaviours they generate means that transfer from controlled setting to actual practice does not work nearly as well, even if the institution as a whole could be operated in an experimental setting.

Another important difference is that because of the ability to routinize, shield, and control, it is often possible to experiment with a part of a physical technology offline, and to transfer an improved version of that piece to the larger system with confidence that it will work in that context and in actual practice. In contrast, the likelihood that a piece of an institution or social technology that works well in an offline experimental setting will work well when embedded in an online system is small. This is not to deny the important role of learning by doing and using regarding the efficacy of physical technologies. However, virtually all learning regarding social technologies and the institutions that mould and support them has to proceed online. And for the reasons suggested above, even that learning is difficult and uncertain.

Relatedly, 'scientific' understanding bearing on institutions, and indicating ways that they might be improved, generally is much weaker than the scientific understanding bearing on physical technologies. The applications oriented natural sciences and engineering disciplines can often provide very helpful illumination of prevailing practice and potential roads to improvement of physical technologies. They can point relatively sharply to what is essential to the performance of a product design, or production process, and what is likely peripheral. The behavioural and social sciences provide much less light on how present institutions work and how to improve them. In trying to understand why, it is important to recognize that the productive knowledge of applied scientists and engineers comes not only from the underlying basic sciences but also from observation, experiment, and analysis of prevailing practices and artefacts, or models of these that are built expressly for experimentation and analysis. Behavioural and social scientists have little opportunity to build this kind of knowledge regarding institutions.

The emergence and adoption of new social technologies can proceed rapidly and fruitfully if there is a reasonably well-defined problem that needs some solution, one can readily identify a new social technology that solves that problem at least broadly, and the needed institutional supports for that social technology are relatively obvious. Under these conditions, the needed new institutions can come relatively quickly into place, at least if those who are in a position to make the institutional changes have an interest in doing so. Thus in the USA the M-form spread relatively rapidly among multi-product multi-market firms. The M-form did at least mitigate the problem of overload of decisions to be made by top management of such firms. The industrial research laboratory provided a way for firms to hire groups of scientists and put them to the task of inventing, and relatively quickly became an 'institution' in industries where the competitiveness of firms depended on their prowess at creating new products and manufacturing processes. Vernon Ruttan (2003, 2006) has argued the case that modern societies in fact have considerable capacity for well-directed institutional reform, based on the strength of the social sciences, as well as ability to learn from experience. Prominent among the examples he uses is the history of agricultural experimentation stations, in the USA, in Japan, and in a number of today's developing countries. The evidence of the efficacy of this institution is very strong.

On the other hand, the history of both the M-form and the industrial research laboratory is one of firms continuing to struggle to fine-tune the structures so that they would work well in their particular context. I read the history of agricultural experimentation as showing the same sort of uncertain groping to find particular structures that work. It is illuminating to contrast the experience here with the evolution of mass production machinery. In the latter, many engineers were involved in designing machines, and getting relatively reliable information on performance from their own testing, and from feedback from users. Efforts to improve design could be guided by that user feedback, and by the ability of designers to experiment offline, with reasonable confidence that what they learned from that experimentation would hold up in actual practice. And designers could learn from studying the characteristics and performance of the machines made by other designers. There is little evidence of anything like this progressive cumulative learning regarding business or research organization. The evolution of social technologies and the institutions that support them is a difficult uncertain process, compared with the evolution of physical technologies.

My reading of the recent writings of Douglass North (1999, 2005) and Thrainn Eggertsson (2005) suggests that they too have come to this judgement. Of course, there are matters of degree here. Feedback from experience and the strength of understanding are certainly greater in the cases of evolution of some social technologies than for others, and for some physical technologies neither of these influences may be particularly strong. But my argument is that there are significant differences on average between physical and social technologies in these respects. Indeed, in some circumstances institutional evolution can result in building into place social technologies that are quite ineffective, or worse. For the most part, evidence of the benefits and costs of using new physical technologies is sharp enough so that few really bad ones ever get into widespread use (although there unfortunately are a number of cases where deleterious side effects, or problems that arose in particular contexts, were discovered only after a technology was around for awhile). In contrast, the introduction and spread of social technologies can be driven by fad, or ideology, and given the difficulties in getting reliable feedback on actual performance, social technologies, and the institutions supporting them, once in place may be difficult to dislodge, even if there is little evidence that they are accomplishing what they were established to do. And reform too may be driven as much by ideology as by solid understanding of the real problems with the existing regime.

## 11.5. The Rise of the Specialized Research Firm, and of University Patenting, in the Evolution of Pharmaceutical Biotechnology

This section of this chapter is concerned with the evolution of institutional structures in the wake of the rise of biotechnology as a new technology for the development of pharmaceuticals. This case displays, in a contemporary setting, many of the same features we have seen in the two historical examples discussed earlier. And more than those earlier cases, this contemporary one nicely illustrates the uncertain and sometimes problematic nature of the processes of institutional evolution highlighted in Section 11.4.

The rise during the 1960s and 1970s of molecular biology as a strong science, and the creation of the basic processes used in modern biotechnology, was clearly a watershed for the American pharmaceutical industry. These developments opened up a new route to pharmaceuticals discovery and development, one in which, at least at the start, established pharmaceutical companies had no particular competences, and at the same time, one where certain academic researchers had expertise. Several lines of university-based research began to appear very promising commercially. A number of new biotech firms were formed, staffed by university researchers and their students, with plans to develop new pharmaceuticals, and either licence the successful results to established pharmaceuticals companies, or themselves go further downstream into the pharmaceuticals business.

Several prevailing broad institutional factors enabled and encouraged these developments. One was the traditional openness of American universities to entrepreneurial activity on the part of their researchers. Another was an established venture capital industry, which quickly came to see the finance of biotech start-ups as a potentially profitable business. These two features of the prevailing institutional framework in the USA should be regarded as part and parcel of a general institutional friendliness towards entrepreneurship. However, the emergence of firms specializing in research, and of university researchers closely linked to these firms, was a quite new institutional development. (For a history see Mowery et al. 2005.)

To make this arrangement viable commercially required that the research firms have control over the new products and techniques they developed. Here, a key legal decision in 1980 assured sceptics that the products of biotechnology could be patented. At about the same time, Congress passed the Bayh–Dole Act, which encouraged universities to take out patents on the results of government-funded research projects, and to try aggressively to commercialize those results. While the language of the act is not specifically focused on biotech, an important part of the argument that led Congress to believe that technology transfer from universities to industry would be encouraged if universities had strong patent rights and could grant exclusive licences to a firm to develop their embryonic products was specifically concerned with pharmaceuticals.

Clearly, one sees in the case of the rise of pharmaceutical biotechnology the same kind of co-evolution of physical and social technologies, and of supporting institutions, that I described earlier in the case of mass production industry in the USA, and of the dyestuff industry in Germany. But there are some interesting differences, particularly on the side of the social technologies that evolved. The major innovations in firm and industry structure that marked the earlier cases—the rise of the large hierarchically organized firm and later the M-form in the Chandler case, and the industrial research laboratory tied to a company that planned itself to employ the inventions that came out of that laboratory in the Murmann case—over time were shown by experience to be generally economically productive and conducive of profitability for firms in the relevant lines of business. However, the new industrial structure that has grown up in biotech has not proved itself, at least not yet. Despite being touted for over a quarter century as being a highly productive new way of organizing industrial research, biotech firms specializing in research, and aiming for profit through joint ventures or licencing agreements with pharmaceutical firms engaged in production and marketing, have with few exceptions failed to earn a profit. And university patenting of research results, as contrasted with placing these in the public domain, has been shown to have some problematic aspects.

It is relevant, that the notion that a firm could be profitable simply by doing research, and without having close organizational linkages to production and marketing, gained enthusiastic credence so readily. This proposition was inconsistent with the history of industrial research that was recounted above, where firms making and selling products learned the advantages of doing R&D internally. While there were a few exceptions, by and large firms that tried to make profit by specializing in R&D were not successful. Regarding the present case, it has been recognized widely for some time that most biotech firms that have specialized in research, and have not moved themselves into production and marketing, are not making any money. However, until relatively recently this problem has been treated as something that time would cure, and not an indication that the business plans and expectations involved in this structure were possibly not viable, except in quite special circumstances. Recently, there has been more recognition of this possibility. Gary Pisano (2006) makes this argument forcefully. And while a number of important drugs have come out of the new regime, the flow has been far less than some enthusiasts had forecasted, and in addition there are signs recently of a slowing down of the flow. In any case, if in fact the research structure that has evolved in biotech potentially is highly productive, but there are still some bugs to iron out, learning certainly has been very slow. If in fact this is not a good way to organize industrial research, it is taking a long time to learn that.

There are also good reasons to be open minded or even sceptical about the economic value, and more generally of the wisdom, of the new policies encouraging universities to patent what they can out of what comes out of their research, an institutional development that, while not tied to biotech, has been exercised especially vigorously in this field. There has been a long history of debate about whether it is appropriate for universities to patent their research results when they can, or rather simply place these in the public domain. Since the end of the Second World War, when the federal government became the dominant funder of academic research, much of the debate has been concerned with the patenting of results coming out of government-funded research. It seems fair to say that, until the testimony and deliberations that led to Bayh–Dole, there was widespread belief that scientific findings would be most productive if placed in the public domain. And when the research in question was funded publicly, there was no need for a patent incentive to induce the work.

The argument that carried the day for Bayh–Dole was that technology transfer would be more strongly motivated if university researchers held a patent on their research findings, and companies that needed to make significant investments on their own to 'commercialize' those results could be assured by the grant of an exclusive patent licence that their profits would not be quickly eroded by competition. However, the evidence for this argument was not extensive. It is clear that since the 1970s many important new products and processes have been made possible by academic research. Over this period, university patenting has increased greatly, as has university revenues from technology licencing. These facts have led some sophisticated observers to argue that Bayh–Dole has amply met its goals. Thus in 2002 *The Economist* opined that 'possibly the most inspired piece of legislation in America over the past half-century was the Bayh–Dole act of 1980'.

However, the enthusiasts for Bayh–Dole have generally suffered from a historical myopia. University research was contributing importantly to industrial innovation long before Bayh–Dole and much of what industry was drawing on was in the public domain, not patented. Bayh–Dole was brought into a university research system that already was strongly oriented to spurring innovation, and quite successful at it. Thus it is not clear that the new university patenting has been as important in facilitating technology transfer as the advocates have claimed. Put another way, contrary to the message of the citation from *The Economist*, it is quite possible that much of the university contribution would have occurred without university patents.

On the other hand, the downsides of Bayh–Dole, and the policies of universities to patent as much as they can, and earn as much money as they can from their patents, are now more visible than they were a few years back (see Nelson 2004). There are several prominent cases where the licencing policy of a university has resulted in a strong monopoly position by a particular company. In at least one such case, a company that was clearly in the lead in developing the technology was effectively shut down by the company that had the exclusive licence. In other cases, the holder of the licence has blocked academic researchers working in a field. A recent court case has clearly signalled that the argument by academic institutions that, since they do basic research, they have a research exemption to any patent blockages is not persuasive in an era when universities themselves are major patentees, and use their patents aggressively. And the issue of possible bias in the articles and public statements of academics has been receiving increasing attention in the press. For all these reasons, recently there has been some backing off from the enthusiasm for university patenting that marked the 1980s and 1990s. A recent issue of *The Economist* (2005) focused on many of the issues raised above, implicitly arguing that the costs of university patenting and often exclusive licencing needed to be weighed against the benefits. The National Institutes of Health have issued guidelines calling for its grantees to licence their patented inventions widely not narrowly. It is uncertain whether or not Bayh–Dole, or rather the set of incentives and practices symbolized as well as reinforced by Bayh–Dole, has been a plus or a minus. The uncertainty here, as the uncertainty regarding whether or not the advantages of specialized research firms in a field like biotechnology have been oversold, shows clearly how difficult it is often to evaluate new social technologies, and the institutions supporting them. Mistakes can be made, and can last a long time.

## 11.6. A Reprise

The thrust of my argument in this chapter is twofold. First, economists are surely right in seeing 'the right institutions' as the key to economic productivity and progressiveness. But second, if we are serious about taking the argument deeper we need to recognize that we have a very real challenge. The magnitude of the challenge, I think, is only beginning to be understood. I read the recent writings of Douglass North (2005) and Thrainn Eggertsson (2005) as presenting a similar point of view. Indications of the intellectual challenge come into view once one recognizes the large number of things distinguished economists, and other social scientists, have called institutions, at least if one continues to believe that, somehow, they all are talking about roughly the same thing. That thing, then, must be very complex and variegated. I have proposed that much of the writing on institutions is concerned with the factors that mould the behaviours of economic agents, in contexts where the effectiveness of their actions depends on the behaviours of other economic agents. Institutions influence the patterns of behaviour that are prominent in a society, and what behaviours are deterred. The complexity and variegation are there because in most cases there are many different factors influencing economic behaviours, and the important ones vary across economic activities. More, given the wide range of human motivations and beliefs, and differences across traditions and cultures, the factors that can induce particular behaviour patterns almost surely differ somewhat from context to context.

If these arguments are accepted, it should be clear that the hunt for a single small set of institutions that are necessary, or sufficient, to support economic productivity and progressiveness is an unpromising quest. Economists, social scientists more generally, are not going to make much headway towards understanding the institutions needed for productivity and progressiveness if we look only at a macroeconomic level, or if we entertain only broad general conceptions like 'support of market organization', or respect for the rule of law, or democratic government. At the most, we may be able to identify a set of broad variables that seem to be associated, more often than not, with good economic performance, or their absence often associated with poor performance. But invariably there are going to be exceptions. Similarly, broad theoretical proposals about the nature of institutions, like that they are 'the rules of the game', or 'governing structures', or 'habits of action and thought common to the generality of man', are not going to take us very far. The devil is in the details. And a major problem for research on institutions is that the relevant details, that is, the details that make a consequential difference regarding the efficacy of action, are often hard to discern. This is at once a problem for positive research that seeks to explain why certain economies have done better than others, and a serious problem for normative analysis concerned with identifying the institutional reforms needed to improve productivity and progressiveness.

Regarding the former problem, earlier I highlighted that perhaps analysts have misread what has been going on in American biotech, putting too positive a gloss on the institutional structure that has evolved. But for an example that has now played out, recall the recent history of attempts by analysts to explain why during the 1970s and 1980s the Japanese industry was doing so well, in competition with American and European, in automobiles and then electronics. Remember the sequence of explanations that today seem rather quaint, or at least at odds with the new conventional wisdom: government guidance under MITI, lifetime employment, long-term financial relationships between banks and firms, cooperative R&D. I am not arguing here that there is nothing to these proposed explanations; they well may have been an important part of the story. Rather, my argument is that it is very hard to identify the key institutions that are behind economic success, and also that is important to recognize that what works well in one country in one era may work quite differently in a different country or as times change. This, of course, makes prescription especially difficult.

The development of a solid understanding of how institutions affect economic productivity and progressiveness is obviously a very challenging task. The basic reason is that the relationships are not simple. But the going will be especially hard if economists do not develop a coherent and broadly agreed-upon way of thinking about what institutions are, and how they affect economic activity, that illuminates the complexities as well as the broad regularities. My central purpose in this chapter has been to sketch out a perspective on institutions and economic change that does that.

## References

Abramovitz, M. (1952). 'Econmics of Growth', in B. Haley (ed.), *A Survey of Contemporary Economics*, Homewood, Ill.: Richard D. Irwin.

——(1956). 'Resource and Output Trends in the United States Since 1870', *American Economic Review*, 46: 5–23.

——(1989). *Thinking About Growth*. Cambridge: Cambridge University Press.

Chandler, A. (1962). *Strategy and Structure*. Cambridge, MA: MIT Press.

——(1977). *The Visible Hand: The Managerial Revolution in American Business*. Cambridge, MA: Harvard University Press.

Commons, J. (1924). *Legal Foundations of Capitalism*. New York: Macmillian.

——(1934). *Institutional Economics*. Madison: University of Wisconsin Press.

Davis, L. and North, D. (1971). *Institutional Change and American Economic Growth*. Cambridge: Cambridge University Press.

Eggertsson, T. (1999) 'The Emergence of Norms in Economics—With Special Reference to Economic Development', Unpublished Manuscript, Jena: Max Plank Institute for Research into Economic Systems.

——(2005). *Imperfect Institutions*. Ann Arbor: University of Michigan Press.

Freeman, C. and Louça, F. (2001). *As Time Goes By: From the Industrial Revolution to the Information Revolution*. Oxford: Oxford University Press.

——and Perez, C. (1988). 'Structural Crises of Adjustment, Business Cycles, and Investment Behavior', in G. Dosi et al. (eds.), *Technical Change and Economic Theory*. London: Pinter.

Glaeser, E., La Porta, R., Lopez de Silanes, F., and Shleifer, A. (2004). 'Do Institutions Cause Growth?', *Journal of Economic Growth*, 9: 271–303.

Granovetter, M. (1985). 'Economic Action and Social Structure: The Problem of Embeddedness', *American Journal of Sociology*, 91: 481–510.

Hayek, F. (1967). *Studies in Philosophy, Politics, and Economics*. London: Routledge and Kegan Paul.

——(1973). *Law, Legislation, and Liberty* vol. i: *Rules and Order*. London: Routledge and Kegan Paul.

Hodgson, G. M. (1988). *Economics and Institutions*. Cambridge: Polity Press.

——(1994), 'The Return of Institutional Economics', in N. Smelser and R. Swedberg (eds.), *The Handbook of Economic Sociology*. Princeton, NJ: Princeton University Press.

——(1998). 'The Approach of Institutional Economics', *Journal of Economic Literature*, 36: 166–92.

—— (2006). 'What Are Institutions', *Journal of Economic Issues*, 40: 1–26.

Kogut, B. (1993). *Country Competitiveness: Technology and the Organization of Work*. Oxford: Oxford University Press.

—— (2000). 'The Transatlantic Exchange of Ideas and Practices: National Institutions and Diffusion', Working Paper 00–13, Reginald H. Jones Center, the Wharton School, University of Pennsylvania.

—— and Zander, U. (1992). 'Knowledge of the Firm, Combinative Capabilities, and the Replication of Technology', *Organization Science*, 3: 383–97.

Mowery, D., Nelson, R., Sampat, B., and Ziedonis, A. (2005). *Ivory Tower And Industrial Innovation*. Stanford: Stanford Business School Press.

Murmann, P. (2003). *Knowledge and Competitive Advantage: The Coevolution of Firms, Technolgies, and National Institutions*. Cambridge: Cambridge University Press.

Nelson R. (ed.) (1993). *National Innovation Systems*. New York: Oxford University Press.

—— (1998). 'The Agenda for Growth Theory: A Different Point of View', *Cambridge Journal of Economics*, 22: 497–520.

—— (2004). 'The Market Economy and the Scientific Commons', *Research Policy*, 33: 455–71.

—— and Sampat, B. (2001). 'Making Sense of Institutions as a Factor Shaping Economic Performance', *Journal of Economic Behavior and Organization*, 44: 31–54.

—— and Winter, S. (1982). *An Evolutionary Theory of Economic Change*. Cambridge, MA: Harvard University Press.

North, D. (1990). *Institutions, Institutional Change, and Economic Performance*. Cambridge: Cambridge University Press.

—— (1999). *Understanding the Process of Economic Change*. London: Institute of Economic Affairs.

—— (2005). *Understanding the Process of Economic Change*. Princeton, NJ: Princeton University Press.

Pisano, G. (2006). *Science Business: Promise, Reality, and the Future of Biotechnology*. Boston, MA: Harvard Business School Press.

Rodrik, D., Subraanian, A., and Trebbi, F. (2004). 'Institutions Rule: The Primacy of Institutions Over Geography and Integration in Economic Development', *Journal of Economic Growth*, 9: 131–65.

Ruttan, V. (2001). *Technology, Growth, and Development: An Induced Innovation Perspective*. New York: Oxford University Press.

—— (2003). *Social Science Knowledge and Economic Development*. Ann Arbor: University of Michigan Press.

—— (2006). 'Social Science Knowledge and Induced Institutional Innovation: An Institutional Design Perspective', Staff Paper P02–07, Department of Applied Economics, University of Minnesota.

—— and Hayami, V. (1984). 'Towards a Theory of Induced Institutional Innovation', *The Journal of Development Studies*, 20: 203–23.

Schumpeter, J. (1934). *The Theory of Economic Development*. Cambridge, MA: Harvard University Press.

—— (1942). *Capitalism, Socialism, and Democracy*. New York: Harper and Row.

*The Economist* (2002). 'Innovation's Golden Goose', 12 December.

—— (2005). 'Bayhing For Blood or Doling for Cash?', 24 December.

Thomke, S. (2003). *Experimentation Matters*. Boston, MA: Harvard Business School Press.

Veblen, T. (1899). *The Theory of the Leisure Class: An Economic Study of Institutions*. New York: Macmillian.

—— (1915). *Imperial Germany and the Industrial Revolution*. New York: MacMillan.

—— (1958). *The Theory of Business Enterprise*. New York: Mentor Books.

Williamson, O. E. (1975). *Markets and Hierarchies: Analysis and Antitrust Implications*. New York: Free Press.

—— (1985). *The Economic Institutions of Capitalism*. New York: Free Press.

# 12

# Institutional Evolution and the Political Economy of Governance

*Alexander Ebner*

## 12.1. Introduction

The relationship between markets and states constitutes a decisive subject for the new institutionalism in the social sciences. It addresses the actually existing variety of governance structures in complex market systems. In this line of reasoning, markets are viewed as ensembles of social relations that are embedded in the institutional variety of a distinct market order. Understanding the evolution of the corresponding governance structures, however, requires further refinements of the research perspective of the new institutionalism. Decisively, the question arises, in what sense the formation and maintenance of markets depends on the organization of economic activity by the state. Also, the feedback of the market process on the institutional field of the state has become a major analytical concern. This co-evolutionary character of the relationship between markets and states makes the exploration of governance structures in the market system so challenging.

Indeed, from the outset, the matter of governance in the new institutionalism has been broadly associated with the analytical concerns of the transaction cost approach in the framework of the new institutional economics. Yet subsequent extensions of the governance debate have covered a more comprehensive theoretical range that includes the analytical strands of evolutionary economics, the new economic sociology and institutional political economy. In approaching the dynamism of institutional change, all of these strands of institutionalist reasoning reflect a sustained shift of analytical interests towards evolutionary positions.

This reorientation is accompanied by a concern with the institutional dynamism that drives the evolution of governance structures. In particular, here, the matter of institutional innovation is taken to the fore. It offers analytical means for perceiving the co-evolution of markets and states as a path-dependent process that reflects the social construction of institutional change.

Addressing these considerations, this chapter reviews the major contributions to the governance approach, as originally provided by the new institutional economics and subsequently extended in the transdisciplinary discourse of the new institutionalism. The presentation proceeds as follows. First, Oliver E. Williamson's transaction cost approach to governance is examined. This review offers insights into the notion of private ordering as a governance device. Second, Douglass C. North's theory of the institutional evolution of markets and states is inspected. In this context, evolutionary positions in North's reasoning are scrutinized. Third, following a critical reconstruction of Mancur Olson's collective action approach to governance, a further reconsideration of institutional variety opens the analytical horizon for the transdisciplinary efforts of the new institutionalism. In particular, this hints at the social construction of institutions. Fourth, the relationship between markets and states is specified as a co-evolutionary process of institutional change which is driven by institutional innovations. Thus, in conclusion, the political economy of governance is most adequately viewed from an evolutionary perspective.

## 12.2. Governance, Transaction Cost and Private Ordering

The concept of governance has become a major analytical device for the new institutionalism in the social sciences. It denotes the structured coordination of actors from the private and public sector in achieving collective action. In addressing the institutional transformation of the state towards less hierarchical modes of regulation, it points to complex patterns of private–public interactions in the regulation of social systems (Pierre 2000: 3–4). These concerns are reconsidered in the more specific perception of governance as a mode of governing in and through the interaction mechanisms of organizational networks (Rhodes 2007: 1246). This allows for perceiving governance structures as evolving sets of institutional rules and norms that constitute distinct coordination modes of social order. Indeed, in particular in the theory of public policy, the notion of governance has become prominent exactly due to its conceptual openness for an understanding of institutional coordination that addresses both formal institutions associated with the state and informal institutions like beliefs and social norms (Hyden 1992). Accordingly, governance research exhibits an inherently transdisciplinary character, quite in line with the methodological pluralism that informs the new institutionalism in the social sciences (van Kersbergen and van Waarden 2004). Yet, the basic understanding of governance as a means for denoting various forms of institutional coordination has been originally outlined in the transaction cost approach of the new institutional economics (Mayntz 2003: 27–8). This specific point of departure has shaped further perceptions of the major problem in the institutional analysis of governance structures, namely the explanation of institutional change (Kjaer 2004: 9). Thus, a closer examination of the transaction cost perspective may provide promising insights into the basic propositions of the governance debate.

Meant to provide an institutional substantiation of neoclassical economic theory, the research agenda of the new institutional economics addresses transactions in economic and political systems, involving diverse agents such as firms and households as well as government and administration. Patterns of monitoring and enforcing exchange relations are perceived as governance structures that confront the problem of economizing on transaction costs (Furubotn and Richter 1997: 2–3). These concerns may be associated with Ronald Coase's pioneering definition of transaction costs as costs of exchange. In the Coasean framework, the developmental interplay of market expansion and increasing specialization depends on the costs of exchange, that is, the transaction costs within an economic setting that is shaped by the diverse institutions of law, politics, education, and culture (Coase 1998: 73). Related governance aspects involve self-enforcement among the contracting parties as well as third-party enforcement, which requires the institutionalized self-restraint of a potentially omnipotent enforcement authority like the state. The first variant is prominent with Oliver E. Williamson's transaction cost approach to economic organization. It provides comparative analyses of markets and hierarchies as governance modes in a setting of established rules and norms. The second variant is commonly related to Douglass North's transaction cost approach to institutional change. It highlights the evolution of rules and norms as a determinant of economic performance.

Actually, in differentiating the explanative range of institutional analysis, Williamson distinguishes four levels of theorizing. The first level denotes the matter of social embeddedness, that is, informal institutions like social norms and belief-systems, which result from long-run evolutionary processes. The formal institutional environment on the second level is subject to restructuring in a much shorter time span. It addresses formal rules of the game such as property rights shaped by government, bureaucracy, and judiciary. Governance on the third level addresses the actual play of the game within established rules. This perspective highlights contractual arrangements that are designed to align governance structures with corresponding transactions. The fourth level deals with continuous change in the agency domain of choices on resource allocation, even pointing to a fifth level of cognitive mechanisms in the evolution of the mind (Williamson 2000*a*: 596–600). In this scheme, the institutional environment and the institutions of governance, denoted as rules of the game and its actual play on the second and third levels of analysis, are of utmost interest for theorizing on governance from a transaction cost perspective (Williamson 1998: 75–6). In related terms, Williamson also distinguishes choice-theoretical and contract-theoretical positions in modern economics, delegating the traditional neoclassical theory of resource allocation to the former and therefore integrating his own transaction cost perspective into the latter. It addresses private ordering in constellations of *ex post* governance, thus complementing constitutional political economy and its concern with public ordering (Williamson 2003: 9–10).

Williamson's transaction cost theory of economic organization approaches the matter of governance from a microeconomic perspective that exhibits similar roots in the behavioural theory of the firm as the modern evolutionary approach. Indeed, it highlights behavioural attributes like bounded rationality in modelling transacting individuals who need to cope with an uncertain and complex environment (Williamson 1975: 252–3). Adding the characteristics of asset specificity and interaction frequency to the transactional dimension of uncertainty then allows for analysing the organizational implications of intertemporal transactions (Williamson 1985: 54–5). *Ex ante* transaction costs may result from negotiating contractual agreements, whereas *ex post* transaction costs contain the costs of running those governance structures that are primarily assigned with monitoring functions, as influenced by social norms and conventions (Williamson 1985: 387–8). The resulting diversity of governance modes is meant to accomplish order through the mitigation of hazards. Private ordering becomes most relevant as a means for safeguarding contract execution when the alternative mechanisms of planning, promise, and competition come to fail due to the impact of bounded rationality, opportunism, and asset specificity (Williamson 1985: 30–2). Thus, the intermediate strategic function of governance is settled between the layer of individuals and their behavioural attributes on the one hand and the layer of the institutional environment with its particular shift parameters on the other hand. It is this mediation between individual action and the institutional context that makes governance a key concern of contractual variations that economize on transaction costs (Williamson 1996: 326–7). In consequence, both behavioural aspects as well as the institutional environment involving the relationship between economy and polity need to be taken into account for understanding the dynamism of governance and institutional change. Thus, particularly in the domain of public policy, any strategy for institutional reform needs to account for the societal embeddedness and related informal cultural dimensions of political–economic governance structures (Williamson 2000b: 117–18).

It follows that the actually existing variety of contractual arrangements reflects diverse types of transactions and modes of monitoring that are meant to inform differentiated governance structures facing asset specificity and uncertainty (Ménard 2000). The underlying reconsideration of bounded rationality and incomplete information allows for an assessment of Williamson's approach as a most advanced line of reasoning in the domain of the new institutional economics. More specifically, it is qualified as a point of departure for a more dynamic mode of theorizing (Brousseau and Glachant 2002). However, it is exactly the aspect of institutional change, which has informed a repeated questioning of the actual substance of Williamson's contributions to the comparative analysis of governance structures (Langlois 1986: 21). First of all, the social structure of markets needs to be taken into account. Thus, Mark Granovetter has repeatedly denounced Williamson's neglect of the role of social relations in governing institutional change (Granovetter 1985: 493–6). Also, the aspect of context-specificity has been identified as a sociological deficit in Williamson's reasoning, which is said to suffer from an inherent functionalism in the explanation of governance structures (Scott 2001: 31). This goes well together with the argument that Williamson's approach overlooks the rationale of market control as a driving force in the evolution of firms and markets, framed by government regulations (Perrow 1990; Lindberg, Campbell, and Hollingsworth

1991: 10). Decisively, Williamson's analytical framework seems to marginalize the relevance of the state as a contract enforcer. A contractual system without legal interventions, as proposed in Williamson's concept of private ordering, bears substantial costs in the face of uncertainty and power asymmetries. Thus, the evolution of a market system with its various governance structures depends fundamentally on the state as an enforcement organ (Hodgson 1988: 154–5, 2003: 378–80). Accounting for these complementarities between markets and states then requires their analysis as co-evolving components of a historical process that is driven by institutional innovation.

## 12.3. The Institutional Scaffold of the Market

The latter consideration hints at key concerns of Douglass North's transaction cost theory of institutional change, which has recently led to the formulation of a framework that characterizes institutions as scaffolds in the cultural evolution of whole societies (North 2005). In North's reasoning, institutions resemble humanly devised constraints that denote the 'rules of the game in a society', that is basically legal rules, social norms, and their enforcement characteristics (North 1990: 3). Institutional arrangements shape transaction costs, which arise from the costliness of information in the transfer of property rights. Accordingly, the state may decisively reduce transaction costs through the provision of an efficient legal system (North 1981: 36–7). The ensuing need for controlling the coercive power of the state for social ends constitutes a central dilemma of political economy. Thus, Williamson's notion of credible commitment as a contractual means for countering *ex post* opportunism through adequate governance structures also applies to the political–economic enforcement dilemma (North and Weingast 1989: 805–6). In the latter context, governance denotes the capacity to commit to specific policies by constitutional rules and institutional procedures. From a developmental perspective, then, the advantages of rule enforcement through the state refer to the reduction of transaction costs associated with a hierarchical mode of policing extended patterns of market exchange (Milgrom, North, and Weingast 1990: 20–1).

Indeed, North originally derives the rationale of the state from its institutional functions in the market system. The evolution of the state remains interconnected with the evolution of markets, market organizations, and the institutional underpinnings of market-oriented production.

Markets and states co-evolve, serving as an interrelated terrain in the variation, transmission, and selection of institutional forms. Thus, the evolution of a differentiated polity is derived from the creation of capital markets and large firm organizations that require a coercive political order, as impersonal forms of exchange require enforcement mechanisms beyond personal ties. Also, a specialized transaction sector becomes crucial for coping with trade, finance, insurance, and related services that promote the coordination of economic activity (North 1990: 120–1). Indeed, from such a qualified property rights perspective, the increasing complexity of the role of government in enforcing an ever extending range of property rights in the private and public sector may be associated with a differentiation of economic activities in the market system (Sened 1997: 179).

In coming to terms with the evolutionary dynamism of institutional change, North introduces the notion of adaptive efficiency. It describes the institutional capability of an economy in the acquisition of knowledge as a means for adapting to altered socio-economic data. The corresponding institutional changes arise from the maximization efforts of entrepreneurs whose patterns of learning induce new bargaining constellations (North 1990: 80–5). The resulting matrix of governance structures involves formal rules and informal constraints that reflect local knowledge as well as the bargaining position of powerful actors. It constitutes the political–economic framework that shapes organizational efforts in learning and innovation (North 1990: 136–7). A pattern of path dependence characterizes this institutional evolution of both markets and states. Thus, due to the impact of lock-in effects, the evolution of the market system resembles a historical chance discovery that is not to be altered voluntarily. This aspect informs also the causal sequence of cultural evolution that ranges from local experiences and associated beliefs via the gradual emergence of informal and formal institutions to the establishment of organizations pursuing specific policies (North 2005: 155).

As indicated by these considerations, the orientation of North's positions towards an evolutionary and behavioural approach entails three major facets: first, a reconsideration of the evolutionary character of economic development in terms of the irreversibility and indeterminateness of historical time; second, an acknowledgement of the subjectivity of perceptions and belief-systems as fundamental aspects of institutional change; third, an appreciation of the impact of environmental experiences for culturally conditioned local learning on both individual and collective levels (North 1994: 381). From that point of view, the cultural dimension of market systems becomes decisive. Culture is defined as an ensemble of socially transmitted knowledge and values that constitutes a framework for encoding and interpreting information (North 1990: 37). In this manner, North's evolutionary conceptualization of institutional change becomes part of a general theory of cultural evolution that reorients the transaction cost perspective from a static property rights framework towards more dynamic problems of knowledge coordination (North 2005: 158).

In line with the reconsideration of path dependence, then, the non-ergodic character of economic and social processes is taken to the fore in terms of continuous change through innovation. In particular, the persistence of inefficient institutions is derived from this novelty-driven disruption of the rational core of historical experiences (North 2005: 21–2). The comparative institutional advantage of market systems is thus associated with the formation of belief systems that embrace novelty and change. In this context, the state as the third-party enforcer of property rights becomes a key component of political–economic governance structures that may effectively integrate dispersed knowledge, reduce transaction costs, and thus promote economic development (North 2005: 70–3). This amounts to the conceptualization of the institutional and technological forces of economic change as a 'cultural scaffold', containing both physical and human capital, that is, the material artefacts as well as the stock of knowledge embodied in institutions. This involves the political structure for framing political choices, the property rights structure for defining formal economic incentives, and the social structure with its distinct norms and conventions that outline the institutional terrain of informal economic incentives (North 2005: 48–50).

Assessing these arguments, North's reasoning has exercised a major impact on related debates in the new institutionalism. This applies primarily to the Northian modelling of the role of the state in the maintenance of property rights as a key element of governance structures in a market system (Lindberg, Campbell, and Hollingsworth 1991: 11). Thus, the major differences between Williamson's and North's analytical perspectives may be interpreted as follows. Williamson provides a normative theory of contractual design that focuses on inter-firm relations while treating transaction costs as the independent variable in a static framework of analysis. North aims at an explanatory approach of economic development that highlights the institutional structure of whole economies and treats transaction costs as the dependent variable in a dynamic framework that accounts for a potentially volitional impact of the institutional context. Again, this implies that North highlights the evolution of the state as a decisive aspect of institutional change (Hirsch and Lounsbury 1996: 878–81). Moreover, North's theoretical appreciation of an evolutionary perspective that accounts for path dependence in institutional change has stimulated major analytical trends in the research framework of the new institutionalism (Nelson and Sampat 2001: 36).

However, critical voices highlight the question whether the conflict-ridden social construction of institutions needs to be taken into account more explicitly in North's theorizing. In this regard, recognizing path dependence may allow for a differentiated line of reasoning beyond functionalist preconceptions. Even so, North's individualist stance allegedly contrasts with the need to reconsider collective action in the social construction of institutional change (Fine 2003; Rutherford 1995; Vandenberg 2002; Zouboulakis 2005). Indeed, North follows Williamson in deriving the logic of transaction cost reasoning exclusively from the exchange sphere of markets. In this manner, power asymmetries that inform social relations and their institutional articulation remain conceptually marginal. A convincing line of reasoning may be derived from augmenting North's positions with Masahiko Aoki's approach to comparative institutional analysis. It views institutions as Nash-equilibria of an $n$-person game with individual adherence to an institutional convention as an optimum response, based on the expectation that a sufficient number of the $n$ players will also adhere to it. Institutions resemble self-sustaining systems of shared beliefs about a salient way a game is played. Thus, they highlight the endogenous character of rules as objectified social constructions (Aoki 2001: 10–12). Such a specification allows for approaching institutional evolution as a reflection of the social construction of institutional change. Institutional innovation as the driving force of institutional evolution thus involves coordination procedures in the search for new equilibrium constellations (Bowles 2004: 368). Still, the question arises in how far institutional change is subject to coercive interventions by powerful social groups aiming at the establishment of rules and norms that are in accordance with their particular interests and still further the common cause of a market order. This fundamental aspect of the political economy of governance is a major concern of the theory of collective action.

## 12.4. The Political Economy of Governance

In his outstanding contribution to the theory of collective action, Mancur Olson differentiates his positions from the transaction cost perspectives in Williamson and North with their image of voluntary exchange in contractual arrangements. Instead, Olson's theory of collective action underlines the role of power and coercion in overcoming collective failure that arises from the rational pursuit of individual interest (Olson 2000: 75–6, 87–8). Olson thus introduces a line of reasoning into the new institutional economics that promotes the key concerns of political economy, namely the interplay of political and economic forces in the governance of market systems. By highlighting the dynamism of collective action in the formation of intermediate institutions, his positions are set apart from conventional transaction cost theorizing. According to Olson's original argumentation, then, group size represents a determining factor in the provision of collective goods. Either small numbers of participants or coercion and selective incentives are required to derive organized collective action from the rational pursuit of individual interest. This leads to a persistent organizational dominance of particular interests over the presumed general interests of society (Olson 1965: 2–3).

Indeed, a key argument in Olson's approach maintains that distributional coalitions among diversified interest groups increase the complexity of policy regulation and thus stimulate crises of political–economic governability. Only those types of organized interest groups may promote economic growth, which encompass a substantial fraction of the population or its resources and thus would come to find such an orientation to be in their own interest (Olson 1982: 48–9). This logic of collective action also informs Olson's theory of the state, which underscores the matter of public good provision through coercive means. In particular, Olson's concept of state formation invokes exchange relations between rulers and constituents. Taxation is defined as a monopoly on theft which furthers the provision of public goods that are required in a productive market order (Olson 1993). Accordingly, differences in the institutional architecture of public policy are identified as the major source of diverging national development trajectories (Olson 1996).

While Olson positions his theorizing explicitly in an evolutionary framework, it is still safe to argue that it remains within the analytical confines of an exchange rationale that has been constitutive for the rather static positions of the new institutional economics. Moreover, related to that issue, Olson's reasoning underestimates the complexity of institutional forms in the evolution of governance structures. After all, it seems that an adequate consideration of the actual variety of institutional forms in the coordination of political–economic processes remains a challenge for institutional analysis (Chang 2002). For instance, in highlighting the basic characteristics of the market system, property rights regimes may be portrayed as highly complex bundles of regulations on diverse levels of individual and collective activity (Ostrom 2003). Accordingly, as outlined in Elinor Ostrom's approach to the governance of common pool resources, both formal arrangements such as legislatures and informal ensembles such as private interest associations need to be taken into account as institutional arenas of collective action (Ostrom 1990: 53–4). Implicitly resounding insights from classical sociology, this assessment goes well together with Masahiko Aoki's claim that property rights are not only exclusively enforced by legal rules, but also by social norms and other informal mechanisms that explain the persistence of institutional variety in modern market economies (Aoki 2001: 85–8).

These aspects are related to the actual complexity of market arrangements. At the level of a single commodity, it may be adequate to define a market as an institution that coordinates *ex-post* strategies of competing traders who interact through price signals (Boyer 1997: 66). However, the actually existing variety of markets for diverse commodities is subject to diverse modes of competition and regulation. In contrast to Williamson's transaction cost theory, therefore, a more adequate conceptualization of governance at the level of industries needs to highlight markets, networks, and hierarchies as distinct sets of exchange relationships. Market economies are actually constituted as hybrid sets of governance modes (Crouch 2005: 120–4). This insight has decisively contributed to recent transdisciplinary extensions of the governance debate that have covered a comprehensive theoretical range including economic sociology and institutional political economy. All of the involved strands of institutionalist reasoning reflect a sustained shift of analytical interests towards evolutionary positions that account for aspects such as institutional variety and path dependence. In this manner, the embeddedness of markets in non-market institutions is perceived as a dynamic component of the market system at large, framed by the regulative impact of the state.

In particular when approaching firms and industries as specific systems of power that operate in a market environment, both market and non-market mechanisms of governance are to be taken into account (Lindberg, Campbell, and Hollingsworth 1991: 5–9, see also Hollingsworth, Schmitter, and Streeck 1994). This is due to the fact that related governance mechanisms usually involve rules of exchange and enforcement mechanisms that contain both coercion and consent. The state plays a decisive role in the establishment of these governance regimes, as it provides an institutional arena for the selective articulation of interest group activities and thus demarcates their legitimate search space (Campbell and Lindberg 1991: 330–2; Lindberg and Campbell 1991: 271–2; Lindberg, Campbell, and Hollingsworth 1991: 29–33). Above all, two types of policy tools contribute to the formation and maintenance of the market system, namely the allocation of resources and information as well as the enforcement of property rights (Lindberg and Campbell 1991: 361–3). Together, they underline the political nature of the market process. Accordingly, it may be argued that markets are inherently political in substance. These aspects have been discussed most promisingly in recent advances of social theory. For instance, Pierre Bourdieu points out that competition among firms usually involves a political dimension that implies competition for power resources over the delineation of property rights (Bourdieu 2005: 203–4). Organization theorists like Scott also describe the state as a unique institutional structure that provides an arena for political conflicts over delineating property rights. Moreover, the state also exerts a major cultural impact on the cognitive orientation of organizational actors in public and private sector alike (Scott 2001: 128–9).

The underlying drive for control in social interaction is well exemplified by the impact of governance structures on the relationship between competition and cooperation among firms. In this line of reasoning, as put forward in Neil Fligstein's sociology of markets, the evolution of governance structures contributes to the control of competition in favour of market stability (Fligstein 2001: 33–4, 39–40). The European Union provides an illustrative case for such a feedback of the governance structures of public policy into the domain of the market process. Thus, historically, the formation of the Common Market stands for the symbiotic development of markets and polities as self-reinforcing institutional fields (Fligstein and Stone Sweet 2002: 1206–8). This symbiotic relationship substantiates the social construction of markets as sets of institutions that are in need of recurring reconstruction by means of political action (Crouch 2005: 6–7). Systemic communication then becomes decisive in the evolution of governance structures. In this context, the law serves as an indispensable medium of interaction between the economic and the political sphere (Stryker 2003).

However, in addition to this concern with legal rules and regulations, the developmental feasibility of effective interactions between state and private sector points once again to the embeddedness of market systems in historically specific patterns of social norms and conventions. From an evolutionary viewpoint, then, markets are perceived as complex sets of institutions, which are embedded in historically rooted social and political frameworks that evolve over time (Zysman 1994: 243–4). In this case, the East Asian development experience provides an illustrative example for a relational pattern of public–private interactions (Bardhan 2005: 29–30). The latter point underlines the institutionalist suggestion that theorizing on institutional change requires a strong emphasis on power relations and innovation efforts, which cannot be reconciled easily with a rational choice perspective and rather needs to account for the impact of ideas, culture, and social practices (Hira and Hira 2000: 279–80). After all, this underlines the role of institutional innovation in the evolution of governance structures.

## 12.5. Institutional Innovation and the Co-evolution of Markets and States

An institutionalist account of governance may perceive the relationship between markets and states as a co-evolutionary process that is driven by institutional innovations. Such a position stands for a well-established line of reasoning in institutionalist thought that may be associated with Schumpeterian as well as Polanyian insights on the institutional evolution of the market system (Ebner 2006, 2007a). Indeed, the underlying segment of evolutionary reasoning has been identified as a most promising terrain for collaboration between the diverse strands of the new institutionalism, involving rational choice, historical and sociological approaches. Evolutionary reasoning stands out as an integrative framework, for it sheds light on the question of efficiency in the selective function of market competition and its political regulation (DiMaggio 1998: 699–700). This is due to the fact that evolutionary change is modelled as an irreversible historical process which is caused by the generation and diffusion of innovations. Economic evolution is defined as the self-transformation of a system over time, based on the generation of change from within, which implies an endogenous capacity for the creation and dissemination of novelty (Nelson 1995: 57–8; Witt 1993: 2). Moreover, evolutionary positions acknowledge the embeddedness of the economy in larger social systems with co-evolving institutional components that include both contractual and non-contractual relationships. Again, institutional variety serves as an indispensable factor of evolutionary change (Bowles 2004: 478–80).

Derived from these considerations, the notion of co-evolution applied to institutional analysis could be interpreted as the joint evolution of particular entities such as populations of firms whose evolutionary transformation is shaped by the parallel evolution of framing institutional constellations (Murmann 2003: 21–2). Yet also the interaction between private and public sector may be viewed as co-evolutionary, as it is subject to both the competitive force of the market process as well as to the impact of power relations and political bargaining in the coordination of economic affairs (Boyer 2002: 330). In such a setting, the actual entities of the evolutionary process of the variation, transmission, and selection of institutional traits are organizations from private and public sector alike. They are subject to a co-evolutionary process in which the rules and regulations enforced by the state mould the dynamism of the market process, whereas market structures and market actors feed back on the formulation and implementation of these rules and regulations. All of this is embedded in a setting of informal institutions such as social norms and conventions which is also part of the evolutionary process. Markets and states thus primarily feed back on each other through the interdependence of institutional innovations in both domains.

This recognition of a co-evolutionary pattern in the development of markets and states implies that the institutional design of complex governance systems remains out of reach. Instead, in pragmatist terms, policy search resembles an experimental process of discovery procedures that is based on the coordination of local knowledge (Ostrom 1999: 519–21). However, the corresponding sets of particular domains—or subsystems, as they are defined in systems theory—all exhibit an internal logic of their own. They are interdependent in their evolution as they constrain as well as enable the dynamism of persistence and change on both the levels of the subsystems and the system as a whole (Coriat and Dosi 1998: 21–3; Nelson 1994). Accordingly, the market system may be viewed as an autopoietic system which functions according to its own rules and logics that may conflict with the alien rationale of those systems from which outside interventions emerge (Jessop 2001: 222–3). This is a decisive reason for arguing that governance procedures are subject to potential failure in the same manner as markets and hierarchies. Following the 'law of requisite variety' of systems theory, which maintains that each functional system contains impurities that allow for its adaptive flexibility as a whole, thus, institutional variety is required as a means for coping with the impact of novelty and uncertainty in complex change (Hodgson 1988: 167–8; Jessop 2003: 110–11).

This hints finally at the matter of institutional innovations in the co-evolution of markets and states. At this point, the focus on search, discovery, and learning, which plays a major role in evolutionary models of institutional change, also refers to the matter of error and imperfection in the dissemination of innovations. Decisively, innovation does not imply a drive for global optimization. Rather, it is about the transformation of local knowledge and the promotion of systemic improvements over time (Dosi and Nelson 1994: 154–5). However, as the process of evolution is conceptually divided into the segments of variation, transmission, and selection, it follows that the mechanism of enhancing variety by innovation needs to be clarified regarding its institutional conditions. For instance, institutional entrepreneurship may be perceived as cognitive leadership in an organization, as it provides cognitive frames which promote a certain strategic orientation (Witt 2000: 744). These aspects also apply to institutional innovation in a more comprehensive manner. Indeed, institutional change results from a process of constrained innovation, that is, a process in which institutions both constrain the range of available options for change as well as enable change procedures by means of certain practices and routines (Campbell 2004: 8). Crucially, then, the question arises how to conceptualize innovation with respect to the role of specific power relations that affect the process of change.

This problem is well illustrated by Neil Fligstein's stylization of markets as distinct fields. In accordance with Bourdieu's social theory, markets are addressed as arenas of social action that contain collective actors who support an institutional system of domination and control by promoting a specific local culture. The latter moulds power relations through frameworks of cognition and legitimization (Fligstein 2001: 12–16). Fligstein maintains that governments focus almost exclusively on promoting those rules that regulate potentially destabilizing market competition and thus endorse the stability of market exchange over time, quite in agreement with the control efforts of dominant market actors (Fligstein 2001: 41–2). Yet such a perspective ignores those aspects of government intervention that stimulate innovation and by doing so willingly disturb market stability and related control patterns. This public support of private sector innovation characterizes the temporary carrying out of entrepreneurial functions by the state, as witnessed most recently by the East Asian countries (Ebner 2006, 2007b). Accordingly, the co-evolution of markets and states is driven by institutional innovations that are introduced by entrepreneurial actors from both the private and the public sector.

A promising way for modelling these aspects defines institutional innovation as the alteration of governance structures through a recombination of their elements. These efforts cannot be understood without an appreciation of their actual context. Institutional innovation involves entrepreneurial actors that are embedded in a set of enabling as well as constraining institutions. Again, this refers to the viewpoint that institutional innovation resembles an effort in entrepreneurial path creation which is enabled as well as constrained by established institutional conditions (Crouch 2005: 20–4). Indeed, institutions and social structures not only constrain but also enable entrepreneurial activity (Garud, Hardy, and Maguire 2007: 961–2). These aspects may be subsumed under the notion of 'embedded entrepreneurship'. It is meant to highlight the creation and dissemination of innovation under conditions of institutional variety, which allows for both systemic coherence and adaptive flexibility (Ebner 2008). Applied to the co-evolution of markets and states, these considerations underline once more the role of feedback mechanisms in the developmental dynamics of the market system. Consequently, accounting for the evolutionary logic of institutional innovation remains decisive for understanding the political economy of governance.

## 12.6. Conclusion

The notion of governance has emerged as a prominent concept of the new institutionalism in the social sciences. It addresses the institutional coordination of the market system with its diverse modes of interaction. The relationship between markets and states belongs to the major topics in the corresponding lines of reasoning. Responding to these concerns, this chapter argues that the relationship between markets and states is well captured by a reconsideration of the evolutionary character of institutional change. Accordingly, understanding the evolution of governance structures requires a reconsideration of the co-evolutionary relationship of markets and states. This proposal is in line with recent advances in institutionalist reasoning, which reflect a shift of analytical interests towards evolutionary positions. In particular, this reorientation promotes an acknowledgement of the dynamic qualities of institutional variety in the set up of market systems. Moreover, it drives a concern with the constraining as well as enabling conditions of institutional innovation.

In accounting for these theoretical constellations, this chapter reconstructs the basic conceptual parameters of the governance approach in the new institutionalism. More specifically, it provides a review of those major contributions that are closely associated with its original domain, namely the transaction cost approach of the new institutional economics. The ensuing survey suggests a set of critical conclusions. Williamson's emphasis on private ordering in economic organization accounts for the behavioural dimension of governance, yet it tends to marginalize the role of the state. North's stylization of the institutional scaffolds of economic development aims at providing an evolutionary account of the relationship between markets and states. Still, it lacks an adequate conceptualization of the social construction of institutions. The latter aspects are also part of Olson's theory of collective action. It accentuates power and coercion in the evolution of governance structures and thus differs markedly from assumptions on the voluntary character of exchange relationships that are prevalent in transaction cost theory. However, it tends to overlook the impact of institutional variety on the developmental dynamism of market systems.

Indeed, in institutionalist reasoning, acknowledging the variety of institutional forms in the evolution of governance structures provides a constructive point of departure for approaching the co-evolution of markets and states. Rules and regulations enforced by the state shape the organization of the market process. However, market structures and market actors also feed back on the formulation and implementation of these rules and regulations. Informal institutions constitute an embedding framework for these interactions. The systemic interdependence of institutional innovations thus informs the evolution of governance structures in the coordination of the market system. In conclusion, this evolutionary perspective points to the need for an intensification of transdisciplinary efforts in governance research, quite in line with the methodological pluralism that informs the new institutionalism in the social sciences.

## References

Aoki, M. (2001). *Toward a Comparative Institutional Analysis*. Cambridge: MIT Press.
Bardhan, P. (2005). *Scarcity, Conflicts, and Cooperation*. Cambridge: MIT Press.
Bourdieu, P. (2005). *The Social Structures of the Economy*. Cambridge: Polity Press.

Bowles, S. (2004). *Microeconomics: Behavior, Institutions, and Evolution*. Princeton: Princeton University Press.

Boyer, R. (1997). 'The Variety and Unequal Performance of Really Existing Markets: Farewell to Doctor Pangloss', in J. R. Hollingsworth and R. Boyer (eds.), *Contemporary Capitalism: The Embeddedness of Institutions*. Cambridge: Cambridge University Press.

—— (2002). 'Is Régulation Theory an Original Theory of Economic Institutions?', in R. Boyer and Y. Saillard (eds.), *Régulation Theory: The State of the Art*. London and New York: Routledge.

Brousseau, E. and Glachant, J.-M. (2002). 'The Economics of Contracts and the Renewal of Economics', in E. Brousseau and J.-M. Glachant (eds.), *The Economics of Contracts*. Cambridge: Cambridge University Press.

Campbell, J. L. (2004). *Institutional Change and Globalization*. Princeton: Princeton University Press.

—— and Lindberg, L. L. (1991). 'The Evolution of Governance Regimes', in J. L. Campbell, J. R. Hollingsworth, and L. N. Lindberg (eds.), *Governance of the American Economy*. Cambridge: Cambridge University Press.

Chang, H.-J. (2002). 'Breaking the Mould: An Institutionalist Political Economy Alternative to the Neo-Liberal Theory of the Market and the State', *Cambridge Journal of Economics*, 26(5): 539–9.

Coase, R. (1998). 'The New Institutional Economics', *American Economic Review*, 88: 72–4.

Coriat, B. and Dosi, G. (1998). 'The Institutional Embeddedness of Economic Change: An Appraisal of the "Evolutionary" and "Regulationist" Research Programmes', in K. Nielsen and B. Johnson (eds.), *Institutions and Economic Change: New Perspectives on Markets, Firms and Technology*. Cheltenham: Elgar.

Crouch, C. (2005). *Capitalist Diversity and Change: Recombinant Governance and Institutional Entrepreneurs*. Oxford and New York: Oxford University Press.

DiMaggio, P. J. (1998). 'The New Institutionalism: Avenues of Collaboration', *Journal of Institutional and Theoretical Economics*, 154: 696–705.

Dosi, G. and Nelson, R. (1994). 'An Introduction to Evolutionary Theories in Economics', *Journal of Evolutionary Economics*, 4: 153–72.

Ebner, A. (2006). 'Institutions, Entrepreneurship and the Rationale of Government: An Outline of the Schumpeterian Theory of the State', *Journal of Economic Behavior and Organization*, 59(4): 497–515.

—— (2007a). *Governance and Public Policy*, Habilitation Thesis, Faculty of Economics, Law, and the Social Sciences, University of Erfurt.

—— (2007b). 'Public Policy, Governance, and Innovation: Entrepreneurial States in East Asian Economic Development', *International Journal of Technology and Globalisation*, 3(1): 103–24.

—— (2008). *Embedded Entrepreneurship: The Institutional Dynamics of Innovation*. London and New York: Routledge.

Fine, B. (2003). 'From Principle of Pricing to Pricing of Principle: Rationality and Irrationality in the Economic History of Douglass North', *Comparative Studies in Society and History*, 5(4): 546–70.

Fligstein, N. (2001). *The Architecture of Markets: An Economic Sociology of Twenty-First Century Capitalist Societies*. Princeton: Princeton University Press.

——and Stone Sweet, A. (2002). 'Constructing Polities and Markets: An Institutionalist Account of European Integration', *American Journal of Sociology*, 107: 1206–43.

Furubotn, E. and Richter, R. (1997). *Institutions and Economic Theory: The Contribution of the New Institutional Economics*. Ann Arbor: University of Michigan Press.

Garud, R., Hardy, C., and Maguire, S. (2007). 'Institutional Entrepreneurship as Embedded Agency: An Introduction to the Special Issue', *Organization Studies*, 28: 957–69.

Granovetter, M. (1985). 'Economic Action and Social Structure: The Problem of Embeddedness', *American Journal of Sociology*, 91: 481–510.

Hira, A. and Hira, R. (2000). 'The New Institutionalism: Contradictory Notions of Change', *American Journal of Economics and Sociology*, 59: 267–82.

Hirsch, P. M. and Lounsbury, M. D. (1996). 'Rediscovering Volition: The Institutional Economics of Douglass C. North', *Academy of Management Review*, 21: 872–84.

Hodgson, G. M. (1988). *Economics and Institutions: A Manifesto for a Modern Institutional Economics*. Cambridge: Polity Press.

——(2003). 'The Enforcement of Contracts and Property Rights: Constitutive Versus Epiphenomenal Conceptions of Law', *International Review of Sociology*, 13(2): 375–91.

Hollingsworth, J. R., Schmitter, P. C., and Streeck, W. (1994). 'Capitalism, Sectors, Institutions, and Performance', in J. R. Hollingsworth, P. C. Schmitter, and W. Streeck (eds.), *Governing Capitalist Economies: Performance and Control of Economic Sectors*. New York and Oxford: Oxford University Press.

Hyden, G. (1992). *Governance and Politics in Africa*. Boulder: Westview Press.

Jessop, B. (2001). 'Institutional (Re)turns and the Strategic-Relational Approach', *Environment and Planning A*, 33: 1213–35.

——(2003). 'Governance and Meta-Governance: On Reflexivity, Requisite Variety and Requisite Irony', in H. P. Bang (ed.), *Governance as Social and Political Communication*. Manchester and New York: Manchester University Press.

Kjaer, A. M. (2004). *Governance*. Cambridge: Polity.

Langlois, R. N. (1986). 'The New Institutional Economics: An Introductory Essay', in R. N. Langlois (ed.), *Economics as a Process: Essays in the New Institutional Economics*. Cambridge: Cambridge University Press.

Lindberg, L. L. and Campbell, J. L. (1991). 'The State and the Organization of Economic Activity', in J. L. Capbell, J. R. Hollingsworth, and L. N. Lindberg (eds.), *Governance of the American Economy*. Cambridge: Cambridge University Press.

Lindberg, L. L., Campbell, J. L., and Hollingsworth, J. R. (1991). 'Economic Governance and the Analysis of Structural Change in the American Economy', in J. L. Capbell, J. R. Hollingsworth, and L. N. Lindberg (eds.), *Governance of the American Economy*. Cambridge: Cambridge University Press.

Mayntz, R. (2003). 'New Challenges to Governance Theory', in H. P. Bang (ed.), *Governance as Social and Political Communication*. Manchester and New York: Manchester University Press.

Ménard, C. (2000). 'Enforcement Procedures and Governance Structures: What Relationship?', in C. Ménard (ed.), *Intuitions, Contracts and Organizations*. Cheltenham: Elgar.

Milgrom, P. R., North, D. C., and Weingast, B. R. (1990). 'The Role of Institutions in the Revival of Trade: The Law Merchant, Private Judges, and the Champagne Fairs', *Economics and Politics*, 2: 1–23.

Murmann, J. P. (2003). *Knowledge and Competitive Advantage: The Coevolution of Firms, Technology, and National Institutions*. Cambridge: Cambridge University Press.

Nelson, R. (1994). 'The Co-Evolution of Technology, Industrial Structure, and Supporting Institutions', *Industrial and Corporate Change*, 3: 47–63.

—— (1995). 'Recent Evolutionary Theorizing About Economic Change', *Journal of Economic Literature*, 33: 48–90.

—— and Sampat, B. N. (2001). 'Making Sense of Institutions as a Factor Shaping Economic Performance', *Journal of Economic Behavior and Organization*, 44: 31–54.

North, D. C. (1981). *Structure and Change in Economic History*. New York: W. W. Norton.

—— (1990). *Institutions, Institutional Change and Economic Performance*. Cambridge: Cambridge University Press.

—— (1994). 'The Historical Evolution of Polities', *International Review of Law and Economics*, 14: 381–91.

—— (2005). *Understanding the Process of Economic Change*. Princeton: Princeton University Press.

—— and Weingast, B. R. (1989). 'Constitutions and Commitment: The Evolution of Institutions Governing Public Choice in Seventeenth-Century England', *Journal of Economic History*, 49: 803–32.

Olson, M. (1965). *The Logic of Collective Action: Public Goods and the Theory of Groups*. Cambridge, MA: Harvard University Press.

—— (1982). *The Rise and Decline of Nations: Economic Growth, Stagflation and Social Rigidities*. New Haven: Yale University Press.

—— (1993). 'Dictatorship, Democracy, and Development', *American Political Science Review*, 87: 567–76.

—— (1996). 'Big Bills Left on the Sidewalk: Why Some Nations are Rich and Others Poor', *Journal of Economic Perspectives*, 10: 3–24.

—— (2000). *Power and Prosperity: Outgrowing Communist and Capitalist Dictatorships*. New York: Basic Books.

Ostrom, E. (1990). *Governing the Commons: The Evolution of Institutions for Collective Action*. Cambridge: Cambridge University Press.

——(1999). 'Coping with Tragedies of the Commons', *Annual Review of Political Science*, 2: 493–535.

——(2003). 'How Types of Goods and Property Rights Jointly Affect Collective Action', *Journal of Theoretical Politics*, 15: 239–70.

Perrow, C. (1990). 'Economic Theories of Organization', in S. Zukin and P. DiMaggio (eds.), *Structures of Capital: The Social Organization of the Economy*. Cambridge: Cambridge University Press.

Pierre, J. (2000). 'Introduction: Understanding Governance', in J. Pierre (ed.), *Debating Governance: Authority, Steering, and Democracy*. Oxford: Oxford University Press.

Rhodes, R. A. W. (2007). 'Understanding Governance: Ten Years On', *Organizational Studies*, 28: 1243–64.

Rutherford, M. (1995). 'The Old and the New Institutionalism: Can Bridges be Built?', *Journal of Economic Issues*, 29: 443–51.

Scott, W. R. (2001). *Institutions and Organizations*, 2nd edn. Thousand Oaks: Sage.

Sened, I. (1997). *The Political Institution of Private Property*. Cambridge: Cambridge University Press.

Stryker, R. (2003). 'Mind the Gap: Law, Institutional Analysis and Socioeconomics', *Socio-Economic Review*, 1: 335–67.

van Kersbergen, K. and van Waarden, F. (2004). ' "Governance" as a Bridge between Disciplines: Cross-Disciplinary Inspiration regarding Shifts in Governance and Problems of Governability, Accountability and Legitimacy', *European Journal of Political Research*, 143: 143–71.

Vandenberg, P. (2002). 'North's Institutionalism and the Prospect of Combining Theoretical Approaches', *Cambridge Journal of Economics*, 26: 217–35.

Williamson, O. E. (1975). *Markets and Hierarchies: Analysis and Antitrust Implications*. New York: Free Press.

——(1985). *The Economic Institutions of Capitalism: Firms, Markets, Relational Contracting*. New York: Free Press.

——(1996). *The Mechanisms of Governance*. New York: Oxford University Press.

——(1998). 'The Institutions of Governance', *American Economic Review*, 88: 75–9.

——(2000a). 'The New Institutional Economics: Taking Stock, Looking Ahead', *Journal of Economic Literature*, 38: 595–613.

——(2000b). 'Economic Institutions and Development: A View from the Bottom', in M. Olson and S. Kähkönen (eds.), *A Not-So Dismal Science: A Broader View of Economies and Societies*. Oxford: Oxford University Press.

——(2003). 'Transaction Cost Economics and Economic Sociology', *CSES Working Paper No. 13*, Ithaca: Cornell University Center for the Study of Economy and Society.

Witt, U. (1993). 'Evolutionary Economics: Some Principles', in U. Witt (ed.), *Evolution in Markets and Institutions*. Heidelberg: Physica.

Witt, U. (2000). 'Changing Cognitive Frames—Changing Organizational Forms: An Entrepreneurial Theory of Organizational Development', *Industrial and Corporate Change*, 9: 733–55.

Zouboulakis, M. (2005). 'On the Evolutionary Character of North's Idea of Institutional Change', *Journal of Institutional Economics*, 1: 139–53.

Zysman, J. (1994). 'How Institutions Create Historically Rooted Trajectories of Growth', *Industrial and Corporate Change*, 3: 243–83.

# 13

# Explaining Economic Change: The Relations of Institutions, Politics, and Culture[1]

*John Harriss*

Such terms as 'values' and 'culture' are not popular with economists, who prefer to deal with quantifiable (more precisely definable) factors. Still, life being what it is, one must talk about these things...

David Landes[2]

## 13.1. The New Institutional Economics (NIE) and Its Analytical Claims

Institutions are, as Geoffrey Hodgson puts it, 'the stuff of socio-economic reality' (2001: 302). They are, as Jeffrey Nugent explains, humanly devised rules that affect behaviour, constraining certain actions, providing incentives for others, and thereby making social life more or less predictable (see Nugent 2006).[3] It is in a way rather curious that so fundamental an aspect of social life should not have been a more important focus of study in the social sciences (outside anthropology) until relatively recently.

---

[1] This is a significantly revised version of a paper entitled 'Institutions, Politics and Culture: A Polanyian Perspective on Economic Change', *International Review of Sociology*, 13: 343–56, which also appears in Wimmer and Kossler (eds.) (2006).

[2] Landes (1998: 215)

[3] See also Nugent, J. (2002). 'The New Institutional Economics: Can It Deliver for Change and Development?', paper presented at the Conference on Paradigms of Change, University of Bonn, May 2002. Nugent (2006) is a revised version, but some of my references are to the original paper.

This reflects the facts that, as Nugent says, mainstream, choice-theoretic economics has not previously problematized institutions, such as even those that are necessary for markets to function, and the expansionary pre-eminence of this kind of economics amongst the social sciences. Hodgson, however, reminds us that the dominance of this particular style of economics, with its pretensions to universality, has overlain and led to the forgetting of a rich tradition of thought about institutions, associated both with the German historical school (in which he includes Polanyi) and with American scholars such as Veblen and John Commons. I shall pick up some of his arguments in this short essay.

Nugent distinguishes between the 'demand' for institutions and their 'supply', pointing out that the former involves in particular problems due to informational asymmetries, and the latter problems of collective action. He then shows us how it is possible to explain, parsimoniously, within the framework of neo-classical economics, why particular institutions are the way they are and why they differ from each other, and how they influence productivity, taking great care as he does so to point out the dangers of making tautological, functionalist assumptions on the lines of the following: these are the institutions that exist; they must therefore reduce transactions costs; therefore they exist, and they must be efficient.

Institutional theorists recognize that it is perfectly possible for a society to get 'locked in' to an inefficient set of institutions because of the interests of power-holders in their reproduction.[4] An example from some of my own work would be the existence of socially inefficient agrarian institutions, such as those that obtained in Eastern India, and which made usurious money-lending and speculative trading in foodgrains privately profitable for a small class of landowners to the extent that, for a long time, there was little or no incentive for them to make productive investments in agriculture, and certainly not those that required collective action, as in the organization of irrigation. I think it can be shown that the institutional arrangements that underpinned this kind of rural economy were socially inefficient; but they supported and were supported by the

---

[4] Compare Douglass North: '... unproductive paths (can) persist. The increasing returns characteristic of an initial set of institutions that provide disincentives to productive activity will create organizations and interest groups with a stake in the existing constraints' (1990: 99). And see also Ha-Joon Chang's historical review of 'Institutions and Economic Development' from which he concludes that 'in many cases institutions were not accepted . . . because of the resistance from those who would (at least in the short run), lose out from the introduction of such institutions' (2002: 117).

power of the landowning oligarchy which thus had a strong interest in their reproduction. This is one way, at least, whereby 'historical path dependence' may arise.[5]

How good is the kind of institutional theory that Nugent describes when it comes to explaining change in institutions? How valuable or effective is it, therefore, in theorizing change in human societies? Nugent is explicit about the limitations of the NIE: most of it is rather static, he says, and 'because of the interdependencies among different institutional arrangements within a given institutional structure and because both demand and supply factors are relevant, it is often difficult to isolate the most relevant institutional change for hypothesis testing' (Nugent 2006: 169). The examples that he gives[6] of NIE explanations of important institutional changes are all interesting, but each of them confirms the modesty of his claims for the NIE as a way of explaining historical change. NIE explanations provide an interesting gloss on current understandings of the emergence of the factory system of production during the Industrial Revolution: the factor of the danger of asset misuse helps to explain why capital owners hired workers in, rather than hiring machines out; the demand for skilled labour probably made the tying of workers into relatively long-term contracts advantageous; there were probably advantages in terms of knowledge and information sharing and the building of trust and cooperation, when workers were brought together in factories. But Nugent says that he would not argue 'that evidence exists to suggest that the traditional economies of scale argument for the rise of the factory system is entirely dominated by these transaction cost and NIE considerations'. The second of his cases, about the emergence and distribution of private property rights involves an interesting study of property rights and coffee production in Central America and the contrasts between Guatemala and El Salvador on the one hand, and Costa Rica and Colombia on the other (Nugent and Robinson 2000). The argument is that the latter pair of countries 'developed coffee quite early thanks to the rapid development of private property rights for mostly smallholders', and the reason for this is said to be 'elite schism' or in other words the fragmentation and consequent development of competition amongst the elites of the two countries—whereas Guatemala

---

[5] My own work on this, first published in 1982 now appears in Harriss (2006, ch. 2). The paper refers in part to Amit Bhaduri's classic 'A Study in Agricultural Backwardness under Semi-Feudalism' (1973). An authoritative study which substantiates my argument is James Boyce's *Agrarian Impasse in Bengal: Institutional Constraints on Technological Change* (1987).

[6] These examples come from the unpublished conference paper referred to in n. 3.

on the other hand 'was dominated by a conservative alliance of church and monopolistic merchants that did not fission' (Nugent 2006: 172). The argument is an interesting one. The application of the NIE in this case, however, does not in itself explain change. It serves to highlight the importance of power considerations and of politics, but it does not in itself explain them at all. Rather it raises interesting questions about the political context which have to be answered through some other, historical (and political) analysis. Thinking of E. H. Carr's metaphor of fishing, in his classic study of the nature of history (1961), the NIE is a useful net that directs our attention to particular facts that then need to be explained historically. It is not in itself a theory of historical change. I believe that John Toye's judgement that the NIE has no theory of history ('The main weakness of the NIE as a grand theory of socio-economic development is that it is empty'[7]) is substantially correct.

I refer back to my East Indian example again. As I said, I think it can be shown that an inefficient set of agrarian institutions persisted over a long period; and it can be shown that this in turn explains the long-run stagnation in the agriculture of Bengal. This stagnation came to an end in the early mid-1980s, and since that time the rate of growth of agricultural output in West Bengal has been amongst the highest, perhaps the highest, in the country. The explanation of this historic change is of course, complex, and exactly as Nugent says 'it is difficult to isolate the most relevant institutional change for hypothesis testing'. The precise role of the modest agrarian reforms implemented by the Marxist-led government of the state has been somewhat controversial; but they were certainly at least partially instrumental in changing the socially ineffi-cient institutions that I have referred to. The reforms, together with the establishment of *panchayats* (elected local councils), brought the middle peasantry to power—a class that was interested in the development of production and used public funds that it came to control through the *panchayats* for productive purposes. 'This ascendant productive class [that replaced the former landowning oligarchy] spearheaded the agricultural surge in the state' (Bandyopadhyay 2003: 881).[8]

---

[7] Toye (in Harriss, Hunter, and Lewis, 1995: 64). Douglass North (one of the leading exponents of the NIE) and Lance Davis conceded in their work on American economic growth that their 'model is not dynamic, and we know very little about the path from one comparative static equilibrium to another' (Davis and North 1971: 263). It is a moot point as to whether North has been able to develop a dynamic theory in his subsequent work, as I explain later in the main text.

[8] I have summarized evidence and argument about West Bengal's agrarian reforms and agricultural performance in a 'Post Script' on the subject (Harriss 2006: 70–4).

It is not too long a jump, then, to argue that the relationships between social classes, and the nature of power structures, which themselves have to be analysed historically, are of particular significance in explaining change or alternatively the lack of it over long periods of time. If we wish to explain the different historical trajectories of Guatemala and Costa Rica, for example, amongst the cases referred to by Nugent, we will also have to take account of the specifics of class relationships, for it is these which appear to underlie the institutional differences that are his focus. As Pranab Bardhan has said 'The history of evolution of institutional arrangements and of the structure of property rights often reflects the changing relative bargaining power of different social groups'; and he points out that 'North [who won the Nobel Prize for Economics in 1993, for his contributions to institutional economics], unlike some other transaction cost theorists, comes close to the view-point traditionally associated with Marxist historians' (Bardhan 2001: 261). North's earlier work, indeed, can be seen as reflecting a constant tension between a commitment to the framework of choice-theoretic economics and awareness of the limitations that this framework imposes when it comes to the analysis of change. This is reflected in his admission that there is 'much to learn' from 'the "old economic historian", the institutionalists of Veblen's and Ayres's persuasion, or the Marxist' (North 1978: 974);[9] and in his concern, as Lazonick has pointed out, to graft onto 'mainstream economics a theory of *political* change' (Lazonick 1991: 311).

If I may extend my point, I have long been interested in the differences between the historical trajectories of the major Indian states, in terms of rates of economic growth and of levels of development. Contrary to the theoretical presuppositions of many economists, in regard to both growth and human development, the Indian states have continued to diverge rather than to converge (e.g. Rao, Shand, and Kalirajan 1999). A large number of different indices show that in many respects the states of the Hindi Heartland in the North, notably Bihar and Uttar Pradesh, lag far behind those of the South and the West. It is a much longer story than I can do justice to here: but there is a lot of evidence to suggest that a major part of the explanation has to do with the persistence of hierarchical social relationships, and of the fairly extreme social fragmentation associated with them, in the Hindi Heartland, while these have

---

[9] For an elaboration of points raised here, see the critical discussion of North's work by Lazonick (1991: 310–18).

been more or less successfully challenged by the political mobilizations for over more than a century of lower caste/class people in the South and the West. I can offer an institutional explanation for different patterns of change, if you will, but one that focuses on the persistence or not of what I have referred to as 'hierarchy', or what Frankel and Rao (1989) call the (traditional) 'dominance' of upper caste/class people who exercise authority that is sanctioned by religious beliefs. With a group of co-authors, these writers have shown how the particular political histories of the major states reflect the workings out of the persistence or not of this upper caste dominance, which is of course linked with the history of lower caste/class mobilizations.[10] Now, in terms of this framework, it becomes difficult to explain how and why two of the states of the Hindi Heartland, Rajasthan and Madhya Pradesh, should have started to grow much more vigorously and to improve levels of human development, clearly distancing themselves from Uttar Pradesh and Bihar. The answer, I think, still lies in political factors, in this case having to do with the nature of party political competition in these two states, by comparison with Bihar and Uttar Pradesh, and with political leadership. In Madhya Pradesh, in particular, a reforming Chief Minister, with a definite vision of development for the state, created a kind of a local version of the 'developmental state'.[11]

## 13.2. Limits of the NIE: Politics and Culture

The question is whether new institutional economists, and notably North, have succeeded in 'grafting a theory of political change onto mainstream economics' (Lazonick 1991: 311). For North, 'a dynamic model of economic change entails as an integral part of that model analysis of the polity'. But it is not at all clear that the NIE actually has a theory of how and why polities differ. It offers no explanation of the fact that the same economic institutions can have very different consequences in distinct contexts. As Robert Bates has argued, this shows 'the necessity of embedding the new institutionalism within the study of politics', for the

[10] Frankel and Rao (1989: 2) define 'dominance' as follows: 'the exercise of authority in society by groups who achieved socio-economic superiority and claimed legitimacy for their commands in terms of superior ritual status'. My development of the Frankel–Rao analysis is in Harriss (1999).

[11] On the recent growth performance of Rajasthan and Madhya Pradesh, see some passing commentary by Rudolph and Rudolph (2001). On the theory of the 'developmental state', elaborated for Japan and other states in East Asia, see White (1988).

reasons for the differences observed—for example, between the outcomes of the establishment of coffee marketing boards in Kenya and Tanzania—have to do with the political context.[12] Ultimately this means studying institutions historically and so integrating theory building and the study of reality.

I have described my analysis of different patterns of change across the various major Indian states as positing an 'institutional' explanation—but, *pace* North's earlier arguments for grafting together an analysis of political change with choice-theoretic economics, I do not think that it is one that fits within the frame of the 'new institutional economics'. This is described as 'new' because, unlike the older traditions of thought about institutions in the German historical school and in early American institutionalism, it operates with the same basic assumptions, about scarcity and individual choice, as mainstream neo-classical economics.[13] The institutions to which my analysis of political regimes across Indian states refers are those of caste, and they involve ideas about authority rooted in religious belief. They have to do, then, with what is commonly referred to as 'culture'. This is one of the most awkward words in the English language, not least because it is polysemic. Here I am referring to culture in the sense of 'the (historically specific) habits of thought and behaviour of a particular group of people', or of 'the ideas, values and symbols—more generally, "meanings"—in terms of which a particular group of people act'.[14] 'Culture', in this sense, is quite often used as a kind of a residual in explanations for social change, or the lack of it, to account for what appears to be 'irrational', or in other words what is not readily explained in terms of the basic model of utility maximization. The NIE engages with the problem of culture, as it does with politics, but with difficulty. Douglass North argues that 'culture defines the way individuals process and utilise information and hence may affect the way informal constraints get specified' (1990: 42), which at least adds to the factors involved in explaining the nature of institutions in any particular case but leaves culture as exogenous to explanation. It remains a residual.

[12] Quotations here are from the Introduction to the collection edited by Harriss, Hunter, and Lewis (1995), which includes essays by Douglass North and Robert Bates.
[13] Douglass North has written of NIE that it 'builds on, modifies and extends neo-classical theory' (North 1995: 17).
[14] I am not implying that these two definitions of culture have absolutely the same meaning (see Hodgson 2001: 292–4), but both assert the historical specificity of cultural patterns. As Platteau has argued 'Ultimately, the cultural endowment of a society plays a determining role in shaping its specific growth trajectory, and history therefore matters' (1994: 534).

Taking serious account of those aspects of social life and experience that are labelled in English as 'culture' (in the particular sense just described) starts to expose the limitations of the universalizing pretensions of neo-classical economics, which depend in part upon quite simplistic assumptions about the preferences that individuals are supposed to be maximizing, and upon a simplified notion of human rationality.[15] Even rather cursory empirical examination of human behaviour shows that people very often act habitually—that is, in ways which are characteristic of their 'culture'—and that preferences too are culturally specific. Of course these preferences and actions may be subjected to rational thought by the social actors themselves,[16] but they are very often not. The strength of the 'old' institutionalism is that it does not treat culture as an awkward (though sometimes convenient) residual, but rather makes it central in analysis. My own analysis of variation in the patterns of change between the Indian states is in line with the 'old' institutionalism rather than with the NIE.

The 'old' institutionalism has been criticized as being 'descriptive' and lacking in the formal rigour of mainstream economics and its off-shoot in the NIE,[17] but as Hodgson has argued there was more to it than this for scholars from the German historical school, and the Americans like Veblen and Commons, at least *sought* to tackle the problem of historical specificity, and the serious limitations of attempts at producing universal theory in the face of the sheer complexity of society and the historical variation between different 'societies'. In doing so they did not retreat into empiricism, but aimed rather to develop 'middle range' theory, or a particular historiography, based—in Hodgson's own exploration of the tradition of the 'old' institutionalism—on certain general propositions concerning the importance for understanding of socio-economic systems of 'the laws . . . that dominate the production and distribution of vital goods and services. Such laws would concern property rights, contracts, markets, corporations, employment and taxation.' These legal rules and contracts, it is held, are always and necessarily 'embedded in deep, informal social strata, often involving such factors as trust, duty and obligation (so that) a formal contract always takes on the particular hue of the informal social

---

[15] Note that Douglass North has more recently argued that though 'The rationality assumption has served economists (and other social scientists) well for a limited range of issues in micro-theory [it] is a shortcoming in dealing with the issues central to [understanding the process of economic change]' (2005: 5).

[16] Amartya Sen shows this in his commentary on identity politics in *Reason Before Identity* (1999).

[17] See, for example, the comments of Harriss, Hunter, and Lewis (1995: 4–5).

culture in which it is embedded'. Further, it is clear that 'The emergence of law, including property rights, is never purely and simply a matter of spontaneous development from individual interactions (but rather) is an outcome of a power struggle between citizens and the state.' Politics and power, as I argued earlier, thus become of central significance in this approach.[18]

Douglass North himself has now very largely conceded these points in his most recent writing, which marks a clear distancing from the neo-classical framework. In *Understanding the Process of Economic Change* (2005), North elaborates the view that neo-classical theory was not created to explain economic change and proves a blunt instrument when it is applied to this task—essentially because 'it does not take into account human intentionality' (2005: 65). In contrast with what is the case in regard to biological evolution, economic and social change 'is for the most part a deliberate process shaped by the perceptions of the actors about the consequences of their actions' (2005: p. viii). Neo-classical theory has nothing to say about where these perceptions come from. The mental constructs that 'individuals form to explain and interpret the world around them [and which underlie their perceptions] are partly a result of their cultural heritage, partly a result of the "local" everyday problems they confront and must solve, and partly a result of non-local learning' (2005: 61). Culture, therefore—'the cumulative learning of a society embodied in language, human memory and symbol storage systems (including) beliefs, myths, ways of doing things' (2005: p. viii)—exercises an important influence upon change through time. North also recognizes that culture is a field of power for, as he puts it 'The way humans structure the decision-making process determines *whose beliefs matter* . . . this is the subject of political economy' (2005: 74, added emphasis); and elsewhere he refers, for example, to the relative power of firms and unions in their relations with the state as a significant influence upon institutional change.[19] Now, too, North advocates the use of a framework for the analysis of change that seems close to that proposed by Hodgson when

[18] Hodgson (2001: 301, 304, and 312). Hodgson notes the continuities with Marx's approach, but argues that 'the analysis goes further than Marx, by grounding property relations in shared habits and by also emphasising the concept of culture' (2001: 309).

[19] 'Economics and political economy have not devoted resources to understanding the complex interdependent character of market structures so as to be self-conscious about the secondary consequences of an initial change. If, for example, a change in a law promoted by a business firm adversely affected the viability of a trade union we would need to know the effective political "clout" of a trade union in obstructing or preventing or repealing such an action. Understanding the structure of the polity would be essential to predicting the outcome' (North 2005: 126).

he draws on the 'old' institutional economics (referred to above): '(the) institutional framework consists of the political structure that specifies the way we develop and aggregate political choices, the property rights structure that defines the formal economic incentives, and the social structure—norms and conventions—that defines the informal incentives in the economy' (2005: 49). Here and elsewhere North, like Hodgson when the latter speaks of the significance of the 'hue of the informal social culture', refers to the importance of the 'complex mix of formal and informal constraints' upon human behaviour (2005: 1). And very much like the 'old' institutionalists, North recognizes the limits of universalizing theory when confronting the complexity of historical experience—though, like them, without retreating into empiricism. He says 'Can we develop a dynamic theory of change comparable in elegance to general equilibrium theory? The answer is probably not. But if we can achieve an understanding of the underlying process of change then we can develop somewhat more limited hypotheses about change ['theory of the middle-range', it might be put] that can enormously improve the usefulness of social science theory in confronting human problems' (2005: p. vii).[20]

## 13.3. Culture Matters: Trust and Indian Economic Development

Let me illustrate the argument further.[21] In Indian society, the values and practices of caste have tended to create relatively tight, closed social networks, so that the society as a whole is pronouncedly segmented or 'cellular'.[22] This in turn has important implications for economic action. Economic transactions involve uncertainty, arising from any one actor's incomplete knowledge about the future actions of others with whom she is transacting. Trust is one way of coping with this uncertainty—uncertainty that is occasioned by the freedom of others—and is never entirely removed, as Hodgson has argued (see above), even in the presence of legal rules and contracts. But where does trust come from? One

---

[20] Note that Kenny and Williams, in reviewing both growth theory and econometric studies of economic growth, reach very similar conclusions. They argue that, given that economic growth 'concerns a complex of interlocking, circular and cumulative changes', there is no substitute for substantial historical analysis of 'the inner workings of actual economies' (2001, passim).

[21] The following discussion draws on Harriss (2003).

[22] This idea appears in some of Marx's writings on India; in Barrington Moore's great classic (1966); and most expressly in Satish Saberwal's *The Crisis of India* (1996).

important source of or basis for trust is the sharing of key characteristics with others, or from knowledge of them in particular social networks (predictability comes with familiarity). Caste relations, involving both shared characteristics and particular social networks, are an important source of trust in Indian society—and it may be said of certain caste communities that they constitute an economic organization. A South Indian caste community, for instance, the *Nattukottai Chettiars*, has functioned very much like a bank, and *Nattukottai Chettiars* have transacted vast sums of money across long distances relying on the specific trust to which their caste relationships have given rise (Rudner 1994).

There is a significant difference, however, between such *specific trust* based on particular shared characteristics or social networks, or that which depends upon personalized transactions, and *generalized trust* running through society as a whole (beyond such networks/relations as caste). Generalized trust is a necessary condition for an effectively and efficiently functioning market economy—as North argues in a discussion of the shift from personal to impersonal exchange (2005: 117–19).[23] I think that it can also be shown that the very strength of the specific trust that is generated in caste relationships stands counterposed to such generalized trust or morality, and that this has constrained India's economic development.

The private sector of the Indian economy has been dominated for a long time by a small number of powerful family business groups, which have been secretive and non-transparent, and have relied heavily on personalized, family, and kinship networks—on 'specific trust', therefore—resisting the professionalization of management. Now, in the context of India's increased integration into the global economy, these great family firms are finding themselves disadvantaged, and they are having to open themselves up more to scrutiny, in order to attract investors. It has come to be recognized, though clearly the argument is resisted in many family businesses, that in addition to the generic problems of family business that have to do with the problems of coordination and collective action between siblings in successor generations,[24] as well as the so-called 'Buddenbrooks Phenomenon' (referring to the declining commitment to business observed in the second and third generations

---

[23] See also Platteau (1994).

[24] Even the biggest and most successful Indian business houses have experienced major problems because of tensions especially between siblings. It is a public secret that the TVS Group, the biggest based in Chennai, was divided between two factions, the members of which scarcely spoke to each other for twenty years, until a recent rapprochement occasioned by a shared concern about the abilities of TVS firms to be globally competitive.

in many business families), Indian family business now confronts new and specific problems in the context of economic globalization. In the highly protected industrial economy of the period up to 1991 the big business houses rarely faced much competition, they did not need to be customer oriented,[25] they were not much subject to shareholder scrutiny, and they invested very little either in product development or in their employees. Joint ventures with foreign companies enabled the big houses to reap monopoly profits. With these features of Indian business, there went highly centralized decision-making by senior family members, organizational informality, and reliance on personal loyalty and on seniority (or personal connections) rather than on competence. Low trust on the part of family members in professional executives became a self-fulfilling prophecy.[26] As companies attempt to meet the demands of a newly competitive business environment so these organizational characteristics are having to be changed—and it is often proving to be a very painful process. At last, many family businesses are replacing family members with professional managers, and a clearer separation is being made between family and business interest, to the extent that in a few cases family members have withdrawn from operational charge of group companies in an organizational set-up in which a clear distinction is made between corporate boards and the family board.[27] What is involved in these organizational moves is a shift away from a heavy reliance upon 'selective trust' deriving from networks centred in close kin groups to a greater reliance on formal institutions of corporate governance.

In summary, there is a shift taking place, both in the way family businesses are organized, and in industrial organization, depending upon institutional innovation, from a reliance on personalized relationships or 'specific trust' (where the 'hue of the informal social culture' is vivid) to a reliance upon abstract principles and professional codes. The problem of trust in India, ironically, is that norms of trust are so strong. The kind of trust that is strong, however, is what I have called 'selective trust', amongst groups of people within specific social networks. It depends

[25] As one senior businessman said to me, it was the time of the 'handkerchief-on-the-seat' culture as customers queued up to wait to be supplied.

[26] See Cohen (1974), for an analysis of this nexus of factors in Indian big business in the 1960s.

[27] See *Business India*, 21 February–5 March 2000, for an account of the organization of the Murugappa Group in Chennai. The clear separation of business management and of family management that has been instituted in this case corresponds with the emphasis that is being placed in recommendations concerning the reform of corporate governance in India, on securing the independence of company boards (see Banaji 2001).

upon what Satish Saberwal (1996) speaks of as 'segmented codes for conduct'. Such selective trust has made possible the development of great business enterprises, as Rudner has shown so well, with regard to the *Nattukottai Chettiars*. Selective trust has to be relied upon when institutionalized sanctions and incentives are weak, as they are in India. But the weakness of the latter—the fact that the enforcement of laws is so poor in India—also has to do with the strength of selective trust. This is reflected now in the problems of corporate governance. At the centre of these is 'the culture of compliance', a boardroom culture shaped by traditions of deference and promoter/management control of boards—a culture that is very resistant to external scrutiny. Business families have not liked to trust outsiders, but have always sought to retain control within a tight circle of kin. They have resisted the claims of what was referred to at the Confederation of Indian Industry Family Business Conclave in 2000 as 'explicitly stated principles and ethical norms'; but then the lack of consistently applied principles in the external environment justifies or leads to reliance on selective trust. There is a kind of a vicious circle in operation. Institutionalized sanctions and incentives are weak because of the weakness of generalized morality in Indian society. The problem of business management in India in the context of economic globalization is that of bringing about a change in the institutional framework and in business behaviour, but in a context in which these changes confront the 'selective trust' that is so strongly rooted in the informal social culture. Change is taking place now, but only against the resistance that derives from the strength of 'selective trust'.[28] In a sense the contest is now on, with different champions on either side from within the business world, between 'traditional', informal institutions, linked to family, caste, and kinship, and formal institutions of corporate governance involving laws and codes of practice.

The case of trust in Indian business shows up key points that together help to support the argument for an approach deriving from the 'old' institutionalism in the analysis of social change, as against the static nature of the NIE. It shows up the interrelations of formal institutions with the 'deep informal social strata' in which they are embedded,

---

[28] See Rudner (1994), on the *Nattukottai Chettiars*. My points here about boardroom culture are supported in the work of Banaji (2001). My argument may seem to be broadly supportive of that concerning generalized morality advanced by Platteau (1994), but I think that his approach is too one-sided and misses the interrelationships of institutions and societal systems of values that I have drawn attention to here.

and hence the importance of those historically specific 'shared habits of thought and behaviour' (or culture). These are not at all easily or satisfactorily explained in the would-be universal theory of mainstream economics, and they remain exogenous in the NIE. Second, explaining institutional change, and hence social change, requires that we take account of power, as Hodgson implies and as Pranab Bardhan explicitly stated in the commentary that I cited earlier. Power is missing from the NIE. Whether or not the rules of corporate governance in India will be changed in such a way as to be effective will depend upon the outcome of a power struggle between different factions of Indian business and their political supporters, and on 'deeper' changes in habits of thought and behaviour. The two are interrelated and the outcomes cannot be predicted.

## 13.4. Culture, Power, and Change

Of course, paraphrasing North (cited earlier), 'the way the decision-making process is structured in a society determines whose beliefs matter'. But simple 'power-distributional' models of institutional formation and change—those 'that view institutions as straightforward reflections of the interests of the powerful, and thus as responding automatically to changes in the balance of power or the preferences of the powerful' (Thelen 2004: 33)—are inadequate. Such models are too 'clunky'—as Kathleen Thelen's work most clearly illustrates.[29]

Thelen shows that the institutions of skill training in Germany, which have latterly served the interests both of employers and of unionized workers, go back to some legislation passed in 1897 that protected and regulated artisanal producers. The legislation was passed for political reasons: the authoritarian government of that period sought to shore up artisanal production as a way of stemming the mounting strength of unionized labour. The legislation was actually opposed at the time by the unions and by the Social Democratic Party, while even if it was not actually opposed by them it was also certainly not driven by large skill-intensive firms. But over time, as a result of negotiation and struggle between capital, unionized labour, and artisans, an institution that was set up to serve one purpose, came to serve other interests: the point is that there is not necessarily a direct connection between the later/current

---

[29] The criticism of 'clunkiness' even applies to the influential work of Acemoglu, Johnson, and Robinson (2004).

effects of an institution and the original intentions that lay behind its establishment. Methodologically, there seems to be no substitute for substantive historical analysis.

This particular case helps to make a nice point, too, about the notion of 'path dependence'—the argument that once an institution has become established then powerful actors will have an interest in its reproduction so that it becomes more or less 'locked in', or frozen in time. This is an argument that is compatible with the common view that institutional change is generally of the kind described in evolutionary theory as that of 'punctuated equilibrium'—long periods of stable equilibrium punctuated by changes brought about by exogenous factors. The case of the German system of skill training, however, shows that while the 1897 legislation exercised a long-running influence—helping to account, for instance, for the major differences between Germany and Britain (where a stable system of apprenticeship failed to develop, and institutions concerned with skill training have often not functioned very well at all)—it did not remain unchanged. Rather there was a series of incremental changes coming about as a result of political realignments amongst the social groups concerned, and renegotiation of the implicit or explicit settlement between them—such as happened in Germany in the 1920s. Thelen sums up: 'institutions are the object of on-going political contestation, and changes in the political coalitions on which institutions rest are what drive changes in the form institutions take and the functions they perform in politics and society' (2004: 31). As the case of the 1897 legislation shows, institutions designed to serve one set of interests often become 'carriers' of others as well—and institutions inevitably have unintended as well as intended effects. They are not necessarily—indeed, probably rather rarely are they—'straightforward reflections of the interests of the powerful', but must rather be seen as the objects of ongoing political negotiation. Institutional evolution and change is the outcome of such negotiation between contending actors.

A comparable point emerges from Atul Kohli's recent analysis (2005) of economic change and development in India, in which he shows that the 'take off' of the Indian economy generally associated with the economic reforms instituted from 1991 (and that have brought about major institutional changes), in fact preceded those reforms. He stresses the importance of the shift in attitude on the part of India's leaders towards private capital already in the 1980s, well before the celebrated economic reforms from 1991, and shows the significance of ideas and in this case of the existence of an influential intellectual critique of India's development policies over the first thirty years or so of Independence (Kohli 2005). This sits somewhat oddly with the same author's comparative analysis of development and change in Korea, Brazil, India, and Nigeria (2004), which lays great emphasis on the significance of their different colonial experiences and the kinds of path-dependent patterns of development to which these gave rise. The model of change underlying this account is certainly one of 'punctuated equilibrium' whereas Kohli's more recent analysis of the Indian experience seems rather to show how institutions are changed through ongoing political contestation in which ideas have a major part to play. The case might also be taken as exemplifying Douglass North's recent statement that 'The key to building a foundation to understand the process of economic change is beliefs—both those held by individuals and shared beliefs that form belief systems' (2005: 83). The changes that started to come about in India's economic development in the 1980s were at least in part the consequence of a cultural shift, in the beliefs and attitudes of some individuals and groups within the political and bureaucratic elites towards the private sector.

## 13.5. Conclusion

Change in human societies can only be satisfactorily explained when such historically specific factors as those discussed in this essay are taken into consideration. They are in an approach based on the 'old' institutionalism, and in other varieties of historical institutionalism, such as that grounded in comparative politics—while they are not in the NIE. What distinguishes historical institutionalists from mainstream economists working within the rational choice framework, who also study institutions, is that they question the basic assumptions of rational choice. It has always been recognized that the model of human behaviour assumed in mainstream economics—that of individual preference maximization—though it has given rise to some parsimonious and therefore powerful theory, is a caricature. It does not account for a wide range of human behaviour—much of which is habitual—and what unites historical institutionalists is the view that the assumptions of rational choice are unduly confining. Essentially, historical institutionalists hold that 'unless something is known about the context, broad assumptions about "self-interested behaviour" are empty' (Thelen and Steinmo 1992: 9)—and hence the 'historical' in their label. Whereas the analysis of institutions within mainstream economics proceeds deductively, historical institutionalism works rather by an inductive logic, and much of the most outstanding research has involved detailed historical comparison of relatively small numbers of cases. From such comparison it is possible to develop 'middle range theory', for example about the characteristics of state structures that are conducive to successful intervention in the economy, rather than attempt to generate universal theory. In his latest work, even so notable an exponent of the NIE as Douglass North seems to have joined hands with the historical institutionalists.

# References

Acemoglu, D., Johnson, S., and Robinson, J. (2004). 'Institutions as the Fundamental Causes of Long-Run Growth', in P. Aghion and S. Durlauf (eds.), *Handbook of Economic Growth*. Amsterdam: Elsevier.

Banaji, J. (2001). *Corporate Governance and in the Indian Private Sector: A Report*. Oxford: Queen Elizabeth House.

Bandyopadhyay, D. (2003). 'Land Reforms and Agriculture: The West Bengal Experience', *Economic and Political Weekly*, 1 March, pp. 879–94.

Bardhan, P. (2001). 'Institutional Impediments to Development', in S. Kahkonen and M. Olson (eds.), *A New Institutional Approach to Economic Development*. Delhi: Vistaar.

Bhaduri, A. (1973). 'A Study in Agricultural Backwardness under Semi-Feudalism', *Economic Journal*, 83: 120–37.

Boyce, J. (1987). *Agrarian Impasse in Bengal: Institutional Constraints on Technological Change*. Oxford: Oxford University Press.

Carr, E. H. (1961). *What is History?* Harmondsworth: Penguin Books.

Chang, H.-J. (2002). *Kicking Away the Ladder: Development Strategy in Historical Perspective*. London: Anthem Press.

Cohen, A. (1974). *Tradition, Change and Conflict in Indian Family Business*. The Hague: Mouton.

Davis, L. and North, D. (1971). *Institutional Change and American Economic Growth*. Cambridge: Cambridge University Press.

Frankel, F. and Rao, M. S. A. (eds.) (1989). *Dominance and State Power in Modern India: Decline of a Social Order*, vol. 1. Delhi: Oxford University Press.

Harriss, J. (1999). 'Comparing Political Regimes Across Indian States: A Preliminary Essay', *Economic and Political Weekly*, 34: 3367–77.

—— (2003). '"Widening the Radius of Trust": Ethnographic Explorations of Trust and Indian Business', *Journal of the Royal Anthropological Institute*, 9: 755–73.

Harriss, J. (2006). *Power Matters: Essays on Institutions, Politics and Society in India*. Delhi: Oxford University Press.

——Hunter, J., and Lewis, C. (eds.) (1995). *The New Institutional Economics and Third World Development*. London: Routledge.

Hodgson, G. (2001). *How Economics Forgot History: The Problem of Historical Specificity in Social Science*. London: Routledge.

Kenny, C. and Williams, D. (2001). 'What Do We Know About Economic Growth? Or, Why Don't We Know Very Much?', *World Development*, 29: 1–22.

Kohli, A. (2004). *State Directed Development: Political Power and Industrialization in the Global Periphery*. Cambridge: Cambridge University Press.

——(2005). 'Politics of Economic Growth in India, 1980–2005', *Economic and Political Weekly*, 41: 13–14.

Landes, D. (1998). *The Wealth and Poverty of Nations*. New York: W. W. Norton.

Lazonick, W. (1991). *Business Organization and the Myth of the Market Economy*. Cambridge: Cambridge University Press.

Moore, B. (1966). *The Social Origins of Dictatorship and Democracy*. New York: Beacon Press.

North, D. (1978). 'Structure and Performance: The Task of Economic History', *Journal of Economic Literature*, 16: 963–78.

——(1990). *Institutions, Institutional Change and Economic Performance*. Cambridge: Cambridge University Press.

——(1995). 'The New Institutional Economics and Third World Development', in J. Harriss, J. Hunter, and C. Lewis (eds.) (1995), *The New Institutional Economics and Third World Development*. London: Routledge.

——(2005). *Understanding the Process of Economic Change*. Princeton: Princeton University Press.

Nugent, J. (2006). 'The New Institutional Economics: Can It Deliver for Change and Development?', in A. Wimmer and R. Kossler (eds.), *Understanding Change: Models, Methodologies and Metaphors*. London: Palgrave Macmillan.

——and Robinson, J. (2000). 'Are Endowments Fate?', Working Paper. Los Angeles: University of Southern California.

Platteau, J.-P. (1994). 'Behind the Market Stage Where Real Societies Exist', *Journal of Development Studies*, 30: 533–77 (Part 1); 30: 753–817 (Part 2).

Rao, M. G., Shand, R., and Kalirajan, K. (1999). 'Convergence of Incomes Across Indian States: A Divergent View', *Economic and Political Weekly*, 27 March.

Rudner, D. W. (1994). *Caste and Capitalism in Colonial India: The Nattukottai Chettiars*. Berkeley: University of California Press.

Rudolph, L. and Rudolph, S. (2001). 'The Iconisation of Chandrababu: Sharing Sovereignty in India's Federal Market Economy', *Economic and Political Weekly*, 5 May.

Saberwal, S. (1996). *The Crisis of India*. Delhi: Oxford University Press.

Sen, A. (1999). *Reason Before Identity*. Delhi: Oxford University Press.

Thelen, K. (2004). *How Institutions Evolve: The Political Economy of Skills in Germany, Britain, the United States and Japan.* Cambridge: Cambridge University Press.

—— and Steinmo, S. (1992). 'Introduction', in S. Steinmo, K. Thelen, and F. Longstreth (eds.), *Structuring Politics: Historical Institutionalism in Comparative Analysis.* Cambridge: Cambridge University Press.

Toye, J. (1995). 'The New Institutional Economics and Its Implications for Economic Theory', in J. Harriss, J. Hunter, and C. Lewis (eds.), *The New Institutional Economics and Third World Development.* London: Routledge.

White, G. (ed.) (1988). *Developmental States in East Asia.* London: Macmillan.

Wimmer, A. and Kossler, R. (eds.) (2006). *Understanding Change: Models, Methodologies and Metaphors.* London: Palgrave Macmillan.

# 14

# Polanyian, Regulationist, and Autopoieticist Reflections on States and Markets and their Implications for the Knowledge-Based Economy

*Bob Jessop*

## 14.1. Introduction

This chapter re-interprets Polanyi's substantive institutionalist analysis of market economies, market societies, and state intervention in the light of two later schools, namely, the Parisian regulation approach to contemporary capitalism and systems-theoretical accounts of the market economy as an autopoietic system. All three regard the modern economy as an operationally autonomous system that is nonetheless socially embedded and needful of complex forms of social regulation. For each, an adequate account of economic activities should explore how they are related to the wider social environment; how they are embedded in a wider nexus of social institutions; how the latter assist in reproducing the capitalist (or market) economy; and how their development is coupled to these and other environing institutions. Crucial differences among the three approaches nonetheless justify exploring their potential complementarities as a basis for further research. Thus, after presenting their respective accounts of economic institutedness and embeddedness, I discuss the stability and reproducibility of the capitalist economy, paying particular attention to governance and meta-governance.[1]

---

[1] This contribution draws on Jessop (2007) and (2001) in line with editorial recommendations.

## 14.2. Polanyi on the Social Embeddedness of Substantively Instituted Economies

Karl Polanyi (1886–1964) developed a distinctive approach to comparative analysis that stressed the substantive institutedness and social embeddedness of economies. Distinguishing formal economics as rational, economizing behaviour from substantive economics as want-satisfying behaviour, he criticized the 'economistic' tendency to assimilate the properties and dynamics of non-capitalist economies to those of market economies based on formally rational economic maximization (Polanyi 1977). He considered the economy, in its substantive sense, as 'an instituted process of interaction between man and his environment, which results in a continuous supply of want-satisfying material means' (1982: 33) and emphasized that the economy's structure and functioning is always 'embedded and enmeshed in institutions' (Polanyi 1982: 34). Polanyi further distinguished profit-oriented, market-mediated exchange from three other principles of distribution of 'want-satisfying material means': (a) reciprocity among similarly arranged or organized groupings (e.g. segmentary kinship groups); (b) redistribution through an allocative centre linked to a political regime; and (c) householding, which is based on production to satisfy the needs of a largely self-sufficient unit such as a family, settlement, or manor (1957: 47–53; 1977: 34–47; 1982: 35). Two or more principles can be combined in actually existing economies and, even where monetary gain is present, it is not always dominant. On this basis, Polanyi wanted to open a debate about alternatives to the prevailing market-based form of economic organization.

Polanyi distinguished capitalist from non-capitalist economic relations in terms of the *separation* (or disembeddness) of capitalist economic relations from non-economic institutions and their extension to the fictitious commodities of land, labour, and money. In pre-capitalist economies, the production process was more or less firmly embedded in a wide variety of institutions such as the family, neighbourhood, community, etc. (1957: 46–53; 1982: 30). This embedding of production relations explains why Polanyi distinguished forms of economic life in terms of their *principles of distribution* rather than their *relations of production*. For, while disentangling *production* from other social activities was often hard, it was relatively easy to identify the principles governing resource *distribution*. Only with the disembedding of production and distribution from all extra-economic institutions could profit-maximization become the dominant organizational principle of capitalist economies. But for this possibility to be realized, non-economic social relations and institutions had to be adapted to the demands of economic reproduction. This, according to Polanyi, was 'the meaning of the familiar assertion that a market economy can function only in a market society' (1957: 57).

This conclusion undermines one-sided readings of Polanyi that focus on the market economy's disembedding from pre-capitalist social arrangements and institutions. For Polanyi argues that 'society' (through diverse social forces) seeks to constrain the destructive anarchy of the free market by subjecting it to various forms of extra-economic regulation that nonetheless support and sustain capital accumulation. Where this occurs, the market economy can be said to have become embedded within a market society. This is especially clear in Polanyi's analysis of the four interconnected pillars that sustained and regularized the liberal regime—the balance of power system, the international gold standard, the self-regulating market, and the liberal state (Polanyi 1957: 3).

In this and other respects, Polanyi anticipated regulationist arguments (see below). Thus, in his history of trade and markets as well as his economic anthropology, he argues that societal (institutional) conditions sustain the (circular) interdependence of economic movements and ensure their 'recurrence' (i.e. their continued reproduction)—without which the unity and stability of the (instituted) economic process is impossible. Thus, he writes that

[t]he instituting of the economic process vests that process with unity and stability; it produces a structure with a definite function in society; it shifts the place of the process in society, thus adding significance to its history; it centers interest on values, motives and policy. Unity and stability, structure and function, history and policy spell out operationally the content of our assertion that the human economy is an instituted process.

(1982: 34)

## 14.3. The Regulation Approach

Like Polanyi, regulationists reject the economistic fallacy that there is a clearly delimited, socially disembedded sphere of economic relations that tends towards a general equilibrium based on self-regulating market exchange among rational economic men. Instead the regulation approach (hereafter RA) focuses on the socially embedded, socially regularized nature of capitalist economies and regards market forces as only one (albeit critically important) factor in capitalist expansion. For institutions, collective identities, shared visions, common rules, norms, and conventions, networks, procedures, and modes of calculation also have key roles in structuring, facilitating, and guiding (in short, 'regulating' or, better, 'regularizing') accumulation. Thus, the RA seeks to integrate analysis of political economy with that of civil society and the state to show how they interact to 'normalize' the capital relation despite the improbability of capital accumulation. It examines the social processes and struggles that define and stabilize modes of economic calculation and norms of economic conduct. Indeed, its concept of 'mode of regulation' covers the social as well as economic modes of economic regulation that secure the conditions for a particular dynamic configuration of production and consumption (for surveys, see Boyer 1990; Boyer and Saillard 2002; Jessop and Sum 2006).

The RA reminds one here of Polanyi's account of the 'double movement' of capitalist development. Polanyi argued that an initial movement based on the disembedding of market forces and the consequent rise of a laissez-faire economy that threatened economic and social stability was eventually met by a counter-movement as social forces sought to re-embed market forces in social institutions and thereby stabilize the market mechanism. In the same way, the RA shows that the 'extensive accumulation regime' of 'liberal capitalism' emerged from *ancien régime* economies, that this entailed the disembedding of market forces from the old order, and that the 'competitive mode of regulation' and night-watchman state had key roles in stabilizing this accumulation regime. Despite these commonalities, the RA rejects Polanyi's views on the 'double movement' because liberal capitalism had its own distinctive forms of social embedding and social regulation. But it does argue that various crisis-tendencies in liberal capitalism and its 'competitive mode of regulation' did eventually lead, after economic, social, and political struggles, to a new accumulation regime based on 'intensive accumulation' and a 'monopolistic mode of regulation'. Thus, whereas Polanyi depicts a two-step movement from unregulated to regulated capitalism, the RA describes a crisis-mediated movement from one regularized regime to another, each with its own dynamic and crisis-tendencies (on *ancien régime* and liberal economies, see Boyer 1990; Delorme and André 1982).

331

## 14.4. Autopoietic Systems Theories and Governance

Another approach to the embedding and regularization of economic activities is the systems-theoretical analysis of autopoiesis in modern, functionally differentiated societies. Autopoiesis (or 'self-production') denotes a class of systems (whether natural, social, or artificial) that are concerned, at least in the first instance, with their own self-reproduction. Yet autopoietic systems co-exist and co-evolve in complex ways with other systems with which they are reciprocally interdependent. This paradoxical combination of operational autonomy and material interdependence poses problems about the external steering (governing, guiding, managing) and/or strategic coordination of different systems.

An autopoietic system is self-constituting because it defines and defends its own boundary vis-à-vis its self-defined external environment. It is also self-organizing because it has its own distinctive operational codes and programmes. Hence, while an autopoietic system may respond to changes in its environment and even reorganize itself in the process, it does so in terms of its own codes and programmes. Interestingly this idea was anticipated, for the market economy, by Polanyi, who notes

A market economy an economic system controlled, regulated, and directed by markets alone; order in the production and distribution of goods is entrusted to this self-regulating mechanism . . . Self-regulation implies that all production is for sale on the market and that all incomes derive from such sales. Accordingly, there are markets for all elements of industry, not only for goods (always including services) but also for labor, land, and money, their prices being called respectively commodity prices, wages, rent, and interest.

(Polanyi 1957: 68–9)

An autopoietic system also reproduces its own elements through the use of its own elements. This feature is well illustrated by the market economy. For, as Polanyi again noted, it deals with 'inputs' such as labour-power, land, and money *as if* they were commodities and subjects them to its own forms of economic calculation. More generally, the market economy is autopoietic in so far as market forces define what will count as exchange-values, secure the exchange of the latter through market mechanisms, and also ensure the recurrence of market relations through the continuing circulation of commodities in exchange for money (cf. Baecker 1988; Luhmann 1986).

An autopoietic system co-exists with other autopoietic systems and depends on them for essential conditions for its own operation and this ensures that it is structurally coupled to them through the co-evolution of the various reciprocally interdependent systems. This co-evolution is also shaped by the 'lifeworld' (or, for Polanyi, 'society') that is formed by various social relations, identities, interests, and values not anchored in specific systems. In short, despite its capacity for self-valorization, the market economy is far from fully self-contained. Indeed, labour-power itself, despite its commodification (or, for Polanyi, its treatment *as if* it were a commodity), is largely reproduced outside any immediate capitalist labour process. This provides an important source of friction or resistance to the logic of capital—although how the market economy responds thereto will still depend primarily on its own profit-and-loss calculations.[2] For, even if changes in an autopoietic system's environment are reflected in changes in its operation or structure, the latter will always be mediated by its own operating codes.

This raises a problem about the governability of functionally differentiated systems that operate according to their own logics and resist external 'steering' based on top-down management or direct intervention. Autopoietic systems analysis connects here to more middle-range research on organizational and institutional governance. This includes work on modes of coordination that could serve as an alternative to the *anarchy* (or invisible hand) of the market and the *hierarchy* of imperative coordination (e.g. the iron fist of the state or bureaucratic command). These alternatives are based on *heterarchy*, that is, self-organization among mutually interdependent actors. Heterarchy can include interpersonal networking, inter-organizational negotiation, and 'de-centred intersystemic context steering' based on efforts to guide a given system by modifying the circumstances in which its operating codes are applied rather than through externally imposed imperative coordination. The use of taxes rather than law to guide market forces illustrates this practice.

## 14.5. Rethinking Market Society

All three approaches offer good reasons to reject the orthodox historical materialist claim that accumulation is the dominant principle of societal organization in every capitalist social formation. Each seems to accept that capital accumulation in its pure form occurs where the key inputs into capitalist production take the form of (perhaps fictitious)

---

[2] Even where profit-making activities are subject to legal or other constraints, firms calculate whether it is cost-effective to break the law or ignore the other constraints.

commodities; where there is effective capitalist control over labour-power in production; where the non-economic social and material environment is sufficiently stable to enable enterprises to orient their activities to opportunities for profit; and where profits can be realized and re-invested in a new round of capitalist production. But this does not mean capitalist societies involve no more than market relations. On the contrary, each approach implies that the universal spread of the commodity form and the resulting dominance of market forces and profit-and-loss calculation throughout society could prove self-destructive.

For accumulation always and everywhere depends on a precarious balance between commodity relations and other forms of social organization. This dependence generates a complex, conflictual, and contradictory process involving recurrent shifts in the relative weight of commodification, decommodification, and recommodification (cf. Offe 1975). This raises the question of how far, and under what conditions, market forces (and their profit-seeking logic) can fully penetrate the social world.

There are four interrelated ways in which market forces and profit-seeking can come to dominate society. First, the commodity form and the logic of exchange can be extended to labour, land, and money (Polanyi 1957: 68–9) and then into new spheres of social life. Neo-liberalism, for example, (re-)commodifies political, educational, health, welfare, scientific, and other activities to organize them as businesses that exploit opportunities for profit without regard to possible extra-economic costs and benefits. Second, even domains or activities that, for whatever reason, retain a primarily non-commercial orientation can acquire a secondary economic coding. This occurs when choices among formally non-commercial activities are influenced by 'profit-and-loss' or economic 'cost–benefit' calculations. Polanyi noted this for nineteenth century liberalism (1957: 33–4) and the same tendency can be seen in neo-liberalism, where educational, health, scientific, and other decision-makers are pressured to assess how their activities impact financially on the individual, organizational, and institutional levels and/or the (perceived or socially constructed) imperatives of a strong, internationally competitive economy. Third, the superior dynamism and reach of a globalizing capitalist economy may cause more problems substantively for other systems than they cause for it. In other words, in the multi-lateral structural coupling of systems, other systems adjust more to the logic of capital than the capitalist economy incurs costs in adjusting to them. This asymmetrical interdependence among institutional orders is rooted in capital's greater capacity to escape the constraints and controls of other systems. This can occur through its own internal operations in time (discounting, insurance, risk management, futures, etc.) or space (capital flight, relocation, extra-territoriality, etc.) or through attempts to corrupt or commodify these systems. Fourth, a successful hegemonic project may establish accumulation as the dominant principle of societal organization. This is seen in the increasing demand to accept that global competition requires wholesale restructuring of any economic *or extra-economic* organizations and institutions that may affect competitiveness.

These tendencies have their own particular bases and may even partly counteract each other. The first is rooted in the search to establish and extend the bases of a self-regulating market economy and find new sources of valorization; the second in attempts to impose the economizing, profit-seeking logic of accumulation on other systems that are not (or cannot be) fully integrated into the market economy; the third in the evolutionary logic of structural coupling or co-evolution; and the fourth in struggles for hegemony and/or in asymmetric interactions between capitalism and other orders. When all four tendencies are mutually reinforcing, the market economy can be consolidated in a market society. Thus, as Polanyi puts it, consolidating the market mechanism 'means no less than the running of society as an adjunct to the market' such that 'society must be shaped in such a manner as to allow that system to function according to its own laws' (1957: 57).

Approaching capitalist societalization in these terms also sheds light on sources of resistance to capitalist dominance or hegemony. Each tendency has its own limits and counter-tendencies and is linked to its own form(s) of resistance. First, in so far as valorization dominates different domains, class struggles proper can develop. They can emerge both in the capitalist economy in its narrow sense—not only in the main field of economic class struggle in the labour market and labour process but also regarding the commodification of land and money—and in the many and varied extra-economic contexts that are essential to capitalist exploitation. Indeed, excessive commodification will generate 'market failures' (or other signs of economic crisis) that threaten the overall social reproduction of capital.

Second, in domains where another code or institutional logic remains primary, agents may resist the imposition of profitability as a secondary code. For this would threaten the codes, programmes, and operational integrity of other systems as well as the rich variety of values, norms,

335

vocabularies, and identities of the lifeworld. It is therefore unsurprising that the representatives of other systems and social forces in the lifeworld will resist attempts at commodification from diverse perspectives. This is why Polanyi criticizes the vulgar Marxist tendency to overemphasize class struggles, highlights non-class bases of resistance to market logic, and identifies a wide range of social forces that respond more or less spontaneously to the many threats posed to 'society' by the expansion of that logic (1957: 132, 149, 152, 154). To this we can add barriers due to market failures (e.g. the continuing limits to the commodification of information and knowledge) and the repercussions of the market economy on social cohesion.

Regarding the third and fourth tendencies, diverse struggles occur over the hegemonic worldviews and naturalized forms of 'common sense' that posit capital accumulation as the desirable and/or necessary condition for accomplishing other social goals. This is where Polanyi's analysis of the double movement, the regulationist analysis of the crucial role of extra-economic regulation of the economy, and autopoieticist analyses of the interdependence of different functional systems and the role of heterarchic coordination all point, in their different ways, to the inherent limits to a one-sided emphasis on capital accumulation. This argument can be taken further not only by noting the different economic and political programmes and ethico-political visions into which economic liberalism is articulated but also by considering the range of counter-hegemonic projects that can be developed to resist the onward march of liberalism. For, if society's fightback is to move beyond dispersed, disorganized, and mutually contradictory struggles, attention must be paid to the ways in which 'society' acquires a relative unity and cohesion in resisting capital's unhampered logic. For the reaction of society to the destructive impact of liberal market forces is not conducted merely in terms of sectional interests but in the name of the general interest of society as a whole. This is where the role of specific economic, political, and social projects, of hegemonic visions, and of associated strategic capacities becomes crucial. Indeed, as Polanyi was well aware, it makes a world of difference whether this resistance is conducted under the dominance of fascism, social democracy, corporate liberalism à la New Deal, a communist regime, or, in his preferred scenario, a maximally decentralized socialism able to 'transcend the self-regulating market by consciously subordinating it to a democratic society' (1957: 234).

This interpretation offers four theoretical advantages over the important analyses offered by Polanyi, the regulation approach, and autopoietic systems theory. First, it provides a more complex and concrete account of the tendency of a market economy to penetrate society, disembedding individuals from the wider ensemble of interpersonal relations, organizational affiliations, institutional and community roots, and broader societal frameworks within which they operate. Second, it provides a more complex and concrete account of how 'society' fights back against this disembedding process. In particular, as Polanyi often notes, this reaction is neither directed against market forces (or capitalism) as such nor is it a reaction of 'society' as such. Instead it is a complex series of reactions at many different points in social space to specific conflicts, crisis-tendencies, and contradictions associated with the unregulated extension of market forces (cf. Olofsson 1995). Third, by integrating Polanyi's conclusions with the arguments of autopoietic systems theory, it offers a theoretically more sophisticated analysis of the limits to external intervention into the market (or capitalist) economy once the latter has reached 'autopoietic takeoff'. This analysis also facilitates research on the structural coupling of the market (or capitalist) economy with other systems (legal, political, educational, medical, etc.) and the lifeworld to produce a social formation dominated by the principles of accumulation. Fourth, drawing on the insights of regulationist and autopoietic systems theories into the modalities and dynamics of governance, this approach provides new ideas about how social relations get embedded into the market economy and the market economy may get re-embedded into the wider society.

## 14.6. Rethinking Social Embeddedness

Social embeddedness is an increasingly popular but confusingly polyvalent concept. The preceding discussion suggests it is useful to distinguish three levels of social embeddedness.[3] The first level is the 'social embeddedness' of interpersonal economic relations (cf. Granovetter 1985) and concerns the multiple networks in which individual economic actors are embedded and how they affect these actors' identities, interests, capacities, and practices. Indeed, theorists of interpersonal embeddedness tend to show what Adam Smith (1937) knew long ago that economic actors

[3] Oloffson writes that Polanyi's concept combines 'three sets of linkages: (a) connections between economic and non-economic institutions (or parts of societies) on the macro-level; (b) relations between actors and institutions on the levels of social relations (cf. the contribution of Granovetter); (c) a second-order systematic linking of these two sets of connections (a macro-micro link)' (1995: 74).

337

tend to make strenuous efforts to re-entangle economic relations in a nexus of social relations as a crucial condition for the stability and predictability of markets. This is reflected in the relative (dis)advantages of strong or loose interpersonal ties and associated problems of trust. However, tempting it might be to claim that Polanyi's historical and/or anthropological studies identified this form of social embedding, this would be anachronistic because pre-capitalist societies were dominated by householding, reciprocity, and redistribution rather than profit-maximization.[4] But one could certainly interpret his discussion of *haute finance,* cooperatives, friendly societies, self-help, etc., as mechanisms for the interpersonal embedding of market-oriented economic action in emerging and/or consolidated market societies.

The second level of embeddedness is what we might describe as the 'institutional embeddedness' of inter-organizational relations (cf. Grabher 1993). These relations have important emergent properties that mean that interpersonal ties and trust are insufficient to secure their reproduction. Thus, organization theorists and 'new institutionalists' have explored the difficulties involved in securing the internal cohesion and adaptability of individual organizations; and in rendering compatible their respective operational unities and independence with their de facto material and social interdependence on other organizations. Negotiation is important here in reconciling these conflicting interests by identifying common short-term objectives and using these to promote longer-term cooperation in joint projects (cf. Mayntz 1993; Scharpf 1994). Studies of this form of economic embeddedness focus on the specificities of strategic alliances, inter-firm networks, etc., their path-dependent character, and the mechanisms of organizational learning. They also suggest that the capacity to steer inter-organizational relations often depends critically on effective interpersonal networks that can stretch social relations over time and space by drawing on interpersonal trust.

The third level is that of the 'societal' embeddedness of functionally differentiated institutional orders in a complex, de-centred society. Polanyi's work is most relevant to this level of analysis—especially, *pace* Swedberg (1997),[5] his concept of embeddedness. For he examined the embedding

---

[4] Swedberg argued that '[w]hereas Karl Polanyi ... introduced the notion of embeddedness to emphasize that the economy was an organic part of society in pre-capitalist times, Granovetter's point was nearly the opposite, namely to show that economic actions are truly social actions in capitalist society' (1997: 165). This claim conflates my first and second levels of embeddedness.

[5] Swedberg (1997: 171) claims that Polanyi mentioned 'embeddedness' only twice in *The Great Transformation* and that his commitment to the concept is 'half-hearted'. This mistakes

of market relations in traditional societies, their disembedding to form a market economy, and the latter's re-articulation with other forms of social relations to create a modern market society. If traditional societies involve, for Polanyi, the embedding of substantive economies in the wider society, modern market economies have two quite different characteristics. First, market forces are institutionally separated (disembedded) from traditional (pre-modern) institutions; and, second, their long-term survival requires not only external regulation but also the interiorization of extra-economic constraints within the very logic of market forces. In exploring the limits of the market mechanism in coordinating the material and social interdependencies between economics, politics, and civil society in the golden age of *laissez-faire*, Polanyi drew special attention to the complex, flexible role of *haute finance* as the main link between the political and the economic organization of the world (1957: 10–11). The importance of interpersonal relations to the governance of inter-organizational relations is taken one stage higher here through the dependence of inter-systemic linkages on inter-organizational relations. For not only did *haute finance* rest on an interpersonal network with diasporic as well as national dimensions, it also depended on a complex web of inter-organizational relations that connected the logics of the economic, political, and military systems on both national and international levels. It is also in regard to this third level that the RA and autopoietic theory have much to offer (cf. Glagow and Willke 1987; Luhmann 1995). Here their key contribution is their account of how inter-systemic heterarchy involves problems of material and social interdependence among operationally autonomous (or closed) functional systems, each with its own codes, programmes, institutional logics, and interests in self-reproduction.

## 14.7. Governance and Meta-Governance as (Re-)Embedding Mechanisms

Polanyi emphasized that the very process of commodification induced by the spread of the market mechanism generates contradictions that it cannot resolve. This raises various problems about market failure and crises. For example, when existing embedding and governance mechanisms failed in nineteenth-century capitalism, including the central role

words and concepts—Polanyi uses many words to denote embeddedness (Oloffson 1995) and overlooks how Polanyi's distinction between substantive and formal accounts of the economy presupposes that between embedded and disembedded economies (Polanyi 1977).

of that heterarchic governance mechanism *par excellence* materialized in *haute finance*, what happened next? Polanyi argues that the state stepped in (1957: 206, cf. 207–8). For the historical record shows that markets work better in the shadow of the state, which would always intervene in the last resort to protect society. But he was also well aware of the limits to intervention and it is here that the autopoieticists' idea of 'de-centred context steering' is useful.

This can be redefined in terms of meta-governance, that is, the collibration of governance mechanisms that continually re-organizes and re-balances different forms of coordination of complex recipro-cal interdependence (on collibration, see Dunsire 1996). In addition to meta-governance practices within the more or less separate fields of anarchic market exchange, hierarchical organizations, and heterar-chic self-organization, there is also extensive scope for meta-governance practices that steer the evolving relationship among these modes of coor-dination. The latter are concerned to provide the ground rules for gover-nance, ensure the compatibility of different governance mechanisms and regimes, deploy a relative monopoly of organizational intelligence and information with which to shape cognitive expectations, act as a 'court of appeal' for disputes arising within and over governance, serve to re-balance power differentials by strengthening weaker parties or systems in the interests of system integration and/or social cohesion, etc. Thus, it involves shaping the context within which governance arrangements are forged rather than developing specific strategies and initiatives for them. To the extent that these practices are oriented to inserting the neo-liberal globalizing market economy into a new cosmopolitan market society, they would provide the basis for that 'co-existence' in market societies for which Polanyi argued and struggled (for further discussion of meta-governance, see Jessop 2002).

## 14.8. Knowledge as a Fictitious Commodity and Its Meta-Governance

Polanyi's analysis of the limits of market forces was primarily concerned with the potentially destructive consequences of the extension of the commodity form to three economic factors that were not produced for sale but nonetheless acquired a price in a market economy. These 'fictitious commodities' were land, labour, and money (Polanyi 1957). It is worth considering whether the contemporary neo-liberal market economy has reinforced the role of a fourth fictitious commodity: knowledge. Well before Polanyi wrote *The Great Transformation* (first published in 1944), Marx had also explored the same three initial fictitious commodities—although he is best known for his analysis of labour-power and the money form (on land and the environment, see Foster 2000). In this context, he observed that the logic of capital accumulation is imprinted by the fundamental contradiction in the commodity form between use-value and exchange-value (Marx 1976). Extending this argument to knowledge, this contradiction is expressed in the form of the intellectual commons versus intellectual property. It becomes more acute in the contemporary knowledge-based economy because knowledge-intensive products become a major source of dynamism and profits—especially when the knowledge-based economy is organized under the dominance of neo-liberal, profit-oriented, market-mediated principles rather than to serve broader social purposes. This raises the question of whether a 'double movement' might occur not only in regard to the neo-liberal re-assertion of commodification regarding land, labour-power, and money but also in relation to the growing commodification of knowledge in all of its various guises.

Among the important forms of appearance of the commodification of knowledge in this regard we can cite: (a) the primitive accumulation of capital through the 'enclosure' of the intellectual commons inherited from the past—biopiracy is the most notorious example but there are many others; (b) the divorce of intellectual labour from control over the means of production that it deploys—achieved through its formalization and codification in smart machines and expert systems—and the resulting appropriation of the knowledge of the collective worker; (c) creeping extension of the limited nature of copyright into broader forms of property right with a consequent erosion of any residual public interest; (d) the dynamics of technological rents generated by new knowledge and their disappearance once the new knowledge and/or knowledge-intensive goods and services become generalized and monopoly profits are competed away—such that the knowledge-based economy is subject to ever-increasing pressure to innovate and to protect vulnerable monopolies in knowledge-intensive products by embedding them in technology, standards, tacit knowledge, or legally entrenched intellectual property rights; (e) the contradiction that each capital wishes to pay nothing for its knowledge inputs but wants to charge a high price for its intellectual output; and (e) the dependence of continuing high profits in knowledge-, design-, or creativity-intensive sectors, despite the general tendency for

341

competition to reduce practical and/or legal monopoly advantages, on uneven development, on unequal exchange, and on downward pressure on the incomes of the surplus population, the unskilled, and producers of commoditized goods and services (cf. Jessop 2007).

Noting these trends invites the question whether there is a new 'double movement' in contemporary capitalism, a new mode of regulation corresponding to the development of a new knowledge-based accumulation regime, or a new form of steering to reflect the tighter coupling between the science, economic, legal, and political systems in a knowledge society (see respectively Boyer 2002, 2004; Petit 2005, Polanyi 1957; Stehr 2001; Willke 1996). This matters because this development is occurring under the dominance of neo-liberalism and it is therefore particularly tempting to ask whether there are equivalent mechanisms to limit, regulate, or steer the potential contradictions and destructive consequences of the development of markets in information, knowledge, and knowledge-intensive goods and services. Currently it seems that the state is still playing a larger role in relation to the initial movement towards the growing (fictitious) commodification of knowledge than it is in mobilizing possible counter-tendencies thereto. But we can certainly discern conflicting tendencies within state action as a whole and in contrasting emphases in action depending on whether the development of a knowledge-based economy in a given economic, political, and/or socio-cultural space is producing more winners or more losers. Let us consider some of these tendencies.

First, states are helping to create the legal and extra-legal conditions for the primitive accumulation of knowledge and/or to protect indigenous resources liable to such dispossession. States tend to polarize in this regard around, first, protecting or enclosing the commons (e.g. North–South) and, second, the most appropriate forms of intellectual property rights and regimes from the global to local scales. States have a key role here in changing intellectual property rights (IPR) laws and protecting domestic firms' appropriation of the intellectual commons at home and abroad. Given its competitive advantage in information and communications technology products, the knowledge revolution, and the so-called creative industries, the US federal state has been especially significant in promoting a neo-liberal form of the knowledge revolution on a global scale. This is evident in its advocacy of the Trade-Related Aspects of Intellectual Property Rights agreement and its use of bi- and multilateral trade agreements, conditionalities, and other pressures to seek to enforce US interests in regard to intellectual property rights.

Second, states are attempting to manage the contradictions of knowledge as a fictitious commodity. They 'must balance the need to protect and maintain the intellectual commons against the need to stimulate inventive activity' (Dawson 1998: 278). Whatever their position on such issues, all states must try to resolve contradictions and dilemmas in knowledge production while eschewing any direct, hierarchical control over it. This is often pursued through state promotion of innovation and diffusion systems (including social capital), broad forms of 'technological foresight', co-involvement and/or negotiated 'guidance' of the production of knowledge, and the development of suitable metagovernance structures (Messner 1998; Willke 1996). Thus, states sponsor information infrastructures and social innovation systems on different scales; develop IPR regimes and new forms of governance for activities in cyberspace; promote movement away from national utility structures with universal supply obligations suited to an era of mass production and mass consumption to more flexible, differential, multiscalar structures suited to a post-Fordist era; and intervene to restructure research in universities to realign it more closely with the perceived needs of business and to encourage the management and exploitation of intellectual property through spin-offs, licensing, partnerships, science parks, technology parks, industry parks, and so on.

Third, states are also promoting the commoditization of knowledge and the integration of knowledge and intellectual labour into production. This is reflected in the increased emphasis on the training of knowledge workers and lifelong learning, including distance learning, the introduction of information and communication technologies into fields of activity for which the state is more or less directly responsible, and the more general prosyletization of the knowledge-based economy and information society. They promote these strategies in the private sphere and third sector. There is also increasing emphasis on flexibility in manufacturing and services (including the public sector) based on new technologies (especially micro-electronics) and more flexible forms of organizing production.

Fourth, states are heavily promoting the dynamics of technological rents generated by new knowledge as part of a more general promotion of innovation. This serves to intensify the self-defeating character of the informational revolution from the viewpoint of capital, in so far as each new round of innovation is prone to ever more rapid devalorization. But capitals nonetheless win temporary advantages and technological rents for the economic spaces they control and, in so far as there are sustainable first-mover advantages, they can consolidate longer-term advantages for a region, nation, or triad. This strategy is an important and quite explicit element in the reassertion of US hegemony since the years of pessimism about the growing threat of the Japanese and East Asian economies, and helps to explain the American commitment to the consolidation of a robust IPR regime (cf. Lehman 1996; Schiller 1988). States also get involved in often-contradictory ways in promoting and retarding the mobility of productive capital.

Nonetheless, despite the current primacy on a global scale of the neo-liberal push to the fictitious commodification and/or quasi-commodification[6] of knowledge and to the extension of intellectual property rights, there are also signs of a counteracting movement even within the heartlands of the neo-liberal, globalizing knowledge-based economy. These reflect variously the resistance of producers to primitive accumulation through the enclosure of traditional knowledge, the struggle by workers in the public sector and professions such as education and health to resist the imposition of commercial logic at the expense of public service and/or professional values, the growing recognition of inefficiencies in capitalist production introduced through intellectual property rights (sometimes referred to as the 'intellectual anti-commons' effect), the rejection by consumers of monopoly prices for knowledge-intensive goods (especially when protected by intellectual property rights and/or by specialized IPR-protecting technologies), and the growing sense that intellectual property rights have become a mechanism for consolidating and entrenching the dominance of advanced capitalist economies and monopolists at the expense of developing economies, more intensely competitive economic sectors, and the low-skilled. This has not yet consolidated into a global 'counter movement' against the treatment of knowledge as a commodity but, in conjunction with the increasingly evident 'fight back' of nature in a growing environmental crisis, we can certainly expect this movement to gather pace. Whether the race against time can be won is, however, another matter.

## 14.9. Concluding Remarks

This chapter has compared three different institutionalist approaches to the market economy, using Polanyi's contributions as a benchmark to

---

[6] On non-commodities, fictitious commodities, quasi-commodities, capitalist commodities, and fictive capital, see Jessop (2007).

assess the contributions of the RA and autopoietic systems theory. Regulationists can extend and refine Polanyi's analyses by proposing how to rethink the economic and extra-economic conditions that help secure an always provisional and unstable capitalist order. In turn, systems theorists provide important insights into the regulatory problems rooted in the modern economy's simultaneous independence as an operationally autonomous system and its complex structural interdependence with other functional systems. I have thereby tried not only to disclose some weaknesses in Polanyi's analysis but also to show how his work can be used to improve the other two accounts of modern economies. Four main innovations have been suggested.

First, I have offered a more detailed analysis of the various forms and levels of social embeddedness and their interconnections. Second, drawing on Marxian and autopoietic insights, I explored the contradictions and dilemmas inherent in the self-organizing logic of a capitalist economy and its implications for the limits of intervention and argued that the capitalist market economy cannot be seen as determinant 'in the last instance' of an entire social formation. Polanyi's account of the dual movement is located at the intersection of these Marxian and systems-theoretical views. Third, I provide a more detailed analysis of capitalist societalization—or what Polanyi called the market society—and the mechanisms through which the logic of the market economy comes to dominate and hegemonize the wider society and the various forms and sites of resistance to market forces. This helps to correct Marxist reductionism by specifying the various economic and extra-economic mechanisms through which a society could become dominated by capitalist logic; and it reveals the richness of Polanyi's own reflections on the dialectics of the dual movement through which a market economy first develops through its disembedding from pre-capitalist institutions and is then (re-)embedded in a market society. Fourth, I suggest that the 'dual movement' that structurally couples the market economy with other systems and the lifeworld can be subjected—always, of course, within certain limits—to appropriate forms of governance and meta-governance. In this way the primary sources of society's counter-movement, i.e. the more extreme manifestations of the formal rationality of market forces, can be tamed through the more reflexive, dialogical rationality of governance. I have illustrated this through an all too brief account of the growing extension of the commodity form of knowledge as a fourth fictitious commodity, of the role of the state as well as market forces in promoting this commodification, and some emerging indications that the state—by virtue of the contradictions involved in this process as well as pressures from a growing range of social forces—is beginning to intervene in this process to limit as well as to promote it. As yet it is too soon to say whether and/or when the counter-tendencies of the double movement will come to dominate the continuing push towards commodification. But it may prove that the resistance of the environment (or, in Polanyi's terms, land) to the dominance of market forces will lead to another great transformation and double movement that requires a new approach to knowledge as intellectual commons before this is generated simply by resistance to its growing commodification.

# References

Baecker, D. (1988). *Information und Risiko in der Marktwirtschaft*. Frankfurt: Suhrkamp.

Boyer, R. (1990). *The Regulation School*. New York: Columbia University Press.

—— (2002). *La Croissance, Début de Siècle*. Paris: Albin Michel.

—— (2004). *Une Théorie du Capitalisme. Est-elle Possible?* Paris: Odile Jacob.

—— and Saillard, Y. (eds.) (2002). *Régulation Theory*. London: Routledge.

Dawson, A. C. (1998). 'The Intellectual Commons: A Rationale for Regulation', *Prometheus*, 16: 275–89.

Delorme, R. and André, C. (1982) L'État et l'économie. Paris: Seuil.

Dunsire, A. (1996). 'Tipping the Balance: Autopoiesis and Governance', *Administration and Society*, 28: 299–334.

Foster, J. B. (2000). *Marx's Ecology: Materialism and Nature*. New York: Monthly Review Press.

Glagow, M. and Willke, H. (eds.) (1987). *Dezentrale Gesellschaftssteuerung: Probleme der Integration polyzentristischer Gesellschaft*. Pfaffenweiler: Centaurus-Verlagsgesellschaft.

Grabher, G. (ed.) (1993). *The Embedded Firm*. London: Routledge.

Granovetter, M. (1985). 'Economic Action and Social Structure', *American Journal of Sociology*, 91: 481–510.

Jessop, B. (2001) 'Regulationist and Autopoieticist Reflections on Polanyi's Account of Market Economies and the Market Society', *New Political Economy*, 6: 213–232.

—— (2002). *The Future of the Capitalist State*. Cambridge: Polity.

—— (2007). 'Knowledge as a Fictitious Commodity: Insights and Limits of a Polanyian Analysis', in A. Bugra and M. Mendell (eds.), *Market Economy as a Political Project: Reading Karl Polanyi for the 21st Century*. Basingstoke: Palgrave.

—— and Sum, N. L. (2006). *Beyond the Regulation Approach*. Cheltenham: Edward Elgar.

Lehman, B. W. (1996). 'Intellectual Property: America's Competitive Advantage in the 21st Century', *Columbia Journal of World Business*, 31: 6–16.

Luhmann, N. (1986). *Die Wirtschaft der Gesellschaft*. Frankfurt: Suhrkamp.

——(1995). *Social Systems*. Stanford: Stanford University Press.

Marx, K. (1976). *Capital*, vol. 1. London: Lawrence and Wishart.

Mayntz, R. (1993) 'Modernization and the Logic of Interorganizational Networks', in J. Child, M. Crozier, R. Mayntz et al. (eds.), *Societal Change between Market and Organization*. Aldershot: Avebury.

Messner, D. (1998). *The Network Society*. London: Cass.

Offe, C. (1975). 'The Theory of the Capitalist State and the Problem of Policy Formation', in L. N. Lindberg, R. Alford, C. Crouch, and C. Offe (eds.), *Stress and Contradiction in Modern Capitalism*. Lexington, DC: Heath.

Olofsson, G. (1995). 'Embeddedness and Integration: An Essay on Karl Polanyi's "The Great Transformation"', in M. Mortensen (ed.), *Social Integration and Marginalization*. Frederiksberg: Samfundslitteratur.

Petit, P. (2005). *Croissance et Richesse des Nations*. Paris: Maspéro.

Polanyi, K. (1957). *The Great Transformation*. Boston: Beacon Press.

——(1977). *The Livelihood of Man*. New York: Academic Press.

——(1982). 'The Economy as Instituted Process', in M. Granovetter and R. Swedberg (eds.), *The Sociology of Economic Life*. Boulder: Westview.

Scharpf, F. W. (1994). 'Games Real Actors Could Play: Positive And Negative Coordination in Embedded Negotiations', *Journal of Theoretical Politics*, 6: 27–53.

Schiller, D. (1988) 'How to Think About Information', in V. Mosco and J. Wasko (eds.), *The Political Economy of Information*. Madison: University of Wisconsin Press.

Smith, A. (1937). *An Inquiry into the Nature and Causes of the Wealth of Nations*. New York: Modern Library.

Stehr, N. (2001). *Wissen und Wirtschaften. Die gesellschaftlichen Grundlagen der modernen Ökonomie*. Frankfurt: Suhrkamp.

Swedberg, R. (1997). 'New Economic Sociology: What has been Accomplished, What is Ahead?', *Acta Sociologica*, 40: 161–82.

Willke, H. (1996). *Supervision des Staates*. Frankfurt: Suhrkamp.

# 15

# Pierre Bourdieu, a Theoretician of Change? The View from *Régulation* Theory

*Robert Boyer*

## 15.1. Introduction

The critical research work that has been carried out by *régulation* theorists on certain hypotheses of neoclassical theory—concerning rationality, the treatment of time, and the notion of equilibrium (Aglietta 1976)—has tended to interpret Bourdieu's sociology as a logic of action, compatible with a historical and institutional approach.[1] The concept of habitus has seemed to be a particularly useful reference point, because it fits in with the stress placed on how actors' behaviour is determined by the institutional context, or, more precisely, by institutionalized compromises. A second phase of enquiry, when *régulation* theory focused on the foundations of institutions, revisited Bourdieu's sociology without necessarily deepening and clarifying the two research programmes. The resulting comparisons and rapprochements tended to concern the economics of conventions, evolutionary theories, and American institutionalism.

Pierre Bourdieu's exit from the scene has forced many disciplines to question themselves about how their respective research programmes relate to his theoretical system. This chapter proposes putting Bourdieu's sociology into perspective by examining the questions that are currently being asked in the research conducted by *régulation* theorists. To be more precise, the goal is to examine Bourdieu's economics and his relationship

---

[1] This chapter has been translated by Philip Wilson from the French original 'Pierre Bourdieu, Analyste Du Changement?', CEPREMAP Couverture Orange 2004-01.

to standard neoclassical theoreticians. The questions of reproduction and change will also be examined, two issues that have given rise to great debate. This will lead to an opportunity to put *régulation* theory into perspective in its turn.

The richness of Bourdieu's work, coupled with the way that it has evolved, has brought a number of commentaries into being. They oppose each other in an almost ritualistic way. On one side are those who fervently admire his work and aim to carry it on, seeing in Bourdieu the founder of a sociology that is both reflective and scientific. On the other side are his detractors, who relativize his work or even deny that this sociologist could have any relevance to our understanding of contemporary societies. Two themes reoccur in the controversy surrounding the debate. Bourdieu is supposed to have sunk into an economism that would only marginally differentiate him from any neoclassical theorist: he therefore ends up being presented as a disciple of Gary Becker. Then again, the stress he places on the concepts of habitus and field supposedly means that his work could only ever form the basis for an analysis of social reproduction, rather than of the transformation of societies.

This chapter is an attempt to respond to these symmetrical criticisms. It is first of all demonstrated that Bourdieu's detractors have too often taken the titles of his works at face value. While these titles may effectively underline the permanent nature of the reproduction of social roles, Bourdieu's argument—once the reader moves beyond the definitions of his basic concepts—is not an attempt to reduce each field's logic to the purely economic level. It then becomes crucial to stress that Bourdieu's defenders have not given sufficient attention to the profoundly dynamic character of his research that effectively forms a totality: from his studies of the Béarn and Kabylia, to his analysis of the market for the single-family house, moving through similar analyses of literature, art, and state nobility.

The chapter finally develops a theme that could surprise the reader: *régulation* theory and Bourdieu's sociology are related. On the one hand, as has already been stressed, regulationist research has turned to the concept of habitus, a term borrowed from Bourdieu, as an alternative to the theory of rational choice as found in economics and the social sciences. On the other hand, both programmes of research can be added to those analyses of contemporary society that set out from a critical evaluation of Marxian insights. They also share this basic hypothesis: that life in society is made possible by the way in which institutions are constructed, just as economic activity is organized by the mode of *régulation*. It is therefore interesting to compare the analysis of change by investigating individual terms one by one: this is the guiding principle of the argument that follows. However, the objectives and the architecture of Bourdieu's sociology and of *régulation* theory obviously remain different. Paradoxically, the theory of fields found in Bourdieu's sociology is, in the final analysis, a theory at the meso level, while the ultimate aim of *régulation* theory is to propose an analysis of macroeconomic systems.

## 15.2. Bourdieu's Economics is Not a Minor Variant of Neoclassical Theory

A common criticism of Bourdieu is that he imported various categories of economic analysis into the social sciences, especially sociology: either consciously or unconsciously (Caillé 1994; Favereau 2001). His work is judged, in the final analysis, as being merely a version of standard neoclassical economics. There are numerous indicators that are supposed to support this judgement, but only a superficial reading—and often a biased one—could authorize this characterization of Bourdieu's work. A more attentive analysis, one that is faithful to both the letter and the spirit, opens up other perspectives. The field of economics is actually only one of the domains in relation to which action and conflicts can structure themselves, while economic institutions are themselves the result of the sort of construction found in the tradition of Norbert Elias (1974).

### 15.2.1. *On the Origins of a Failure of Comprehension*

In most of the books and articles produced by Bourdieu are found many terms that refer to economics: *interest, profit, capital,* and even *market* are frequently employed in fields other than the economic. It is the recurring use of these terms that has brought about the criticism frequently made of Bourdieu: going beyond his own specific project, he is supposed to have applied economic reasoning to a variety of other fields (the world of art, academic life, linguistic practice, relations between the sexes, etc.) and by doing so he has devalued the logic that is proper to those fields. This interpretation shows a lack of comprehension of both the spirit and the letter of the texts (Table 15.1). The terms that have been borrowed from economics take on a different sense in each field. They are only a point of

**Table 15.1.** Interest, profit, capital, and market: their use in Bourdieu's sociology

| Basic concept | Definition according to field | Use in the sociology of Bourdieu |
|---|---|---|
| Interest | • Each field is characterized by a particular and different form of interest.<br>• Action, even if apparently disinterested, nonetheless obeys the logic of the field (e.g. academic or artistic). | • Economic interest is not the general equivalent of the interests found in the various fields.<br>• The application of the logic of *homo economicus* leads to a contradiction in the majority of fields. The role of illusion. |
| Profit | • The term in fact designates the result of action, so that profit can be symbolic just as much, if not more than, economic. | • A more exact term would be this: the distribution of the advantages that result when the specific attributes of a field come into play: for example, reputation. |
| Capital | • Economic capital is not the only form of capital.<br>• There are numerous forms of capital that coexist autonomously: cultural capital (diplomacy, acquaintance, good manners), social capital (networking). Then there is symbolic capital that enables the acquisition of what is delivered by other forms of capital (physical or economic). | • No doubt it is somewhat clumsy to refer to one of the most problematic categories of neoclassical theory: this is not a measurement theoretically founded on economic capital.<br>• The term evokes a differentiated accumulation of attributes according to the space occupied in the field under consideration. It therefore refers to a relationship of domination, just as economic capital expresses the domination of capital over labour. |
| Market | • This is a clear notion in the economic field: a construction in which certain key actors participate.<br>• Use is metaphorical in most of the other fields (the marriage market?), unless they tend to be dominated by economic logic (the art market). | • The equivalent of the art of the judoka? A dominant concept in contemporary societies is imported in order to make the logic of interactions stand out within fields that are not economic.<br>• A superficial reading can give the impression of being a variant of the theory of Gary Becker. |

departure, for analyses that introduce very different determining factors from those postulated by standard neoclassical theory, or its extension into the analysis of social facts in the tradition of Gary Becker (1996) and those inspired by him (Cameron 2002). In effect, Pierre Bourdieu's work is a 'sociology of interest' only in the sense that it is opposed to sociology that is trying to be general.

What can be deceptive is that, just like neomarginalist economists, I give priority, among all the different forms of social conduct, to a specific form of interest, of investment. But the words themselves are the only things we have in common. The interest of which I speak has nothing to do with the self-interest of Adam Smith—ahistorical, natural and universal, but ultimately the unconscious universalisation of interest that is created and assumed by capitalist economy.

(Bourdieu 1980*b*: 33)

In effect, there are as many definitions of these key notions borrowed from economics as there are fields. By field it is necessary to understand a delimitation of the social world, one that is governed by its own laws and codes: this could be the university, journalism, or the spheres of literature, art, and politics. In each of these fields, we find self-contained role-playing. The key notions can now be reviewed.

- In Bourdieu's writings, each *field* is characterized by a particular and different form of *interest*. In certain cases, even the most apparently disinterested form of action will nevertheless obey the logic of the field (e.g. the academic or the artistic field). But the main point to note is that economic interest is not the general equivalent of the interests that are to be found in the various fields. This is a fundamental difference from sociological research inspired by the issue of rational choice. The logic of *homo economicus* brings out contradiction after contradiction when it is applied to most fields, as can be seen by looking at the examples of the aristocrat at the court of Louis XIV, or the scientist: it is nonsensical to make them both into types of the contemporary capitalist entrepreneur, where an entire way of life is based on the maximization of temporal profit.

Bourdieu's own use of the notion of *profit* is more metaphorical than typically economic. The term designates the result of action, and finds a specific definition within each field, so that profit can be symbolic as much as economic, if not more so. Everything depends on the nature and the organization of the field in which individuals operate. A more exact term would actually seem to be that of the (unequal) distribution of attributes or of benefits within a given field. In the academic field, for example, profits are above all symbolic: peer recognition through the frequency of quotations, or responsibilities taken on in learned societies.... The only academic market where this sort of recognition gets converted into a differentiation in income, with all the corresponding advantages (or the opposite), is the American!

- The case is the same for *capital*: it cannot be reduced to economic capital alone. In effect there are various forms that coexist and are endowed a priori with fairly radical autonomy. We could think of the characteristics and the determining features of cultural capital (diplomacy, acquaintance, good manners) or even of social capital, which in turn depends on the network that is maintained by the agent. And yet another logic operates for symbolic capital: in effect it permits agents to obtain the equivalent of what is offered by the other forms of capital, whether physical or economic. It is of course true that these various forms of capital can eventually be converted into each other, but the process is in no way automatic in the way that Becker's theory of human capital would postulate. Bourdieu's use of such a problematic category of neoclassical theory is clumsy, especially so because since the Two Cambridges Capital Controversy it has been shown that there is no theoretical measurement of economic capital. So exactly what is the significance of this concept within Bourdieu's system? The answer to this question lies in recognizing the way that accumulation differs according to the positions that are occupied within whichever field is under consideration. Accumulation refers to a network of domination, just as economic capital expresses the domination of labour by capital. In this sense, Bourdieu's sociology cuts itself off from the sociology of rational choice, according to which all players have equal standing by right, if not de facto.

- The limits of the transposition become even clearer in the use of the term *market*.

This concept has a clear sense for the economic field. Economic sociology goes on to emphasize that this means of coordination is the result of a construction that involves the participation of key actors. In most of the other fields, the term is used metaphorically. Is it really possible to refer to the marriage market without postulating that the power of economic logic is taking over the other fields, to the extent of making them into markets in the strict sense of the term? It can be assumed that this risk of confusion has been taken into account by Bourdieu, who practises the equivalent of the art of the judoka: he brings in a key notion in the interpretation of contemporary societies so that he can make the logic of interactions within a field become clear. In the academic world, for example, a logic of disinterestedness replaces interest as it is properly understood within the economic sphere, and yet this reversal of logic still has to obey an a priori model that never varies within a field. However, by taking this step,

353

Bourdieu exposes himself to the possibility of being misunderstood, for a superficial reading can give the impression that he adheres to a variant of standard neoclassical theory.

This ambiguity has often concealed any relevance that Bourdieu's system might have for contemporary research on the frontier between sociology and economics.

### 15.2.2. *An Antidote to the Naiveties of Neoclassical Theory*

It can be asked whether economic agents are playing with the same cognitive cards in their everyday decisions as professional economists. Is it really possible to sum up economic relationships by the single market relationship between individuals endowed with the same powers, capacities, and information? Doesn't the type of *homo economicus*, considered as a representative agent, conceal the fact that there is no solution to the problem of the passage from micro to macro? Why does it have to be assumed that, everywhere and in almost every time, the state destabilizes the course of economic activity? Do theories of equilibrium really permit the conception of historical time and the transformations that are implied by this? Finally, is it reasonable to postulate economic rules that never vary through time and space?

Bourdieu's work offers ways of starting to answer these questions, forming an epistemological and methodological critique of the presuppositions of the theory of rational choice. Even more importantly, there is an original conception of fields and how they are articulated. Economic activity can be analysed with reference to this construction (Table 15.2).

- The *theorists* see themselves as exclusively rational and are generous enough to attribute this rationality to concrete economic agents, so as to end up with a pure form of economics. But what claims to be a positive analysis is actually a normative project: any empirical observations that do not fit in with the assumptions of the theory are explained as being due to agents' irrationalities or incomplete aspects within markets (Boyer 2003). This will be recognized by the reader as the project of neoclassical fundamentalism. The rationality and the equilibrium of the market are never questioned and the existence of an economic equilibrium and its character are justified by the appeal to the Paretan optimum (Amable, Boyer, and Lordon 1995).

**Table 15.2.** Bourdieu's economic sociology as an alternative to the scholastic illusion of neoclassical theories

| Characteristic | Neoclassical economics | Economic sociology |
| --- | --- | --- |
| Epistemology | The existence of natural laws within an autonomous economic space. | Economics, as a field and as a discipline, is a social construct. |
| Logic of action | The theory of rational choice is as formulated by the professional economist. | Interaction between habitus and field and possible interactions between fields. |
| Interrelationship of agents | Horizontal and fundamentally egalitarian relations between agents, via the market. | The rapport between the dominant and the dominated is fundamental within each field and/or market. |
| Nature of agents | Identity or similarity of agents' objectives and preferences. | The historical formation of habitus implies the heterogeneity of agents. |
| Treatment of time | A succession of states of equilibrium within time (conceived as virtual and instrumental). | Fields and habitus are reproduced but can possibly be desynchronized, or can enter into crisis. |
| Role of the state | Its exclusive or fundamental role is to interfere with the *private calculations* of agents. | Often the instigator of the market and of basic economic relationships. |
| Political position of the analyst | Essentially committed, the engineer of the market. | The critical role of the analyst and the researcher. |
| | Tendency towards the naturalization of the economy. | Historical constructivism and contingency. |
| | Sensitive to the interests of the dominant economic actors. | Support for the dominated sectors of society. |

- Relations between *microeconomic approach and macroeconomic analysis* appear to be problematic for most of the social sciences and in particular for neoclassical economic theory. The concept of the invisible hand finds its culmination in the attempts of theories of general equilibrium to demonstrate the existence of an equilibrium that derives precisely from the diversity of methods of production and of preferences, whereas the majority of macroeconomic theories postulate the equivalent of a representative agent. Theoretical analysis shows that, except in extremely restrictive conditions—that are actually never satisfied in actually existing economies—a perfect match turns out to be impossible. Even if the most recent research, which aims at finding an approximate aggregation, appeals to the hypothesis of the heterogeneity of people, the economist still finds himself or herself unable to recognize this heterogeneity. The importance of economic sociology and in particular of Bourdieu's concept of habitus lies in the clarification of the reasons—that to some extent are endogenous—for this differentiation. The characteristics of a field are not the simple transposition of agents' characteristics, but are the result of their interaction.

- Addressing the concept of time poses a considerable problem for any attempt to formulate all-encompassing economic theories. In effect, *time* as considered by the economist is that of calculation, of anticipation, of movement towards equilibrium. It is a *cinematic time*, essentially virtual in that it is nothing more than the context for the experience of thinking: as thinking is carried out by the theoretician! The question of *historical time* is actually at the heart of the construct of the economic agent, as the very definition of habitus by Bourdieu stresses. A second factor of change is introduced through the evolution of the game-rules that govern the functioning of a field and more generally the historical transformation of economic institutions. Sociological economics, because of its interest in the genesis of categories, institutions, and markets, is a point of departure for a historicizing economic analysis. This is therefore an alternative to neoclassical theory, where predictions are permanently frustrated by recurrent innovations that tend to be perceived as radical, whereas they are in fact minor; or vice versa the reoccurrence of initially marginal changes that lead to the entire transformation of the mode of *régulation* (Boyer 2001*a*).

- For most economic theories, the role of the state and of the political is problematic. The very nature of an analysis that formalizes the interactions of rational agents across markets means that any state intervention has to be detrimental. If the teachings of standard neo-classical theory are taken literally, the economist has only one role: to be the defender and the propagandist of the market. A quick glance at economic history brings out a remarkably complementary relationship between state and market, however. In numerous cases, and not only that of France (a country characterized by state capitalism), public forces actually set up the market. A purely economic theory of the market appears to be a contradiction in terms. It may come as a surprise, but the foundation of market economy, a monetary institution, is inseparable from the sovereignty and the legitimacy of the state (Aglietta and Orléan 1998, 2002).

Neoclassical theory holds that it is possible for the *economic field to bring about self-closure* through the explanation of the economy by reference only to economic factors. This claim is untenable because it assumes that the economy is a separate entity, an assumption that is undermined by numerous pieces of empirical evidence. It turns out to be the case that the institution of the market corresponds to a process that mobilizes the strategies of social actors and very often the power of state legitimation. This theme is essential.

### 15.2.3. *All Economic Space is Socially Constructed*

For Bourdieu and the work that he has inspired in economic sociology, every market is the result of interactions between actors, who then codify rules to permit the smooth adjustment of supply and demand. Neoclassical theoreticians assume the existence of the process without ever asking themselves how the market came about in the first place. Just as for the theory of general equilibrium, the majority of research in economics postulates the existence of a market and studies its qualities, but fails to propose a general underlying theory. It is too often supposed that when the protagonists know what they want and have realized that the market is superior to a barter economy, then the market's institution is inevitable. This is to forget, as has been shown by Alfred Marshall, that a market only takes shape if intermediaries manage to convert information about sources of supply and demand into profit, something that happens precisely because of the organization of a market that they have set up (Lesourne 1991). Economists themselves have shown over the last two decades various factors that limit the coordination of markets: the imperfection and asymmetry of information (Stiglitz 1987), the impact of representation on the functioning of markets (Spence 1973), and the constitutive character of certain social norms (Akerlof 1990). Even once it has been constituted, there is no assurance that the market can ever be self-balancing, because it is unable to deliver a solution to any coordinated series of decentralized actions, given a change in scale or in the quality, number, or coordination of agents (White 2002).

The general picture is that most economists consider the market to be the *solution* to the problems of coordination between interdependent agents, while for the sociologist the constitution of the market is the *problem* that has to be analysed (Table 15.3). In the first case we find the market's function and method of functioning, in the second case we have its emergence and its construction. This leads to the paradox of economic research: it actually postulates a central mechanism without supplying any theory, still less an explanation, of the origin of the mechanism. In contrast to this, the works of economic sociology provide an analysis of

**Table 15.3.** The alternative sociological approach to the neoclassic conception of the market

| The neoclassic conception of markets | The sociological approach to markets |
| --- | --- |
| A *mechanism* that delivers a single price for the same goods, as a result of competition from supply and demand. | An *institution* that reproduces the strategy and the concept of control of the dominant actors. |
| A *black hole*, an empty set. | The place of *social, political, and economic interactions*. |
| The *parametric* behaviour of individuals who are—a priori—*equal*, and who consider the environment to be a given fact, thus conforming to the paradigm of *homo economicus*. | *Strategic interactions* between heterogeneous social actors who are trying to stabilize or transform their environment. |
| *Pure and perfect* competition is the ideal. | *Imperfect* competition between unequal agents is the rule. |
| An *exclusively economic* mechanism, bringing about its own equilibrium and endowed with the capacity to institute itself. | An *institutional construct* that emerges from new social movements. |
| A mechanism that is *easily accessible* and therefore guarantees liberty of transaction. | A *very sophisticated social construction*: only *extremely precise conditions* in law, jurisprudence, compatibility, monetary regime, etc. permit the emergence of the market. |
| A coordinated *universal* vocation. | *Partial diffusion*, with theoretical and practical limits to the market. |
| *Structurally stable* by nature. | The typical evolution of a market: *emergence, development, obsolescence, crisis*, and disappearance. |

how markets emerge. This is why the market of pure and perfect competition is not the result of some state of nature but the result of the application of the normative framework of neoclassical theory. In the computerized market studied by Marie-France Garcia (1986), the emergence of a form of the market corresponding to the concept of perfect competition actually resulted from an alliance formed against the wholesalers between an official of the chamber of agriculture—whose formation had been in neoclassical theory—and local producers. A much more subtle mechanism can be seen to be at work in the study by Gilles Laferté (2002) on the presentation and marketing of Burgundy wine. While, at the beginning of the twenties, the wholesalers had organized the market in their favour by regulating the labels of origin and by creating new brands, the emergence of a small number of new actors, such as Jules Lafon, enabled an entire tradition to be invented, or possibly reinvented. This brought down the organizational model in favour of the owners and the labels of origin, and thereby created a new image for Burgundy wine. Here is a remarkable example of the market analysed as a social construct, and it is all the more interesting in that its constitution involved a complete break with previous tendencies. This means that the concept of a field as a space for identical reproduction is no longer tenable. A third example can be found in the analysis that Bourdieu himself carried out on the emergence of the market of the single-family house: this results from a twofold construction relating both to demand (when agents form preferences and are then given aid, i.e. access to credit or public subsidies) and to supply (by means of directives given to the construction industry) (Bourdieu 2000*a*). In both cases, the state contributes to create these two component parts of what appears to be—*ex post*—a market. The relationship between the state and the market is therefore more complementary than competitive.

There could be no better antidote to the naturalization of economic relations, especially commercial ones, that is being promoted by the research of contemporary economists. Economic theories are themselves the products of history, and their structure and style are highly dependent on the role of the state in the very process of the setting up of any market economy. Even national academic traditions can be related to the history of markets and the constitution of capitalism within the individual countries (Fourcade-Gourinchas 2002). And the concept of field can be used to analyse the distribution of economists' positions (Lebaron 2000), which can lead to a renewed understanding of various rival programmes of research.

### 15.2.4. *Power Relationships Structure the Various Fields*

According to most economic theories, the market is the main authority—perhaps the only one—for coordinating a set of behaviours of decentralized agents. As a mechanism it is perceived as a horizontal relationship that links agents who have the same amount of influence over it, or no influence at all in the case of perfect competition. Furthermore, the market is presented as not just efficient but also as just, because each individual contributes to the formation of prices in proportion to his or her income or wealth. Bourdieu's economic sociology again insists on this fundamental property: whatever the field, certain actors will have more power than others. This means that competition is not about equality of opportunity but about the reproduction of an unequal distribution of capital. All fields are affected by the opposition between the dominant and the dominated, which characterizes their structure as much as their dynamic and their transformation. A priori, this opposition inevitably recalls Marx's distinction between market relationships and relations of production, but it cannot be reduced to this. There is an inevitable division in the way that power operates within the various fields. Each field is characterized by specific power relationships that are founded on possession of one of the various forms of capital. This differentiation prevents the imposition of a single hierarchy that would integrate the various forms of power. Bourdieu's theory is here in opposition to Marxist conceptions that would make political power the simple expression of economic capital, for example. Even if fields are brought together by a certain solidarity, based on homologous positions, they still remain in opposition because of competition and conflict, cf. the rate of exchange between the different types of capital that constitute the various fields (Bourdieu 1997: 124). Therefore, it is not possible to construct a global indicator of capital independently of the field in which an agent operates.

This is a long way from the fiction of the representative agent that is still being used by a number of contemporary researchers, even though it has been shown that this notion was a contradiction in terms and that it would make the theory incapable of any relevance at all in the analysis of change, even if this change were conceived as the transition from one state of equilibrium to another (Kirman 1992). The characteristics of a field can only be analysed and understood by taking into account the interaction of individuals who are not equally endowed in terms of capital: and here the volume of capital is specified as much as the division between economic, social, and symbolic capital. Therefore, it is principally the heterogeneity of social positions that creates habitus and lifestyle (Bourdieu 1979, 1980a). While the economist tends to categorize as exogenous the heterogeneity of individual preferences and competences, Bourdieu's approach is to examine the factors that determine the distribution of various forms of capital and their evolution through time. This is a great help in clarifying the well-known unresolved dilemma of the relationship between microanalysis and the presentation of macroscopic regularities. Bourdieu helps the economist come to an understanding of why every effort has failed to produce a perfect (or even approximate) aggregation of serialized individuals whose only distinguishing trait was their level of income (Hildenbrand 1997). It is the dynamic interactions between unequal agents that define the characteristics of a field, and this characteristic can also be applied to the various markets.

What is also of significance in this gap between the dominant and the dominated is how it immediately introduces a dynamic aspect into the analysis. Each field is the site for struggles to conserve or to transform capital distribution, and this is true even in scientific fields (Bourdieu 2001*a*: 69). The dominant are in a good position to deploy strategies that would permit them to preserve their position and to extend their capital; but the dominated, as well as any new entrants, share the opposite ambition. Their aim is to destabilize the current positions of strength and as a result they develop innovations designed to devalue the capital that is held by the establishment. It is clear that the destabilization of a field is not a very frequent phenomenon, but it would be an error to conclude that every single field is the scene of a reproduction ad infinitum of the same structure. What is necessary is to ask why so many critics of Bourdieu have set him up as a theoretician of reproduction, when there is the constant assertion in his works that 'it is not possible to separate the analysis of structure (the static) and the analysis of change (the dynamic)' (Bourdieu 2001*a*: 121). It appears that many readers confuse his affirmation that invariable laws govern the way that the various fields operate with the impossibility of any analysis of the historical dynamic that operates within each field.

### 15.2.5. *Under the Appearance of Reproduction: A Theory of Change*

A paradoxical interpretation of Bourdieu's work might be attempted: although a superficial reading suggests the inevitability of social reproduction, a full analysis brings out factors of change and transformation. It is true that his earliest writing, highly aphoristic in character, referred to the education system in a way that seemed to indicate a pure theory of reproduction with absolutely no possibility of historical transformation (Bourdieu and Passeron 1970). Subsequent elaborations, however, in particular with respect to the concepts of habitus and field, bring in a historical approach that aims to work out a field's *genesis*, its institutionalization and the factors that can transform it or bring it into crisis.

### 15.2.6. *Habitus: Acquired but Powerfully Generative*

Critical incomprehension is greatest concerning the concept of habitus. In the majority of cases, critics have taken the easy way out by going for an etymological analysis: habitus can be reduced to habit, that is, the mechanical reproduction of invariables, which leads to the disappearance of individual autonomy and therefore to a static history marked by the permanent domination of the same holders of capital over the dominated (Caillé 1994; Favereau 2001). Bourdieu finds it necessary to expose this lack of understanding in practically every work, however, and this can be proved by direct quotation.

Habitus...is what has been acquired but has become permanently incorporated in the body under the form of permanent dispositions....The concept is in line with a mode of *genetic* thought that is opposed to essentialist modes of thought....Habitus is something that is powerfully *generative*...Habitus is a principle of *invention*, which, produced by history, is relatively independent of history: dispositions are lasting, something that leads to all sorts of effects of *hysteresis* (delay, *discrepancy*...).

(Bourdieu 1980*b*: 134–5)

History also becomes relevant because any investment in a field is the result of an interaction between a playing area (that sets the stakes) and a system of dispositions adjusted to the game in question. 'In other words, investment is the historical effect of agreement between two realisations of the social: in things (by institution) and in bodies (by incorporation)' (Bourdieu 1980*b*: 35). The match of one to the other is only a special case when institutions and habitus are both the product of the same historical process. Bourdieu's earliest works address the discrepancies and the small problems that occur in a field that is basically functioning well, but where it is hard to see the logic.

What appears to have happened is that the special case of habitus and structure has often been taken to be a principle of repetition and conservation. In fact the concept of conservation, like that of habitus itself, was the only way in which I could describe the sort of discrepancies to be found in an economy such as that of Algeria in the sixties (...) between objective structures and incorporated structures, between economic institutions imported and imposed by colonization (which today would take the form of market constraints) and the economic dispositions held by agents whose origin was in the precapitalist world.

(Bourdieu 1987: 189)

Furthermore, it is not built into the concept of habitus that it has to obey some sort of monolithic, immutable, fatal, and exclusive principle. This is seen again in the example of the Algerian underclass, which showed 'instances of habitus that are broken and torn and that carry tensions and contradictions that show the contradictory conditions in which they were formed' (Bourdieu 1997: 79).

Habitus is therefore neither necessarily adapted nor necessarily coherent (...) it can happen that—just as in the paradigm of Don Quixote—dispositions fail to match the field and the 'collective expectations' that control its working. This is

especially relevant when a field goes into a profound crisis and sees a corresponding disruption of its regularities, even of its rules.

(Bourdieu 1997: 190)

This theoretical perspective is found throughout Bourdieu's works, no
matter which topic he addresses: labour in Algeria (Bourdieu 1958); the
evolution of farming society in the Béarn (Bourdieu 1962, 2002*b*); the
university crisis (Bourdieu 1984); redeployment strategies of the French
elites (Bourdieu 1989); and the question of women (Bourdieu 1998*a*). And
this is not to forget the parallel question, that of the emergence of a new
field, for example the sector of the single-family house (Bourdieu 2000*a*).

A certain analogy with the reception of *régulation* theory is striking.
The level of analysis is certainly different: more microeconomic in the
case of habitus and field, macroeconomic in the case of *régulation* theory,
which originated in the realization that the post-war growth regime was
in a growing crisis that finally exploded (Aglietta 1976), and which has
been constantly denounced for its static character and its postulate of an
identical reproduction of capitalist institutions. Critical understanding is
for the most part linked to the connotations of the term *régulation* (the
homeostatic reproduction of a system), which tend to be taken over into
the precise definition of a mode of *régulation*, which is understood as a
transitional equilibrium between the forces bringing about the endogenous destabilization of a regime of accumulation (Boyer and Saillard
2002). This is quite paradoxical. In both cases, concepts that had been
elaborated to take into account the social and historical construction of
individuals and of institutions are interpreted as defending and illustrating a pattern of identical reproduction where there is no possibility of
transformation, either marginal or radical. Bourdieu has been constantly
criticized like this, even though his intention was to offer a reflective
analysis that would in turn provide tools that could bring to an end the
apparent inevitability of domination in each field.

### 15.2.7. *The Genesis of Fields and of Markets*

It is essential to refer to history in any characterization of contemporary
configurations and to avoid any attempts at naturalization. An example
of this is Bourdieu's own view of his analysis of Flaubert's work: Bourdieu
held that he had shown the process through which the nineteenth century literary field had become *autonomous* (Bourdieu 1992*b*). It can similarly be recalled that one of his significant contributions to economics was

**Table 15.4.** The genesis of fields and markets: some examples

| Fields/markets | References | Factors of emergence | | |
|---|---|---|---|---|
| | | Specialization/ autonomy | Dominant actors | State power |
| Artistic | *L'amour de l'art* | | | |
| | Bourdieu 1966 | + | | |
| Computerized market | *La construction sociale d'un marché parfait* | | | |
| | Garcia 1986 | | + | + |
| Literary | *Les règles de l'art* | | | |
| | Bourdieu 1992b | + | + | |
| Media | *Sur la télévision* | | | |
| | Bourdieu 1996 | + | + | |
| Market of the individual home | *Les structures sociales de l'économie* | | | |
| | Bourdieu 2000a | + | | + |
| Burgundy wines | *Folklore savant et folklore commercial* | | | |
| | Laferté 2002 | | + | + |

to use the example of the single-family house to bring out the conditions in which markets emerge (Bourdieu 2000*a*): this was a special case but a significant one. The results accumulated in his various works have never been systemized (Table 15.4) and this remains a matter for regret. It is the same research that is still being carried out by economic sociology, more systematically in the United States than in France (Fligstein 2001; White 2002), paradoxically enough.

## 15.2.8. *The Multiple Forms of Change: A Taxonomy*

Once a field has been set up, its functioning sets in motion a series of forces of change. These are historical in origin. It is lamentable that so few economists seem to have actually read the section 'Principles of an Economic Anthropology' that closes the work on the social structures of the economy (Bourdieu 2000*a*). At least five factors contribute to change and this typology goes beyond the strict framework of the market that is being studied.

- The first factor is linked to the fact that the *dominant actors* in a field have a certain ability to impose 'the speed of transformation.... The use of temporal differentiations is one of the principal sources of their power' (Bourdieu 2000*a*: 248). The reproduction of the positions within a field assumes that the forms of capital that characterize the field will always be unequally distributed and this means that the perpetuation of domination cannot be based on any identical reproduction of strategies, because it is assumed that there will be innovation as well. The artistic field and the literary field are both exemplary in this sense, because the pressure for novelty becomes a major characteristic.

- The entry of *new agents* is highly likely to modify the structure of the field. This is certainly a crucial factor in the economic field, because any pressure to innovate in order to free up new sources of profit has led, in certain historical periods, to the collapse of productive structures. This dynamic is reinforced by the fact that economic competition can come from other nations or sectors. It is a factor of change found in most fields: increased access to education changes the way the system functions, just as the renewal of the teaching body in a university inevitably changes the dynamic (Bourdieu 1984).

- A third factor is that 'changes within a field are often linked to changes outside a field. To the concept of crossing frontiers has to be added that of the *redefinition of frontiers* between fields' (Bourdieu 2000a: 249). It is the behaviour of the field's elite that leads to the redefinition of frontiers. Economic examples are not hard to find, in that specialization has led to the creation of new sectors. In information technology, for instance, software production has become independent of hardware production to a point where the hierarchy within the sector has been reversed, as can be seen in the change in profit distribution. *A contrario*, certain radical innovations can lead to the creation of a new sector by uniting former sectors. The encounter between information technology and telecommunications, for example, has brought down some of the best established monopolies of the sixties. This move towards the redefinition of frontiers is especially notable in the economic field, but it does characterize most of the others. Hence the field of the media has a growing effect on the academic field (Bourdieu 1996) and market relationships are starting to infiltrate artistic activity, etc.

- Among all the exchanges that are possible between a field and the outside world, Bourdieu has stressed the importance of interactions with the state. *Competition for power over state power* introduces a fourth powerful factor of change. This factor is again absolutely fundamental for the economic field, if only because the liberal strategy of a return to the market is actually making a noted and notable

365

appeal to state power. This is why the contemporary evolution of the various fields is so marked by conflicts over public intervention (Bourdieu 1997: 209). Bourdieu's many appearances in the political arena (with increasing frequency after 1995) can be explained by this understanding (Bourdieu 2002*a*). His activism matched his ongoing reflections on the characteristics of state nobility and on the nature of the opposition between the public and the private (Bourdieu 1989).

- The final (and frequent) source of change (if not of crisis) is *when habitus and field become desynchronized* because of the *changes* that affect the way that different fields are constructed. This is the case with general transformations affecting demography, lifestyle, and gender relationships across various fields (Bourdieu 2000*a*: 251). Or the simple fact of a change in the rate of equivalence between various forms of capital can be passed on into an entire series of fields, destabilizing the capacity for reaction of any habitus that had been formed in a completely different context. In certain instances, the very complexity of the interdependencies between fields can itself cause *crises*. These crises will come to affect the conditions and the factors of the relevant power relationships. There are many examples of this destabilization in Bourdieu's work.

A conceptual framework that initially appears to privilege reproduction is actually asking the question of how a field can be transformed (Figure 15.1). To use Bourdieu's terminology, the field is endowed with a certain plasticity, and because of this it does not have to be seen as mechanistic, because 'a field only becomes mechanistic when the dominant have the means to destroy the resistance and the responses of the dominated' (Bourdieu 1980*b*: 136). Or again, 'the permanent struggle within the field drives the field. It can be seen incidentally that there is no antimony between structure and history. (...) The structure of the field...is also the principle of its dynamic' (Bourdieu 1980*b*: 200).

### 15.2.9. *The Analysis of Change and of Crises: A Permanent Trait in Bourdieu's Work*

If the above interpretation is correct, then a paradox seems to be at the heart of Bourdieu's work. His writings constantly addressed the general theory of fields and attempted to describe it and to elaborate it, but Bourdieu did not have the time to give a complete formalization. His

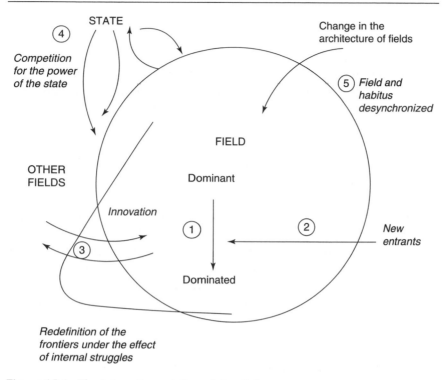

**Figure 15.1.** The interactions at the origin of change

theoretical writings have therefore favoured a superficial reading that has tended to underestimate Bourdieu's contribution to how change and crisis can be understood. Is it not true that the power that underlies reproduction is revealed during a period of crisis? This is why most of his works lead into the analysis of a field's crisis, or show field and habitus becoming desynchronized. The inability of the older generation to adapt to a local marriage market, in the Béarn society of the sixties (Bourdieu 2002*b*). The distress of the Kabyle people, faced with colonial domination of the economy and the heteronomy of the local concept of work (Bourdieu 1972). The crisis in the institution of the university under the effect of the changing student population and the growing heterogeneity of those recruited to teach there (Bourdieu 1984). The suffering and disillusionment of the various categories of wage earners when work changed under the impact of an economic crisis (Bourdieu 1993). The difficulties faced by feminism when it was realized that the invisible structures governing relationships between men and women were permanent (Bourdieu 1998*a*). All these examples call for a re-evaluation of his contribution to the understanding of contemporary societies. They show that theoretical work has not lost its ability to provoke a programme of original research (Table 15.5). Bourdieu's increasingly frequent interventions in the political arena are surely yet another proof of the importance he attached to change: clarifying the general laws of reproduction was only one of the conditions necessary to bring about truly transformative collective action.

## 15.3. Theory of Fields, Mode of *Régulation*: A Homology but Different Aims

Certain rapprochements between Bourdieu's work and regulationist research would support this categorization, which invites reflection on the common traits and the differences in the two approaches (Table 15.6). Bourdieu's project was essentially sociological but it also addressed a programme within the social sciences; *régulation* theory moved away from economics to form links with history and subsequently with political analysis and law.

### 15.3.1. *From Habitus to Institutionally Situated Rationality*

Works with an essentially macroeconomic aim—that is, the investigation of the nature and evolution of accumulation regimes and of modes of *régulation*—have always found it necessary to specify which theory of action should be adopted. The rejection of *homo economicus*—endowed with substantial rationality, an exceptional capacity for calculation, and an almost perfect power of anticipation—has led to the use of the concept of habitus, defined as the matrix where behaviour is formed, where the historical context is crucial (Boyer 1986a). The way that regulationist research has developed has then involved—more implicitly than explicitly—specifying and redefining this contribution.

- The concept of habitus firstly assumes that there is a *restricted sphere* for the definition of action. Neoclassical theory is committed to the supposition that each agent knows the totality of the system of prices, but in fact, as it is costly to gather the necessary information, what happens is that agents form routines that allow them to find their way around the economic sphere in which they usually operate. This is why wage earners and especially the collective organizations known as unions only take into account a limited number of variables—costs

**Table 15.5.** Change at the heart of the analysis of fields

| Field/actors | References | Habitus and field desynchronized | Strategy of dominant actors | Factors of change | | | |
|---|---|---|---|---|---|---|---|
| | | | | New entrants | Endogenous displacement of frontiers between fields | Competition for power over the power of the state |
| Béarn farmers | 'Célibat et condition paysanne' Bourdieu 1962; *Le bal des célibataires* Bourdieu 2002b | Inability of older generation to adapt to a marriage market that is no longer local. | | Competition from non-farmers. | Consequence of the progression of the market economy into access to marriage. | |
| Kabyle society | *Esquisse d'une théorie de la pratique* Bourdieu 1972 | The process of Kablye socialization makes the notion of work alien. | Imposition of colonial norms. | | | Consequence of colonial domination over the organization of social relations. |
| Universities | *Homo academicus* Bourdieu 1984 | The opening of access to university study destabilizes the field. | | Growing heterogeneity of the teaching body as a result of the enlarging of recruitment. | Change of the social composition of the student population. | |

*(cont.)*

**Table 15.5.** (*Continued*)

| Field/actors | References | Habitus and field desynchronized | Strategy of dominant actors | Factors of change | | |
|---|---|---|---|---|---|---|
| | | | | New entrants | Endogenous displacement of frontiers between fields | Competition for power over the power of the state |
| Economic elites | *La noblesse d'État* Bourdieu 1989 | Transformation of the economic regime and impact on the higher education system. | Strategy of redeployment of children from middle-class families. | Creation of new courses of study and business schools. | Internationalization displaces the public frontier. | |
| Wage earners | *La misère du monde* Bourdieu 1993 | Divorce between the expectations built up by a previous configuration of the field and the constraints associated with a new economic regime. | Technological and social innovations in companies and management. | | | Change of economic policies in the direction of liberalism. |

**Table 15.6.** The theory of fields, *régulation* theory: a homology of theoretical constructions?

| | Theory of fields | *Régulation* theory |
|---|---|---|
| 1. Vision | • Society as a series of more or less interdependent fields. | • The mode of *régulation*, the conjunction of a series of institutional forms. |
| 2. Grounds for action | • Habitus as the result of confrontation within one or more fields. | • Institutionally situated rationality. |
| 3. Relations on the micro/intermediate/ macro levels | • The properties of a field hold for all its structural characteristics.<br>• Differentiation is at the heart of each field. | • Evidencing the macro institutional bases of individual behaviours.<br>• Possible complementarity or hierarchy between institutional forms. |
| 4. Conditions of reproduction | • The adjustment of habitus to field, of expectations to the positions actually held. | • Compatibility of the macroeconomic dynamic introduced by the various institutional forms. |
| 5. Factors of change | • Struggles within each field.<br>• Displacement of frontiers and relations between fields as a result of these struggles.<br>• Struggles for the power of the state. | • Struggles around/for the institutional forms.<br>• Alteration of the mode of *régulation* under the effect of the extension of its logic.<br>• Destabilization of the complementarity between political coalition and mode of *régulation*. |
| 6. Forms of crisis | • Lasting (structural) mismatch between habitus and fields.<br>• Competition between the dominant agents opens up possibilities for the dominated. | • Destabilization of institutional forms, the support of the mode of *régulation*.<br>• Incapacity to construct a political coalition capable of bringing about a reconfiguration of institutional forces. |
| 7. Criticisms made of the theory | • A theory of reproduction.<br>• Incapable of analysing transformation. | • An apology for eternal capitalism.<br>• A simple description of the past. |

of consumption, unemployment, productivity (Boyer 1978)—and are generally not capable of internalizing the indirect consequences that will affect them through the macroeconomic impact of the conjunction of a series of decentralized negotiations. Behaviour is inevitably specified in relation to the five *institutional forms* used by *régulation* theory.

371

- Secondly, there are other indicators than price, because the *interiorization of the rules of the game* is essential, as are the effects that this causes in the other actors. This is again illustrated by the example of wage negotiations. It can be shown that even if wage earners and employers share the same preferences and the same objectives, the level of wages and of employment itself depends on the interchanges that take place between the actors. The macroeconomic results come from a number of variables, such as whether only the employers are organized or only the unions, or whether a professional organization has to negotiate with a single union (Bowles and Boyer 1990), and they can differ radically. Most *régulation* theorists, being economists, would be tempted to assert the rules of the game over habitus, but they would not deny the importance of habitus, in that it can explain social differentiation and heterogeneity. If the institutional context changes significantly because of institutional upheavals, it still remains possible to explain a change in macroeconomic regularities without necessarily postulating an equivalent change in the objectives being pursued by the actors (Boyer 1991). To take one example among many: French farmers, who were supposed to be so emblematically Malthusian in the period between the wars, actually became in the sixties the producers responsible for the sort of surpluses that would draw criticism from ecologists. *Régulation* theory tends to stress institutional change, with learning being incorporated in individual agents, when it comes to explaining the transformation of macroeconomic realities.

- It is still possible to maintain that agents' objectives and preferences are shaped in history and by history, as is affirmed by a strong version of institutionalist theory (Douglas 1989). This *malleability of habitus* adds a further evolutionary factor because it links with the political drive towards institutional change, a duality that is again illustrated by an example. In order to interpret the transformation of French capitalism in the nineties, it is of course necessary to analyse the impact of financial deregulation and the opening up to international norms of good governance, but it would also be possible to refer to the conceptual changes that took place within the major French groups and their leaders and to stress how capital became an almost omnipotent driving force in society (Lordon 2002), possibly as a result of the revitalization that came over several generations of state functionaries and entrepreneurs. Whatever the cause, there could never have been such a high incidence of massive share exchange offers and takeovers without a change in institutional context.

Therefore, for *régulation* theory, the institutional forms have a predominant role in the genesis of macroeconomic regularities.

## 15.3.2. *Fields Versus Institutional Forms*

If the two issues are compared term by term, a homology appears between Bourdieu's concept of the field and *régulation* theory's institutional forms. This is not to deny that the two constructions have different objectives and areas of concern.

- Bourdieu's vision of what is known as society is this: the conjunction of a certain number of fields that tend to become autonomous with respect to their foundational logic, but which are in fact interdependent across a series of mechanisms that have previously been specified. (Hence actors are able to move from one field to another and capital can be converted into new forms.) For *régulation* theory, an economic regime emerges from the *compatibility of the set of five institutional forms*, a set that is established *ex post* through the behaviours created by the forms.

- There is a major difference in the respective visions of society and economy that goes beyond this similarity. Bourdieu's sociology aims at the construction of a general theory of fields but makes no attempt to question the fields' *connection* or their coherence as a set. *Régulation* theory only ever analyses the institutional forms as an intermediary stage in the construction of modes of *régulation*, which are conceived as the explanation for a set of institutionalized compromises, autonomous either a priori or in theory.

- Both field and institutional form ensure a twofold movement: from the intermediate level to the micro level, and vice versa. As has already been stressed, the properties of a field do not result from the behaviour of *homo sociologicus* but from the dynamic reproduction of a set of differentiated habituses and inequalities in how the various forms of capital are allocated. Similarly, the partial macroeconomic regularities that *régulation* theory associates with each form are not the simple extrapolation of what is observed for each of the actors. This can be compared to the way in which the Fordist equation for wages is not based on the behaviour of any single firm but is the result of a set of interactions, involving the participation of a large number of heterogeneous firms, whose strategies then become rules in the playing of the game.

- The two approaches generally show the *co-evolution* of habitus and field (Bourdieu) and the *co-evolution* of actors' strategies and institutional forms (*régulation* theory). This trait is particularly notable in Bourdieu's sociology, so much so that it has drawn the criticism— an excessive one, as has been shown—that Bourdieu is trying to bring about a quasi-automatic fit (amounting to a tautology) between expectation and achievement in a field, between disposition and position. The analyses of *régulation* theory are constructed in such a way that they can deliver results only on what goes on at the meso economic level. It is not possible—given the lack of data and of analyses—for *régulation* theory to explain institutional change or the changes in preference described by microeconomic theory. The major indicator of a co-evolution between institutions and individual behaviours is seen in what happens when institutions are brought in from other spheres in an attempt to replicate a mode of *régulation* (Berger and Dore 1996; Boyer and Freyssenet 2000). In very general terms, the result is that individual behaviour and the new institutions become desynchronized, which tends to prove that the malleability of habitus is a long way from being governed by a simple system of incentives carried by the institutions. This is how things work in the real world, as opposed to the theoretical world. The concept of hybridization can be used to explain the mutual adaptation of behaviours and institutions (Boyer et al. 1998) when two economic spaces come into contact.

- Finally, *the intermediate scale* constituted by the *meso level* is important in both theoretical systems. In Bourdieu's sociology, this is the field. In *régulation* theory, this is the institutional form. Even if the same general laws were to be found governing the workings of all the fields, it would still be necessary to consider their interactions in order to arrive at a characterization of the evolution of the whole. This means that there is no direct relation between the actor and the totality that is being analysed. In the same way, the viability of a particular institutional form can only be analysed at the level of micro/meso relations, but it is absolutely necessary to consider the compatibility of the changes it causes on the frontier with other

institutional forms or even within them. The recent work done by
*régulation* theory with respect to institutional hierarchy (Boyer 1999)
and institutional complementarity (Amable 2000; Amable, Ekkehard,
and Palombarini 2000) assumes a movement in two stages from
micro to macro, and this is possible because of the research done
on the complementarity between institutional forms at the meso
level.

At a certain level of abstraction the two issues follow a similar path, even
if *régulation* theory can be seen to diverge as it tries to expound a methodology that could overcome the *macro/micro dilemma* common to all the
social sciences, which seem to be characterized by their search for multiple
scales of analysis. The conflict between methodological individualism and
holism has perhaps obscured the relations between micro and macro for
too long and vice versa.

### 15.3.3. *Under the Appearance of Invariability: Two Analyses of Historical Change*

Both Bourdieu's sociology and *régulation* theory have been criticized for
presenting an analysis of how fields or economic systems can be reproduced, with actors being under the sway of an implacable determinism
that prevents change in any form. Critics take the terms 'habitus' and
*régulation* literally, forgetting that both projects aim to examine the conditions under which change is possible. Two quotations can illustrate this
parallel development. From Bourdieu's sociology:

> To exclude 'subjects' is not to destroy *agents* in favour of some underlying structure,
> the way that certain Marxist structuralists have done. ('Subjects' are valued within
> the philosophy of consciousness and remain a permanent possibility, the ideal
> type of limited case.) This is true even if agents are the products of the structure
> in question, even if they contribute to keeping it viable while remaining within
> it, even if they are able to transform it radically, given well-defined structural
> conditions.

> (Bourdieu 1992*a*: 114–15)

This essay has already outlined in various ways in which Bourdieu has
put this approach into practice. From foundational writings in *régulation*
theory:

> To speak of the *régulation* of a means of production is to try to express how the
> determining structure of a society is reproduced in its general laws. (. . .) A theory

375

of social *régulation* is a global alternative to the theory of general equilibrium. (...) The study of the *régulation* of capitalism cannot be reduced to research into abstract economic laws. It is the study of the transformation of social relations, and the consequent creation of new forms that are both economic and non-economic, that are structured and that in their turn reproduce a determining structure, i.e. the mode of production.

(Aglietta 1976)

Since its origin, the research carried out by *régulation* theory has constantly attempted to work out any changes in the institutional forms and has tried to offer a diagnostic analysis of accumulation regimes and future modes of *régulation* (Aglietta 1998; Boyer 1986*b*, 2000, 2002; Coriat 1991; Petit 1986, 1998; Taddei and Coriat 1993). The similarities are also found at a more analytical level, as has already been stressed in Bourdieu's case: 'There are conflicts within each field and therefore there is history' (Bourdieu 1992*a*: 78). For *régulation* theory, conflict is guided and polarized by the architecture of the institutional forms. These forms are the expression of how *régulation* functions, but in certain crucial historical periods they can determine the form that the institutions will take. *Régulation* theory therefore concentrates on the decline in the mode of *régulation* over time, as the logic of *régulation* and the success of its economic reproduction has an effect; this contrasts with Bourdieu's sociology, where interest centres on the displacement of frontiers and how fields function when there are internal struggles. The difference is caused by a difference in scale between the two programmes of research. For Bourdieu's sociology the scale is principally meso/micro, while for *régulation* theory it is essentially meso/macro.

There is a final convergence and this is the role attributed to the state. In both cases, state power drives change in most fields and most institutional forms. This applies especially to the economic field as analysed by Bourdieu. For some time now, *régulation* theory has been characterized by the way it has made the state the quasi-obligatory point of passage in a number of areas: transformations in the wage-labour nexus (Boyer and Orléan 1991); forms of competition; connections with the international world (Chartres 2002). Its role is even more evident in the institutionalized compromises that fashion social security, the finance system, and the nature of public spending (Delorme and André 1983). For many economic theories, public intervention has a destabilizing character, but for Bourdieu's sociology and *régulation* theory it is both constitutive and constructive.

### 15.3.4. *From the Possibility of Crises to a Typology of Their Various Forms*

It has already been shown that Bourdieu's sociology can be characterized by the permanent possibility and reality of crises (cf. Table 15.5, *supra*); similarly, *régulation* theory places equal stress on investigating *régulation* and on investigating the crises that are found in the same analytic framework. The homology between these two approaches operates on a twofold level. Both systems address the issue of how a crisis can arise. For Bourdieu, it is the result of a clash between *habitus* and *field*; for *régulation* theory, it is the clash between the mode of *régulation* and the permanence of the institutional forms. An example of this is a transformation that takes place outside a field, causing a clash between expectations and strategies for any agent whose habitus was formed in a previous context, perhaps through a shift in power relations. This is also true, *mutatis mutandis*, for *régulation* theory, where a transformation of the international regime can bring out inadequacies in individual and collective behaviour that would normally be sustained by local institutional forms. Such events can change or even radically transform what had previously been determined and can open up struggles for the redefinition of the principles that structure the field or its institutional architecture. The second convergence is when, in a context of crisis for Bourdieu's sociology, competition between the dominant opens up the possibility for the dominated to redefine the rules of the game; in *régulation* theory any inability of the actors to form a viable political coalition can bring about a crisis that would be different in kind from the normal course of events under a stabilized mode of *régulation*.

This has led to *régulation* theory developing a systematic typology of different forms of crisis. This is done much more systematically than in Bourdieu's work. It means that a crucial distinction has to be made within *régulation* theory's economic discipline and theoretical tradition. There are certain macroeconomic adjustments that reduce any instabilities that have previously been accumulated, and that actually consolidate the institutional forms. Examples would be a small crisis or an expression of the mode of *régulation*. These adjustments must not be categorized with episodes where the institutional forms are destabilized, eroded or even destroyed by the economic dynamic, for in these circumstances the mode of *régulation* has entered crisis. Even more seriously, attempts at reconstructing the institutional forms sometimes prove incapable of redressing the unfavourable course of accumulation. It could be claimed that

Bourdieu's work has a parallel configuration, showing how the difficulties in one field can spread to another and result in a crisis of legitimation across the whole set (Bourdieu 1992*a*).

### 15.3.5. *A Critical Position Within the Disciplines*

There is a final similarity: the way that these two theories have been received by the research community. Epistemological and methodological criteria are obviously different in both disciplines, but certain convergences do stand out, with both issues being perceived as going against current practices. Sociology of American inspiration sees in Bourdieu's work an ambitious and therefore limited approach, where reflection flirts with philosophy. It also deplores the way that his empirical works give more attention to breaking down the main components, in order to categorize and analyse them, than they do on the application of proper statistical tests. Secondly, supporters of the application to sociology of rational choice theory stress the heuristic capacity of formulations that unite *homo sociologicus* and *homo economicus,* claiming a power to generate ideas that is absent from Bourdieu's sociology. The response to the first criticism would consist in stressing that Bourdieu's sociology has established itself as a project for the comprehension of the reproduction (and in certain cases the evolution) of the heterogeneity of dispositions, habitus and *illusio*. As has been shown, this challenges that extremely useful fiction: the representative agent. Statistical techniques to evidence the distribution are therefore appropriate. The second criticism shows a radical miscomprehension of Bourdieu. His work consists in extending the concept of interest. He makes the term much broader than the economic interest that is given such a privileged status by those researchers who have been seduced by the economist's model of rational action, in which they see a generative power that is too often merely tautological.

Critics of *régulation* theory develop similar arguments. It is asked why it should be necessary to question the genesis of institutional forms when it ought to be sufficient to examine their impact on economic activity. The use of traditional econometric methods, where economic measurements are used along with variable institutional indicators, runs into difficulties when it tries to show how institutional organization could ever determine performance. Similarly, the hypothesis that rationality is institutionally situated gives the impression of being a simple description, an ad hoc hypothesis in line with the extreme parsimony of the standard neoclassical view. However, the different econometric projects carried out within regulationist research have offered some responses. First of all it has been stressed that institutional parameters do not need to make a linear intervention in a reduced equation explaining growth, for example (Boyer 1988). Secondly, and most importantly, studies over a long period (Boyer 1978) and analyses of international control with reference to the contemporary period (Boyer 1990) confirm the change of *régulation* that becomes associated with the decline in the institutional forms after a period of one to two decades. Finally, it is possible to show analytically that the hypothesis that agents do what is in their best interests, given their particular institutional context (Bowles and Boyer 1990), is sufficient to make the mode of *régulation* highly sensitive to whatever historical conditions have been inherited.

This is not to use the equivalent of Lebaron's analysis of the economists' field, in order to categorize Bourdieu and his school as professional sociologists (Lebaron 2000). The various programmes of sociological research have a priori a greater degree of heterogeneity and autonomy, which contrasts with the drive to integration that seems to hold sway with professional economists. Although regulationist researchers seem to have a lower status, the recognition of Pierre Bourdieu by the Collège de France bears witness to his influence, even if it is an influence that is most clearly seen in the polarization that exists between disciples and violent critics. Whatever the cause, Bourdieu's sociology forms a point of reference, at least in the French academic context, which has both good and bad effects. The case is different with *régulation* theory, which for some time now has had the distinction of attracting the anger of political orthodoxy and of mainstream economic methodology (Mingat, Salmon, and Wolfelsperger 1985). Ironically, the strongest criticisms continue to come from economists who are engaged in similar programmes of conventionalist research (Favereau 1993), or Marxist research (Duménil and Lévy 2002).

### 15.3.6. *Analyses of Contemporary Societies and Economics: Convergences and Cross-Referencing*

The rapprochements do not just concern the general approach adopted in the social sciences (Bourdieu, Passeron, and Chamboredon 1967) and the relative position held in the respective academic field. They are also of significance for some important axes of research and the results of this research. This is hardly surprising in view of the fact that Bourdieu's aim was to intervene in the evolution of a number of social sciences—ethnology, linguistics, history, economics—and that the development of regulationist research has led to the extension of the economic field (understood *strictu sensu*) into areas such as history, political science, law, and anthropology: an example of this has been the attempt to explain the institution of money. There are five points of intersection that ought to be mentioned (Table 15.7).

### 15.3.7. On the Origins of Social Stratification and of Emergent Growth Regimes: the Role of School

The role played by the education system in social reproduction is a constant theme in Bourdieu's sociology, found in the early analytical work (Bourdieu and Passeron 1964, 1970) and the subject of further study and elaboration over the course of time (Bourdieu 1984, 1989). One basic concept stands out: school and, more generally, the education system are matrices that form dispositions, and therefore the positions that will be held in various fields. This invariant remains compatible with significant variations in the way that schools, universities, and higher education are actually organized. Bourdieu's central hypothesis is that the conjunction of family membership and schooling—two factors that are inextricably linked—results in a social heterogeneity that then finds expression in relationships of domination in the various fields.

The contrast is striking with the foundational works of *régulation* theory (Aglietta 1976; Boyer 1978; CEPREMAP-CORDES 1977). This is because the reproduction and differentiation of wages in the Fordist growth regime—as in every other historical precedent—had been driven by the firm, which is why so many regulationist works continue to address the wage-labour nexus (Boyer and Saillard 2002). But the breakdown of the Fordist wage-labour nexus from the end of the seventies showed a growing differentiation of wage relationships (Aglietta and Brender 1983), that is, the definition of the wage-labour nexus according to the sector, the individual, or the firm. Which factor could explain the different paths that wage earners took in the eighties and the nineties? In the French case, there is little doubt that a determining role was played by the school or the university that an agent attended, and in turn this led to broadening the concept of the wage-labour nexus to that of the *relationship between employment and education* (Boyer and Caroli 1993). The long history of the wage-labour nexus can therefore be interpreted as the interaction between the dynamic of the education system (seen both in the sense

**Table 15.7.** Theory of fields, *régulation* theory: a cross-réferencing of themes and results

|  | Theory of fields | *Régulation* theory |
|---|---|---|
| The educational institution | • Matrix for the reproduction of dispositions/habitus.<br>• This theme of research is foundational and recurrent.<br>• Simultaneous analysis of the reproduction and transformation of a hierarchy. | • The firm more than the school is the matrix for the reproduction of wages.<br>• Eventually examined in order to explain the transformations following on from the crisis of Fordism.<br>• Recent research refers to the relation between work and education. |
| The wage-labour nexus/wage relationships. | • This form of domination is not supposed to go across the various fields.<br>• Unhappiness at work, following on from the economic crisis, reveals the transverse nature of the wage connection. | • The wage-labour nexus, especially under Fordism, forms the foundation of an institutional configuration.<br>• The differentiation of sectors and the specialization of competencies lead to an explosion of wage relationships. |
| Economic/social relations | • In theory, the economy is only one of the fields and is subject to a general logic.<br>• Contemporary evolution reflects economic logic in almost every field. | • An economic theory, embedded in a set of social (and political) connections.<br>• Crises overwhelm the economy, which leads to a reinforcement of relations with sociology, law, and politics. |
| The political | • Hardly present in an explicit form in the foundational research.<br>• Progressive recognition of the roles played by: economic policies; the state; politicians; the specific attributes of the political field.<br>• Engagement since 1995 against liberal politics. | • Politics of the exit from the crisis of Fordism as the horizon of the theoretical contribution.<br>• Explicit work on the political and the economic.<br>• An analytic criticism of the likelihood and the merits of competitive *régulation*. |
| The symbolic | • Importance of the symbolic as specific capital, formed from violence and in the form of domination: present in each field.<br>• Recognition of the role of the economic in the dynamics of the fields. | • Originally an approach of 'materialist' inspiration, even if representations are present, in the institutional forms.<br>• Recognition of the role of the symbolic in the legitimation of mode of *régulation* and the acceptance of disequilibria in the economic sphere. |

of general education as well as professional formation) and the evolution of the division of labour within the firm (Caroli 1995).

Introducing the heterogeneity of the relationship between employment and education changes the perspective taken on institutional reconstruction and the emergence of new growth regimes (Boyer 1995): an example is the growing inequality in remuneration that results from the skills learned in the education system and later in the productive system (Beffa, Boyer, and Touffut 1999). This joint evolution of wage relationships and educational pathways brings in a new element: life-long professional development makes a link between skills (generic and transferable) and know-how (specialized and localized) (Boyer 2001*b*). A surprising, if partial, convergence emerges with an issue that is emblematic for Bourdieu's sociology. The role of education takes central place in the production and reproduction of inequalities. This is a theme that *régulation* theory had neglected for some time.

### 15.3.8. *From Varied Relations of Domination to the General Domination of Wage Earners*

When a *régulation* theorist reads the works produced by Bourdieu before the nineties, a remarkable absence is evident: there is no mention of wage relationships as a constituting factor for any of the various fields, not even the economic field. This is surprising, given that Bourdieu is known to have been a critical but attentive reader of Marx. A change came with his work on the suffering of wage earners in various sectors of French society (Bourdieu (ed.) 1993). At this time he was also becoming politically engaged in response to the social and human damage that was being caused by both liberal and conservative policies (Bourdieu 1998*a*, 2002*a*). Therefore, even if there was no theory to support it, contemporary domination could be seen to be hitting wage earners especially hard. This showed how French society had been transformed under the effects of the Fordist crisis, which should give no grounds for surprise when it is recalled that Bourdieu always insisted that the social sciences were historically situated.

This is why it is possible to talk of cross-referencing Bourdieu's sociology with *régulation* theory. Bourdieu's work takes into account the effects of the economic crisis within each field. It was therefore forced to incorporate the fact that the wage-labour nexus is the essential factor that determines the individual worker's situation. *Régulation* theory, as has just been shown, had been forced to account for the consequences of the differentiation of skills and the growth in specialization as societies moved out of crisis. It no longer made any sense to refer to a canonical wage-labour nexus, that is, the typical wage earner's contact within Fordist industries. Instead, attention had to be given to re-examining the role played by wage relationships within the coherence and the reactivity of the mode of *régulation*. The merits of flexible wage relationships have been rediscovered in such sectors as the construction industry (Campinos-Dubernet 1984; Du Tertre 2002) and the service industry (Petit 1998). Parallel to this, certain works of economic sociology have made the same discovery: some ways of organizing wage relationships that were considered atypical in periods of high growth—such as for show business contract workers—have expanded in the last decade. This is because they correspond to the constraints—or even to the opportunities—of an economic context that is marked by uncertainty, by the transformation of the processes of production, and by strong competition for access to employment (Menger 2002).

It can therefore be seen how economic sociology has rediscovered the centrality of the wage-labour nexus, while institutionalist macroeconomics has been forced to take into account the heterogeneity in status among wage earners. Both approaches are moving towards a diagnostic that is close, if not identical: the dominated and recessive forms of yesterday tend to develop and impose their logic today.

## 15.3.9. *From Society to Economy . . . and Vice Versa*

For Bourdieu, the economic field was in his early works only one among many, located in a set subject to general laws. The categories of economics—interest, capital, profit, and market—were used in order to form a better understanding of the logic (often concealed under *illusio*) of how such fields as art and science are structured. From the start of the nineties, particular attention was given to investigating the economic field, and this should not only be seen as Bourdieu applying his theory to a field that he had previously neglected, but also as a response to the way that capital (understood in the strictest economic form) had begun to structure fields that had once been autonomous: art, sport, and the media. To read the successive works of Bourdieu is to be struck by increasingly precise references to the work of economists (Bourdieu 2000*a*) and by increasingly frequent interventions in the sphere of political economy in order to denounce the consequences of neoliberalism (Bourdieu 2001*c*, 2002*a*). It may seem paradoxical, but some of Bourdieu's media appearances make him look like a committed member of the anti-globalization group ATTAC (Carles 2001; Grass 1999): the economic field is the object both of analysis and—with increasing frequency—of denunciation.

Regulationist research has followed a similar path. The original work came from economists who were working in what might be called economic administration and who therefore had to use economic criteria. However, things have moved on since the foundational research and the hypothesis has been rejected that economic analysis could be carried out completely independently of social relations (Aglietta 1976; Boyer and Mistral 1978). As the issues have deepened, interest in the political aspect has grown. The crisis of Fordism was seen to have had a direct effect, in the surge in public deficit and debt. Controversy also grew up about just how viable and legitimate were the institutions associated with the post-war growth years. It was only logical for research to investigate how social movements relate to institutional change. Other questions that have been raised include the reversal of the rule of law (when it protects the dominated for a time) and the formation of political coalitions and credible and legitimate economic policies (Lordon 1997*a*; Théret 1999*b*).

The importance of this shift can be seen in the way that regulationist work is now involved with issues from the other social sciences, such as the anthropological foundation of currency or the factors underlying monetary sovereignty (Aglietta and Orléan 1998, 2002). A new generation of work on *régulation* theory has brought about a complete reinterpretation of the very concept of Fordism in the light of an analysis in terms of social mediation. This has led to the concepts of *régulation* and crisis being broadened to take into account the possibility of a mismatch between the viability of a macroeconomic regime and the legitimation of a societal mode of *régulation* (Théret 1999*b*). This is why a crisis at the level of the economic regime does not necessarily cause a social or political crisis. The symbolic order has a range of possibilities within it that tend to legitimize any actual evolutions, no matter how dramatic they may seem to an economist (Aglietta et al. 2000, summed up in Boyer and Saillard 2002: 543–50). After the bursting of the dotcom bubble in the United States, for example, there was a marked contrast between the growing number of bankruptcies and financial scandals and the silence of the political opposition, not to mention the complete absence of the sort of popular political unrest that has always accompanied equivalent scandals throughout American history.

## 15.3.10. *Politics: A Vision and a Division of the Social World and a Vehicle for Institutional Forms*

The theme of politics can be found throughout Bourdieu's work, taking different forms over time and according to which field was under analysis. In his first works on Algeria, it was present in the way that colonialism is shown to have affected daily living and to have destabilized the environment. When the analysis shifted to seventies French society, politics became an endogenous factor in the setting up of groups: 'The change from being a practical group to being an instituted group (class, nation etc.) presupposes this construction: a principle of classification that is capable of producing the set of distinctive properties that would characterise the group' (Bourdieu 1981: 70). This is an essentially political concept, hence this original definition: 'Politics begins, properly speaking, with the denunciation of the tacit contract of membership of the established order that defined the original *doxa*; in other words, political subversion presupposes cognitive subversion and a conversion in the way that the world is seen' (Bourdieu 1981: 69). A third characteristic stressed by Bourdieu is the way that conflict is necessary in this institutionalization of the social: 'The struggle is to be found therefore in the very principle of the construction of class (social, ethnic, sexual etc.): no group exists that is not the site for a struggle for the imposition of the legitimate principle of how groups should be constructed' (Bourdieu 1981: 71), while 'orthodoxy will always resist the forward motion of any heretical criticism'.

It is striking just how original this approach is in its attempt to synthesize the *double origin—cognitive and political—of a group's social identity*. It anticipates certain currents in contemporary research (Figure 15.2). *Régulation* theory (in its historical analysis of the growth regime of the post-war years) narrates the emergence of institutionalized compromises that supported and were mostly caused by the *political conflicts* provoked by the crisis of the thirties and the years just after the war, although it runs the risk of underestimating those aspects linked to representations (Chanteau 2003). The theory of conventions insists in its turn on aspects of the emergence of institutions and organizations that are more directly *cognitive*, but this approach neglects somewhat the struggles that take place for state power, unless this is being very indirectly addressed through the concept of testing (Boltanski and Thévenot 1991).

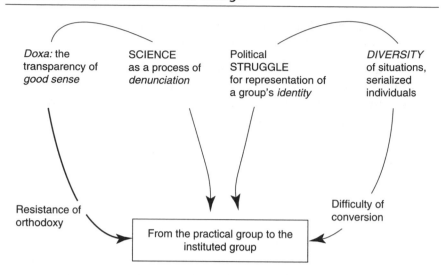

**Figure 15.2.** Politics: a conversion in the way the world is seen

*Source*: Elaborated after Bordieu (1981, 2000b).

The later works of Bourdieu's sociology brought a shift in how analysis is applied: it no longer limits itself to examining the impact of politics on a given field, looking at how the field is being destabilized or reinforced. What matters is to analyse the *political field* in its own right, and to examine to what extent the general theory—that has been progressively elaborated across such fields as the religious, the artistic, or the scientific—can be said to apply to the political field or not, or whether any typical characteristics of the political field emerge (Bourdieu 2000*b*). The tendency of the field to close on itself is actually counterbalanced by the fact that politicians have to justify themselves vis-à-vis the popular verdict and that, in addition, they are struggling for power over the state and not just for their own advancement or for political space as these are defined *strictu sensu*. The gap between professionals and non-professionals is somewhat reminiscent of that between clergy and laity in the religious field, but in this case there are actors who are not explicitly political—such as journalists—who can form part of the field and play a significant role, perhaps even an essential one. The comparative method can offer an analysis of how the political field functions. Both general traits and specific characteristics can be seen (Table 15.8).

**Table 15.8.** The political field: the general and the specific

| Components | Characteristics | |
| --- | --- | --- |
| | General | Specific |
| Degree of autonomy | Tendency of the field to close on itself. | ... but policies have to be justified by popular verdict. ... and by struggle for power over the state. |
| Definition of the field | Gap between professionals and non-professionals. | ... Non-politicians (journalists) may take part. |
| Configuration of the field | The hierarchy of the dominant and the dominated is permanent but individuals may change position. | Concentration of power in an oligarchy. |
| Type of capital | Reputation and celebrity. | ... Sensitivity to scandal. |
| Metaphor | Actors' game within the field. | The theatre of politics: the stage and the wings. |

*Source:* After Bourdieu 2000*b*.

Bourdieu's political engagement became increasingly evident from the nineties (Bourdieu 1998*b*, 2002*a*; Carles 2001; Grass 1999). A critical reader might note that the positions he adopted in this final evolution were not always the result of applying his sociological theories to the political field. His engagement actually came from having observed the consequences that conservative policies were having for certain social groups. His political intervention has been perceived by his sociological opponents as purely polemical and ideological, but the same canonical definition can be found in this work as he proposed in his earliest writings: '*The political field (can) be described as a game in which the stake is the legitimate imposition of how the social world should be seen and divided*' (Bourdieu 2001*b*: 67).

The authors of *régulation* theory have followed a different trajectory. They have become aware of the paradoxical consequences of their analyses and their suggestions concerning the conduct of those economic policies introduced by governments of the left after 1981: their analysis of the crisis of Fordism has often been used by those responsible for the changes or by socialist ministers, but the politics of governments of the left is inspired far more by the politicians' own left-wing traditions, traditions that have nothing to say about the fact that the crisis of Fordism is unresolved, and that the internationalization of the economy considerably changes the possibilities open to the institutionalized compromises carried by the left. There has also been a significant divergence in the personal and professional paths of the founders of *régulation* theory. Certain authors have tried to put into practice the political programmes drawn from previous research, either as politicians (Lipietz 1984, 1993) or as consultants (Gauron 1999). Others have tried to reconcile political and economic consultancy with the pursuit of their own research, which has moved to addressing the weightier themes of the day, such as international finance or Europe (Aglietta 1998). And others have preferred to stay apart from any advocacy in political economy, even though their research could well have been of relevance for an understanding of the political scene (Lordon 1997*a*, 1997*b*, 2002; Théret 1992, 1999*a*, 1999*b*). None of this has stopped these same authors making vigorous interventions in public debate (Lordon 2000, 2003).

The most remarkable evolution in the programme of *régulation* theory came when the relationship between the economic and the political spheres became central. Two explanations for this can be offered. Firstly, the somewhat naive question had to be answered why the suggestions of *régulation* theorists did not find any supporters, that is, a hegemonic bloc that would put these suggestions into effect. Secondly, the events of the nineties showed the close connection between economic crisis and the collapse of political coalitions, for example in Italy (Palombarini 2001) or in Japan (Boyer and Yamada 2000). It might even be asserted that regulationist economists became increasingly preoccupied with an integrated treatment of economics and politics because this stage would seem to be essential before any recommendations or interventions can be made in the sphere of economic policy (Boyer 2001*c*). Given the pressure of events and the urgent need to intervene, from 1995 onwards Bourdieu seems to have made the opposite choice (Bourdieu 1998*a*, 2001*c*), probably because he had access to a much greater stock of social recognition than the economists who still represented *régulation* theory.

### 15.3.11. *The Position of the Symbolic Within* Régulation *and the Impact of the Economic in the Various Fields*

*Régulation* theory was part of the critical re-evaluation of the Marxist heritage and therefore actors' representations and ideologies are inevitably present in the way that the institutional forms function on a day-to-day basis, but there is never any specific analysis in the foundational writing. Symbolic capital is by contrast an essential category in Bourdieu's sociology. It appears in his very first works and has made a major contribution to the social sciences (Terray 2002). The specialized nature of their work—rather than deliberately ignoring other issues—led *régulation* theorists to concentrate on the treatment of economic capital, given that their early work aimed at explaining essentially economic phenomena: inflation, growth, productivity, the evolution of long-term profit rates, etc.

To examine how the two research programmes have developed is to see a growing number of common concerns. Bourdieu's sociology has given increasing attention to the impact of capital, as understood in the proper economic sense, and has researched how capital has penetrated and taken root in every field. It has already been stressed how Bourdieu made greater reference to economics from the mid-nineties: as a discipline, an object, and a function within other fields. *Régulation* theory, on the other hand, began to ask implicit and explicit questions on the nature of the symbolic during the course of its research on the five institutional forms, as has been noted with reference to the nineties. An example is the research carried out into the frames of reference that legitimized the return to power of neoliberal ideology (Théret 1999*a*). The question of symbolic power came into play when it was considered how the economic policies of the post-war growth years were initially changed and then completely reversed (Lordon 1999). The development of research proving the impossibility of an individualist foundation for currency led to the question of violence (Aglietta and Orléan 1982) and then to more general questions on the nature of legitimacy and sovereignty (Aglietta and Orléan 1998, 2002). The determining nature of beliefs was again significant in the analysis of technological innovation (information and communications technology) and/or organizational innovation (start-ups), or in the process of evaluating those financiers who were active in the new sectors (Boyer 2002; Orléan 2002).

Belief and the symbolic (i.e. representations that are for the most part non-economic) were therefore found to be at the very heart of the one field that is supposed to be emblematic of pure economic rationality: the financial markets. These factors have had an impact on the evolution of stock exchanges, on rates of exchange, and consequently on macroeconomic evolutions themselves. *Nolens volens, régulation* theory has found itself engaged in one of the most difficult programmes of research in the contemporary social sciences. The *symbolic* has come to be seen as

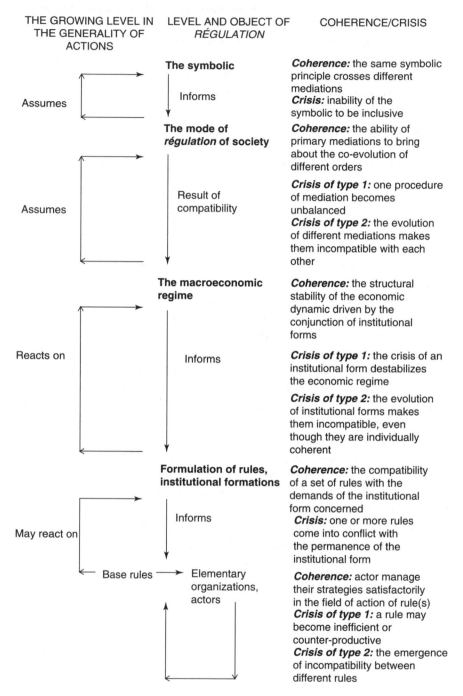

**Figure 15.3.** The symbolic as a guarantor of modes of regulation

*Source*: Aglietta, Boyer, Lordon, Oreléan, Theret (2000).

a determining factor in the light of transformations observed over the last two decades, particularly in the domain of the legitimation of economic policies. Social mediations are somehow legitimized by the symbolic: it crowns the macroeconomic regime (Figure 15.3). *A contrario*, it would appear that the severest crises are those that affect the symbolic order itself, and this has led to *régulation* theory renewing its understanding of the different levels and types of crisis.

The aim of forming a general theory is at the heart of Bourdieu's project, while *régulation* theory originally presented itself as a theory with an apparently somewhat limited aim: to form an understanding of capitalism's transformation, its modes of *régulation*, and its crises. The project of giving an economic treatment to these themes turned out to be formidable enough, but, several decades later, *régulation* theory set itself an even more ambitious task (Aglietta et al. 2000). Economics, considered as a formal discipline, had seen the triumph of an economism without precedent, and many social sciences were continuing to trade their particular versions of methodological individualism (founded on hypotheses of rationality that are typical of economics), and yet here were economists who were ready to open up their work to the social sciences (Figures 15.3).

## 15.4. Conclusion

This attempt to put Bourdieu's work into perspective has shown how certain elements in it need reinterpretation, while there are also important similarities with some heterodox approaches in economics. The preceding arguments suggest four main conclusions: (1) Bourdieu's use of the vocabulary of neoclassical theory—that is, the concepts of interest, profit, capital, and market—has led to a reductionist interpretation of his work. Bourdieu defines interest in terms that have nothing to do with any utilitarian or economic project. Profit designates simply the remunerations that are specific to each field, rather than their monetary conversion. Capital refers to the accumulation of the skills necessary to operate within a field, not to the sum total of capital in the economic sense. Finally, the stress placed on the relations between the dominant and the dominated is far from being a statement of support for the irenic vision of the market that has been developed by those theories that posit equality—*de jure* and thus de facto—of agents within markets. The theory of fields, when each element is elaborated in turn, constitutes a truly original system, and it can serve to inspire *alternative economic research*. (2) It is a serious error to see Bourdieu as only able to conceive of the *reproduction* of invariant positions in a field. The opposite is true. To put his historical analysis into perspective and to elucidate his basic concepts brings out a multiplicity of *factors of evolution and change*, not to say *of open conflict*. Most of Bourdieu's works can be seen as moving towards an analysis of the crisis that could result from the strategies of innovation adopted by the dominant in a field, from the entry of new actors (whose habitus has been formed in other fields and contexts) or from the endogenous redefinition of the frontiers between fields under the effect of the struggles taking place within these fields. The role played by competition for power over state power is also essential and must not be forgotten: by this is meant the role played by the state in setting up the evolution of a field. Finally, a change in the general context can make habitus and field desynchronized, something that is frequently observed in contemporary societies. (3) Bourdieu's theory therefore carries a number of implications for the programme of *regulationist research*. The *concept of habitus* originally seemed to be relevant because it could account for the historicity of preferences (as characterized by microeconomic theories) and their subsequent evolution under changes in the institutional context. A significant proportion of new institutionalist theories— following on for example from Douglass North—can be said to have adopted this point of view (North 1990). This applies particularly to those Anglo-Saxon researchers working in the programme of economic sociology, and Bourdieu was one of the initiators of this programme. Recent work on regulationist issues has brought deeper understanding and the development of a holistic individualism that sees *rationality defined by context*, particularly the institutional context. In the long term, the structuring of the institutional forms determines the dynamic of habitus, but as a model this remains approximate and temporally limited. (4) It is clear that Bourdieu's sociology and *régulation* theory do not have the same objectives, nor do they develop identical notions and concepts. It is therefore all the more remarkable to note a convergence regarding the hypothesis of the *central role played by the political*: both systems see politics as constituting the social identity of a group and as guaranteeing the institutionalized compromises that are at the heart of all modes of *régulation* and growth regimes. It is therefore not possible to bring about a closure of the discipline of sociology (in an attempt to explain the social by the social) and it is equally impossible to bring about a closure of the discipline of economics (in an attempt to found the economy on strict economic rationality). Involvement with the political aspect is essential: firstly, in order to understand how a field functions or what characteristics a mode of *régulation* has; secondly, in order to analyse the crises that arise.

If this analysis is accepted, then it follows that Bourdieu's thought still has considerable generative power. It is to be hoped that it will inspire new interpretations and research in the various fields of the social sciences.

# References

Aglietta, M. (1976). *Régulation et Crises du Capitalisme*. Paris: Calmann-Lévy.

——(1998). 'Le Capitaisme de Demain', *Notes de la Fondation Saint-Simon*, Novembre.

——and Brender, A. (1983). *Métamorphoses de la Société Salariale*. Paris: Calmann-Lévy.

——and Orléan, A. (1982). *La Violence de la Monnaie*. Paris: PUF.

————(1998). *La Monnaie Souveraine*. Paris: Éditions Odile Jacob.

————(2002). *La Monnaie entre Violence et Confiance*. Paris: Éditions Odile Jacob.

——Boyer, R., Lordon, F., Orléan, A., and Théret, B. (2000). 'La Théorie de la Régulation: Noveaux Fondements, Analyses et Propositions', CEPREMAP Ronéotype, Paris: CEPREMAP.

Akerlof, G. (1990). 'The Fair-Wage Hypothesis and Unemployment', *Quarterly Journal of Economics*, 105: 255–83.

Amable, B. (2000). 'Institutional Complementarity and Diversity of Social Systems of Innovation and Production', *Review of International Political Economy*, 7: 645–87.

——Boyer, R., and Lordon, F. (1995). 'L'ad hoc en Économie: La Paille de la Poutre', in A. D'Autume and J. Cartelier (eds.), *L'Économie devient-elle une Science Dure?* Paris: Economica.

——Ekkehard, E., and Palombarini, S. (2000). 'Institutional Complementarity: Labor Markets and Finance', CEPREMAP Mimeograph, Paris: CEPREMAP.

Becker, G. (1996). *Accounting for Tastes*. Cambridge, MA: Harvard University Press.

Beffa, J. L., Boyer, R., and Touffut, J.-P. (1999). 'Les Relations Salarieles en France: État, Enterprises, Marchés Financiers', *Notes de la Fondation Saint-Simon*, Juin.

Berger, S. and Dore, R. (eds.) (1996). *National Diversity and Global Capitalism*. Ithaca: Cornell University Press.

Boltanski, L. and Thévenot, L. (1991). *De la Justification: Les Économies de la Grandeur*. Paris: Gallimard.

Bourdieu, P. (1958). *Sociologie de l'Algérie*. Paris: PUF.

——(1962). 'Célibat et Condition Paysanne', *Études Rurales*, 5–6: 32–135.

——(1966). *L'Amour de l'Art. Les Musées et Leur Public*. Paris: Minuit.

——(1972). *Esquisse d'une Théorie de la Pratique*. Paris: Seuil.

——(1979). *La Distinction. Critique Sociale du Jugement*. Paris: Minuit.

Bourdieu, P. (1980a). *Le Sens Pratique*. Paris: Minuit.

—— (1980b). *Questions de Sociologie*. Paris: Minuit.

—— (1981). 'Décrire et Prescrire: Note sur les Conditions de Possibilité et les Limites de l'Efficacité Politique', *Actes de la Recherche en Sciences Sociales*, 38: 69–74.

—— (1984). *Homo Academicus*. Paris: Minuit.

—— (1987). *Choses Dites*. Paris: Minuit.

—— (1989). *La Noblesse d'État. Grandes Ecoles et Esprit de Corps*. Paris: Minuit.

—— (1992a). *Réponses. Pour une Anthropologie Réflexive*. Entretien avec L. Wacquant, Paris: Seuil.

—— (1992b). *Les Règles de l'Art. Genèse et Structure du Champ Littéraire*. Paris: Seuil.

—— (ed.) (1993). *La Misère du Monde*. Paris: Seuil.

—— (1996). *Sur la Télévision*. Paris: Liber.

—— (1997). *Méditations Pascaliennes*. Paris: Seuil.

—— (1998a). *La Domination Masculine*. Paris: Seuil.

—— (1998b). *Contre-Feux 1. Propos pour Servir à la Résistance contre l'Invasion Neo-Libérale*. Paris: Liber.

—— (2000a). *Les Structures Sociales de l'Économie*. Paris: Seuil.

—— (2000b). *Propos sur le Champ Politique*. Lyon: Presses Universitaires de Lyon.

—— (2001a). *Science de la Science et Réflexivité*. Paris: Raisons d'Agir.

—— (2001b). *Langue et Pouvoir Symbolique*. Paris: Seuil.

—— (2001c). *Contre-Feux 2. Pour un Mouvement Social Européen*. Paris: Raisons d'Agir.

—— (2002a). *Interventions Politiques 1961–2001*. Paris: Agone Èditeur.

—— (2002b). *Le Bal des Célibataires. Crise de la Société Paysanne en Béarn*. Paris: Seuil.

—— and Passeron, J.-C. (1964). *Les Héritiers: Les Étudiants et la Culture*. Paris: Minuit.

—— —— (1970). *La Reproduction: Éléments pour une Théorie du Système d'Enseignement*. Paris: Minuit.

—— —— and Chamboredon, J.-C. (1967). *Le Métier de Sociologue*. Paris: EHESS.

Bowles, P. and Boyer, R. (1990). 'Labour Market Flexibility and Decentralisation as Barriers to High Employment?', in R. Brunetta and C. dell'Aringa (eds.), *Labour Relations and Economic Performance*. London: Macmillan.

Boyer, R. (1978). 'Les Salaires en Longue Période', *Économie et Statistique*, 103: 27–57.

—— (1986a). *La Théorie de la Régulation: Une Analyse Critique*. Paris: La Découverte.

—— (1986b). *La Flexibilité du Travail en Europe*. Paris: La Découverte.

—— (1988). 'Formalizing Growth Regimes Within a Regulation Approach: A Method for Assessing the Economic Consequences of Technological Change', in G. Dosi, C. Freeman, R. Nelson, G. Silverberg, and L. Soete (eds.), *Technical Change and Economic Theory*. London: Pinter.

—— (1990). 'Le Bout du Tunnel? Stratégies Conservatrices et Nouveau Régime d'Accumulation', *Économies et Societes*, 5: 5–66.

—— (1991). 'Capital Labor Relation and Wage Formation: Continuities and Changes of National Trajectories among OECD Countries', in T. Mizoguchi (ed.),

*Making Economies More Efficient and More Equitable: Factors Determining Income Distribution.* Oxford: Oxford University Press.

——(1995). 'Wage Austerity or/and an Educational Push: The French Dilemma', *Labour,* Special Issue 1995: S19–S65.

——(1999). 'Le Politique à l'Ère de la Mondialisation et de la Finance: Le Point sur Quelques Recherches Régulationnistes', *L'Année de la Régulation 1999,* 3: 13–75.

——(2000). 'Is a Finance-led Growth Regime a Viable Alternative to Fordism? A Preliminary Analysis', *Economy and Society,* 29: 111–45.

——(2001*a*). 'Les Économistes Face aux Innovations qui Font Epoque', *Revue Economique,* 52: 1065–115.

——(2001*b*). 'Promoting Learning in the Enterprise', Communication prepared for the OECD Conference on Adult Learning Policies, Seoul, Korea, 5–7 December 2001.

——(2001*c*). 'Lorsque l'Economiste Rencontre le Politique', Préface à S. Palombarini, in *La Rupture du Compromis Social Italien.* Paris: CNRS Editions.

——(2002). *La Croissance Début de Siècle.* Paris: Albin Michel.

——(2003). 'L'Avenir de l'Économie Comme Discipline', *Alternatives Économiques,* 57: 60–3.

——and Caroli, E. (1993). 'Changement du Paradigme Productif et Rapport Éducatif', CEPREMAP Discussion Paper, Paris: CEPREMAP.

——and Freyssenet, M. (2000). *Les Modèles Productifs.* Paris: La Découverte.

——and Mistral, J. (1978). *Accumulation, Inflation, Crises.* Paris: PUF.

——and Orléan, A. (1991). 'Les Transformations des Conventions Salariales entre Théorie et Histoires: D'Henry Ford au Fordisme', *Revue Economique,* 42: 233–72.

——and Saillard, Y. (2002). *Théorie de la Régulation: L'Etat des Savoirs.* Paris: La Découverte.

——and Yamada, T. (eds.) (2000). *Japanese Capitalism in Crisis.* London: Routledge.

——Charron, E., Jürgens, U., and Tolliday, S. (eds.) (1998). *Between Imitation and Innovation.* Oxford: Oxford University Press.

Caillé, A. (1994). *Don, Intérêt et Désintéressement.* Paris: La Découverte.

Cameron, S. (2002). *The Economics of Sin: Rational Choice or No Choice At All?* Cheltenham: Elgar.

Campinos-Dubernet, M. (1984). 'Emploi et Gestion de la Main-d'Oeuvre dans la BTP', *Dossier du CEREQ,* 34.

Carles, P. (2001). *La Sociologie est un Sport du Combat.* Buena Vista: Video.

Caroli, E. (1995). *Formation, Institutions, et Croissance Économique,* Doctoral Thesis. Paris: Institut d'Etudes Politiques.

Chanteau, J.-P. (2003). 'La Dimension Socio-Cognitive des Institutions et de la Rationalité', in *L'Année de la Régulation,* vol. 7. Paris: Presses Sciences Po.

Chartres, J.-A. (2002). 'Le Changement de Modes de Régulation: Apports et Limits de la Formalisation', in R. Boyer and Y. Saillard (eds.), *Théorie de la Régulation: L'État des Savoirs.* Paris: La Découverte.

Coriat, B. (1991). *Penser à l'Envers: Travail et Organisation dans la Firme Japonais.* Paris: C. Bourgois.

Delorme, R. and André, C. (1983). *L'État et l'Economie.* Paris: Seuil.

Douglas, M. (1989). *Ainsi Pensent les Institutions.* Paris: Editions Usher.

Duménil, G. and Lévy, D. (2002). *Économie Marxiste du Capitalisme.* Paris: La Découverte.

Du Tertre, C. (2002). 'Une approche Sectorielle du Travail', in R. Boyer and Y. Saillard (eds.), *Théorie de la Régulation: L'État des Savoirs.* Paris: La Découverte.

Elias, N. (1974). *La Sociéte de Cour.* Paris: Calmann-Levy.

Favereau, O. (1993). 'Théorie de la Régulation et Economie des Conventions: Canevas pour une Confrontation', *La Lettre de la Régulation,* no. 7.

—— (2001). 'L'Économie du Sociologue ou: Penser (l'Orthodoxie) a Partir de Pierre Bourdieu', in B. Lahire (ed.), *Le Travail Sociologique de Pierre Bourdieu.* Paris: La Decouverte.

Fligstein, N. (2001). *The Architecture of Markets.* Princeton: Princeton University Press.

Fourcade-Gourinchas, M. (2002). 'Les Économistes et Leurs Discours: Traditions Nationales et Science Universelle', *Sciences de la Societé,* no. 53.

Garcia, M. F. (1986). 'La Construction Sociale d'un Marche Parfait: Le Marche au Cadran de Fontaines-en-Sologne', *Actes de la Recherche en Sciences Sociales,* 65: 2–13.

Gauron, A. (1999). *L'Oeuvre Réformatrice de Pierre Bérégovoy.* Paris: Comité pour l'Histoire Économique et Financière.

Grass, G. (1999). *Vu d'en Bas: Entretien avec Pierre Bourdieu.* Cologne: Arte Video.

Hildenbrand, W. (1997). 'On the Empirical Evidence of Microeconomic Demand Theory', in A. d'Autume and J. Cartelier (eds.), *Is Economics Becoming a Hard Science?* Cheltenham: Edward Elgar.

Kirman, A. (1992). 'Whom and What Does the Representative Individual Represent?', *Journal of Economic Perspectives,* 6: 117–36.

Laferté, G. (2002). *Folklore Sauvant et Folklore Commercial.* Paris: These EHESS.

Lebaron, F. (2000). *La Croyance Économique. Les Économistes entre Science et Politique.* Paris: Seuil.

Lesourne, J. (1991). *Économie de l'Ordre et du Désordre.* Paris: Économisa.

Lipietz, A. (1984). *L'Audace ou l'Enlisement.* Paris: La Découverte.

—— (1993). *Vert-espérance. L'Avenir de l'Écologie Politique.* Paris: La Découverte.

Lordon, F. (1997a). *Les Quadratures de la Politique Économique.* Paris: Albin Michel.

—— (1997b). 'Endogenous Structural Change and Crisis in a Multiple Time Scales Growth Model', *Journal of Evolutionary Economies,* 7: 1–21.

—— (1999). 'Croyances Économiques et Pouvoir Symbolique', *L'Année de la Régulation 1999,* vol. 3. Paris: La Découverte.

—— (2000). *Fonds de Pension: Piège a Cons? Mirage de la Démocratie Salariale.* Paris: Raison d'Agir.

—— (2002). *La Politique du Capital.* Paris: Odile Jacob.

—— (2003). *Et la Vertu Sauvera Le monde . . . : Après la Débâcle Financière, le Salut par l'Éthique*. Paris: Raisons d'Agir.

Menger, P.-M. (2002). *Portrait de l'Artiste en Travailleur: Métamorphose du Capitalisme*. Paris: Seuil.

Mingat, A., Salmon, P., and Wolfelsperger, A. (1985). *Méthodologie Économique*. Paris: PUF.

North, D. C. (1990). *Institutions, Institutional Change and Economic Performance*. Cambridge: Cambridge University Press.

Palombarini, S. (2001). *La Rupture du Compromis Social Italien*. Paris: CNRS Editions.

Petit, P. (1986). *Slow Growth and the Service Economy*. London: Pinter.

—— (1998). 'Formes Structurelles et Régimes de Croissance de l'Après Fordisme', *L'Année de la Régulation 1998*. Paris: La Découverte.

Spence, M. (1973). 'Job Market Signaling', *Quarterly Journal of Economics*, 87: 353–74.

Stiglitz, J. (1987). 'The Causes and the Consequences of the Dependence of Quality on Price', *Journal of Economic Literature*, 25: 1–48.

Taddei, D. and Coriat, B. (1993). *Made in France*. Paris: Librairie Générale Française.

Terray, E. (2002). 'Réflexions sur la Violence Symbolique', in J. Lojkine (ed.), *Les Sociologies Critiques du Capitalisme*. Paris: PUF.

Théret, B. (1992). *Régimes Économiques de l'Ordre Politique*. Paris: PUF.

—— (1999a). 'La Régulation Politique: Le Point de Vue d'un Économiste', in J. Commaille and B. Jobert (eds.), *Les Métamorphoses de la Régulation Politique*. Paris: LGDJ.

—— (1999b). 'L'Effectivité de la Politique Economique: De l'Autopoièse des Systèmes Sociaux à la Typologie du Social', in *L'Année de la Régulation 1999*. Paris: La Découverte.

White, H. (2002). *From Network to Market*. Princeton: Princeton University Press.

# Index

abandonment, and organizational
  change 94
Abolafia, M., and commodity
  exchanges 168–9
Abramovitz, Moses 255–6
*Academy of Management Journal* 113
action, and structuration theory 187, 188
actors:
  and organizational
    institutionalism 180–1, 184
  agency for other actors 185–6
  agency for principles 186
  agency for the self 185
  agentic actors 186
  conceptions of 181
  decentring of 181–2, 183
  paradox of embedded agency 186
  social agency 184–5
  and social network analysis, actor
    attributes 160–1
  and structuration theory 187
adaptation:
  and organizational ecology 205, 206,
    216
  and problemistic search 90
adaptive efficiency, and institutional
  change 293
agency:
  for other actors 185–6
  and paradox of embedded 186
  for principles 186
  for the self 185
  and structuration theory 187
Aglietta, M. 375–6
agricultural experimentation stations 277
allocation, and economic distribution 329
Allport, Floyd 32
ambiguity, and learning under 75, 76
Aoki, Masahiko 295, 297
AOL-Time-Warner 147
Apple 141
archetypes, *see* institutional archetypes

Argyris, Chris, and organizational
  knowledge 33
aspiration levels:
  and organizational change 89, 91
  and reference groups 92
asset specificity, and transaction cost
  theory 290
ATT 147
audience learning 74, 75
autopoietic systems:
  and economic relations 332–3
  and governance 333

Bacdayam, Paul, and routines 34
Baker, W. E., and security exchanges 169–71
Bardhan, Pranab 313, 322
Bates, Robert 314–15
Baxter, William 138
Bayh–Dole Act (USA) 279, 280, 281, 282
Becker, Gary 349, 351
behavioural theory, and organizational
  learning 73–6
belief systems:
  and economic change 324
  and institutional change 273
  and institutional entrepreneurship 195
  and institutionalized belief systems 108
  and market systems 294
  and régulation theory 389
Bell Telephone Laboratories 53
Bihar 313, 314
biotechnology industry 153
  and co-evolution of social and physical
    technologies 278–9
  and patenting of university research
    results 279, 280–2
  and unprofitability of research firms
    279–80
boardroom, as institutional archetype 111
bounded rationality:
  and rational choice institutionalism 6
  and transaction cost theory 290, 291